KODU
for Kids

James Floyd Kelly

D1304265

The Official Guide to Creating Your Own Video Games

Kodu for Kids

ISBN-13: 978-0-7897-5076-1

ISBN-10: 0-7897-5076-7

Library of Congress Control Number: 2013936931

Printed in the United States of America

First Printing: April 2013

Trademarks

All terms mentioned in this book that are known to be trademarks or service marks have been appropriately capitalized. Que Publishing cannot attest to the accuracy of this information. Use of a term in this book should not be regarded as affecting the validity of any trademark or service mark.

Warning and Disclaimer

Every effort has been made to make this book as complete and as accurate as possible, but no warranty or fitness is implied. The information provided is on an "as is" basis. The author and the publisher shall have neither liability nor responsibility to any person or entity with respect to any loss or damages arising from the information contained in this book or from programs accompanying it.

Bulk Sales

Que Publishing offers excellent discounts on this book when ordered in quantity for bulk purchases or special sales. For more information, please contact

U.S. Corporate and Government Sales
1-800-382-3419
corpsales@pearsontechgroup.com

For sales outside of the U.S., please contact

International Sales
international@pearsoned.com

Editor-in-Chief
Greg Wiegand

Acquisitions Editor
Laura Norman

Managing Editor
Kristy Hart

Senior Project Editor
Jovana Shirley

Copy Editor
Seth Kerney

Indexer
Erika Millen

Proofreader
Dan Knott

Technical Editors
Kodu Game Lab Team

Editorial Assistant
Cindy Teeters

Cover Designer
Mark Shirar

Compositor
Nonie Ratcliff

Contents at a Glance

Online Files

There are videos and other resources available for download with this book. In the back of this book, you will find instructions on how to register your book and download the files. Check back to the Downloads page in case new or updated material is posted for this book.

Table of Contents

Forewords

Perhaps the biggest barrier to teaching children to create programs has nothing to do with the child but rather with the preconceptions of adults and the relative dearth of people willing or able to teach children basic software skills. This is a shame, really, because the ability to program is the ability to create. If we could give our children those skills early in life, it would empower them to be not just participants in our digital society but also agents. It would give them both an understanding of how our increasingly technology-driven world works and the confidence of knowing they can change it if they so choose. It would also go a long way toward satisfying an increasing need for technical skills in our society that is calling out for people who can make our tools, gadgets, and services deliver more value and work better.

Despite the fact that we live in an increasingly technical world, the creation of software—one of the most fundamental skills of the information age—remains shrouded in mystery for most and at minimum is viewed as a difficult and perhaps arcane art. Society sees "programming" as something that, if you learn it at all, you learn in the later stages of high school or in college. If a younger child learns to program, we are more likely to think of that child as a prodigy (or at least as a special case).

The reality, though, is that there are actually very few true prerequisites to teaching a child the fundamentals of software creation. About all a child needs to know to begin learning about software engineering is basic reading and writing, very basic arithmetic, simple notions of logic ("true and true equal true," "true and false equal false") and basic notions of abstraction. Most children have those skills by the age of 6 or 7.

What excited me most when I first saw Kodu was the realization that it not only provided a fun "play" environment for children, but that it was an engaging and exciting way to teach young children how to create software. It is approachable enough that even young children can learn from it without needing an adult to help them, but at the same time it can give a child basic engineering skills in a way that is fun and unintimidating. It also provides an environment in which older children, young adults, and grown-ups can enjoy and create—a great introduction and first step into the skills needed in our digital society.

—Rick Rashid, Chief Research Officer, Microsoft

Our group in Microsoft Research, FUSE (Future Social Experiences) Labs, creates experiences that help people express themselves in rich, beautiful, and novel ways. The idea for Kodu began when we asked people this: "If you could make anything on the computer, what would you create?" So many people dream of making and sharing the kind of games they play but don't know how to begin. We challenged ourselves to enable 6-year-olds who can't yet type to create in 15 minutes a game or story that they can share with their friends or classmates.

We dream of deeply affecting education. We believe that students who know how to program and build the experiences they use online all day will have more life opportunities. We are disheartened by the fact that most high schools in the United States don't even offer computer science—and we are even more disheartened by the fact that by middle school many kids feel they aren't "technical." Using Kodu—a simple tool with big aspirations—we hope to inspire everyone to be creative, tell stories, share the creative work, and "get hooked" on (and be empowered by) programming.

One of the first experiments we ran more than 5 years ago was to have two middle school kids, Nicky and Julian Boss, write the first curriculum and teach the first Kodu class at a local elementary school. We learned so much from their criticism and teaching prowess. I remember them saying how slow the parents were in comparison to the kids, and how they incorporated turn-taking and helped the really excited kids think about what they were making before just jumping in. The "show" during the last class was so incredible: about 20 little kids, divided evenly between boys and girls, all telling us how they had coded their games. They were sitting around playing the games they had made, sharing stories about coding Kodu, and all the while talking about a maiden being rescued from a castle. Kids teaching kids! All this let us know that we were doing something right.

Since then, we've seen Kodu used by many different groups. Last summer, we went down to Los Angeles to help a local education group teach Kodu. This was absolutely my favorite photo, which pretty much sums up why we love working with kids. Hope you enjoy reading about Kodu and give it a try.

Here's a 5-year-old little rock star girl creating away!

—Lili Cheng, General Manager, FUSE Research

About the Author

James Floyd Kelly is a technology writer with degrees in English and Industrial Engineering. James has written on a wide variety of topics, including LEGO robotics, open-source software, and building 3D printers. James is a DIYer—a tinkerer and a maker who enjoys learning new skills whenever possible. He lives in Atlanta, Georgia, with his wife and two young boys.

Dedication

For Ashley—Thank you for always supporting me. XO

Acknowledgments

Writing this book was a real team effort. My name might be on the cover, but if you really want to know who's responsible for making this book a reality, I've got a long list of names for you.

My first big thank you must go to my wife and two children. Writing is time-consuming work, and there were days when I was hidden away in my office until the wee hours. I always appreciate the patience and understanding they give to me when deadlines loom. Thanks, Ashley. Thanks, boys.

Next, Laura Norman at Pearson deserves a big round of applause. She listened to my early pitch for the book and then proceeded to start opening doors that made this book a reality. She's always been supportive of my book proposals, but this one is special to me… and Laura saw the potential and gave me the chance to write it. Thanks, Laura.

I have to say I've absolutely enjoyed working with Scott Fintel and Stephen Coy of Microsoft. They offered up ideas, examples, corrections, and support, and this book would not have been possible without their help.

Jumping back to Pearson, I'd like to thank Keith Cline, Seth Kerney, and Jovana San Nicolas-Shirley for their hard work in taking my chapters and turning them into the final book you're holding in your hands. And please flip back a few pages and look at the list of Pearson folks who also had a hand in making this book—a big thank you to all of them!

Finally, Kodu Game Lab isn't a software tool that just magically appeared. There are a lot of folks who are responsible for giving us this great-looking and fun-to-use tool. Huge thanks go to each person in this list for all their work with Kodu Game Lab:

Saxs Persson, Senior Director, Microsoft Studios

Stephen Coy, Senior Software Development Engineer, Microsoft Research

Scott Fintel, Technical Producer, Microsoft Studios

Kiki McMillan, Release Manager, Microsoft Studios

Alex Games, Director of Curriculum Development, Microsoft Studios

Tom Guzewich, Producer, Microsoft Studios

Matt Skelton, Legal, Microsoft Studios

Carla Woo, Legal, Microsoft Studios

Lili Cheng, General Manager, Microsoft Research

Karen Cowan, Business Administrator, Microsoft Research

Eric Anderson, Senior Software Development Engineer, Microsoft Studios

Brad Gibson, Senior Producer, Microsoft Research

Eric Havir, Developer Evangelist, Microsoft

Matt MacLaurin, Senior Director, Microsoft Research

James Rogers, Senior Technical Art Director, Microsoft Studios

Lee Steg, Art Director, Microsoft Studios

Jason Cowan, Senior Business and Strategy Manager, Microsoft Studios

Michael Miller, Senior Software Development Engineer, Microsoft

Mark Finch, Senior Research Software Development Engineer, Microsoft

Rich Rashid, Chief Research Officer, Microsoft Research

John Scott Tynes, Senior Academic Evangelist, Microsoft

Kent Foster, Director, University Incubation, Microsoft

Mike Jacob, Group Program Manager, Microsoft Studios

Kodu Community, for creating great levels

We Want to Hear from You!

As the reader of this book, *you* are our most important critic and commentator. We value your opinion and want to know what we're doing right, what we could do better, what areas you'd like to see us publish in, and any other words of wisdom you're willing to pass our way.

We welcome your comments. You can email or write to let us know what you did or didn't like about this book—as well as what we can do to make our books better.

Please note that we cannot help you with technical problems related to the topic of this book.

When you write, please be sure to include this book's title and author as well as your name and email address. We will carefully review your comments and share them with the author and editors who worked on the book.

Email: feedback@quepublishing.com

Mail: Que Publishing
          ATTN: Reader Feedback
          800 East 96th Street
          Indianapolis, IN 46240 USA

Reader Services

Visit our website and register this book at quepublishing.com/register for convenient access to any updates, downloads, or errata that might be available for this book.

Introduction

In This Introduction

Yes, You Can Be a Game Designer

Have you ever played a game on your computer or gaming console and wondered how the game was actually made? And have you ever played a game and then wondered whether you could make something just as fun? I know I have.

But, like me, you might have heard something like this:

○ Game design is difficult and can be tricky.

○ Cool games (especially the really complex ones with lots of fancy graphics and complicated storylines) often take years to create before anyone ever plays them.

○ Most games are created by teams working long hours (and that can cost a lot of money).

○ Many of the games are created using complicated software that can take years to learn.

Years to make, lots of cash required to develop, and an understanding of complex software—these requirements make it sound like game design is beyond the reach of people like us, don't they?

Well, game design is *not* out of our reach.

What if you and I could make your own games and it didn't take years (or even months)? What if the software needed to make our own games was free for Windows users (or under $6 for Xbox owners)? And what if that software were not only extremely simple to understand and use but also *fun*? Do you want to hear more?

Of course you do.

Kodu Is Way Fun!

I'm not going to keep you in suspense about the software needed to create your own games. (And you're holding this book in your hands with a title that says *Kodu for Kids*, which sort of gives away the big secret, anyway.) It's called Kodu Game Lab, and it is one of the most fun and easy ways to create your own games.

Just how fun and how easy? Glad you asked.

It's fun because you control it all: You can design the rules of your games, the characters that players see, the environments in the background, the points system for scoring, and much more.

It's easy because everything you do is visual. You drag items around the screen to place them where you like, you tweak settings in your games using either the mouse or a game controller (and if you've got a tablet like the Surface that has a touchscreen, you can even use your finger), and you can immediately test your game at any point to see what works… and what might need a little more tweaking.

Does that sound fun and easy? Yeah? But wait… there's more.

You can share games you create with Kodu Game Lab with your family, your friends and classmates, even with other students on the other side of the world. Students from around the world are using Kodu Game Lab to create games. Just imagine how much fun it will be to create a game and get feedback on it from a student in Israel, Australia, or a dozen other countries? Kodu Game Lab is currently available in 13 languages: Arabic, German, Greek, English, Spanish, French, Hebrew, Icelandic, Italian, Dutch, Polish, Russian, and Portuguese.

Another super-cool thing about Kodu Game Lab is how easy it is to connect with other Kodu fans. Do you have a question and just cannot find an answer? There are safe and kid-friendly online resources where you can post your questions and get answers from other Kodu users. And you might even be able to answer questions from other Kodu users. After all, when you finish this book, you're going to be a Kodu guru.

Kodu Offers So Much

Is there anything else that Kodu Game Lab offers to budding game designers? Yes, there is.

Kodu Game Lab is an outstanding tool for helping with special projects at school. Did your teacher just assign you to do a presentation about how white blood cells attack foreign bodies in your bloodstream? Don't reach for a sheet of boring posterboard. Use Kodu to draw a blood vessel (the terrain or environment), drop in some characters that represent the white blood cells and maybe a flu bug, and use the software to control their movements and use colorful animation to show just how white blood cells react. Even better? Turn it into a game where one player controls the flu bug and the other player controls a white blood cell—the flu bug players must run away, and the white blood cell players must try and catch the flu bug. (And because Kodu can support up to four players, you could really make it fun.) I'd give you an A for the presentation.

Kodu will also teach you some real-life skills that will help you throughout your education and into your future career. You see, the ability to create a game requires some logical and critical-thinking skills. Those might not sound important to you now, but to your parents and teachers, it's a big deal. Even if you don't know what you want to do when you "grow up," trust me, some of the skills you will learn as you develop your own games will never leave you and will benefit you no matter what career you choose later in life.

Kodu Game Lab is always changing. Updates are occasionally released that add new features, new characters, and much more. So, there will always be new features to figure out that can make your games even more crazy, advanced, and fun. You should never stop learning. Instead, always be on the lookout for new things to try out in your games. Think of Kodu as a toolbox. I want you to try out each and every tool inside it. You'll find your favorites, and you'll discover some tools that you might never use. But by learning them all, you'll have the maximum number of skills and features available to make your games the best they can be.

Walk Before You Run

Creating great games means starting at the beginning. You've probably heard the phrase "you need to learn to walk before you can run," and that's definitely true with Kodu Game Lab. You need to learn the basics of Kodu before you can start creating that dream game that's floating around in your head.

I know you're probably anxious to learn everything there is to know as fast as possible, but let me tell you why this isn't such a great idea. You need to let all this Kodu information sink in a bit. That means learning something new in one chapter, and then playing with Kodu Game Lab to try it out. You'll remember something if you read it and then use it. This means opening Kodu and actually performing the tasks that I put in front of you in the book's chapters.

Kodu has its own rules and expects you to do things in certain ways, but they're extremely easy to remember. You'll learn all about them in later chapters, but what I want you to know right now is that this book teaches you things in a very specific order. Don't skip ahead or jump around—you might miss something super-important.

> **NOTE**
>
> I cannot stress enough just how important it is to read and work through the book in the proper order. If you want to skip ahead to see what's coming, that's fine. But be sure to return to your original place in the book. Skipping ahead means you might miss a technique or skill in an earlier chapter that is required later in the book. You'll be confused, and the games you design might not work properly. Even worse, you might miss a topic on a cool feature that your future games will lack because you don't know it exists.

There's no rush here. Take your time and work through the chapters at your own pace. You'll be rewarded with an understanding of all the great features that Kodu offers, and that will make your games shine.

How to Use This Book

One of the things I hope you most enjoy about this book is the frequent use of screenshots. I took snapshots of the screen as I was working, which means that you can follow along in each chapter and use the figures to make certain that you're keeping pace with the game development.

Sometimes, however, a figure just isn't enough. In those instances, just refer back to the text for exact instructions on what to do. Because Kodu Game Lab is so simple to use, though, and because so much game design in Kodu is done onscreen, many tasks are covered with just a few sentences that explain what to do with your mouse or game controller and then refer you to a screenshot to see the final results.

Don't let this bother you if your preferred method of Kodu game design is using a game controller. After all, just about every Kodu feature can be accessed and every task performed using a game controller. I prefer the keyboard, but I'll do my best to ensure that you game controller fans are covered.

Finally, I've mentioned it earlier and I'll repeat it here: Follow along with the chapters and actually create the games. You'll become more familiar with all the buttons and tools, and the concepts will sink in and stick with you over time. This book is really more of a workbook. Your goal should be to tackle (*in order*) every page, every task, and every game so that you move quickly from Kodu novice to Kodu guru.

In addition to the instructions provided in this book, you can also access some narrated videos that demonstrate how to use Kodu Game Lab. Some of these videos show actual games from the book being programmed, and other videos show one or two short techniques to further explain a concept mentioned in the book. See the instructions in the back of this book for how to register and view these videos.

Introducing Two New Friends: Kodu and Rover

Throughout the book, you're going to enjoy learning about some additional features and fun things about Kodu from two of the creatables found in the Kodu software: Kodu and Rover.

Kodu is a cool little fellow—the software's named after him. He knows everything about the software. And that's a good thing, too, because Rover is fairly new and is still learning. Occasionally Rover has some questions, and you'll see conversations between Kodu and Rover in the various chapters. Their conversations are often about the current chapter's topics, but sometimes they're about other things related to Kodu.

Rover: Sorry to interrupt, but I've been listening in and have a question. How long has Kodu been around?

Kodu: I can answer that. Kodu began with Microsoft Research's FUSE Labs, a group at Microsoft that develops really cool software. The first version was released in 2010, and the most recent update was released in 2013.

Get in Touch

I've enjoyed writing this book for you! And I'd love to see and hear from you about the games you're creating with Kodu. If you'd like to email me, you can send your message to feedback@quepublishing.com, and my publisher will forward your message to me. I can't promise I'll be able to respond to every email, but I'll definitely take a look at your game, especially if you've shared it online.

And if you find any errors in the book, I'd like to know about those, as well. Although I've done my best to avoid mistakes, they sometimes manage to sneak by. Email me at the same address and I'll do my best to make sure the error is fixed. Any errors that are reported will have their corrections shared online at www.quepublishing.com/kodu.

And now, it's time to learn Kodu!

Get Kodu: Download and Installation

In This Chapter

○ Downloading Kodu

○ Installing Kodu

○ Checking Whether Kodu Installed Properly

○ Adding a Game Controller

○ Moving On

Downloading Kodu

Before you can start having fun with Kodu, you need to download a copy of it from the Kodu Game Lab website. It's free, but you're not going to find it already installed on your computer. Well, that's not 100% true—a parent, teacher, or other student might have installed it. If it's already installed on your computer, you're in luck and can jump to Chapter 2, "Explore Kodu Game Lab: Basic User Controls and Tools." If you want to see whether it's installed already, jump ahead to the "Checking Whether Kodu Installed Properly" section and follow the instructions.

If you know that Kodu is *not* installed on your computer, go and find it (a task Microsoft has made easy). Just open a web browser (such as Internet Explorer or Firefox) and type in www. kodugamelab.com. A page that looks like Figure 1.1 will open.

FIGURE 1.1   The Kodu Game Lab website is the official home of Kodu.

You should see a big green button in the upper-left corner of the screen that says Get Kodu. You want to click that button now. Your web browser then opens to the Microsoft Download Center. This page gives you all you need to know about the Kodu Game Lab Setup program, including its version number, the language it supports, and the file size. (From here on out, for easier reading, I refer to the Kodu Game Lab program simply as Kodu or the Kodu program.)

Figure 1.2 shows that I'm downloading the Kodu installation file and the file is 191.5 megabytes (MB) in size. Version 1.2.88.0 is the one I'm downloading today. This web page always provides the latest version. After you've installed Kodu, though, you can install updates automatically from within the Kodu program without going back to the Microsoft Download Center.

CAUTION
Pay careful attention to the System Requirements section. This section provides you with the minimum hardware and software requirements to install the Kodu Game Lab. Notice that Kodu currently runs only on Windows 8, Windows 7, Windows Vista, and Windows XP.

Click the Download button in the Quick Details section of the Download Center web page. A pop-up window appears, offering a few options. Click the Save button, shown in Figure 1.3.

FIGURE 1.2 Microsoft Download Center gives you all the information you need to know about how to download and install Kodu and about which version you are installing.

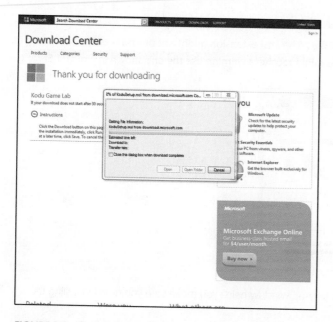

FIGURE 1.3 Saving the Kodu Setup file to your computer might take a while if you have a slow Internet connection.

The Kodu Setup program begins to download. The name of the file you're downloading is KoduSetup.msi. Pay attention to where this file is being saved on your computer; it can be saved to the desktop or to a special folder on the computer's hard drive. If you are given an option, create a folder on the computer, name it Kodu Setup File, and then save the file there until you are ready to install Kodu.

When the file has finished downloading, go to the folder (or desktop) where you saved the KoduSetup.msi file. If you saved it to your desktop, you will see an icon like the one shown in Figure 1.4.

FIGURE 1.4   The Kodu Setup program puts an icon on your desktop so you know it is the file you use to install Kodu.

Now, it's time to install Kodu.

Installing Kodu

Double-click the KoduSetup.msi file . (The .msi extension might not be visible, so just look for KoduSetup as the filename.) You might receive a warning like the one shown in Figure 1.5.

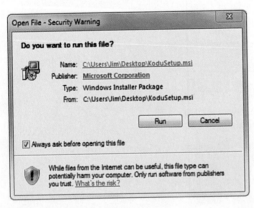

FIGURE 1.5   The Security Warning pop-up window helps you make sure you aren't installing the wrong software.

If you're certain this is the file you downloaded directly from the Microsoft Download Center, go ahead and click the Run button.

> **TIP**
>
> If you didn't download the file and want to be absolutely certain you've got the correct file (including version number), it might be a good idea to click the Cancel button and follow the instructions in the previous section to download a new Kodu Setup file.

Click the Run button and the Kodu Game Lab Setup process begins. You might see one or two screens flash by before the Kodu Game Lab License Agreement appears, as shown in Figure 1.6.

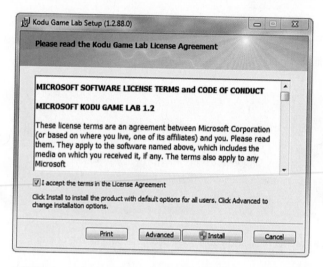

FIGURE 1.6 The Kodu Game Lab License Agreement requires that you accept certain terms if you want to use the software.

If you (or your teacher/parent) have read over the agreement and are okay with the terms of use, click the I Accept the Terms in the License Agreement check box, and then click the Install button.

After you click the Install button, you are asked whether you want Kodu to check for updates automatically. If you check the box next to that question, Kodu goes out and looks for updates to its program whenever you start it. You are also asked whether Microsoft can receive usage information from your computer to help the company fix errors and find ways to make Kodu better. Check with your teacher, parent, or other adult to see how they want you to respond to those questions. Then click one or both boxes (or leave them blank if you don't want automatic updates to Kodu, or you don't want to send usage information to Microsoft), and then click the Next button, shown in Figure 1.7.

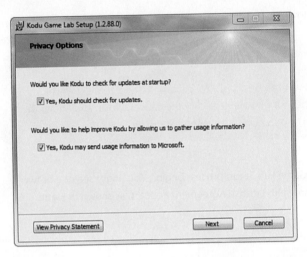

FIGURE 1.7   Choose your privacy options for Kodu.

CAUTION

A User Account Control pop-up window might appear, asking whether you want to allow the program to install software on your computer. First, make sure that the program name is Kodu Game Lab and that the verified publisher is Microsoft Corporation. Then, if this information is correct, click the Yes button. If the information doesn't match, click the No button and download another copy of the Kodu Setup program.

The Kodu Setup program begins installing files, and you'll see a progress bar like the one in Figure 1.8.

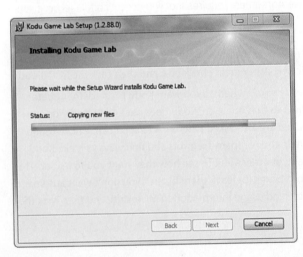

FIGURE 1.8   A progress bar during the installation process lets you know when the installation has finished.

When the installation process finishes, a screen like the one shown in Figure 1.9 tells you that Kodu has been installed.

FIGURE 1.9   Successful installation of Kodu.

Click the Finish button and you're done with the Kodu Setup file.

Checking Whether Kodu Installed Properly

If you saw a screen like the one shown in Figure 1.9, you probably installed Kodu correctly. However, there are a couple of other easy and fast ways to check that Kodu is actually installed on your computer.

Look on your desktop for the Kodu Game Lab and the Configure Kodu Game Lab icons. Figure 1.10 shows the two icons. If they are both there, you are ready to begin.

FIGURE 1.10   The two Kodu-related icons look like this on the desktop.

The other way to check, if you don't see the icons on your desktop, is to click the Start button and look in the Programs or All Programs folder. You should see either a Kodu Game Lab listing, or a Microsoft Research folder that contains Kodu Game Lab icons.

There's another way to test that Kodu installed properly: Just double-click the Kodu Game Lab icon (see Figure 1.10) and start Kodu.

Rover: Hey, that's you, Kodu! But why two icons?

Kodu: Yep, that's me. One icon is bright green, the other is metallic gray. The green icon opens the actual Kodu Game Lab, where you can make games. The metallic gray icon is for when you want to change Game Lab display settings for different-sized screens. Kodu Game Lab is pretty good at determining the proper settings, so don't mess with the metallic gray icon unless you know what you're doing.

Let's hold off on that until Chapter 2, okay? I know you're anxious to get started, but you need to do a few more things to prepare yourself (and your computer) to use Kodu.

Adding a Game Controller

As mentioned in the Introduction, you can use Kodu with both a keyboard and a game controller. Your computer already has a keyboard but doesn't necessarily have a game controller. If you have access to a game controller and want to use it to design and play games with Kodu, all you need to do is insert the game controller into a free USB port. With Vista, Windows 7, and Windows 8, the software needed to communicate with the game controller is already installed, so you're ready to go.

If you find that the game controller still isn't working after inserting it into the USB port, then carefully read the instructions that come with the game controller you use. I'm using an official Microsoft Xbox 360 Controller for Windows, but if you have a slightly different controller, the steps for installing and using it might differ a little from the ones shown here. You may be asked to insert a DVD before you connect the game controller; again, read the instructions carefully.

CAUTION

If a User Account Control pop-up window appears, verify that the program name is the name of the controller you are installing (mine is Xbox 360 Accessories 1.2) and check that the verified publisher name matches the controller's manufacturer (mine is Microsoft Corporation). Click the Yes button only if you are certain of the origin of the software you are about to install.

If you are required to insert a DVD, a screen like the one you see in Figure 1.11 may appear.

FIGURE 1.11   The Microsoft Xbox 360 Accessories Setup screen looks like this. Yours might look different if you have a different controller.

Click the I Accept This Agreement check box, and then click the Next button.

The installation files start copying, and a progress bar shows the status of the installation. When it's done, an Installation Complete window like the one in Figure 1.12 appears.

FIGURE 1.12   The game controller has been installed and is ready to use.

Click the Finish button. The game controller is now installed. You're done.

Moving On

You are probably super excited to begin playing with Kodu. The word *playing* works better here than the word *learning* because playing is exactly what using Kodu feels like. Kodu is fun, and even as you're figuring out all the special features and techniques, it will feel more like playing than working.

So, here's some simple advice:

○ Enjoy the trip: Look around. Take breaks. Show your friends and family what you're doing. There is nothing wrong with doing a little exploring on your own with Kodu, so feel free to look around and click buttons and menus to see what they do. (Remember, there's a great Undo feature that you'll learn about, so any mistakes you make can easily be reversed.) There's no rush. You're not under any time limit; so before moving on to the next chapter, be sure you're comfortable with everything you learned in this chapter.

○ Explore: When you learn something new, push it to the limits. If it has a setting from 1 to 100, and I tell you to use a value of 50, go ahead and try it with settings of 1, 25, 75, and 100. See what happens. If you get curious about something that you see while learning about a specific part of the program, go ahead and check it out. It won't bother me a bit. Keep in mind that the more you learn about Kodu as you explore every little nook and cranny, the better Kodu game designer you'll be.

○ Don't get frustrated: Kodu can get complicated, especially if your goal is to design complex games. You're going to make mistakes. You're going to get stuck on a problem. The secret is to not let it get to you. Smile, take a deep breath, and then look at the issue again. Post a question on a Kodu forum or ask a fellow Kodu programmer. Someone has the answer, and if you can't figure it out on your own, there's help out there.

And now, let's move on to Chapter 2 and start creating some games with Kodu.

2

Explore Kodu Game Lab: Basic User Controls and Tools

In This Chapter

- ○ Opening the Kodu Game Lab
- ○ Navigating a New World
- ○ Adding and Modifying an Object
- ○ Moving On

Opening the Kodu Game Lab

In the last chapter, you installed the Kodu Game Lab and verified that it installed properly. Now it's time to actually open Kodu and try it out. To do that, just double-click the Kodu Game Lab icon (refer back to Figure 1.10).

NOTE

For most of this book, I use a mouse and keyboard. Occasionally I switch to the game controller when there's something unusually different or unique in how the game controller works. Rest assured, however, that if I'm doing something with the mouse and keyboard, you can do it the game controller, as well.

Kodu opens with the Main Menu, as shown in Figure 2.1.

FIGURE 2.1   Open the Kodu Game Lab to get started learning how to build games.

> **NOTE**
> If you chose during the installation process to let Kodu look for and install updates automatically, you may see a window or two open and close when you double-click the Kodu Game Lab icon. When the updates complete, the Kodu Main Menu appears.

The Main Menu contains a list of items in the center of the screen, with Kodu floating and dancing to the right of the menu. The Main Menu offers the following selections:

○ **Resume:** This option opens the Kodu Game Lab at the point where Kodu was last shut down. If you were the last user, whatever game you were designing during your previous visit will open and be ready to go.

○ **New World:** Choose this option when you want to start building a new game. It opens Kodu with a blank game and no other items on screen. (You'll be using this option shortly.)

○ **Load World:** Game files that you save to the computer can be stored anywhere you want, and this option lets you retrieve a previously saved game and open it in the Kodu Game Lab. (Open the Kodu Configuration Tool to specify where game files are stored.)

○ **Community:** Choose this option to load and play games created by other Kodu users. You can also access Lessons and view sample games that are a great resource for ideas and training.

○ **Options:** Choose this option to adjust controls related to how the Kodu Game Lab works (such as showing hints when you hover the mouse pointer over a button or menu item, or increasing/decreasing the sound effects and music that play during game design). You'll learn more about the Options feature later in Chapter 17, "The Big Bag of Tricks."

○ **Help:** This is a great place to find reminders about using a game controller with Kodu. It offers some basic explanations about a few of the Kodu Game Design tools, but you'll learn them all if you finish this book. This option also lists all the names of the Kodu design team members who have helped bring Kodu to life.

○ **Quit Kodu:** This option closes down Kodu.

You can select any of these options in any of the following three ways:

○ With your mouse (left-clicking an option to select it)

○ By using the up/down arrows on the keyboard followed by the Enter key

○ By using a game controller's left thumb joystick, or the D-Pad to move up and down, followed by pressing the A button to activate the selected option

Figure 2.2 shows the two locations on the Microsoft Xbox 360 game controller from which users make selections.

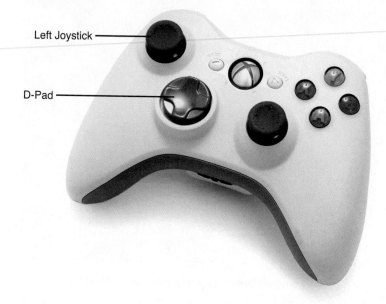

Left Joystick ———

D-Pad ———

FIGURE 2.2 Use a game controller to make a selection from the Kodu Main Menu.

You can also read news and updates about Kodu in the News section on the Main Menu. Click the More! link to expand the window a little bit and scroll up or down using the mouse wheel, keyboard up/down arrows, or the game controller.

I know you're excited to start playing with Kodu Game Lab, so I'm not going to review every feature, button, and menu here. Instead, I scatter them throughout the rest of this book. You'll find information about the important features you need to know about earlier in the book; the less-important features and controls appear in later chapters.

Now, go ahead and select the New World option from the Main Menu. It's time to have some fun and learn how to add and control characters, one of the fundamentals of game design.

Navigating a New World

When you create a new world, the Kodu Game Lab opens and displays a patch of ground (in the shape of a square) directly in the center of the screen. There are no trees. There are no vehicles. There's no water or mountains. Nothing. It's up to you to shape the world as you see fit! Figure 2.3 shows your new world and some important tools and features that I explain next.

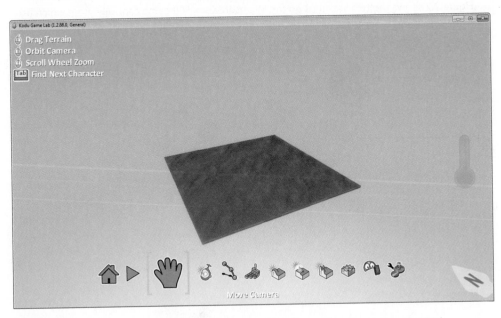

FIGURE 2.3 A new world without any characters, buildings, water, mountains, or vehicles.

You will always find a short list of tips in the upper-left corner of the screen. These change depending on whether you are using a mouse/keyboard or a game controller. If you have a game controller plugged in and then move the mouse or touch a key on the keyboard, these tips change to mouse/keyboard tips, and vice versa.

These tips also change depending on which of the Kodu Game Lab tools you select. (And from now on, I refer to the Kodu Game Lab tools as just tools, okay?)

The Tools

The tools run along the lower edge of the window. Figure 2.3 shows a House, a Play button, a Hand, and more. You'll learn about each of these as you progress through this book, but for now, focus on the Move Camera tool (the Hand icon) and the Object tool (it looks like Kodu) to the right of the Move Camera tool.

> **TIP**
>
> Don't see the Move Camera tool? Then you're most likely using a game controller! The Move Camera tool is visible only when you are using the mouse/keyboard option. Don't worry, though. If you select the Object tool, you have access to the same features (Drag Terrain, Orbit Camera, Zoom In/Out, and Find Next Character) that are available to mouse/keyboard users who click the Hand.

Move Camera Tool

The Move Camera tool enables you to use your mouse to change the location of the camera's view of the single square of terrain when you click and hold down the left mouse button. Click anywhere on the terrain or just outside it and hold down the left mouse button. Now move the mouse around, and you should see the camera's view move to wherever you drag the mouse. Release the left mouse button to "drop" the camera; it stays there until you move it again. Figure 2.4 shows that I've dragged the camera view all the way to the left of the screen.

The Object Tool

You can do the same thing with a game controller, but instead of selecting the Move Camera tool, you select the Object tool. Figure 2.5 shows the tools available when using a game controller. Notice that they are slightly larger in size than the ones visible when using a mouse/keyboard. (You may also notice the Hand icon is missing.)

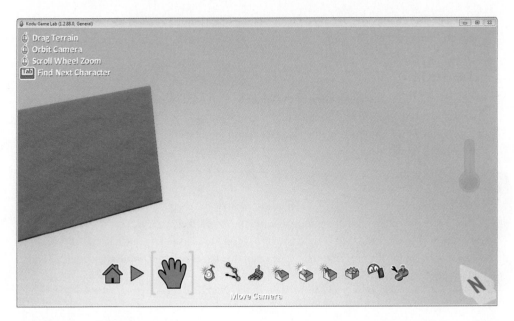

FIGURE 2.4   Drag the camera around the screen and drop it where you want by clicking and holding down the left mouse button.

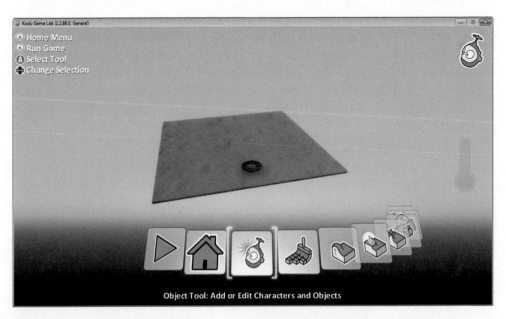

FIGURE 2.5   To use a game controller to move the camera, you must select the Object tool.

Changing the camera view works a little differently with the game controller. You move between tools with a game controller using the left thumbstick—a yellow bracket appears around the tool to let you know that it's the tool that will be selected when you press the A button.

When you select the Object tool and press A, the tools disappear, as shown in Figure 2.6, and all you'll see are the terrain, a cursor on the terrain to indicate where the game controller does its magic, and tips in the upper-left corner of the screen for using the game controller.

FIGURE 2.6   Use the game controller's left thumbstick control to move the camera's view.

TIP

Using the game controller with the camera is a little different from using the mouse. With the mouse, when you want to drag the camera to the right, you just click and hold down the left mouse button and drag the mouse to the left. But that won't work with the game controller.

With the game controller, if you use the left thumbstick control and direct the cursor to the left, the camera moves to the right, as shown in Figure 2.7.

NOTE

At first this might seem a bit strange to have the controller moving the camera to the right if you move the Control Circle to the left. But you'll adjust once you've used the game controller for a while. I go back and forth between using a mouse/keyboard and the game controller, and it usually takes my brain only a minute or so to get used to the change.

FIGURE 2.7   Moving the cursor to the left moves the camera to the right.

If you've got a game controller, experiment with moving the cursor around. Move it up, down, left, and right and watch how it affects the location of the terrain.

Before you place a character on the terrain, I want to show you how to use two more controls: the Zoom feature and the Orbit Camera control.

The Zoom Feature

Using your mouse's scroll wheel, you can spin it forward to zoom the camera in on the terrain and see the details of the surface more clearly. Spinning the scroll wheel backward makes the camera view zoom out, providing a less-detailed view of the terrain. I've zoomed in as far as possible with my mouse's scroll wheel, and you can see what it looks like in Figure 2.8.

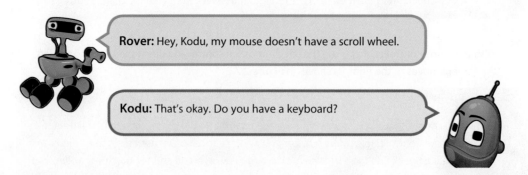

Rover: Hey, Kodu, my mouse doesn't have a scroll wheel.

Kodu: That's okay. Do you have a keyboard?

Rover: Yes.

Kodu: You can use the Page Up and Page Down keys to zoom in and out. Just make sure that NumLock is turned off.

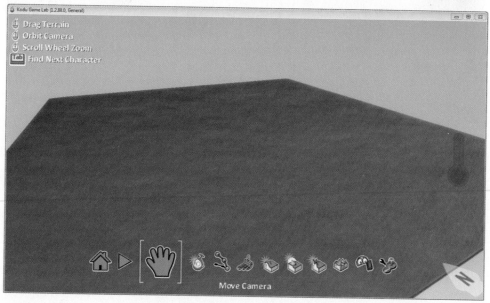

FIGURE 2.8 Zooming in on the terrain with the mouse scroll wheel.

If you're using the game controller, select the Object tool (Kodu icon) and press the A button. Then, you can zoom in with the Right Shoulder button or Right Bumper and zoom out with the Left Shoulder button or Left Bumper. Figure 2.9 shows that I've zoomed out quite a bit. I can still see the cursor, but just barely!

Experiment a bit with either the mouse's scroll wheel or the Shoulder buttons on the game controller. Combine the activities of zooming in and out with moving the camera view around on the screen until you're comfortable with these two controls.

In addition to moving the camera view around the screen and zooming in and out, I want you to have one final skill before we drop a character on the terrain. This skill is important, so pay attention!

FIGURE 2.9   Zoomed out using the game controller's Left Shoulder button.

The Orbit Camera Feature

You can move the camera view around the terrain by dragging it left, right, up, and down. But what if there's a mountain on the screen like the one shown in Figure 2.10? How can you determine whether there's something hiding behind it?

Kodu Game Lab allows you to not only move the camera view around terrain on the screen but also to rotate it as if the camera were on top of a merry-go-round. This is called the Orbit Camera feature.

If you're a mouse user, select the Move Camera tool (hand icon), and then click and hold down the right mouse button and move the mouse around. Notice how the camera view rotates as you move the mouse. You can even move the mouse down and the camera view will rotate so that you can view terrain from above. (No matter how high you push the mouse while clicking and holding down the right button, you won't be able to view underneath the terrain. Sorry.)

If you're a game controller user, you can also use the Orbit Camera feature by selecting the Object tool (Kodu icon) and then using both the left and right thumbsticks to rotate the camera view. This definitely takes some practice, but it's a skill that will pay off later if you spend some time experimenting.

Figure 2.11 shows that our friend Rover was hiding behind that mountain. All it took was using the Orbit Camera feature to rotate the camera to take a look.

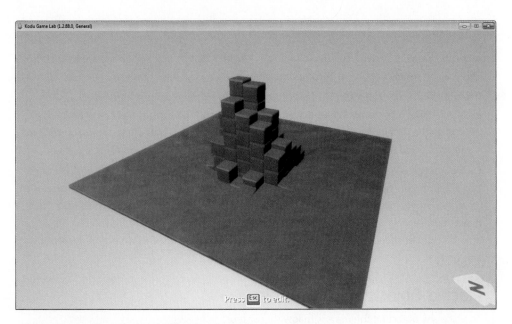

FIGURE 2.10   What's hiding behind that mountain?

FIGURE 2.11   Rover hides behind the mountain, but the Orbit Camera feature lets you find him.

Are you ready to drop a character on the terrain? I know that Rover and Kodu are probably going to try to convince you to pick them, but don't make your decision just yet. Let me show you the options available to you in the next section, and you can pick any one you like.

Objects

All items that you place on the terrain (vehicles, rocks, robots, trees, and so on) are called *objects*. This is a commonly used term in computer programming, but for now all you need to know is that every character that you can use to create games in Kodu Game Lab starts out as an object.

Each object has a name: rock, tree, Rover, Kodu, apple (and more). And you can place multiple objects on the terrain in a Kodu game. You can even place duplicates of the same object. This means you could have two Kodus, three Rovers, four apples, five rocks, and six cannons.

Each object behaves differently depending on the instructions you specify. One of Kodu Game Lab's really great features is the capability to customize objects. You can change their size, their color, even their speed. So, you could have a red Kodu that is half the size of a blue Kodu, but moves twice as fast. All of this is done with simple programming, but before you change an object's color or speed or other characteristics, you've got to place that object on the terrain, so let's do that.

Placing Objects on the Terrain

To place any object on the terrain, follow these steps:

1. Start Kodu Game Lab and open a new world if you haven't already done so. A blank screen like the one back in Figure 2.3 will appear.

2. Zoom in a bit until you have a good view of the single square of terrain.

   Why do I want you to do this? To demonstrate that the single block of terrain on the screen really isn't all that large. You can add more terrain, grow mountains, add rivers and lakes, and much more, and I show you how to do all this in upcoming chapters. The single block of terrain that exists right now in your new world doesn't have enough room for too many objects.

3. After zooming in, select the Object tool.

4. For mouse users, move the mouse pointer to the center of the terrain and click and release the left mouse button. A large circular-shaped window like the one shown in Figure 2.12 will appear.

   This is called a *pie menu*, and it consists of individual "slices" that you can select by moving the mouse pointer over that slice. In Figure 2.12, notice how the Apple slice is pulled out slightly and the color changes from green to yellow. If I click the left mouse button again while the Apple slice is selected, a single apple is placed on the terrain where I left-clicked.

   This works the same way for game controller users, but there is one additional slice (called the Path slice) on the pie menu, as shown in Figure 2.13. Don't worry about that right now; the Path feature is available to mouse/keyboard users in a different location.

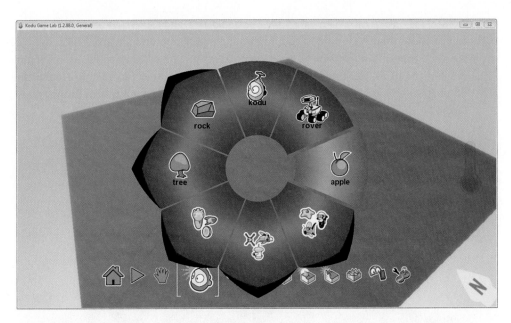

FIGURE 2.12   A pie menu appears when you left-click the mouse button using the Object tool.

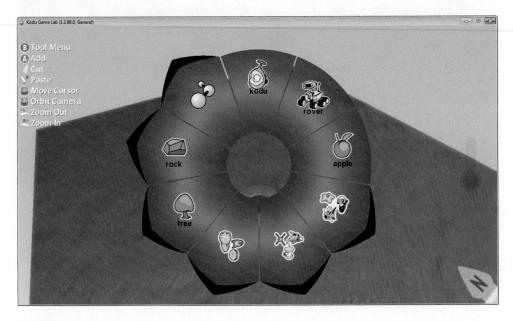

FIGURE 2.13   The pie menu is available to game controller users.

Some of the objects have names: Kodu, Rover, apple, tree, and rock. A few others do not have names. Click the one that shows a coin, rocket, and a castle, for instance, and you'll see another pie menu appear over the original, as shown in Figure 2.14. Any time an additional set of tools or selections are available, you get another pie menu. To return to a preceding pie menu, click off and outside it, or just press the Escape key on the keyboard or the B button on the game controller.

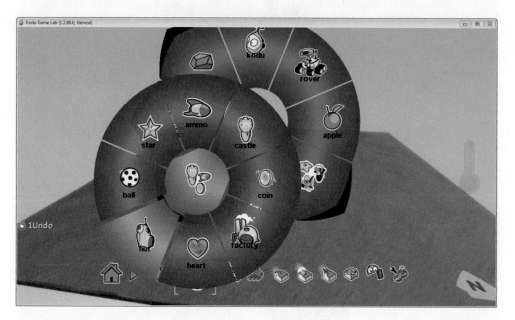

FIGURE 2.14   Additional pie menus offering more options may appear.

Although there are dozens of objects you can choose to place on the terrain, not all of these objects are capable of being controlled by a player. So right now, choose one that can move around the terrain. This means selecting either Kodu or Rover or one of the vehicles found on the Vehicle slice (see Figure 2.15).

5. Use your mouse or game controller to select a vehicle's slice, and then left-click or press the A button to select and place it on the terrain.

I've selected the Cycle, a single-wheeled speedy robot with exhaust pipes, but feel free to select any vehicle (including Kodu or Rover) that you like.

FIGURE 2.15   Place an object in the center of the terrain by selecting it from a pie menu.

Changing an Object's Characteristics

Now that you've placed a vehicle on the terrain, let's make some changes to it. To change an object after you've placed it on the terrain, follow these steps:

1. Select the Object tool.

2. Move the pointer/cursor over the object you want to modify until it is glowing.

3. Left-click or right-click the object, depending on what you want to do to the object.

I'm going to change the Cycle's color first. To do this, use the Object tool, so go ahead and select that tool with the mouse or game controller.

Changing an object's color is easy. Move the mouse pointer or game controller's cursor over the object until a slight glow appears around the object, as shown in Figure 2.16.

Just above the object is a series of colored dots. The largest one represents the current color of the object. Use the tips on screen to change the color. Game controller users can use the D-Pad to move left or right. The object changes color as you move between dots. For mouse/keyboard users, use the left or right arrow keys on the keyboard to move between colors. When you're happy with the color, move the mouse pointer or cursor away from the object; the color is locked in.

FIGURE 2.16 A glow appears around a selected object.

I mentioned earlier that we can also change an object's size. To do this, select the Object tool and move the mouse pointer over the object until it is glowing. Now right-click the mouse and you'll see a small menu of options appear, like the one shown in Figure 2.17.

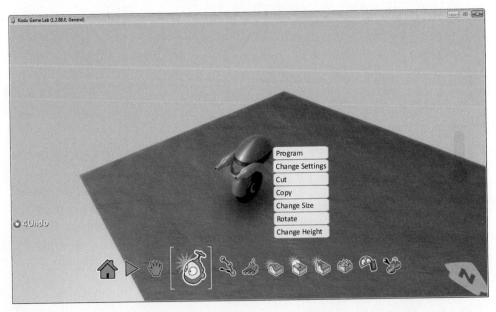

FIGURE 2.17 Additional options are available for modifying objects with a single right-click.

Most of the options shown in Figure 2.17 are also available to game controller users, but instead of right-clicking the object, game controller users just use the Object tool and move the cursor over the object until it glows. Instead of in the small menu, the options are now listed as tips in the upper-left corner of the screen, as shown in Figure 2.18.

FIGURE 2.18 Additional options are also available to game controller users via tips.

To change an object's size with a game controller, you simply tap Up or Down using the D-Pad. For mouse users, select the Change Size option and a drag bar will appear below the object, as shown in Figure 2.19.

Click the green drag bar and move it left or right until you are happy with the object's new size. Figure 2.20 shows that I've dragged the bar almost all the way to the right, increasing the Cycle's size immensely. As you can see, I even had to zoom out a bit on the camera view to fit most of the Cycle in the image.

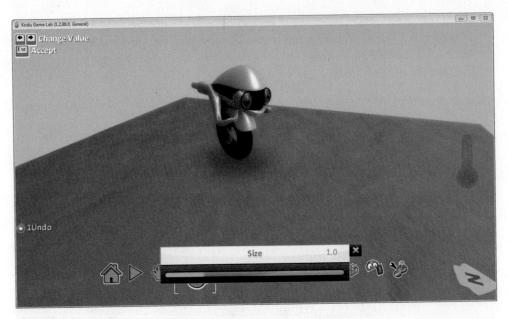

FIGURE 2.19   You resize an object with the mouse using a drag bar.

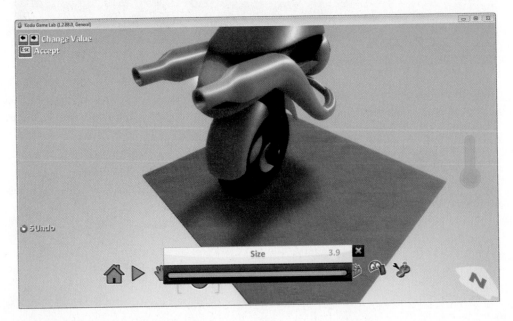

FIGURE 2.20   That's one big Cycle!

You can also change the height of the object. This doesn't make an object taller; you use the Resize option to do that. The Height option moves the object up off the ground. As shown in Figure 2.21, a Height drag bar appears (for mouse users) and the object appears to hover over the terrain. (For game controller users, the Height feature is called the Move Up/Down option, and it uses the D-Pad's up/down buttons; remember that the D-Pad's Left/Right buttons change the object's color.)

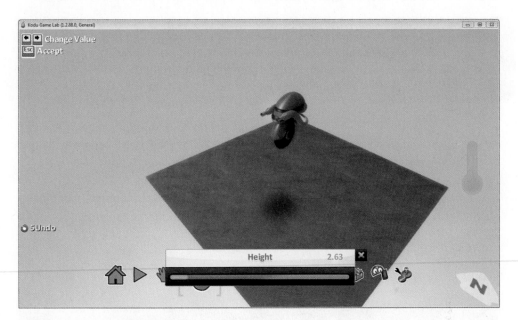

FIGURE 2.21   Give an object flight capability by using the Height feature.

Set the Height to 0.00 to return the object safely to the ground.

As always, even after you've changed the characteristics of an object, you can always move the object around the terrain again. To do so, left-click and hold on the object, or select the object with the game controller (so that it glows) and press the A button before moving it.

Rotating an Object

The last thing I show you how to do in this chapter is how to rotate your object.

There are many objects you can place on the terrain; trees, apples, and rocks are just a few. But these objects don't have a "face." That is, they typically don't have front, back, and left/right sides. Where you drop them doesn't matter because they'll usually look the same from whatever point on the terrain you are viewing them.

Many objects do have a face (such as Kodu) or at least an identifiable front and back. Some objects, such as cannons, have a dangerous end; where they point is where the cannonball is fired. So, placing these objects requires that you not only determine where you want the object on the terrain but also the direction to point it.

To change the direction that an object is pointing, follow these steps:

1. Select the Object tool and move the mouse pointer over the object.

2. Right-click the object and choose Rotate from the pop-up menu (refer back to Figure 2.17).

> **NOTE**
> You can also use a game controller to rotate an object after it's been placed. You must use the Orbit Camera tool to move around the terrain and then place an object. The object will be facing in the direction that you, the programmer, are also looking at the terrain.

3. A Rotation drag bar will appear, as shown in Figure 2.22. Drag the bar left or right to rotate the object in place on screen and thus fine-tune the direction it is facing.

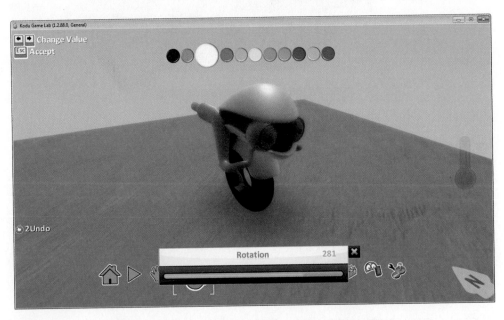

FIGURE 2.22 Change the direction an object is facing with the Rotate option.

You can modify many more characteristics for objects, but now you at least know the basics so that you can enable your new object to move around on the screen. You learn how to do this in Chapter 3, "Take a Test Drive: Controlling Objects and Terrain," so go ahead and pick a character that you like, change its color, maybe increase its height a bit, and play around with the direction it's facing.

When you're comfortable placing an object on the terrain and modifying some of its characteristics, you're ready to start learning how to actually program that object to do things. Fun things!

Moving On

You learned a lot in this chapter. Not only can you move around the terrain however you like, zooming in and out, and rotating it all around, but you also now know how easy it is to add objects to the terrain.

And objects are what Kodu game design is all about. Without objects, your game would consist of players just staring at the pretty, flat terrain. But that's not a fun game at all!

In later chapters, you learn how to take that terrain and make all kinds of crazy changes to it. You learn how to add mountains, lakes, buildings, and other things that moving objects can actually visit and drive around, and maybe even shoot missiles in their direction.

Before you leave Chapter 2, however, I've got a little bit of homework for you. It's not hard, and it won't take long:

1. Drop another object on the terrain. It doesn't matter what it is: a rock, building, or vehicle. Just drop one on there and make some changes to it. Get comfortable with changing an object's color, size, and the direction it's facing. If you're feeling confident, drop another one and do the same thing.

2. After you've got two or three objects on the terrain, spend a little time moving them around with the mouse or game controller. You need some good practice with moving objects around, so having two or three objects on screen will give you some training in dealing with multiple objects.

3. Finally, click the Home Menu button (the icon that looks like a house) and choose the Save My World option. Give it a name at the top and maybe type into the Description field a short description of what you've done. When you're finished, click the Save button.

If you're done for the day, go ahead and click the Home Menu button one more time and select Exit to Main Menu. From the Main Menu, select the Quit Kodu option to close down Kodu Game Lab until you're ready for the next chapter. (And feel free to go tell your teacher, parent, or best friend something about what you learned in this chapter.)

3

Take a Test Drive: Controlling Objects and Terrain

In This Chapter

❍ Programming an Object to Move and Jump

❍ Taking Rover for a Spin

❍ Adding and Modifying an Object

❍ Moving On

Now that you know how to add objects to your game world, it's time to give them some life; this means movement. In this chapter, you learn how to enable an object to move around the screen using the built-in programming capabilities of Kodu Game Lab. You also learn how to test your programming by taking one of Kodu Game Lab's characters for a spin around your world. Finally, because your character won't have a lot of room to actually move around in, you'll see how easy it is to modify your world by adding some more terrain to explore.

Programming an Object to Move and Jump

In Chapter 2, "Explore Kodu Game Lab: Basic User Controls and Tools," you learned how to drop various objects on to the terrain. You also learned how to change some of their characteristics, such as color and size. But right now, no matter how many changes in size or color you make, or which direction you point the character (using the Rotate feature), the character just sits there. Let's change that and add some control that will let us steer the character.

Go ahead and open up a new world and drop in a either Kodu or Rover. I've selected Rover in Figure 3.1, the vehicle submenu. (Refer back to Figure 2.13 to see the submenu that contains the other vehicles.)

FIGURE 3.1   Drop in a vehicle and get ready to add some steering controls.

I'm going to go over programming objects in much more detail throughout this book, but right now I just want to give you some simple steering capabilities so that you can see how easy it is to create a game in Kodu Game Lab:

1. It all starts with selecting the Object tool and then right-clicking (with the mouse) the object. For a game controller, use the Object tool and move the Control Circle over the object and press the Y button.

2. Select the Program option indicated in Figure 3.2.

   With the Kodu Game Lab, everything you do to create a game is going to involve completing a series of When Something Happens, Do This commands. As shown in Figure 3.3, after you select the Program option, a numbered row appears onscreen with two other items inside: a When selection box and a Do selection box. Notice also that the When and Do boxes have a large plus sign (+) inside of them. The pencil cursor also indicates which of the boxes is currently selected.

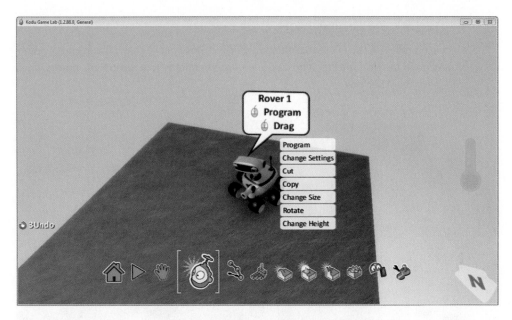

FIGURE 3.2   Select the Program option for the object you want to modify.

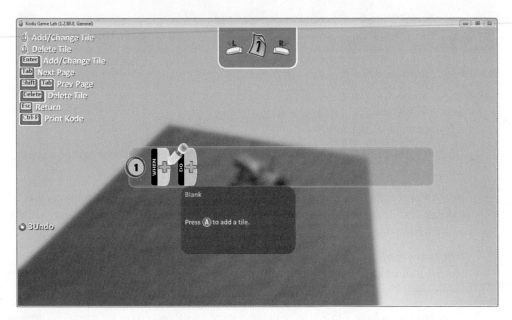

FIGURE 3.3   Programming starts with the When and Do programming boxes.

3. Select the When box by left-clicking it.

   Game controller users can use the left thumbstick to move between the boxes and pressing the A button to select the When box. Figure 3.4 shows another pie menu that appears when you select the When box.

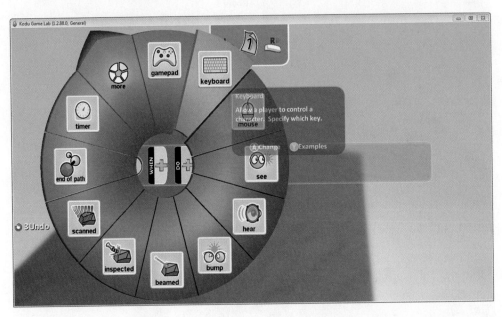

FIGURE 3.4   Select the When box and a pie menu appears with various options.

4. Select the Keyboard option if you're using a mouse/keyboard, and choose the Gamepad option if you're using a game controller.

   Figure 3.5 shows that I've selected the Keyboard option; it appears inside the When box now. (The Gamepad option appears if you select that option.)

   Notice now that there's still a + to the right of the Keyboard option. This lets me know that there are additional selections that can be made (but are not always required). Can you guess why this happens?

   First, I want to be able to control Rover using some keys on the keyboard. But which keys? I've specified in the When box to monitor the Keyboard, but Kodu Game Lab needs more information.

5. Go ahead and click the + to add more details. Figure 3.6 shows another pie menu that appears.

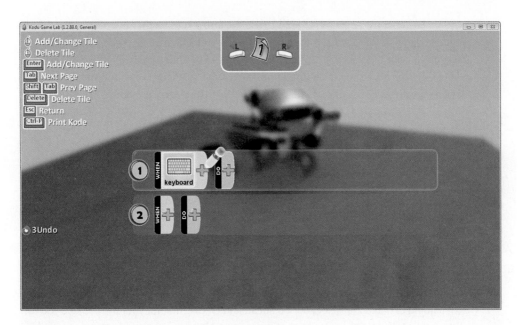

FIGURE 3.5   Adding the Keyboard option to the When box.

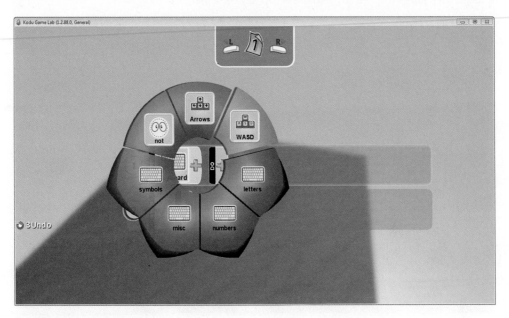

FIGURE 3.6   Another pie menu appears, allowing me to provide more details about the Keyboard option I selected.

I have many options here! I can choose to use the arrow keys on the keyboard or the WASD keyboard keys (W for forward, A for left, D for right, and S for reverse). I can also choose to program specific letters and assign them certain tasks by choosing the Letters option. (Kodu Game Lab even allows me to choose number keys, miscellaneous keys, and special symbol keys; all these can be assigned to do certain special things when pressed.)

> **NOTE**
>
> If you're a game controller user, I'm going to assume that you've got the hang of using the game controller for moving the Control Circle and making selections. Remember that Tips in the upper-left corner of the screen can always help you figure out how to do things. Rather than switch back and forth between mouse/keyboard instructions and game controller instructions, I'm going to stick with the mouse and keyboard, and will use Notes and Tips to alert you when something unusual or different happens for game controller users.

For now, I just want to be able to steer Rover, and I've played plenty of games that use WASD, so I'm going to make that selection. Go ahead and choose that for your own object; you can change it later if you like.

Figure 3.7 shows that I've selected the WASD key combinations.

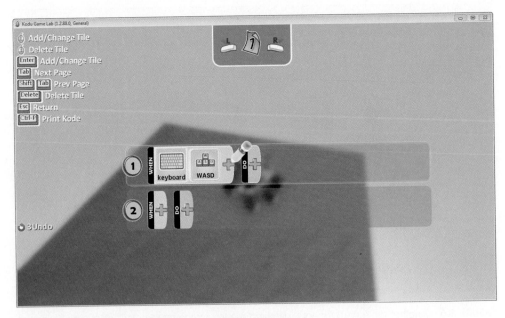

FIGURE 3.7   Adding the WASD keys to the Keyboard option.

Now the WASD keys are added to the When box, just after the Keyboard option. But there's that + again!

Go ahead and click it and you should see just one option: Not.

6.   Select the Not option and add it to the When box, as shown in Figure 3.8.

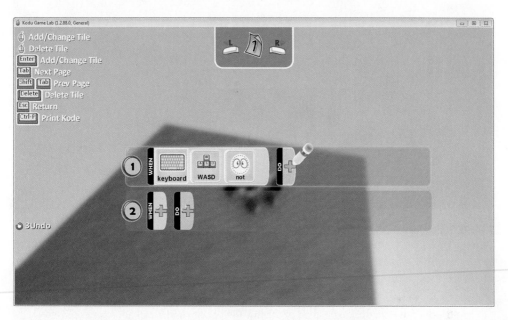

FIGURE 3.8   Adding another option to the When box that really isn't needed.

I'm not going to do anything with the Not feature right now, but I wanted you to add it so that I could show you how easy it is to undo an action. By adding the Not feature, I'm going to be telling Rover to do something when the WASD keys are *not* pressed—this could be just roaming around randomly, shooting missiles, or some other action. But that's not what I really want to program in right now; I only want Rover to move when I press the WASD keys, and I want him to stay in one place when I'm not pressing those keys.

7.   You need to remove the Not feature, and to do this right-click it and choose the Cut Tile option shown in Figure 3.9.

To delete any tile, just right-click it and choose Cut Tile. You'll use this feature a lot as you test your games. You might add tiles and find that they don't do what you need them to do. In that case, you simply delete them and try something else.

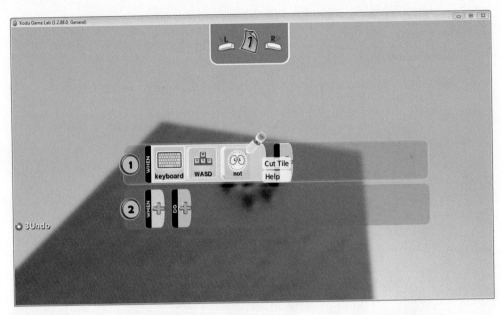

FIGURE 3.9 Delete a tile by right-clicking it and choosing Cut Tile.

> **NOTE**
>
> One more really cool feature of the Kodu Game Lab is the built-in Help tool. Right-click a tile and choose the Help option (instead of the Cut Tile option) and you'll get a pop-up window like the one shown in Figure 3.10. The Help option provides you with an example of how the selection looks in a box (either the When or Do box) as well as a short description of its function.

At this point, I've defined in the When box that I want to monitor the keyboard and the WASD keys. But I haven't yet programmed what happens when these keys are pressed. And that's where the Do box comes into play.

8. Go ahead and click **+** in the Do box and you'll see a pie menu like the one in Figure 3.11.

Many of the options available on the Do box's pie menu won't make sense at this point. What is Switch or Inline, for instance? Don't worry. You learn about these in later chapters. For now, I want to introduce you to the Move pie slice shown in Figure 3.11.

9. That's the one I'm going to select, and I want you to do the same. Select the Move pie slice.

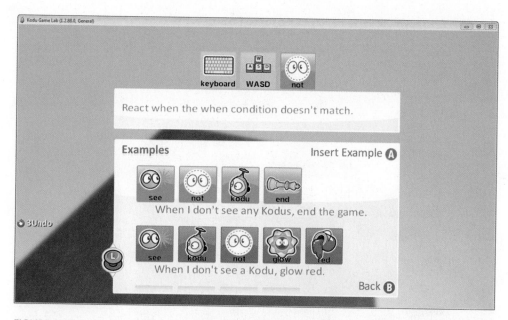

FIGURE 3.10 Use the Help feature to understand the various tiles and how they work.

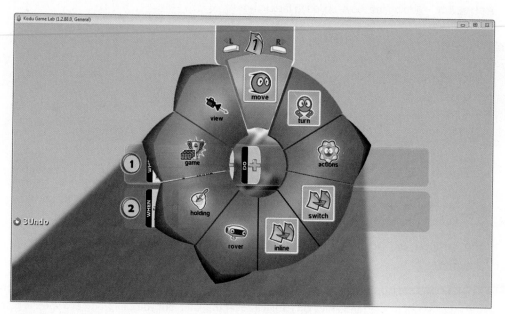

FIGURE 3.11 Another pie menu, but this one is for the Do box.

Figure 3.12 shows the Move option added to the Do box.

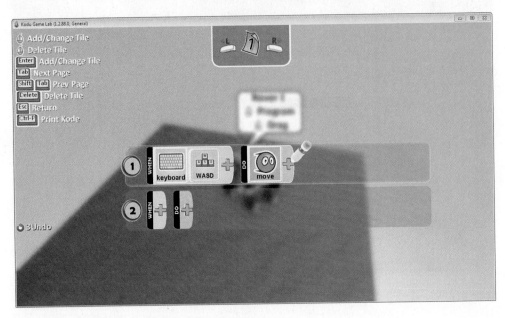

FIGURE 3.12   Adding the Move option to the Do box.

TIP

If you choose the Turn option by mistake, you can quickly change your selection by selecting the wrong tile and choosing the correct one from the pie menu that appears. You don't have to use the Cut Tile feature to delete the incorrect one if you simply want to exchange it for another.

Once again, there's a + after the Move option. This makes sense if you think about it for a moment. I've used the When box to monitor when I press the WASD keys, and I'm now telling Rover to move when one of those keys is pressed. But where, and in what direction?

10. Go ahead and click the + after the Move option to display a pie menu like the one shown in Figure 3.13.

Options include Forward (Rover's wheels will always spin forward, even when turning left or right), Wander (Rover moves randomly), On Path (I'll cover this later, but you can program a specific path you want an object to follow), and other options. You can even specify a speed: Quickly or Slowly. Figure 3.14 shows that I've selected Wander.

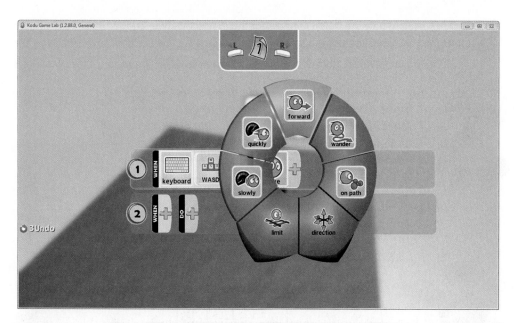

FIGURE 3.13   Specify what type of movement is needed using this pie menu.

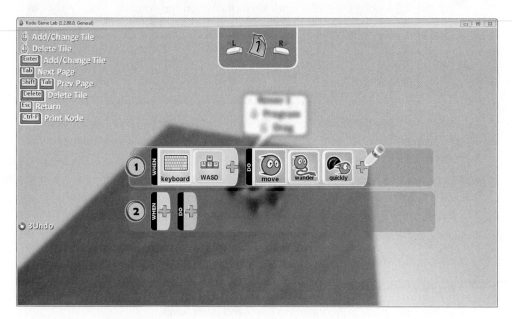

FIGURE 3.14   Programming Rover to wander… quickly.

If you're wondering how the Quickly option got there, select Wander and see if you have another +. Click it and you'll see additional options; I chose Quickly, but you can choose Slowly if you like.

I've now programmed Rover to wander around at a fast pace when I press any of the WASD keys.

Rover: I like the WASD keys for controlling my movements, but can other keys be used for forward or left or right?

Kodu: Yes, but that requires more programming.

Rover: How do you do it?

Kodu: For each movement, you need to specify the Keyboard tile and a letter tile in the When box, and then in the Do box select the movement you want to assign to the letter you picked. Using this, you can make the T key, for example, control forward movement.

You might have noticed that after we added a tile to the Programming Row 1 (refer back to Figure 3.3), another programming row appeared below it: Programming Row 2. What do you think this means?

Well, it means that you can add more complex programming to Rover. I could go back and specify that when the left mouse button is pressed, Rover jumps high into the air. Take a look at Figure 3.15 and you'll see that I've programmed in that ability. See if you can duplicate it.

If you need some help, here's a quick explanation:

1. Click the new When box in Programming Row 2 and select the Mouse option.

2. Click the + next to the Mouse option and select Left.

3. Click the new Do box in Programming Row 2 and select Jump.

4. Click the + next to the Jump option and select High.

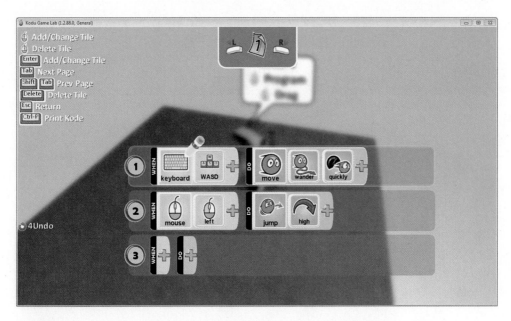

FIGURE 3.15   Rover can now jump super-high when the mouse is left-clicked.

That's it!

Want to drive Rover and get him to jump? Okay, here's how.

Taking Rover for a Spin

It's time to let Rover go and explore his world. To do this, follow these steps:

1. Exit the programming screen.

   For mouse/keyboard users, just press the Esc key. Don't worry; your program did not get deleted! It's still there. (To double-check, just right-click the object again and choose Program; you'll see your program again.)

2. Click the Play button on the toolbar shown in Figure 3.16.

> **TIP**
>
> Frequent use of the Play button is crucial to designing a good game. You need to develop a habit of making one or two changes or additions to your game and then testing the results. Don't create an entire game and then press the Play button; you'll likely be disappointed. Instead, develop a pattern of Add – Play/Test – Add/Modify – Play/Test – Add/Modify – Play/Test…. Should you make a mistake with a small bit of programming, you'll easily know where to go back and look for the error.

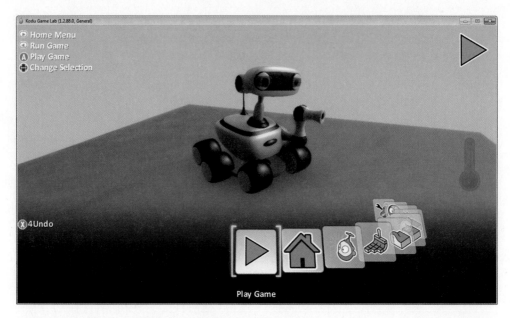

FIGURE 3.16 Click the Play button to test your new program.

The toolbar has now disappeared and I'm seeing Rover sitting still on the terrain. Time to get him moving.

My first test will be to move him forward. I press the W key on the keyboard and…

Rover's moving around randomly.

Now, he doesn't really have a whole lot of room to move around though, does he? I'm going to fix that in a moment. But while I'm in testing mode, I want to go ahead and press the A and D and S keys and make sure that they work. I press them and…

Rover continues to move around randomly.

But what about his jumping capability? Time to check that. I left-click and…

Rover jumps.

He's fast, but I managed to rotate the terrain a little bit (remember how to do that?) and take a screenshot so you can see underneath him as he jumps. Figure 3.17 shows him getting off the ground.

Congratulations! You just programmed an object to move and jump. It might not seem like much, but consider this: In many games, you must control an object by moving it around the screen. And sometimes you need that object to jump over obstacles or jump high to collect a treasure that's floating in the air. You've just learned how to program those two movements that are essential to many games. And you did it with only two programming rows. Imagine how powerful your games are going to be when you start adding more objects, more programming rows, and more terrain. Are you beginning to see the potential for your own games?

FIGURE 3.17 Rover jumps when I press the J key.

And speaking of adding more terrain, let's return to Rover for a minute and examine his world. It's not very big, is it? One patch of square, green grass. He could probably use some more terrain to move around on, couldn't he? Let's see how that is done.

Adding More Terrain

Over the next few chapters, you learn how to modify the terrain in different ways. You learn to add water, mountains, and much more, but let's start simply and just give Rover some more ground to roll around on:

1. To start, zoom out a bit so you can see the surrounding empty space around Rover and his single patch of terrain.

Figure 3.18 shows all that empty space waiting to be filled. Remember, you can use the Move Camera tool to move the terrain around the screen, left or right, but in Figure 3.18 I've centered the existing terrain right in the middle of the screen.

2. Select the Ground Brush from the toolbar, shown in Figure 3.19. This tool works the same for both the mouse/keyboard and the game controller.

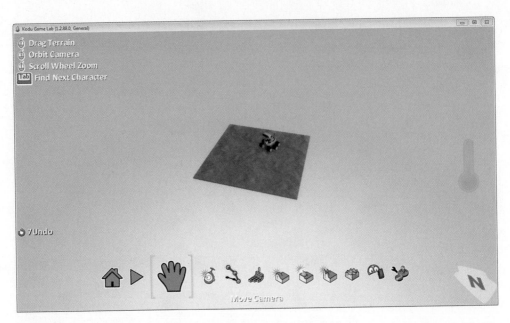

FIGURE 3.18   Zoom out to see how much empty space is available.

FIGURE 3.19   Select the Ground Brush to add more terrain.

Terrain is added using the Ground Brush. (In a later chapter, I show you how to resize the brush so that you can add bigger or smaller bits of terrain.)

3. After selecting the Ground Brush, use the mouse or the game controller's left thumbstick to move the glowing brush seen in Figure 3.20 to where I want to place a bit of new terrain, and I left-click with the mouse (or the Right trigger with the D-Pad) to add the new terrain.

FIGURE 3.20   Move the glowing white square to where you want to put some new terrain.

Notice in Figure 3.21 that the terrain doesn't quite match the original. Oops. That's easy to fix:

Notice in the Tips in the upper-left corner of the screen that you have an option called Pick Material from Terrain. To do so, just move the mouse pointer (or Control Circle) to the old patch of green grass and hold down the Alt key on the keyboard. A small cone appears that points down; move it over the terrain you want to copy and left-click. You'll hear a ding sound to indicate the color has been copied.

Now, move the mouse pointer (or Control Circle) over the terrain that doesn't match. Consult the Tips again and you'll see an option for Paint Material. It requires that you hold down the Shift key and left-click. I drag the mouse pointer over the new terrain, hold down the Shift key and left-click, and the terrain now matches, as shown in Figure 3.22. As a matter of fact, I went ahead and added three additional patches (at each corner).

FIGURE 3.21 The new patch of terrain doesn't match.

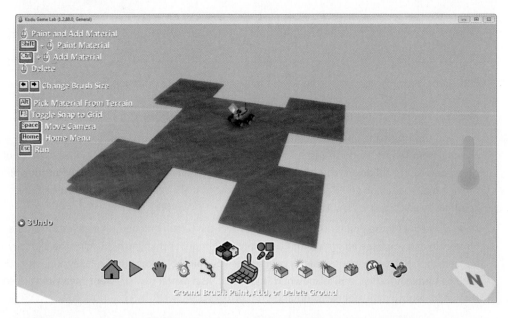

FIGURE 3.22 I've changed the terrain color to match and added additional squares.

Before I end this chapter, let me show you a few more terrain editing features, and then I'm going to give you some homework that will let you explore the programming rows a bit more.

Changing the Terrain Color/Material

I'm already bored with the green grass. Are you? Let's add some new terrain for Rover to explore and change the material (and color). To do this, follow these steps:

1. Select the Ground Brush.

   Notice when you select the Ground Brush, however, that there are two small icons that appear above it (one to the left and one to the right, as shown in Figure 3.23).

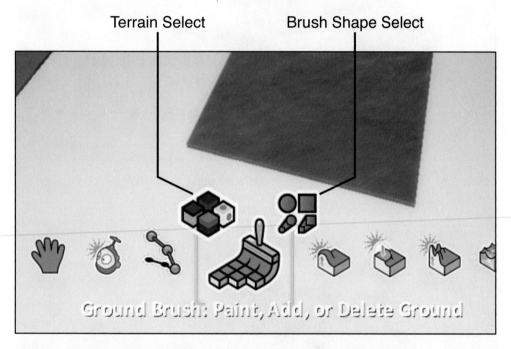

FIGURE 3.23   Changing the terrain material and color is easy.

2. Let's start with the Materials icon on the left. Select this option with the mouse (or press the Y button on a game controller) and you'll get a numbered row of small cubes, each with a different color or material. You can use the mouse scroll wheel to cycle through all of them (over 100 in all!); just click with the mouse on the one you like, and that's the material that will now be "painted" when you place new terrain.

Let's try it. Figure 3.24 shows me selecting option 13, a marble-like material that looks like clouds over a blue ocean.

Now I can click anywhere I like and add a small square of terrain with that pattern and color. Figure 3.25 shows that I've had some fun and added a mix of green grass and marbled terrain for Rover to explore.

FIGURE 3.24   Select a terrain that you want to add to the world.

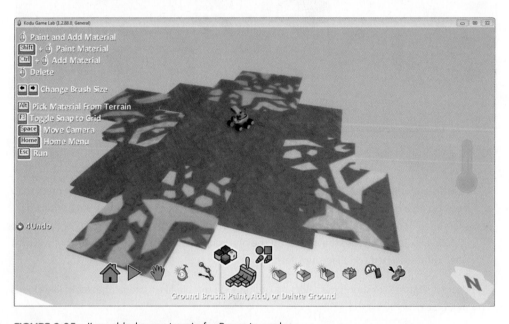

FIGURE 3.25   I've added more terrain for Rover to explore.

That square pattern, however, doesn't look very lifelike, does it? Fortunately, there's a way to change the shape of new terrain from square to round:

1. I just need to select the Ground Brush again, but this time I pick the Brush Shape option that sits above and to the right (refer back to Figure 3.23).

2. When I select this option, I can change the brush shape from Square Brush to Hard Round Brush, Linear Square Brush, Linear Hard Round Brush, or Magic Brush. I'm going to choose Hard Round Brush right now, but feel free to experiment with the other three options.

> **NOTE**
>
> The other three brushes offer different behaviors when creating new terrain. The Magic Brush simply lets you recolor existing terrain by first choosing the new material/color and then moving the mouse pointer over existing terrain; it will change color automatically. (It can also be used to raise and lower terrain; you learn how to do this later in the book.) The other two Linear brushes are used to put down terrain between Point A and Point B. You click once at Point A where you want a bit of terrain to be added and then move the mouse to Point B and click; terrain is added between these two points. The Linear brushes are much more accurate (in terms of drawing a straight line of terrain) than trying to draw a straight line by clicking and holding down the mouse as you paint the terrain with a continuous brush stroke.

You can place a single piece of terrain by clicking and releasing the left mouse button where you want that terrain to be located. You can also hold down the left mouse button and drag the mouse to apply a continuous "brushstroke" that will leave a piece of terrain wherever you move the mouse. Figure 3.26 shows that I used the Hard Round Brush to put some marbled terrain in the gaps between the green grass.

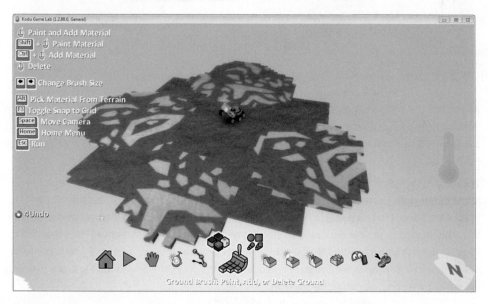

FIGURE 3.26 Add terrain bit by bit or hold down the mouse button and go crazy.

After you add a bit more terrain for Rover, go ahead and press the Play button again and take him for a spin. Now that he has more room to explore, you'll be able to see a bit more randomness to his movements. Also, you can press the left mouse key as he drives and jump at the same time.

Save Your Progress

You've done a lot of work in this chapter, and I don't want you to lose it. So, when you're done playing and driving Rover around, go ahead and click the Home Menu button (the house icon) and select the Save My World option shown in Figure 3.27.

FIGURE 3.27   Save your world so that you do not lose the programming and terrain additions.

As you can see in Figure 3.28, I've given my new world a temporary name (Wander Jump and New Terrain). I can change that at any time. I also added in some text to the Description box so that I can remember what I did with this version of the game. I also typed my name into the Creator text box.

Speaking of the game version, take a look again at Figure 3.28 and locate the version number in the upper-right corner of the screen. Right now it's set to V00 (version 00), but the next time I make any changes to this game I'm going to increment that by one using the up/down arrows to V01. This allows me to save multiple versions of my game as it develops. Should I find that version 10 (V10) doesn't work the way I like because of a new programming row I added, I can choose to delete that row, or I can simply go back and open up version 9 (V09) and I won't lose any previous work—just the addition of that buggy row.

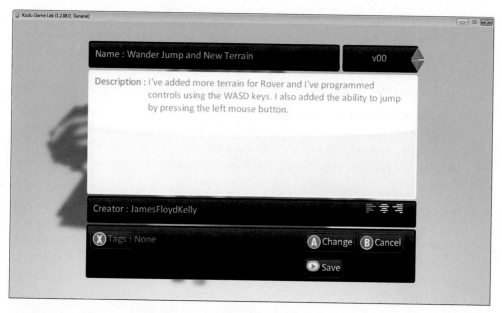

FIGURE 3.28 Give your game a name and provide a description.

Click the Save button and you're returned to the Kodu Game Lab to continue your game design, or you can quit and return to it later.

Moving On

How does it feel to be a game designer? You did quite a lot in this chapter, including programming an object to obey your move commands. You also gave your object a special ability (jump) and created some additional terrain for it to explore.

Games that you design are going to depend on you not only placing and programming the right objects into your game but also on some smart terrain design. A game that sits on nothing but a flat bit of terrain will work, but it better have some amazing objects and controls and objectives for the player to overlook the lack of terrain. Likewise, you can design the coolest-looking terrain, complete with mountains and cities and lakes, but if there's nothing fun to do on top of that terrain, your game player is going to get bored. Fast.

But you're taking your time and exploring the tools and experimenting with all the buttons and pie menus and terrain options, aren't you? You know that it's going to be a combination of good terrain design and good object placement and programming that's going to make your game stand out, so pat yourself on the back and smile because you're well on your way to designing some great games.

I did tell you I would have some homework, but I promise it won't be hard or boring. Here's what I'd like you to do before moving on to the next chapter:

1. Drop another object on the new terrain you've just added. Right-click that object and experiment with the When and Do boxes to give that object something different to do. Don't make it move around; explore a bit and see whether you can find a way for it to add a point to a scoreboard every time you press the P key. Or, maybe drop in a Danger Tree that fires a missile every time the right mouse button is pressed.

2. Save your work and then open up a new world. For this assignment, I want you to try and design a world that consists of a piece of terrain that looks like a dartboard. Make the center dot one color, and then add a ring around it of a different color, and then a larger ring around that one. Add five or six rings until you get the hang of selecting terrain and painting it on the screen.

3. And last, explore the Home Menu a bit more. Close out of Kodu Game Lab, open it up again, and choose the Load World option. Click the My Worlds button shown in Figure 3.29 and scroll through the various games you've saved. Practice opening one game, closing it down, and opening another. I want you to gain experience with moving between not only different games but also different version numbers. So, if you don't have multiple versions of a game, make a few fake ones and save them as Game 1, Game 2, Game 2 v01, and so on.

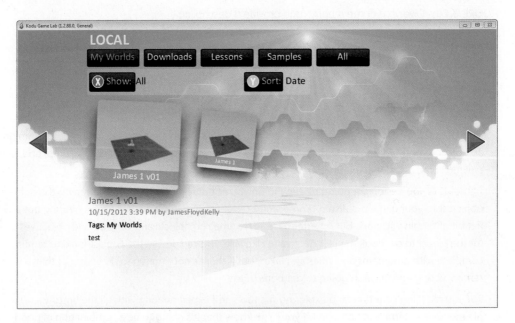

FIGURE 3.29   The My Worlds screen shows you all your games.

When you finish with the homework, click the Home Menu button and select Exit to Main Menu. From the Main Menu, select Quit Kodu to close down Kodu Game Lab.

Missiles Locked and Loaded: Adding Targets and Firing Controls

If a game involved nothing more than just moving a character around the screen, you would now know everything you need to create a game with Kodu Game Lab. But that would make for one seriously boring game. (Or maybe not; Google the game titled Journey.) Games usually need a bit more complexity than just moving around the screen, and although you'll learn about a number of game elements in this book, one of the best ways to add this complexity is to enable your players to shoot at targets. After you've figured out how to fire some missiles, you're also going to be shown how to make some tweaks to your world that can have fun and interesting consequences to a game.

Adding Nonmoving Obstacles

Now that you know how to create new terrain and add objects, it's time to see what you can do in Kodu Game Lab when objects interact with one another. You can take a number of actions when one object touches another: increment a score counter, cause one of the objects to explode, and much more. But before you learn how to do some of these things, let's create a new world that gives us room to explore the results of two objects interacting:

1. Add some terrain to increase the size of the world. The color doesn't matter; just use your new skills in adding terrain to create something similar to the world shown in Figure 4.1.

FIGURE 4.1   Add some terrain to expand your new world.

2. Drop in Kodu, as shown in Figure 4.2. Place the object to the far left. I'm using Kodu.

> **NOTE**
> Notice that the new object I added is named Kodu 1. If I drop another Kodu, its name will be Kodu 2. The unique name given to each similar object you dropped will come in handy later, but for now I am working with just one Kodu object.

3. Drop in some rocks and trees. Add two rocks and one tree, as shown in Figure 4.3.

FIGURE 4.2 Drop in Kodu to your new world.

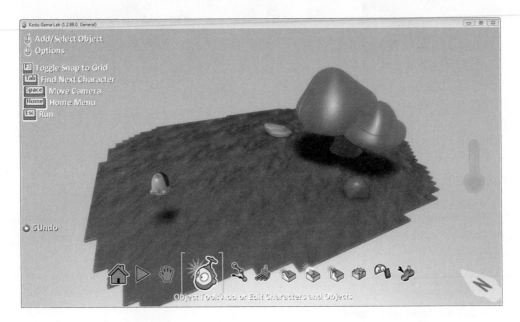

FIGURE 4.3 Add some rocks and a tree and move them to the right side of the world.

Rock and Tree are two of the objects you can select from the pie submenu that appears when you click the terrain to place an object. When you click the Rock or Tree leaf, you are given additional variations of those items, so pick any that you like. Feel free to modify each of them to change their size, but keep them to the right of Kodu for now.

Making Objects Disappear

Now it's time to have some fun. First, I need to give myself steering control over Kodu, so I've added a short program shown in Figure 4.4 that gives me basic steering controls. (Refer back to Chapter 3, "Take a Test Drive: Controlling Objects and Terrain," if you need help with this bit of programming.)

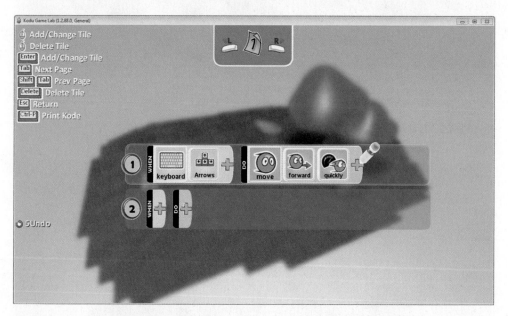

FIGURE 4.4 Add basic movement controls to Kodu.

Press the Play button and take Kodu for a test drive. For my world, the rocks are small enough that Kodu flies right over them, but he cannot fly over the tree and instead bumps into it, shown in Figure 4.5.

Next, I increased the size of the rocks to maximum. This time, when I run Kodu into a rock, instead of flying over it, he pushes it!

Figure 4.6 shows what happens.

FIGURE 4.5   Try to push the tree with Kodu and see what happens.

FIGURE 4.6   Objects will run right up against the invisible boundary surrounding your world.

For objects you control, a glass wall circling your world prevents objects from falling off. (Trees, though, no matter how small, are locked in place; they must have some really strong roots!) (And you'll see in a later chapter how to lock any object in place, preventing it from moving.)

> **NOTE**
> You can turn off the glass wall that surrounds the terrain, and I show you how to do that later. For now, I keep the shield in place to prevent Kodu from falling off, too.

I like trees, but Kodu is feeling the need to clear some room for him to roam and explore. Let me show you how to give Kodu the special ability to clear the tree off the terrain:

1. Select Kodu and right-click him to choose the Program option.

   Programming Row 1 already contains the steps I added that gave me control of his movement. It's Programming Row 2 that I use to make the tree disappear when Kodu bumps it.

2. Click in the When box in Row 2 and select Bump, as shown in Figure 4.7. I select the Bump action because I want to define what happens when two objects touch (or bump).

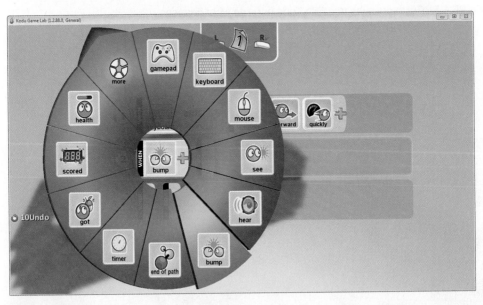

FIGURE 4.7 Choose the Bump option when you want to create an action that occurs when Kodu bumps the Tree object.

3. Click + to the right of the Bump tile and select the Objects pie piece, as shown in Figure 4.8.

4. You'll see a variety of objects that are included in Kodu Game Lab: Factory, Hut, Castle, Apple, Rock, and more. Tree is in that list, as shown in Figure 4.9, so go ahead and select Tree because

we want to control what happens when Kodu bumps a Tree object. (You can also add a Programming Row 3 and define what happens when Kodu bumps a Rock object if you want.)

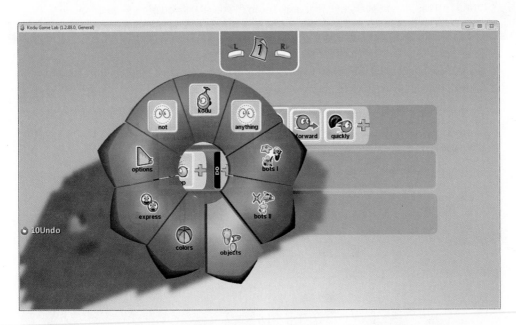

FIGURE 4.8   Selecting what will be watched for a bump to occur.

FIGURE 4.9   The Tree object is selected and will have something done to it if Kodu bumps it.

> **NOTE**
>
> This action applies to every tree that appears on the terrain. If you drop 50 trees on the terrain and Kodu bumps any of them, what you define in the Do box will happen to that tree.

You've now defined the When box that will monitor for some action (Kodu bumps Tree) to occur. Now it's time to define what happens when that action is detected:

1. Click + in the Do box and select the Combat pie slice, as shown in Figure 4.10. Notice also you can choose to Eat, Turn, Shoot, and many more. You'll learn about many of these in later chapters, but the one we want is Vanish, and it's hidden in the Combat leaf.

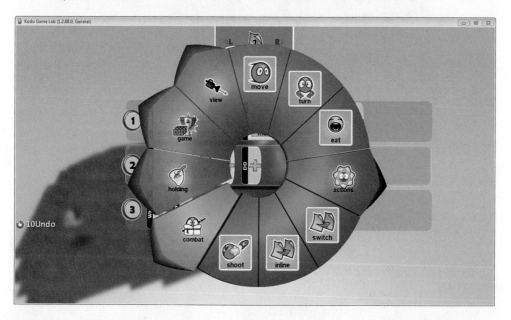

FIGURE 4.10 Select the Combat pie slice to see things that will occur to the object that has been bumped by Kodu.

2. Look at all the things you can do to an object that is bumped by Kodu: Boom, Damage, Heal, Stun, and Knockout. Is your imagination starting to run with all the possible game ideas these fun-sounding actions offer? Don't worry; I show you many of these options in upcoming chapters, but for now, I just want you to make the tree go away, which you do by selecting the Vanish option, as shown in Figure 4.11.

3. You might think you can just leave the Vanish tile as it is and run the game. But there's one thing still left to do: You must choose which object disappears, Kodu or the tree. So, click + to the right of the Vanish tile and select It (meaning the Tree) and your final program will be ready, as shown in Figure 4.12. (If you were to select Me, you would make Kodu disappear.)

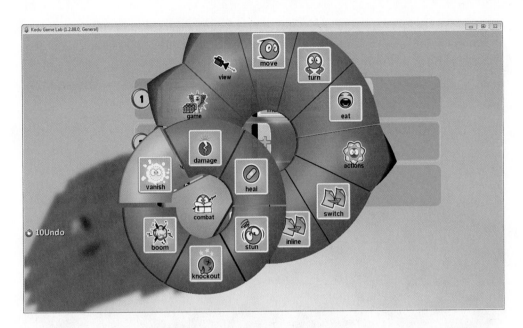

FIGURE 4.11   Select Vanish to make the Tree object disappear.

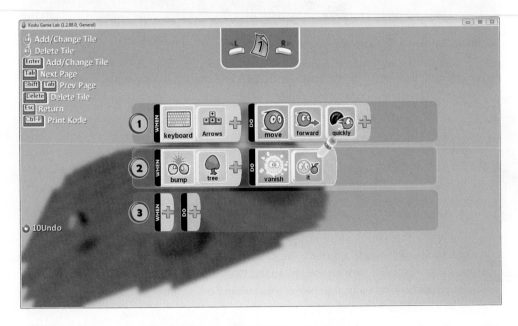

FIGURE 4.12   Your program to make trees disappear is complete.

Tap the Esc (Escape) key on the keyboard to exit the programming screen and then click the Play button. Use the arrow keys (or your game controller) to steer Kodu into the tree and see what happens. Figure 4.13 shows that I programmed the bump correctly because...

FIGURE 4.13   I just bumped Kodu into the tree. What tree?

The tree disappeared! If it didn't disappear, go back and check your programming to make sure it matches the programming shown in Figure 4.12.

> **TIP**
>
> Sometimes in a game, you do want your controllable character to disappear. Normally this also ends a game. Consider a game that has a dangerous magical rock that when touched causes Kodu to disappear. In that instance, rather than choose the It option for when Kodu bumps the rock, you would choose the Me option, and Kodu would be gone with a poof!

I've got a quick challenge for you here. Create a new world with Kodu or Rover and program that object so that you can drive it around the screen. Next, drop in some trees on your world. Now, can you figure out how to change the color of a tree when Kodu or Rover bump into it?

I hope you're having some fun here and getting lots of ideas for games you want to create, so let's not stop. I want you to modify the existing program a bit and enable Kodu to fire missiles. Does that sound fun?

Here Come the Missiles

Exit the game (if you're playing it) and use the Object Tool to select Kodu and right-click him. Choose Program to pull up the existing program. You're going to create Programming Row 3, so start by clicking + to the right of the When box and selecting the Mouse option. Click + to the right of the Mouse tile and choose the Left button, as shown in Figure 4.14.

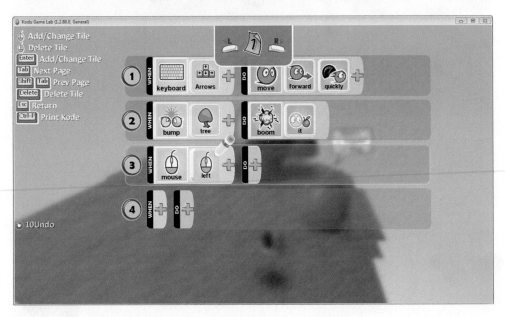

FIGURE 4.14   Add the left mouse click option to the When box.

Next, let's define what happens when the left button is pressed. We do this by clicking + to the right of the Do box and selecting the Shoot action. Click + to the right of the Shoot tile and specify the Missile option, as shown in Figure 4.15.

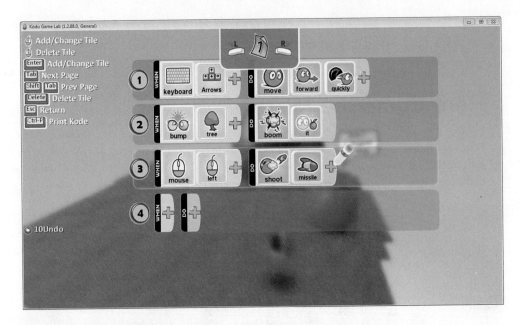

Figure 4.15 Choose the Shoot action and select Missile as the option.

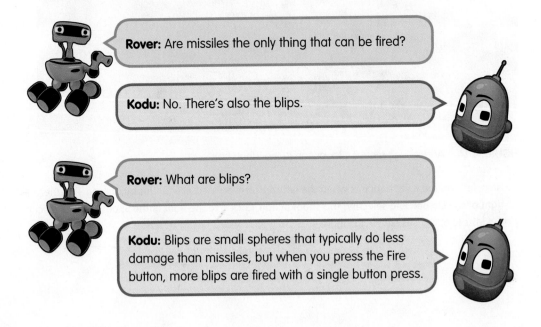

Rover: Are missiles the only thing that can be fired?

Kodu: No. There's also the blips.

Rover: What are blips?

Kodu: Blips are small spheres that typically do less damage than missiles, but when you press the Fire button, more blips are fired with a single button press.

Go ahead and test your new game. Fire a few missiles in the direction of the tree and rocks and see what happens. The missiles will self-guide themselves to the target, so you'll need to use the mouse pointer to pick the target or turn and face the target if you're using a D-Pad controller. Figure 4.16 shows a missile heading to its target.

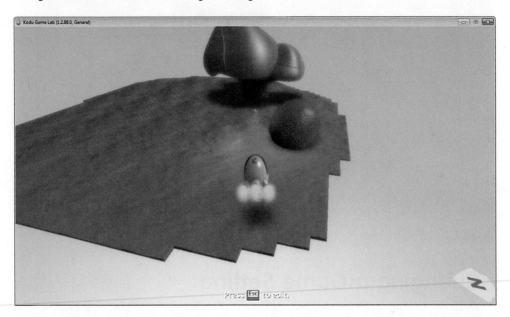

Figure 4.16 Fire a missile at a rock or tree.

Did the tree or rock disappear? (A short rock might not get hit, so increase the size of the rocks if you want to see an explosion!)

If you'd rather not have to use the mouse to set the direction of the missile, go back into your program and click + to the right of the Missile tile. Select Direction and then choose Forward. Your program should look like the one in Figure 4.17, and when you play it the missile will always fire in the direction that Kodu is facing. Try it.

I don't know about you, but that missile is firing just a bit too slowly. I want lots of missiles! To change the speed that the missile fires, I need to modify the game settings. Up to now, you haven't had to tweak any game settings, but now it's time to learn how to do it. When you complete the next section of this chapter, you'll have enough information to figure out how to increase the missile firing speed on your own.

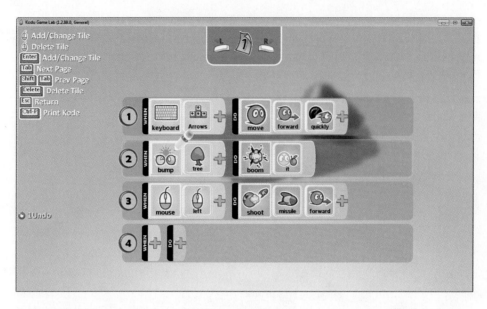

Figure 4.17   Firing missiles that go where Kodu is facing.

Changing a Game Setting

When you have an object selected and you right-click it, you have a lot of options available. You've used some of them already, such as Program, Change Size, and Rotate. But have you noticed the Change Settings option in the list shown in Figure 4.18?

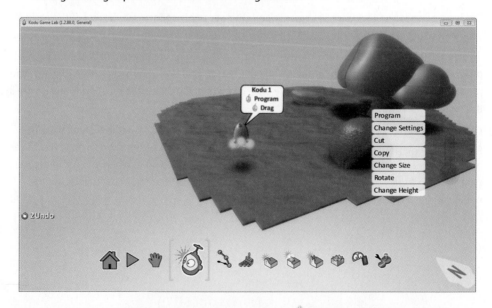

Figure 4.18   Change Settings is an option available to all objects you place in a game.

In Figure 4.18, I've right-clicked one of the rocks. When you think of a rock, you probably think of things like its color, shape, or size. But in a game, a rock has many more characteristics. It can have hit points. (For instance, if a missile does 50 damage and the rock has 100 hit points, it'll take two missiles to destroy the rock.) It can also be indestructible; no number of missiles will destroy it.

Every object has its own characteristics that can be tweaked, and to access and view these options, select the Change Settings option after right-clicking an object. A scrollable list of settings appears on screen, as shown in Figure 4.19.

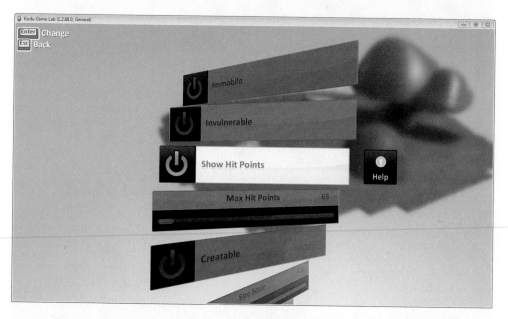

Figure 4.19   An object's settings are listed in a scrollable list.

You use the mouse's scroll wheel to move up and down the list. The setting in the center of the screen is slightly brighter (others are dimmed or grayed out), and a Help box appears to the right of it. In Figure 4.19, for example, Show Hit Points (of the rock) is selected, and I can click the Help box (or press the Y button on a game controller) to read more details about a particular setting. In this instance, to enable the Show Hit Points box, I simply click the Power icon (it turns green to indicate it is active), and a small health bar appears over the rock, as shown in Figure 4.20.

Drag bars like the one shown in Figure 4.21 work by moving the green bar left or right. A number in the upper-right corner of the box changes as you move the drag bar. Figure 4.20 shows that I've made the Max Hit Points of the selected Rock object equal to 200. Tap the Esc key to exit the Change Settings screen when you're done.

Figure 4.20 View an object's health to see how many hit points it has left.

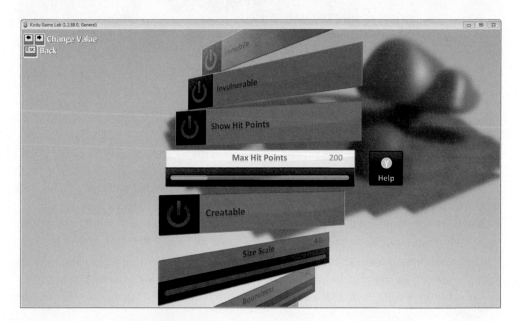

Figure 4.21 Increase the maximum hit points of an object by using a drag bar.

Some objects will have settings that are not available to other objects. Kodu, for example, has settings related to his speed; the Rock object doesn't move and therefore doesn't have speed settings to tweak.

There are so many settings available in Kodu Game Lab that unfortunately I cannot cover them all. The good news is that every setting has a Help box to its right that can provide you with more details about what it does and how it works.

I encourage you to spend some time right-clicking on your current objects (Kodu, Tree, Rock) and changing a setting here or there. Click some Help boxes and see what certain settings are all about. At this stage in the book, you really can't do anything wrong that cannot be undone. Have some fun, look around, and make some changes to see what happens.

Now that you've seen how to access the settings for an object, let's have some fun with our current game by tweaking some of Kodu's settings and the tree's settings.

Having Fun with Settings

First, I want to turn the damage done by one of Kodu's missiles down a bit, which I do as follows:

1. Right-click Kodu.

2. Select Change Settings.

3. Scroll down the list to find Missile Damage, as shown in Figure 4.22.

4. Use the drag bar to set the value to 10.

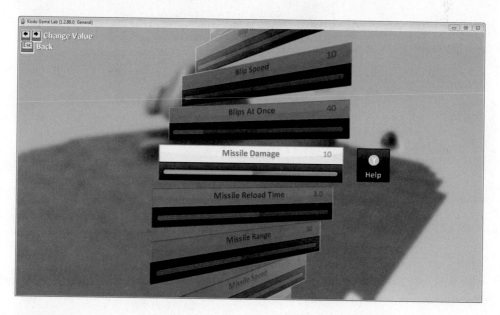

FIGURE 4.22   Change the damage done by a missile using Change Settings.

Next, I want to increase the hit points of the Tree object, which I do like this:

1. Right-click the Tree.

2. Select Change Settings.

3. Scroll down to the Max Hit Points setting and change it to 100 using the drag bar, as shown in Figure 4.23.

> **NOTE**
>
> If you're not familiar with the term *hit points*, it's an easy concept. Hit points are how much damage an object can take before it is destroyed. Hit points are given as a value (such as 50 or 100). If the Missile Damage is set to 10, and a tree's hit points are 100, it will take 10 hits from a missile to destroy it. Likewise, if the missile damage is 1, it will take 100 hits to destroy that tree. Keep in mind that objects can also be programmed to be invulnerable, meaning they cannot be destroyed.

FIGURE 4.23 Increase the hit points for the Tree object.

Now it's going to take more than a single missile to destroy the tree!

One last tweak: I want a health bar over the top of the tree just like the one I added to the rock. Scroll up just one setting and enable the Show Hit Points option (refer to Figure 4.23); the Power icon should turn green when you click it.

Now it's time to play. Figure 4.24 shows that I've taken five successful missile shots at the tree (half of the health bar is gone).

FIGURE 4.24   Poor tree! Only half of its hit points are left.

As you can imagine, when you start designing your own games, you can define how many hit points enemies have, how much damage your weapons can do (as well as the damage done by enemy weapons), and other game-related settings.

CAUTION

Every object you place on the terrain is considered unique. That means if you place two rocks and change the hit points of Rock 1 to 500, the hit points of Rock 2 will still remain at 50 (the default setting). When you change the settings of one object, it does not automatically update that same setting on an identical object. There is a way to do this, however, and I cover that later in this book.

Save Your Progress

Go ahead and save your work here. Give it a new name; perhaps "Chapter 4 Test," or "Missiles Versus Tree." Whatever name you choose, be sure to fill in some basic information about the game in the Description box, as shown in Figure 4.25.

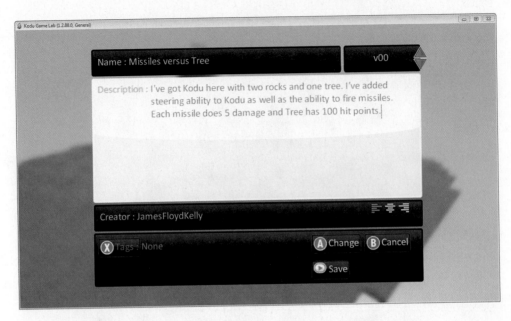

FIGURE 4.25 Save the current world so that you don't lose your work.

Moving On

You've learned enough so far to create a basic and fun game. You now know how to drop in objects (including vehicles and nonmoving obstacles such as trees and rocks) and how to tweak some of their settings, such as hit points and their size.

You've also learned how to add driving/steering controls and program what happens when two objects bump or touch. You had some fun with missiles, and you now understand how to tweak settings, such as the missile damage and from which direction a missile is fired.

At this point, however, you're firing at objects that cannot run away. (Simply point Kodu in the direction you want him to fire a missile and any object in its path is destroyed, or its hit points are reduced.) What's needed to make this more fun is some objects that are moving and maybe even trying to avoid your missiles. And what about keeping track of the score? Yeah, it'd be great if we could learn how to keep track of the objects we've hit with our missiles, wouldn't it?

You've still got a lot to learn about Kodu Game Lab, and fortunately it's all really fun stuff. But before you continue on to Chapter 5, "Player 1 Versus Player 2: Adding Players and Awarding Points," I've got some homework for you to give you just a bit more practice with what you've learned so far.

Here's what I want you to try to tackle before continuing to Chapter 5:

1. I mentioned earlier in the chapter that I wanted to change the speed at which missiles fired, but I never showed you how to do it. Trust me, you've now got the skills to do this yourself, but here's a hint: Right-click Kodu and select Change Settings. Look for a setting related to how fast the missile reloads and increase or decrease that setting's value to get a faster-firing missile. Which setting did you choose, and what value gives you the fastest firing rate? How might you increase the speed at which the missile crosses the terrain?

2. Drop Rover on the terrain (or Kodu if you originally selected Rover) and maybe a building like a castle or factory. Right-click these objects and investigate the settings that you can change for each. Select some settings that you've not yet seen or used and use the Help box if necessary to learn about them.

3. Instead of Missiles, select Blip for the weapon. (In Programming Row 3, click the existing Missile tile and then choose Blip in the pie menu that appears to replace the missile with blip balls.) Play around with the game to see the difference between shooting missiles and shooting small blip balls.

When you're done with the homework, click the Home Menu button and select Exit to Main Menu. From the Main Menu, select Quit Kodu to close down Kodu Game Lab.

Player 1 Versus Player 2: Adding Players and Awarding Points

In This Chapter

When you're playing a game against a friend, how do you determine who is winning? This chapter introduces you to the programming needed to keep score in a game. So far, you've been creating games with a single player, too… and that's going to change. Now it's time to learn how to add a second player so that keeping score actually makes sense.

Basic Game Elements

We've all played video games, and I bet that if you take a moment to think about it, you'll agree that all games share a number of similarities. (Well, similarities that all *good* and *fun* games share.) I'm not talking about shooting at enemies; not all games are shooters. And I'm not talking about inventories or even power-ups, because some of the best games out there have no objects to be collected (and stored in an inventory) and certainly no power-ups (which give bonus powers or skills to you briefly or permanently).

No, when I talk about similar features, I'm talking about standard game elements, such as:

○ **Scoring**: Okay, not every game keeps score, but most do. Keeping score is one of the best methods for players to gauge how well they are doing in a game.

○ **Instructions**: In Chapter 4, "Missiles Locked and Loaded: Adding Targets and Firing Controls," if you handed the game controller over to a friend and said "Play this," but forgot to tell him how to fire the missiles, he'd find wandering around the tree and rocks a bit dull after a few moments. All good games provide players with the basics of how to play the game and explain the controls and special buttons or keyboard options available.

Later chapters discuss other game elements, but right now I want to demonstrate how to integrate the first element (scoring) into a simple game so that you'll know how to include it later in your more advanced games. (You'll learn about instructions later in this book.)

Keeping Score

To save time, I want you to open up an existing world: the mini-game we created in Chapter 4. It consists of Kodu, two rocks, and a tree on a bit of land. Figure 5.1 shows this world. We're going to modify this little game to see how the success of shooting missiles at trees and rocks can be displayed using a scoreboard.

FIGURE 5.1 Kodu's world consists of two rocks and a tree.

If you don't have this world saved, return to Chapter 4 and create it. Be sure to include the programming that enables you to move Kodu and fire missiles. You can tweak the hit points of the trees and rocks to whatever values you like, and you can set the value of the damage done by a missile to any value.

Back in Chapter 4, I also configured one rock's settings and the tree's settings to show the health bar above them so that I would know how much damage my missiles had done. You can see a single health bar above the rock in Figure 5.1. Although the health bar is a good visual indicator of how much damage my missiles have done, I would much rather have a counter on the screen that shows how many trees and missiles I've destroyed. Here's how I can do that.

First, I have a question for you. If I want to keep score, to which object do you think I'll add the additional programming to create the scoreboard?

Ask yourself another question: What would add a point to the scoreboard? When Kodu fires a missile, should that add +1 to my score? The answer to that question is no. Simply firing a missile shouldn't add to my score. If that were the case, the winner would simply be someone who can fire the most missiles before the game ends.

What about when a missile hits a tree or rock? Should that add +1 to the score? If a game has multiple players who are each firing missiles at the same tree or rock, would it make sense to give all players a point when any one of their missiles strikes a target?

And there's my answer: I should increment the score each time a missile successfully strikes a target. So that means I should add some new programming steps that monitor when a player's missile fires and increment the score only when a missile hits an object.

But before I add that bit of programming, you might be wondering what the scoreboard looks like. Figure 5.2 shows you. Notice the number 1 in the upper-right corner in white. You might also notice that the rock is missing. I destroyed it with missiles, and that added 1 to my score.

I could easily have programmed the game to earn me 5, 10, or even 100 points every time a missile hits a rock or tree. For example, if the tree has more hit points than the rock, it is harder to destroy (it takes more missiles). In the next section, you'll learn how to control not only the points earned but also how to assign the player those points using a color of your choice.

Configuring the Scorekeeping

The simplest scorekeeping configuration is for one-player games. To configure scorekeeping for one player, complete the following steps:

1. Select the player's object, right-click it, and choose Program.

2. Add programming that checks for a hit on an existing object.

3. If a hit is detected, award points to that player.

FIGURE 5.2   A point is added to the scoreboard when the rock is destroyed.

Let's start by configuring the scoring for only one player: the White Kodu. As mentioned earlier, we want to monitor the missiles that have been fired and award points for each missile strike. This requires that we add some programming to the White Kodu so that each time a white missile hits an object, the player is awarded five points.

First, I select the White Kodu, right-click it, and choose Program. Figure 5.3 shows the current program.

As this book progresses and the games get more advanced, I won't be able to explain to you every option I select. Instead, I show you an entire programming row and then briefly explain my selections to create it. For example, Figure 5.4 shows the new programming row that monitors when white missiles hit any object (rock, tree, other player) and awards the White Kodu player five points.

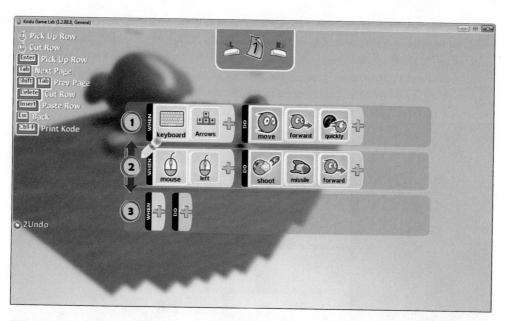

FIGURE 5.3 White Kodu's current programming has only movement and missile-firing programming.

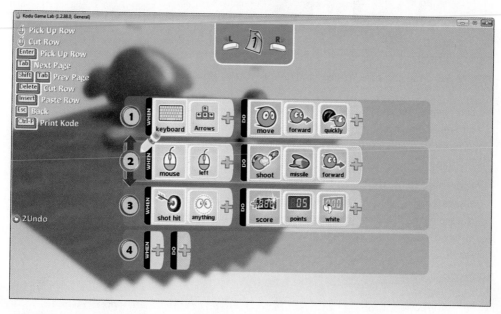

FIGURE 5.4 A new programming row for tracking missile hits and awarding points.

Let me explain what you're seeing in Programming Row 3. The When box contains two tiles: Shot Hit and Anything. This is saying, "When a white missile that I fire hits anything," but I can change the Anything tile to something more specific. I could select a rock, a tree, or even a specifically colored object. For example, Figure 5.5 shows that I've changed the Anything tile to monitor for a missile hit on a blue apple. You can get that specific in what a missile (or blips) targets.

FIGURE 5.5 You can select a color and an object for specific scoring needs.

Later in this chapter, you learn how to copy entire programming rows so that you can create different point awards for different objects. For now, though, I want to award the single player (White Kodu) with just five points when a missile hits a tree or a rock, so I change the tile back to Anything.

I now need to use the Do box to define what happens when a missile hit is detected. Figure 5.4 shows that I've selected the +Score, Points, and White tiles. The +Score tile is used to increment the score by a specific number; you use the Points tile to select that number of points. Notice in Figure 5.6 that I have options of 1, 2, 3, 4, 5, 10, 20, 50, and 100 points. Alternatively, I can select the Random tile to award a number, but I don't recommend this.

> **TIP**
>
> What do you do if you want to award 15 points? As you can see, there is no 15 Point tile. You'll see this put into practice later in the book, but if you're just itching to know how to do it, try placing two numbered tiles side by side. For example, add a 10 Point tile and then click the plus

sign (+) to the right of the 10 Point tile. See the 5 Point tile? Select it and it's added. Easy! When value tiles are side by side, they are added together. Using this method, you can program any value you need, even if it's not seen on an actual tile.

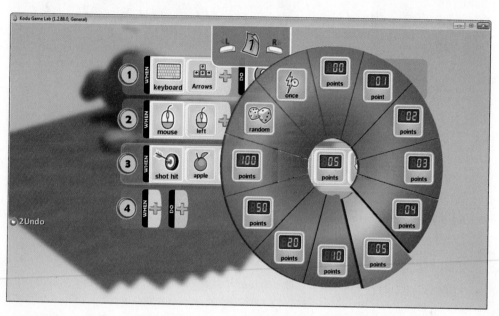

FIGURE 5.6 Select the number of points to award the player for a successful missile hit.

Awarding Points

Right now, there's only one player: White Kodu. But if I add a second player (let's say Blue Kodu), I need a way to award points to that player and not to the White Kodu player. To award points to a second player, follow these steps:

1. Select the second player's object, right-click it, and choose Program.

2. Add programming that checks for a hit on an existing object.

3. If a hit is detected, award points to that player using a unique color tile.

So, I need to add an additional tile that specifies where to award the points. Click the + to the right of the Points tile and select the Scores+Paint leaf shown in Figure 5.7. (See the paint bucket in the upper-right corner of the leaf's icon?)

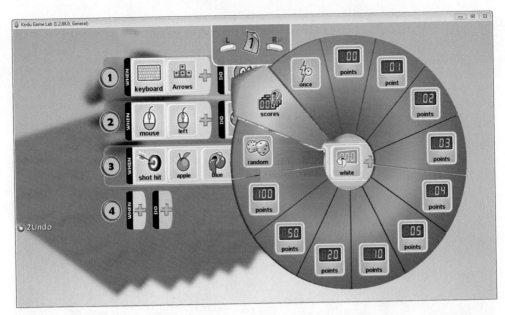

FIGURE 5.7   The Scores+Paint leaf allows you to select a color to assign points.

CAUTION

If you don't assign a color for a missile hit, the points are awarded to just a single scoreboard listing (the only one there). In this case, players' scores are combined into one score. You might like this option in games where players must cooperate, but if the players are competing against each other, you definitely want to have different colors for each player's points for the scoreboard.

When you click the Scores+Paint leaf, you get a pie menu like the one shown in Figure 5.8. I'm going to select White.

Figure 5.9 shows the completed Programming Row 3. Read it like this: "When my shot hits anything, increment the score by five points for the white player."

Rover: How would I subtract points from my opponent's score?

Kodu: You've seen the + Score tile, and there's a matching - Score tile.

Rover: Great! A way to take points away from my opponent.

Kodu: Just don't forget to assign the color scoreboard tile after the - Score tile; otherwise, your own score will decrease.

FIGURE 5.8   Select a color from the pie menu for White Kodu's score.

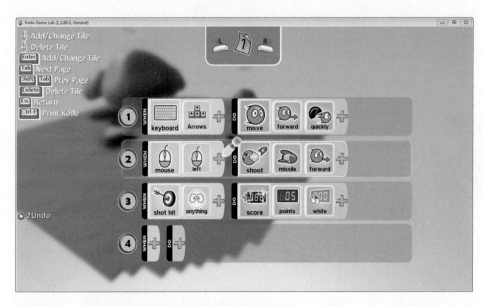

FIGURE 5.9   The updated program for White Kodu.

Testing the Scorekeeping

Now test your game. Click the Play button and fire off some missiles at the tree or rock. Figure 5.10 shows that I've hit the rock five times (25 points). How do you know it was the rock and not the tree? Look at their health bars. (Also notice that the score is in white.)

FIGURE 5.10   Firing missiles at the rock to get some points for White Kodu.

Shooting missiles at rocks and trees will get a bit boring after a while, so in the next section you learn how to add another player. Before we create a real two-player game, though, I want to show you how to quickly and easily create different types of point awards.

Creating Different Point Awards

In the preceding section, I added some programming to award five points anytime White Kodu's missiles hit any other object. But what if I want to award more points for smaller objects and fewer points for large objects? (Hitting that large tree is fairly easy, but the smaller rock requires a little more accuracy from the player; I should give more points for hitting the smaller, more-difficult-to-hit objects.)

To create different point awards for hitting different objects, complete these steps:

1. Access an object's programming.

2. Identify the When condition that determines a hit on that object.

3. Add correct programming to assign points to the proper player's scoreboard.

I start by opening White Kodu's programming page shown back in Figure 5.9. What I'm going to change is the Anything tile. When I click the Anything tile, a pie menu opens, as shown in Figure 5.11. From that, I select the Objects leaf.

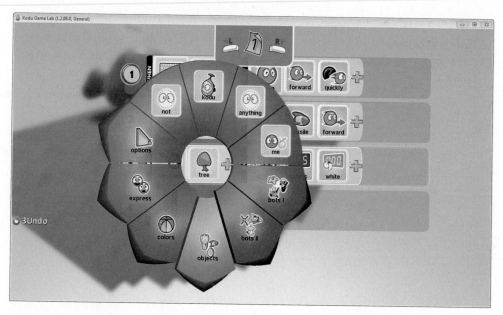

FIGURE 5.11   Replace the Anything tile with a more specific object.

After selecting the Object leaf, I click the Tree leaf, as shown in Figure 5.12.

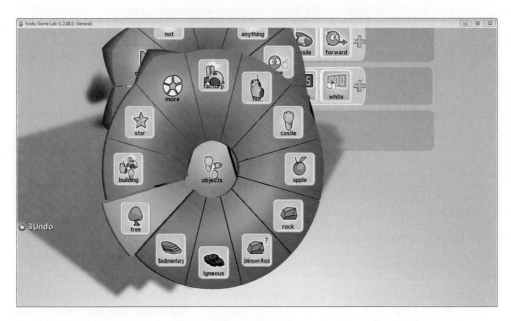

FIGURE 5.12 Select the Tree object to specify points to award for missile hits.

Because I'm still awarding points for hitting objects, all I have to do at this point is click the Points tile in the Do box and select a lesser value. The large tree is easier to hit, so I want to award a player only two points for hitting the tree. Figure 5.13 shows that I've replaced the original five points with two points. (I've left the color as white because I'm programming White Kodu.)

But what about the rocks? Because I removed the Anything tile, the rocks won't award any points when they are hit. Let me fix that.

To quickly add additional objects that award points when hit by White Kodu's missile, I right-click the number 3 at the start of Programming Row 3. I get a small pop-up menu like the one shown in Figure 5.14.

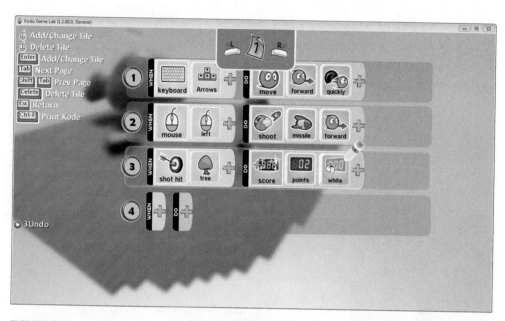

FIGURE 5.13 Decrease the points awarded for larger objects because they are easier to hit.

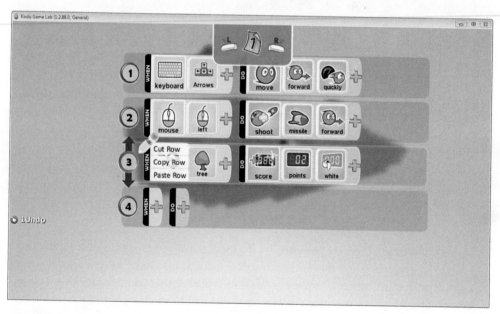

FIGURE 5.14 Right-click a programming row's number for a small pop-up window.

I am provided with three options: Cut Row, Copy Row, and Paste Row. I want to leave Programming Row 3 alone and just make a copy of it, so I choose Copy Row.

Then, I right-click the number 4 (it's a blank programming row right now), but this time I choose Paste Row. A copy of Programming Row 3 is added to the list, as shown in Figure 5.15.

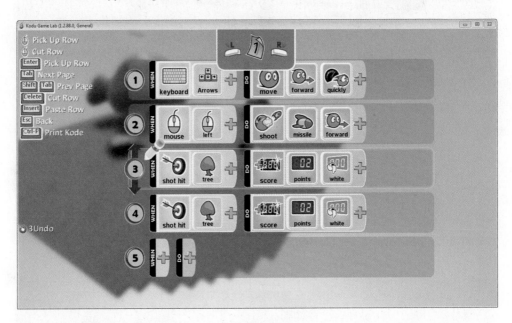

FIGURE 5.15   Copy a programming row and paste it into a new row.

As you can see, Programming Row 4 is identical to Programming Row 3. In both rows, the Tree object is being monitored for a missile hit.

> **NOTE**
> What do you think will happen if you play the game now with these two identical rows and you fire one missile at the tree? Try it and see what happens. Why did you get a score of 4 and not 2?

Now it's time to add some programming for the rocks. But as you can see in Figure 5.16, I've changed the color of one of the rocks: It's red. (If you don't remember how to change an object's color, refer back to Chapter 2, "Explore Kodu Game Lab: Basic User Controls and Tools.") I want to award a player 5 points for hitting the larger gray rock and 10 points for hitting the smaller red rock.

Once again, I open White Kodu's programming page. In Programming Row 4, click the Tree tile and change it to the Rock tile. Click the + to the right of the Rock tile and choose the color Gray. Next, click the Points tile in the Do box and select 5 points. You can see the modified Row 4 in Figure 5.17.

FIGURE 5.16   Modify the world and change the color of one of the rocks.

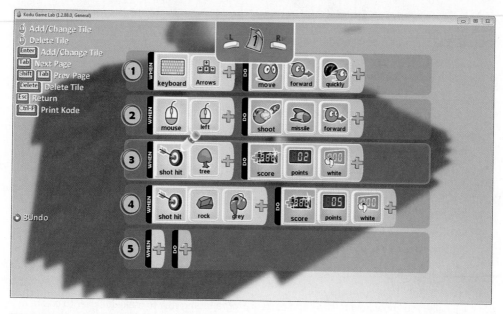

FIGURE 5.17   Create a point award for the gray rock.

I've got one more point award to program: the red rock. I copied Row 3 and all those tiles are still on the clipboard (in memory), so all I need to do is right-click on the number 5 below

Programming Row 4 and choose Paste Row again. Figure 5.18 shows a copy of Row 3 now in Row 5. (You can also right-click on Row 4, copy it, and paste into Row 5; this keeps the Rock tile, and all you have to modify is the color, type of rock, and the points.)

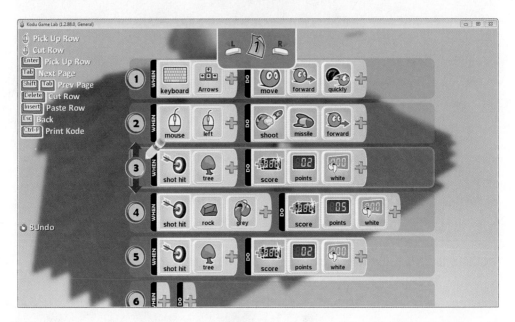

FIGURE 5.18   Create a point award for the red rock.

Try your hand at modifying Row 5 so that it awards 10 points for a missile hit on a sedimentary rock. Figure 5.19 shows the modified Row 5 that now awards 10 points.

As you can see, the capability to copy and paste a programming row and all its tiles can really save you some time. I can continue to add more rows as I add new targets (one for a castle, another for a building, and another for apples).

Let me recap quickly what you currently know how to do when it comes to scoring:

○ You know how to add points to a player's scoreboard by specifying the color of the scoreboard to be changed.

○ You know how to add tiles that specify the number of points to be added when an action is met (such as a missile hitting a tree).

○ You also know how to program using different objects with colors assigned, such as a red rock or a blue tree.

○ Finally, you know how to copy and paste a programming row to make it easier to create new point awards.

FIGURE 5.19   Now the red rock awards 10 points when hit with a missile.

All of these are skills you've developed for a one-player game. But what about a two-player game? What if you add a Blue Kodu to the world so that two players can try to score the most points before the objects are destroyed? Now that's a game! Let me show you how to do it.

Adding a Second Player

Remember how easy it was to copy and paste all of the tiles from a programming row? Well, to add a second player (Blue Kodu) you're going to do something similar. To add a second player, complete these steps:

1. Copy the White Kodu object.

2. Paste a copy of the White Kodu object and change its color.

3. Change the movement and firing controls to a different game controller or to mouse/keyboard (if the original object uses the only game controller).

4. Change any programming of the new object that affects scoring.

If you right-click the White Kodu, you'll see an option called Copy, as shown in Figure 5.20.

Select the Copy option, and then click anywhere on the open terrain. A second White Kodu will be placed there, as shown in Figure 5.21.

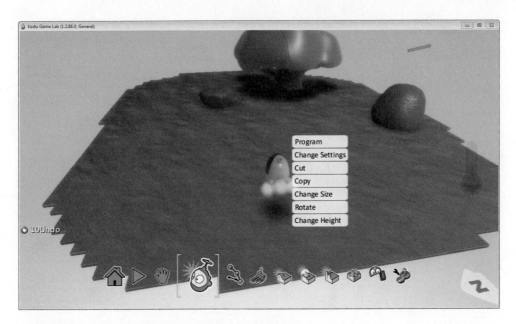

FIGURE 5.20   Right-click the White Kodu and select Copy.

FIGURE 5.21   Paste a copy of White Kodu on the terrain of your world.

All the programming you've done for White Kodu comes along for the ride when you paste a copy on the terrain. This includes the steering and missile-firing programming, as well as the scoring. In fact, if you play the game right now, your steering and firing (using the keyboard/mouse) will affect both White Kodus. To make this a two-player game, I need to change that.

First, let's start with the color. That's the easy one. Select the new White Kodu and change its color to blue. If you're using a keyboard, click the new White Kodu, and then use the Left/Right arrows to select a color, as shown in Figure 5.22. (Game controller users use the center D-Pad's Left and Right movements to select Blue.)

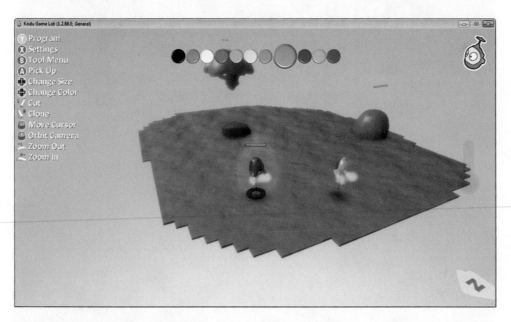

FIGURE 5.22   Change the color of the new Kodu.

But just changing the color isn't enough. Right-click Blue Kodu and choose Program to open its programming page, as shown in Figure 5.23.

As you can see in Figure 5.23, Blue Kodu is still programmed to use the arrow keys for movement and the left mouse button to fire missiles, and all points awarded will go to the White scoreboard.

I'm going to just go down the list of programming rows and make the changes as they are needed. First, I need to modify the movement. I could easily program Blue Kodu to use the game controller, but instead I'm going to keep the Keyboard tile and select the WASD keys, as shown in Figure 5.24. No other changes to Programming Row 1 are necessary.

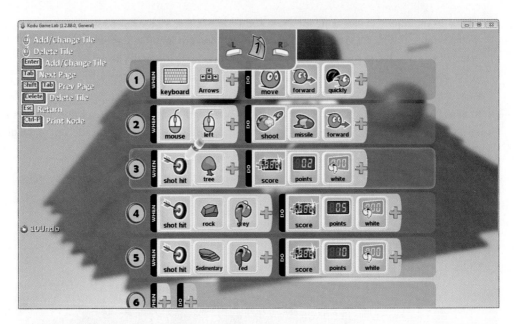

FIGURE 5.23   Blue Kodu's programming page.

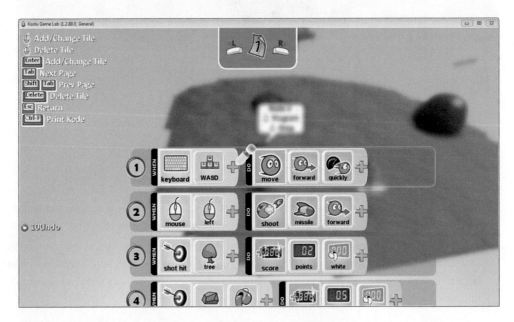

FIGURE 5.24   Now Player 2 can control Blue Kodu with the WASD keys.

Next to be fixed is the ability to fire missiles. Player 1 (White Kodu) uses the left mouse button, but that won't work for Player 2. Instead, I'm going to change it so that when the spacebar is pressed, Player 2 fires a missile. To do this, I first click the Mouse tile and select the Keyboard leaf. Next, I click + to the right of the Keyboard tile and select the Misc leaf, which opens a pie menu like the one in Figure 5.25. Notice that the Space key is at the top; that's the one I want.

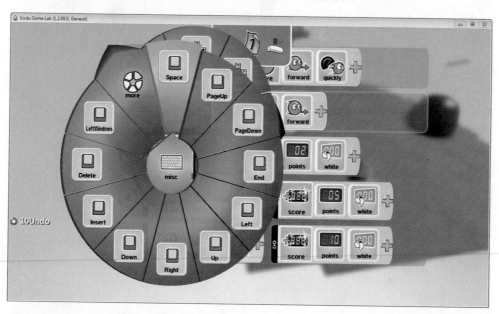

FIGURE 5.25 Make the spacebar launch missiles for Player 2.

Programming Rows 3, 4, and 5 are all fine except that they award points to White Kodu (Player 1). I can change this quickly by just clicking the White tiles in each row and changing them to Blue. Figure 5.26 shows the final programming page for Blue Kodu.

If you're ready, go ahead and invite a friend or family member over for a friendly game. Be sure to explain to them the controls (WASD or arrow keys for movement, left mouse button or spacebar for firing) and how to score points. As you can see in Figure 5.27, Blue Kodu is clobbering me in points. She completely destroyed the red rock (for more points) while I was spending time firing at the gray rock (fewer points awarded).

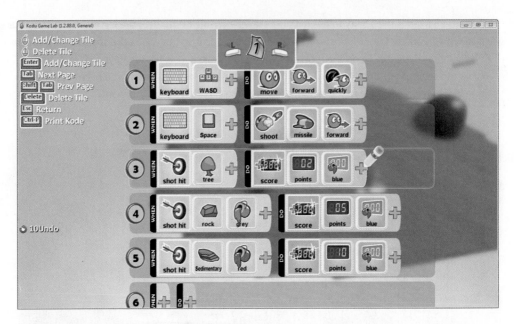

FIGURE 5.26 The programming page for Blue Kodu.

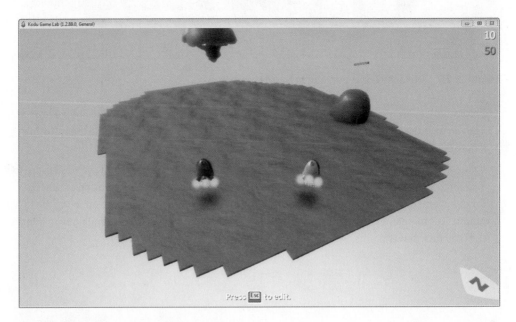

FIGURE 5.27 Player 1 versus Player 2: Have fun!

Moving On

You're only five chapters into the book and you've already created a game in which two players compete by firing missiles at nonmoving targets. Congratulations!

But maybe you're wondering if it would be more fun if the rock and trees were moving and running away. Of course, it would!

One of the most basic types of games out there involves the player trying to hit a moving target. Do a Bing search for "Space Invaders" or "Asteroids." You might not have heard of these games before, but they are the early versions of the types of games you'll be designing with the Kodu Game Lab.

Upcoming games in this book are going to start getting a bit harder, but if you've come this far and understand all the concepts covered in Chapters 1 through 5, you're definitely ready.

Of course, I can't let you leave this chapter and move on to Chapter 6, "Build Your Own World: Moving Mountains andf Painting Terrain," without giving you some additional tasks to try out. So see whether you can handle the following extra assignments, and then move on to the next chapter:

1. Guess what? A third friend has just watched you pulverize Player 2 (getting most of the points) and wants to play. But Player 2 wants to keep playing as well. Do you think you could figure out how to add a Red Kodu to the game? What if Player 3 wants to use the game controller? Think you can figure out how to give Player 3 the option to use the game controller? Give it a try.

2. Try firing at the other player. What happens? Are you able to destroy your opponent's Kodu? Experiment with each of the Kodu object's settings (right-click a Kodu and choose Change Settings) and see whether you can find a setting in the list that will prevent players from firing at one another. (Hint: Look for another word for *indestructible*.)

3. Experiment with changing one player's firing. Change it from missiles to blip balls. (You might have to modify the damage done by either missiles or blip balls to make the game fair.)

When you're done with these experiments, click the Home Menu button and choose Exit to Main Menu. From the main menu, choose Quit Kodu to close down Kodu Game Lab.

6

Build Your Own World: Moving Mountains and Painting Terrain

It's Not All About the Objects

Kodu Game Lab has some fun and entertaining objects. There's Kodu to start with, and let's not forget Rover, the Cycle, and one of my favorite vehicles, Blimp. Plus you've already encountered nonmoving objects such as trees and rocks, but there are plenty more, such as coins, stars, castles, and factories. You'll find all these objects useful in your games as either playable characters, targets, or treasure (or something else). You'll be designing the games, so it will be up to you to assign roles to the objects in your games.

But one character in almost all games goes unrecognized. This character is easy to spot but almost always never makes any noise. This character is absolutely required for your game to be a good one, and thankfully it's also a character that you can program. Do you know what it is? Give up?

Okay, here's the answer: It's the world! Yes, it's the actual terrain that defines the boundaries of your game, provides obstacles for your players to move around or hide behind, and gives your game new and exciting places to visit. Without the capability to add and modify terrain, your game would exist on nothing but the initial flat square of land shown in Figure 6.1 and that appears whenever you select New World from the Home Menu.

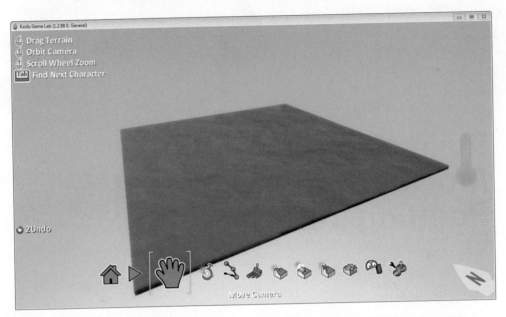

FIGURE 6.1 This small square of land is not enough for a great game.

Professional game designers often spend just as much time on the environment as they do on the in-game characters (and maybe more). One of the secrets to a good game is making certain the terrain (buildings, hills, rivers, and more) enhances the fun, provides players with a visually pleasing background, and is integrated into the design of the gameplay. That is, you can use the terrain to create rules that make a game more challenging. Imagine a game called *Stay Off the Grass*, for example, which penalizes players who wander off a path and onto the green grass. Or imagine another game called *Pothole City* that has holes scattered around that end the game if a player falls into one.

With most games, it's not the terrain that provides the primary objective; instead, the terrain adds complexity or dangers, or just fun visuals. And because interacting with the terrain is not usually the way to win a game (but it can sometimes end a game), the game relies on other aspects such as the programming of objects that you've been learning.

The key is to learn to manipulate and control the terrain so that it can add to the fun of your game, not take away. And that's what this chapter is all about: learning about the available tools that enable you to add, modify, and take away terrain. If you've got a solid understanding of how to control your new world's terrain, you're well on your way to creating some impressive-looking games.

Let's take a look at the available tools and how to use them. Open up Kodu Game Lab and select New World so that you begin with that single square of terrain. You're going to be making some major changes to it in this chapter.

The Ground Brush

I want to start with the simplest of tools first: the Ground Brush. This is the tool selected in Figure 6.2 and is represented by the white square.

FIGURE 6.2   Select the Ground Brush to make basic additions and color changes.

You already learned about the terrain selection feature and the tool brush shapes in Chapter 3, "Take a Test Drive: Controlling Objects and Terrain," but I want to go over them with a little more detail here. Before I show you all the ways the Ground Brush works, let me explain a few modifications that you can make while it is selected.

First, if you're using a keyboard and mouse, you can change the size of the brush by using the Left Arrow and Right Arrow keys. Notice in Figure 6.2 that the brush shape is square and that the size is about a quarter of the single block of green terrain. If I tap the Left Arrow key, the brush shape shrinks in size, as shown in Figure 6.3.

FIGURE 6.3 Shrink the Ground Brush by tapping the Left Arrow key.

Game controller users can shrink the Ground Brush by tapping Left or Right on the D-Pad.

To increase the size of the Ground Brush, tap the Right Arrow key on the keyboard or tap Right on the D-Pad. Notice in Figure 6.4 that I can make the Ground Brush size quite large, even larger than the original single square of green terrain.

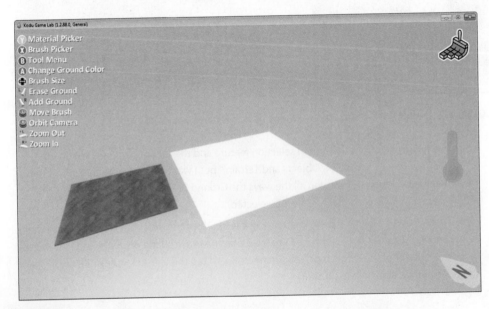

FIGURE 6.4 Increase the size of the Ground Brush.

Changing the Brush Shape

If you want to change the Ground Brush shape, you can select from Square, Round, Linear Square Brush, Linear Round Brush, or the Magic Brush. The Square and Round brush shapes work the same, but simply apply terrain or change color using a round or square brush head.

The Linear brush shapes enable you to select a starting point and an ending point and then apply your terrain to all points in between. For example, in Figure 6.5, I've selected the Linear Round Brush and moved the brush head from one end to the other by holding down the left mouse button and moving the brush head to its end position. (You can do the same thing by using the game controller's left thumbstick.)

FIGURE 6.5 Move the Linear Brush from a starting point to an ending point.

With the mouse, the terrain is applied when I release the left mouse button, but with the game controller you press the R trigger. Figure 6.6 shows the final stretch of terrain I added with the Linear Round Brush.

If when you are adding new terrain the brush head moves over existing terrain, that terrain is replaced with whatever color/texture you currently have selected. For example, in Figure 6.7, I've placed a new square of terrain to the right of the current terrain. Notice they are not touching and are two different colors.

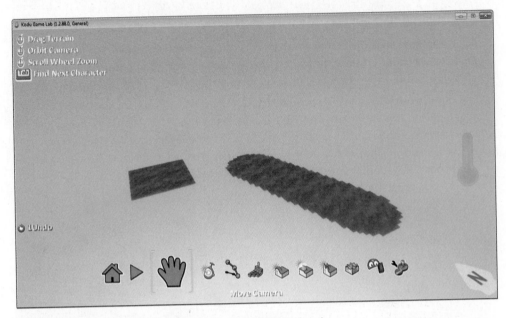

FIGURE 6.6   A new stretch of terrain added with a Linear brush.

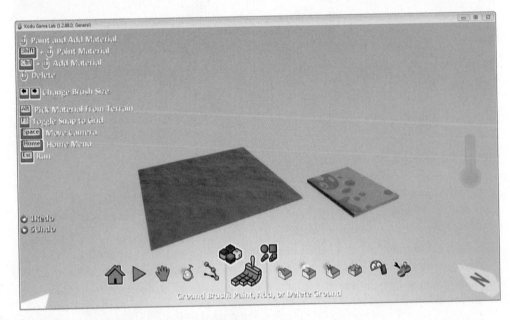

FIGURE 6.7   A new piece of terrain is added.

Rover: Just how many possible terrain colors and patterns are available?

Kodu: There are more than 100 different options.

Rover: That would be one amazing game that used all 100 colors, wouldn't it?

Kodu: Well, it might also be so difficult to look at that it would make playing the game almost impossible!

Rover: But you just know someone is going to try it.

Kodu: And they can call the game Insane Rainbow. Sounds fun, actually!

But watch what happens when I add another square of the new terrain in the space between large and small squares. Figure 6.8 shows that part of the larger (green) terrain has been replaced with the new color.

When you're using the Ground Brush, any movement of the Square, Round, or Linear brushes replaces old terrain with new when you drag over the old terrain. But there's a way to avoid that.

If you hold down the Control key on your keyboard while dragging the Ground Brush around, existing terrain will not be modified if the brush moves over it. Instead, the new terrain is placed anywhere terrain does not already exist. Figure 6.9 shows that I've painted a new terrain around the original green square while holding down the Control key. See how the original terrain is left unmodified?

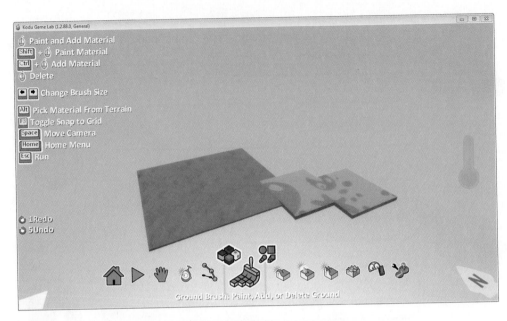

FIGURE 6.8   Old terrain is replaced with new terrain.

FIGURE 6.9   Use the Control key to keep existing terrain.

> **NOTE**
>
> If you look closely at Figure 6.9 near the bottom-left corner, you'll see 6Undo. Kodu Game Lab keeps track of the changes you make and can let you undo certain actions such as changing the color of terrain or growing a mountain. Tap the Undo option once to undo the last edit you made. In this instance, Kodu can undo the last six modifications you've made, but this number will sometimes be more… and sometimes less.

What if you want to replace some existing terrain with a new color while avoiding adding any new land to your world? In that case, hold down the Shift key while dragging the Ground Brush over existing terrain. As you can see in Figure 6.10, the original (green) square of terrain now has a completely new color.

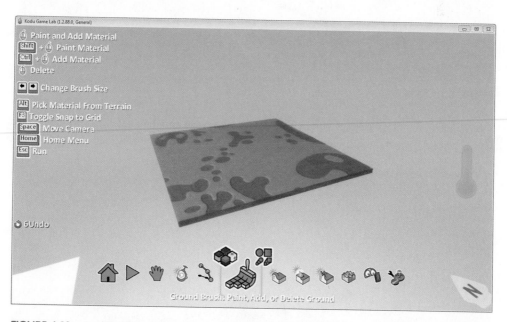

FIGURE 6.10   Replace an existing piece of terrain with a new color only.

When you have a Square or Round brush selected, right-click with the mouse and drag over some terrain to erase it; you can use the Left Arrow or Right Arrow keys on a keyboard to increase or decrease the size of the brush head to control how much terrain you erase. In Figure 6.11, I've decreased the brush head to a small square and then erased some terrain from the center.

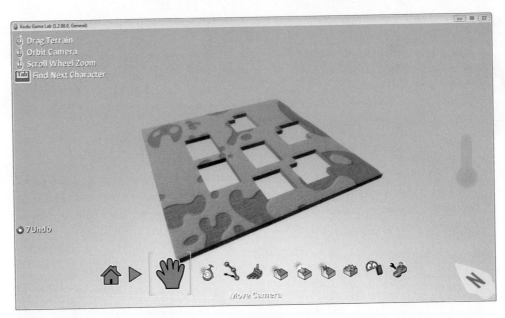

FIGURE 6.11 Right-click to erase with the Ground Brush.

I can fill those holes easily enough by selecting a new terrain and then holding down the Control key while dragging the brush over those holes. Figure 6.12 shows the new look of the terrain.

FIGURE 6.12 Fill in holes with new terrain using the Control key.

The Magic Brush

Before I move on to a different tool, I want to show you how the Magic Brush works. Before you select the Magic Brush, click the Ground Brush and select a different terrain. I've selected a dark red painted terrain, but you can pick anything that you're not already using.

Next, select the Magic Brush (it's the last one to the right, just beyond the Linear Round Brush) and move it over any bit of existing terrain.

It's a bit difficult to tell in Figure 6.13, but whatever terrain you have selected will glow and fade repeatedly while you are using the Magic Brush. You can then modify whatever terrain is glowing by using the tools you've already learned about; you selected a new terrain color, so tap the left mouse button and that color will be applied to any flashing terrain. Notice in Figure 6.14 that I changed the overall color of the terrain with the Magic Brush but that the smaller squares were not modified.

FIGURE 6.13   Use the Magic Brush to make large changes to terrain.

I showed you earlier how to use the Control key while using the Square or Round brush to change the color of existing terrain. If you had done this over the large square of terrain, however, it would have also changed the small squares. Using the Magic Brush, I was able to select just the color of the larger square and change it without changing the smaller squares.

FIGURE 6.14 Magic Brush can apply colors selectively.

Rover: Will the Right and Left Arrow keys also change the size of the Brush?

Kodu: Absolutely! Shrink it down to a thin line and you could draw or write words on the terrain that would be easy to read.

Rover: And I'm guessing that it would be helpful in creating outlines of shapes.

Kodu: Yep! Imagine drawing the outline of a castle's outer walls using the thin line. Then you could use the Up/Down tool to raise the outline and create a three dimensional castle instantly.

You'll definitely want to experiment with all five brushes (Square, Round, Linear Square, Linear Round, and Magic Brush) until you're good and comfortable with them. The Ground Brush is the primary tool you'll use to create larger worlds, such as the battle ring I've created and shown in Figure 6.15.

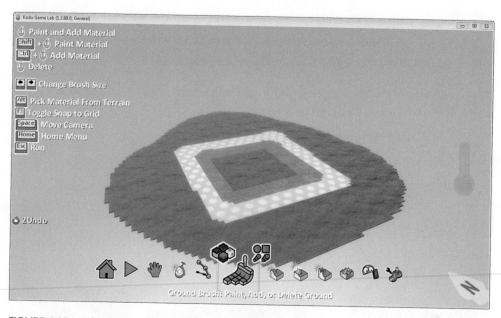

FIGURE 6.15   A battle ring for a fighting robot game, perhaps?

Mountains and Molehills

Look at Figure 6.15 again. Notice that although the terrain is colorful, it's also quite flat. Flat isn't always bad, though. Sometimes a game needs to exist on a flat surface; the rules of the game or maybe how you've programmed the objects in it might not be suitable for a world of hills and mountains and lakes. But if you want them, it's really easy to add them to your new world.

The tool to the right of the Ground Brush is called the Up/Down tool, and it lets you add hills and valleys. As with the Ground Brush, you can increase or decrease the size of the tool with the Left Arrow and Right Arrow keys on the keyboard (or by pressing Left or Right on the D-Pad).

Now it's easy to create hills or mountains, as follows:

1. Select the Up/Down tool and its brush size.

2. Move your cursor over an existing bit of terrain and hold down the left mouse button.

3. Maintain your left mouse button press until you achieve your desired hill or mountain height.

4. Move the cursor, as desired, to widen or narrow your hill/mountain.

5. Release the left mouse button press when you're happy with the look of your terrain.

Figure 6.16 shows that I've added a small hill right in the center of my terrain. Notice that the hill/mountain gets its coloration from the terrain that it affects.

FIGURE 6.16 A small hill in the center of my new world.

If you don't like a hill/mountain you have created, just get rid of it by pressing and holding down the right mouse button and moving the cursor over the hill until the hill is reduced in size (or completely gone), as shown in Figure 6.17.

FIGURE 6.17   Reverse the direction of a hill with the right mouse button.

Brush Shape Options

You can change the shape of the Up/Down tool just as you did with the Ground Brush, but this tool has some different options, as shown in Figure 6.18.

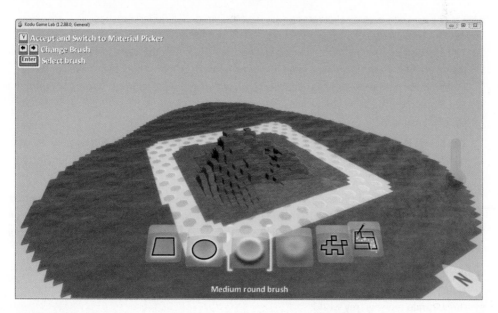

FIGURE 6.18   The tool has its own options for adding and removing hills.

○ **Square and Round Brushes:** The Square and Round brushes apply the raising and lowering effect equally across the entire area of the brush shape. With the Medium Round Brush or Soft Round Brush, however, the raising or lowering effect is subtle on the outer edges of the tool. Figure 6.19 shows that I've added another hill, but this time the brown terrain (surrounding the inner green terrain) is smoother and less "blocky" looking.

FIGURE 6.19   You can obtain softer terrain with the Medium or Soft Round Brushes.

○ **The Mottled Brush:** The Mottled Brush (second selection from the right, just next to the Magic Brush) enables you to raise the terrain in a more random fashion. Think about a hill or lake or other natural terrain; there's a randomness to it, with no straight edges or 90 degree bends. The Mottled Brush allows you to give your terrain that same natural look and making it more realistic looking.

○ **The Magic Brush:** With the Magic Brush, you can pick one type of terrain (such as the dotted patch of terrain surrounding the inner green patch) and then raise or lower only the selected terrain.

Figure 6.20 shows that I've used the Magic Brush to raise the terrain only on the yellow dotted terrain going around the inner green and brown terrain. Notice that unlike the randomness of a growing hill or mountain, the terrain is grown up at a consistent rate, enabling me to make a fence around the inner area.

Right-clicking with the Magic Brush enables me to lower the fence or completely remove it. Figure 6.21 shows that I've used the Magic Brush to create a "birthday cake" effect with the three terrain types on my world.

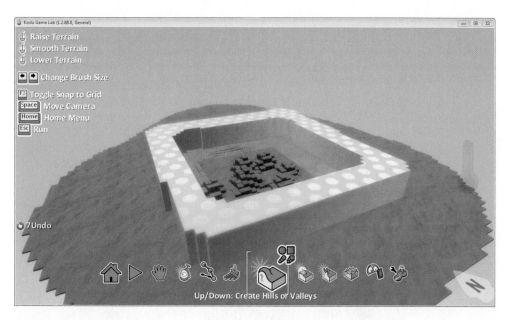

FIGURE 6.20   Use the Magic Brush to raise and lower terrain at a constant rate.

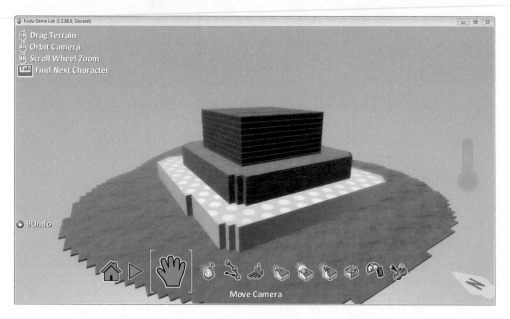

FIGURE 6.21   Three levels of playing field are created (four if you count the surrounding terrain).

Smoothing or Roughing Terrain

If you are using a mouse with a scroll wheel in the center, press and hold the scroll wheel while moving it over terrain to apply a smoothing effect to any raised terrain. It's subtle and sometimes difficult to see with some terrain, but I've applied the smoothing effect to the top of the rough mountain back in Figure 6.19. Figure 6.22 shows a smoother mountaintop thanks to my use of the center scroll wheel.

FIGURE 6.22   Use the center scroll wheel to smooth terrain.

If you don't have a center scroll wheel, you can select the Flatten tool to the right of the Up/Down tool to get the same results. The only difference with using the Flatten tool is that you can select the shape of the brush: Square, Round, or Magic Brush. Once again, Square and Round apply the flattening effect somewhat equally across the size of the brush, whereas the Magic Brush enables you to select an entire terrain type (that's also connected) and then apply a consistent flattening effect all at once.

To give hills and valleys a smoother and more natural look, use the Flatten tool slowly and methodically. Figure 6.23 shows how I've used it to give my center hill a rounded and more gradual incline.

Finally, the Roughen tool (to the right of the Flatten tool) is used to grow terrain in faster and spikier manner. It grows the terrain faster and gives a random forest or urban look (depending on the terrain you've selected). Figure 6.24 shows how I've added a wild forest area to the outer ring surrounding my hill.

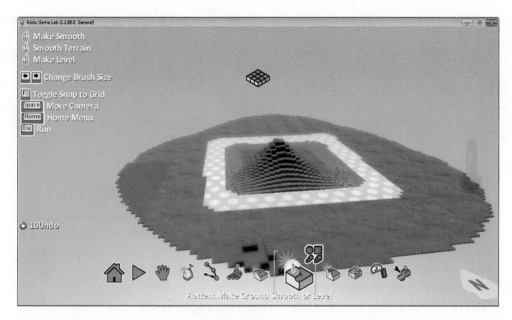

FIGURE 6.23 The Flatten tool is more of a polishing tool for rough terrain.

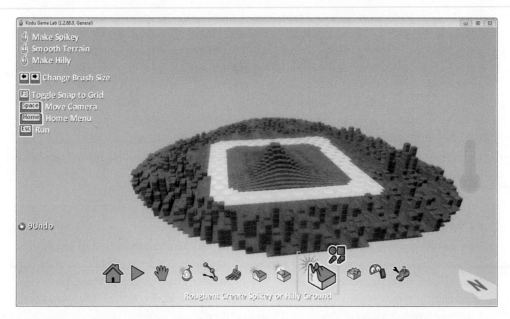

FIGURE 6.24 Give your world a rougher and spikier look with the Roughen tool.

> **CAUTION**
> Rough terrain can be difficult or even impossible for players to navigate. This is why it is so important to constantly test your games. When you're creating terrain, drop in Kodu and add some basic movement controls and then drive him all over the game world. Look for areas where he cannot move or access such as between thin walls or up a steep cliff. You'll have to modify these areas if you want players to be able to access those areas.

Much More World Building to Come

I'm one of those people who likes to push buttons and click features just to see what they do, so I'm not going to tell you to stop poking around Kodu Game Lab's other tools. Feel free! But I will be covering the topics of water and roads in a later chapter. For now, you should have enough hands-on experience with the basic Ground Brush and terrain-modifying tools to start creating some wild and crazy worlds of your own.

And that's a good thing, because as I said earlier in this chapter, a good game is more than just throwing some objects on the screen and programming them to shoot at one another. If you've got a great game idea growing in your head, you absolutely cannot forget to include the look and feel of the terrain in your plans.

The world that your game exists in needs to be eye-catching, of course, but it also needs to make sense in terms of the rules of the game. If you've put pits everywhere that look good but that frustrate your players because they keep falling in, that's not a good thing (well, unless the point of the game is to avoid the pits). Instead, the pits should be used sparingly, a few here and there, to make a game more exciting, not frustrating. Your players should be focused on the main goals of the game (such as collecting coins or shooting flying enemies), and the terrain and obstacles you've created should be adding to the fun, not taking away from it.

A good balance of goals, game rules, and world design is what makes a game great. And you'll get better at it over time, I promise.

Moving On

Let's create a short list of your Kodu Game Lab skills to this point. You know how to add objects to a world, including objects controlled by players and objects that simply sit still and make good targets. Speaking of targets, you've learned how to program player objects to shoot missiles or other projectiles, and you've learned how to create a simple scoring system. You know how to change colors and sizes of objects, and how to make multiple copies of objects that you've programmed.

As for the terrain, you now know how to add, modify, and remove terrain as needed. You know how to select different colors/styles of terrain that can best be used in certain types of games you might have planned, and you've gotten quite good at using the Move Camera tool (the Hand) to rotate your world and zoom in and out.

If I'm correct, you are ready to create a game—maybe not the most advanced Kodu game ever made, but certainly something that is fun and can provide some entertainment to you and your friends. (And I have to add, you're also ready to design a game that will impress your family, your teachers, pretty much anyone you want to show off your game to.)

So, in anticipation of the upcoming chapters in which you'll learn more advanced programming features that give your games even more punch and power, I want you give you a few extra tasks to try and perform before moving on, okay?

Here's what I want you to do before moving on to Chapter 7, "Difficult Targets to Hit: Increasing Game Difficulty and Path Following":

1. Use the Ground Brush and similar tools and create a big world. Make it round or rectangular-shaped, but give it four or five different terrain types—maybe a grassy inner terrain surrounded by a more urban cement-and-steel look. You decide, but give yourself some time to experiment with the world design tools until you're confident with adding, removing, and editing terrain.

2. After you've created a new world, drop in Kodu or Rover and add basic programming to steer it around your new world. Take your object for a spin, zoom in a bit, and roll around your terrain. Did you add any hills or mountains that prevent Kodu or Rover from moving on or over? If not, do so now. Try to find out just how steep of a hill you can add before Kodu or Rover are blocked and cannot roll up.

When you finish this homework, click the Home Menu button and save your newly created world before selecting Exit to Main Menu. From the Main Menu, select Quit Kodu to close down Kodu Game Lab.

7

Difficult Targets to Hit: Increasing Game Difficulty and Path Following

In This Chapter

○ Increasing the Difficulty Level

○ Where Did That Target Go?

○ Score Programming

○ Moving On

Increasing the Difficulty Level

You've learned quite a bit about Kodu Game Lab to this point. You've certainly got enough information to build some fairly fun one-player or two-player games that involve missiles, targets, and scoring. But not all games involve shooting, not all targets stand still like trees and rocks, and a numeric score isn't always the best method for determining a winner in a game.

Even with a two-player game that tracks who shoots and destroys the most trees and rocks, the gameplay is going to get old quickly. What's needed is some added complexity. You saw in the preceding chapter how creating some interesting terrain can add complexity to a game: Throwing up some small hills that you and your opponent must race around to find trees and rocks to fire at will certainly make the game more complex, but really all you're doing is delaying the actual gameplay (shooting the targets) rather than making it more complex.

No, complexity in a game often comes from adding threats and risks to a player. Imagine if those trees and rocks could fire back. And what if the trees and rocks could move and dodge your missiles? Even better, what if your score decreased if you shot friendly targets, or if an opponent hit you with a missile while you were hunting for nonfriendly targets?

As you can see, it's easy to take a basic game with few rules and increase the complexity. Every time you add another threat to your player, you increase the game's complexity. Giving a tree the capability to fire a missile right back at a player is one major threat.

Add a risk to your player (such as holes the player can fall in or an unfriendly object that, if touched, poisons you and reduces your health) and the complexity continues to advance.

The trick is balancing complexity with fun. If you increase the difficulty too much, you will find the fun of the game decreasing. Likewise, make a game too easy and it will lose all its fun fast.

This chapter introduces you to a few ways to increase complexity in a game. You'll learn more methods in later chapters, but it's best to pick up a few tricks at a time and then discover ways to implement them in your own games. And Kodu Game Labs has plenty of tricks to learn, so hang in there.

Let's take a look at one of the easiest ways to increase the complexity of a game involving shooting at targets: enabling the targets to move and even run away.

Where Did That Target Go?

Think back to the earlier game where you and a second player were shooting missiles at trees and rocks. You probably had some fun with it for a while, but shooting at poor trees and rocks that just sit there gets old fast, doesn't it?

Let's change up that game a little bit. First, I'm going to have you change the trees and rocks to different types of objects. After you've selected the types of targets you want to create, you'll then enable those targets to run away.

> **NOTE**
>
> As the book progresses, I do not show you how to re-create every power or every trick that you've learned in every chapter. Instead, I'm relying on your ability to return to earlier chapters if you need a reminder of how to perform a programming task. For example, I won't be showing you how to give the player's object (Kodu, Rover, or another character) the capability to move. If you forget how to program that object with WASD or the game controller or other keys, just flip back to a chapter that provides figures showing how to perform that task. This will save space in the chapters for me to give you more examples and introduce you to more programming concepts.

Let's start with a simple world that has four small mountains and one large empty area in the center. Feel free to create your own new world using whatever colors/textures of terrain you like. Figure 7.1 shows the world that I created, but as long as your world has at least one large obstacle that obstructs a player's view, you'll be fine.

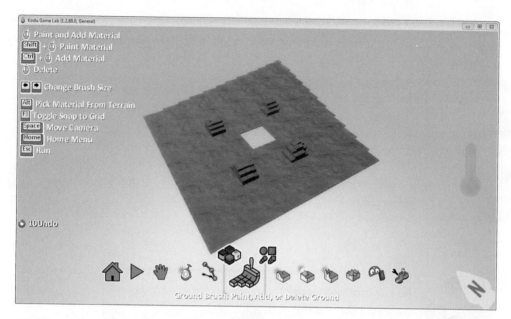

FIGURE 7.1 My new world is called Square Donut World.

Why did I put a large hole in the center of the world? Complexity. I'm going to show you later in this chapter how to turn off a world setting that prevents players from falling off the edges of the world. If you haven't tried to drive your Kodu or Rover objects off the screen yet, go ahead and run a previous game and try it. What happens? That's right. It's like an invisible wall running around the outer boundaries of the terrain, but it also prevents a player from falling into the hole like the one in Figure 7.1. I'm going to change that after I've got the new game created so that players will need to avoid not just the outer edge but also the big hole in the center of their world.

After I've created my world, it's time to drop in my Player 1 and Player 2 objects. I want one player to be controlled by the keyboard and the other player to use a game controller, and both players should be able to shoot missiles. You can refer back to Chapter 5, "Player 1 Versus Player 2: Adding Players and Awarding Points," if you need help creating the two player characters and enabling them to move and fire missiles, but let me show you a little trick that can save you some time:

1. Open the game you saved in Chapter 5 (you did save it, right?) and click the Object tool.

2. Select either Kodu (White or Blue) and right-click that object and select Copy.

3. Close down the Chapter 5 game, open up your new game with your new world, and select the Object tool.

4. Right-click anywhere on the terrain and choose Paste.

A copy of the Kodu from the Chapter 5 game now exists in your Chapter 7 game.

How cool! You can copy and paste objects from one game into a completely different game.

This will save me a lot of time, especially because the programming of the object comes along for the ride. All I have to do is modify the programming a little bit for each of the objects to fit into my new game.

CAUTION

The only downside to copying and pasting a character from one game to the other is that you can only modify the character's color and nothing else. This means that I can't change the White Kodu I just pasted and make him into a Red Rover object. But there's still a benefit to copying and pasting an object from game to game; you can create a new character (such as a Red Rover) and then copy the programming rows from the White Kodu into the Red Rover object. It's still faster than creating the programming from scratch.

Rover: That's convenient. A programmer can simply copy your programming over to my own.

Kodu: Well... not completely. For example, I can shoot missiles, but you cannot.

Rover: Oh, that's right. And I have special abilities like the Beam Tool for examining rocks, and you do not.

Kodu: Yep! If a programmer tries to copy a bit of programming from one object to a second object for a capability that doesn't exist for the second object (like shooting missiles) some parts of the program won't get copied.

Figure 7.2 shows that I've added White Kodu on one side of the world and Blue Kodu on the other side of the world. Their programming has remained the same: Blue Kodu uses the keyboard, and White Kodu uses the game controller. Before you do any additional programming, go ahead and play the game and make certain that you can move and fire with both Kodus.

FIGURE 7.2   Two Kodus added to Square Donut World.

Just testing the game as it is, I discovered a few things. First, both Kodus easily climb the small mountains. Second, the missiles they fire follow the curve of the mountains instead of impacting them, allowing the missiles to go over the hills to hit a target hiding behind them. And third, the scores stay at zero because the programming only increments the scoreboard when a tree or rock is hit.

I'll fix these issues later, but right now I want to add some targets for the two Kodus to try and hit. I say *try* because I'm going to give them the capability to move, making it more difficult for a player to hit.

Figure 7.3 shows that I've dropped in a single saucer on the terrain. Why one and not four? Because after I program the single saucer, I can copy and paste three more saucers on the terrain, each having identical programming as the original. So, let's start with the original.

You have multiple options when it comes to a target's capability to move:

○ You can make it wander randomly around the screen. This will make it difficult to hit, especially if we increase the object's movement speed.

○ You can make an object follow a set path. This can also make it difficult to hit a high-speed object, but players might be able to figure out the path and time their shots.

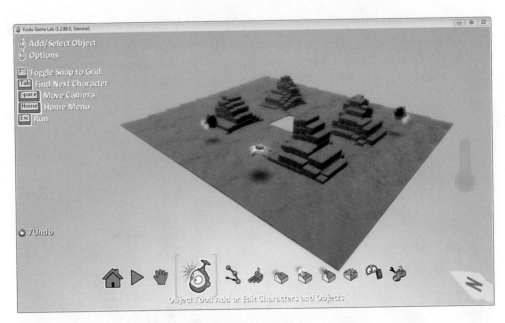

FIGURE 7.3   Drop in a saucer that will become Target 1.

○ You can make an object actually run from a player. If you give an object a high rate of movement speed, you can really make a target hard to hit.

Let's go through all three options here so that you can see how they work.

Random Movement

First we enable the saucer to move randomly around the world, as follows:

1. Click the Object tool and then right-click the saucer and select Program. Programming Row 1's When and Do tiles will be empty.

   If you leave the When tile empty, any actions you program in the Do tile will always be performed. Yes, you can leave the When tile empty (but not in every case), but it's just good programming technique to fill it with a condition. Right now, I just want the saucer to move randomly around the world and keep moving (never stopping). I want it to *always* move and wander. And guess what? There's an Always tile. Figure 7.4 shows where it's hidden.

2. Tap the When tile's + to open the first pie menu, and from that select the More option. Tucked in the second pie menu that opens is the Always tile.

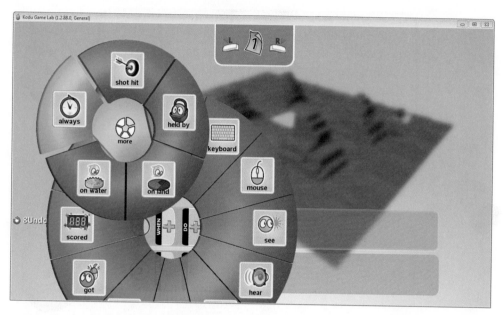

FIGURE 7.4 Set the When condition to Always.

Now I can select what happens when the Always condition is triggered. (Hint: The Always condition is triggered… always!)

3. Tap the Do tile and select Move. Follow that with the Wander option, and then with the Quickly option. Figure 7.5 shows the completed Programming Row 1.

Rover: So, a Quickly tile can increase an object's speed? That's cool!

Kodu: Yes, and you can add up to three Quickly tiles, one right after the other. And the same goes for the Slowly tiles.

Rover: Wow. I'll bet that using three Quickly tiles is like putting a rocket on the back of an object.

Kodu: Unfortunately, that's not the case. The Quickly and Slowly tiles only bump the speed up or down in small increments, so you're not going to see a big difference. They're really useful for giving an object a very small edge over another object.

Rover: So, how can you make certain one object is blazing-fast compared to another?

Kodu: For that, you have to modify the object's base speed by right-clicking the object and choosing Change Settings.

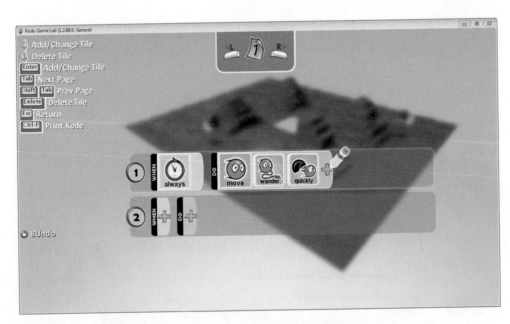

FIGURE 7.5   Programming the saucer to move really fast around the world.

Now run the game and watch what happens. That saucer is F-A-S-T! It's going to be difficult to hit with a missile. (If I find it's just too difficult, I can always go in and change the Quickly tile to

Slowly.) Feel free to take the controls and try to hit the saucer with a missile. When you're done, we'll look at the next option: following a path.

> **TIP**
>
> Feel free to right-click the saucer and choose Change Settings. Scroll down the list and change the Max Hit Points to 10 or fewer. A single missile hit should destroy the saucer now. But even if you hit the saucer and destroy it, you'll get zero points. You haven't modified the Kodu's programming yet to award points for a successful saucer hit.

Path Following

The random movement of the saucer can make it difficult to hit, especially at high speed. You can reduce the complexity of the game a bit by putting the object on a fixed path. This path can be a straight line, a star-shaped pattern, or something completely wild and random. You will be drawing that path, too, so let me show you how it's done:

1. Move the saucer object to one of the edges of the world so that it's out of the way; I can do the same with the Kodu objects.

2. Use the Move Camera tool and rotate the world so that you're looking at it almost completely from the top. Figure 7.6 shows that I've rotated my world so that I can see all its terrain easily.

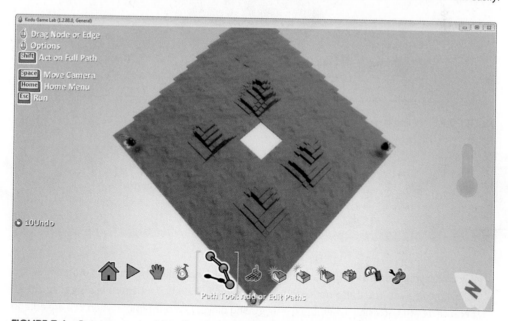

FIGURE 7.6   Rotate your world so that you can see it all, even terrain behind mountains.

3. Select the Path tool indicated in Figure 7.6. It's to the right of the Object tool and looks like three balls connected with tubes. If you're using a game controller, you can find the Path tool by using the Object tool and selecting it as one of the pie slices when you press the A button.

   The Path tool lets you click the terrain to place small spheres. Every time you left-click with the mouse, a small sphere is placed, and a tube connects it to the nearest sphere or spheres.

4. If you click once in the lower corner of your square world, and then again in each of the other corners of your square world, and then one final click on your starting sphere, you'll see a path placed like the one in Figure 7.7.

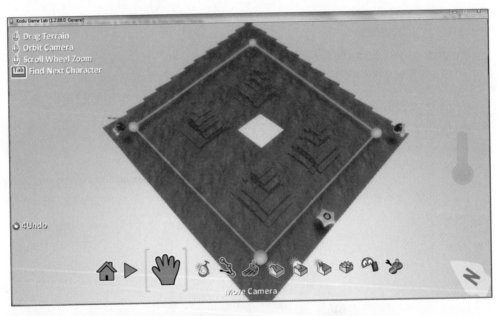

FIGURE 7.7 Adding a path for an object to follow.

> **NOTE**
> The path will be closed only if you click your starting sphere. You do not have to close a path. Paths can consist of a straight line such as one with three spheres, one on each end, and one in the center.

If you play your game now, the saucer will still wander randomly. It hasn't been programmed to follow the line yet. You'll also notice that the path you just drew on the terrain disappears. That's because a path is invisible when the game is being played; it's only visible when you are editing your game, and it does not disappear if you select a tool other than the Path tool. Feel free to press the Play button to see what happens.

> **TIP**
>
> If you need to modify a path, simply left-click and hold on a sphere to drag it; you'll notice that the tubes that connect the spheres will adjust in length and angle so they can stay connected. Hold down the Shift key if you want to move the entire path but not modify its shape.

Now you need to program the saucer to follow the path:

1. Right-click the saucer, select Program, and delete the Wander and Quickly tiles (right-click on them and choose Cut Tile), leaving the Move tile.

2. Click the + to the right of the Move tile and select On Path. You can further modify the On Path tile by specifying a speed (Slowly or Quickly).

> **NOTE**
>
> If you do not specify a speed, it moves at a medium speed (which you can adjust in the object's Change Settings list by using the Forward Speed Multiplier option).

Figure 7.8 shows the modified Programming Row 1 for the saucer. I've changed the saucer to move on the path, but slowly.

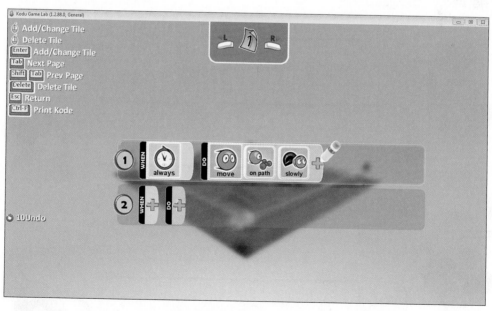

FIGURE 7.8   The saucer's new programming has it moving slowly on the path.

Notice in Figure 7.9 that I can also specify a path color to follow. The current path I drew is white, but I can modify a path's color easily enough. Use the Path tool and place the cursor over one of the existing spheres; you can then use the Left or Right Arrow buttons to change the color of the path.

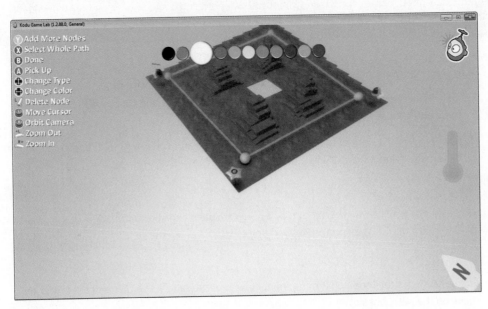

FIGURE 7.9 Change the color of a path.

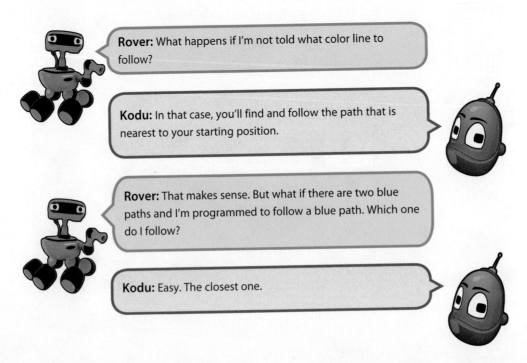

Rover: What happens if I'm not told what color line to follow?

Kodu: In that case, you'll find and follow the path that is nearest to your starting position.

Rover: That makes sense. But what if there are two blue paths and I'm programmed to follow a blue path. Which one do I follow?

Kodu: Easy. The closest one.

I've changed the path color to green and added a second path that is yellow. Figure 7.10 shows that the yellow path follows a diamond shape over the green square path and that the paths cross at certain points. Don't worry about where the paths cross; objects will avoid colliding all on their own.

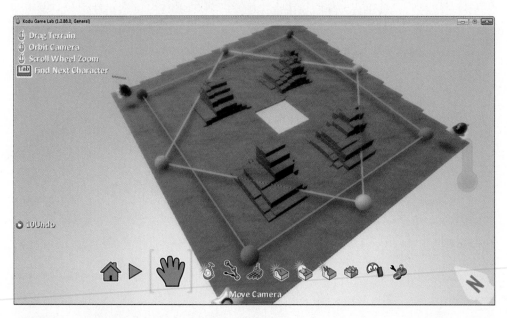

FIGURE 7.10 Create a new path using a different color.

Paths can also have height. I've added a new path (purple) that is a straight line with three spheres (two on the ends and one in the middle). I've also right-clicked the middle sphere, which offers the menu shown in Figure 7.11.

Right now, I'm only concerned with the Change Height option. (The Change Type option lets you cycle through various styles of paths and roads. The Delete option lets you remove a sphere, and the Add More Nodes option lets you click an existing path to add spheres.)

The Change Height option displays a drag bar as shown in Figure 7.12. Dragging the bar to the right raises the selected sphere up and away from the ground.

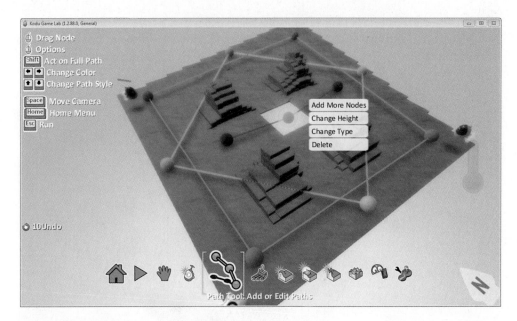

FIGURE 7.11 Right-click a sphere for options.

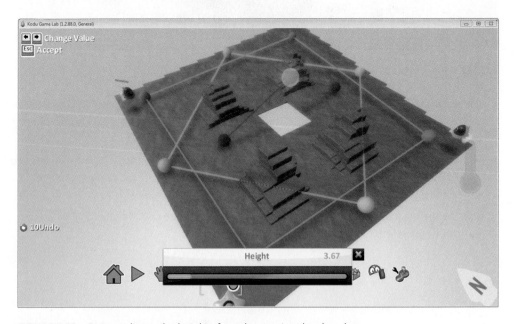

FIGURE 7.12 Raise or lower the height of a sphere using the drag bar.

It can be a bit difficult to tell when a sphere is higher than other spheres, so in Figure 7.13 I've used the Move Camera option to rotate the terrain so that you can view it from the side and see the raised sphere.

FIGURE 7.13 The raised sphere changes the path from a straight line to angled.

I'll add a fourth and final path (orange) that runs underneath the purple path, as shown in Figure 7.14.

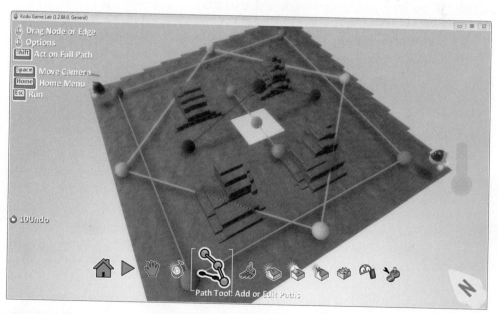

FIGURE 7.14 Four paths, one for each of the four saucers to follow.

Now I'll return to the program for my saucer and modify the Do box by adding a color (green) for the first saucer to follow. Figure 7.15 shows the Programming Row 1 that instructs the saucer to move slowly and to follow the green line.

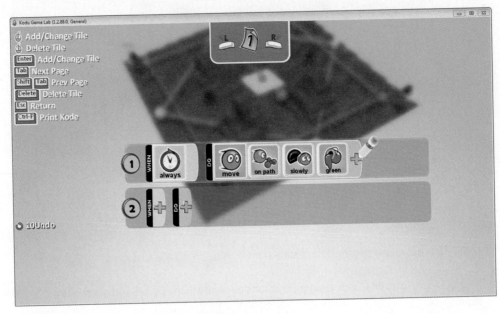

FIGURE 7.15   Finishing the programming for a Saucer object.

I've now got four paths, each a different color, and only one saucer. Now it's time to copy and paste three copies of the saucer:

1. Right-click the Saucer object.

2. Select Copy.

3. Paste a copy near each of the other three paths (yellow, purple, orange), as shown in Figure 7.16.

> **NOTE**
> It doesn't matter where you place a saucer. After you've programmed it to follow a path of a particular color, when the game starts it will move toward the path it is programmed to follow and then stay on that path until the game ends or until it is destroyed.

I right-click each of the other three saucers and change the color in their Programming Row 1 to one of the three remaining colors. When I'm done, I play the game to see whether the four saucers follow their programmed paths.

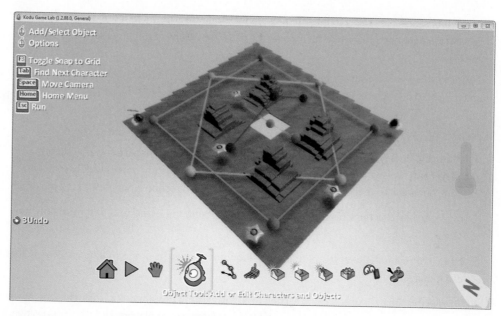

FIGURE 7.16   Four saucers and four colored paths.

It's a bit difficult to tell in Figure 7.17, but my four saucers are indeed following their respective paths.

FIGURE 7.17   Four flying saucers following invisible paths.

These four saucers are tricky to hit, but because they follow a path, all that's needed is a patient player to watch their movement to discover the path they follow and then time the firing of her missiles.

I want to add one more saucer to the mix, but I want this saucer to not only be fast but also smart—smart enough to run from players and make it difficult to hit.

Run Away!

The third and final type of movement option I have available is to enable a saucer to detect the player and run away. This saucer will not follow a path, so its movements will be somewhat random, but it will have the capability to quickly change its direction when it detects a player:

1. I start by selecting the Object tool and then right-clicking the terrain and pasting in one more saucer.

2. I then right-click the new saucer and select Program to open its programming window so that I can modify it.

3. To give this Smart Saucer a chance, I delete all the existing programming, including the Always tile. Instead, I want this saucer to be watching and listening for players, and this requires two When conditions.

    The first When condition I select is shown in Figure 7.18: the See tile.

FIGURE 7.18 When the Smart Saucer sees something, it will do something.

4. I click the + to the right of the See tile and choose Kodu from the pie menu that appears. Figure 7.19 shows that I've added the Kodu condition. I could click the + again to specify a color, but because Player 1 and Player 2 are both playing Kodu objects, I don't need to specify a color.

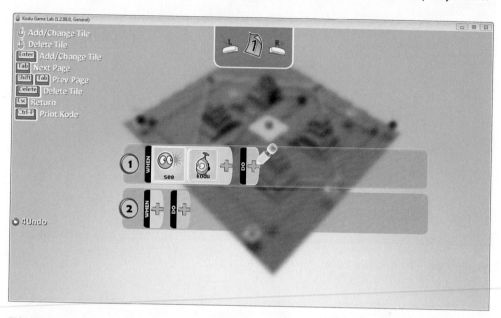

FIGURE 7.19   The Kodu condition is added so that the Smart Saucer will watch out for a Kodu.

5. When the Smart Saucer sees a Kodu, what do I want it to do? That's obvious: run away! To enable this, I click the Do box and select the Move option followed by the Circle and Quickly options, as shown in Figure 7.20.

Take a look at Figure 7.21, which shows another pie menu with options I could have selected by clicking the + to the right of the Move tile.

Why did I choose the Circle option rather than the Away or Avoid options shown in Figure 7.21? The answer is easy: I tested all of them and Circle worked the best. When I selected the Away option, believe it or not, the moment the saucer saw a Kodu, it took off in the opposite direction, leaving the world and disappearing from the screen. Don't believe me? Try it.

Next, I tried the Avoid option, but even with its speed set to Quickly, it was an easy target to hit because it just made small moves away from me, allowing my fast missiles to hit it as long as I stayed far away.

Nope, it was the Circle option that gave me the fastest and most fun results. With the Circle option, when the saucer saw one or both Kodus, it would swing out wide and circle the Kodu, never letting the Kodu get too close. And because it was making a circular path, my missiles that only shoot straight made it difficult to hit. Fun!

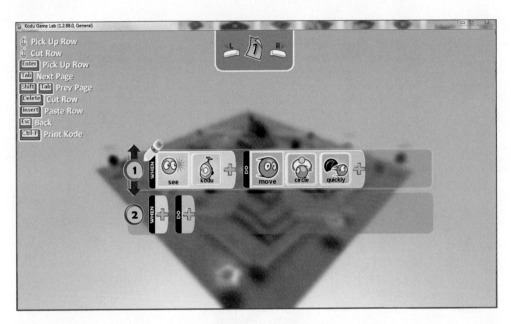

FIGURE 7.20   The Smart Saucer will move away from a Kodu player quickly.

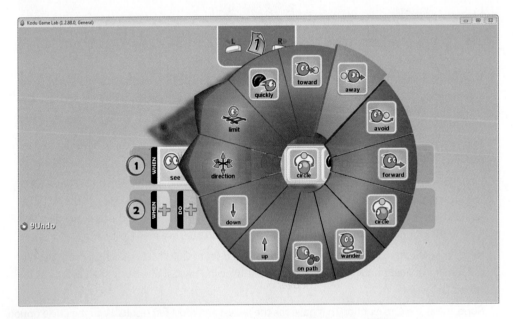

FIGURE 7.21   Other options for movement: Away, Avoid, Toward, and Wander.

I suggest you try all the options yourself, just to see what happens. And definitely try the Toward option—whichever Kodu (White or Blue) the Smart Saucer sees first, it races toward it, making for an easy shot.

Yes, the Circle option definitely makes that Smart Saucer hard to hit, but if I want to make it smarter, I can add more programming that goes beyond just giving it the capability to see a Kodu.

What I need to make the Smart Saucer even sneakier is to enable it to listen, which is what I've done in Figure 7.22. I've created the Programming Row 2 to be identical to Programming Row 1, but instead of the See tile, I've used the Hear tile.

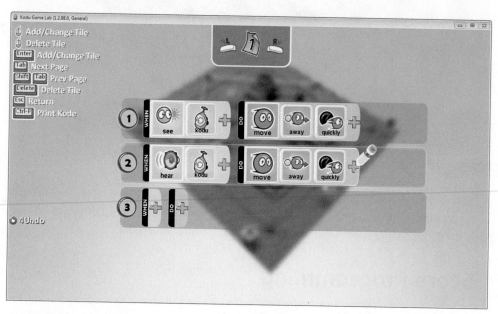

FIGURE 7.22 Giving the Smart Saucer the ability to listen.

Now it's time to play!

A few small tweaks are in order, too. First, I've upped the Maximum Hit Points of the four saucers following paths to 50 and set each Kodu's missile damage to 10. It'll take five hits to destroy a path-following saucer.

Next, I set the Smart Saucer's Maximum Hit Points to 20 and turned the Show Hit Points option to On. It will take two hits to destroy it, and if one player gets in a lucky hit, both players will see its Hit Points bar cut in half and can fight over getting the final hit. I'm also going to change the color of the Smart Saucer to red.

I'll add some programming in a minute that awards bonus points to the player who destroys the red Smart Saucer. Saucer 5 is the Smart Saucer's real name, as you can see in Figure 7.23 when the object is selected. I point this out because the entire saucer isn't colored red, just the small gaps between its starfish-like hull.

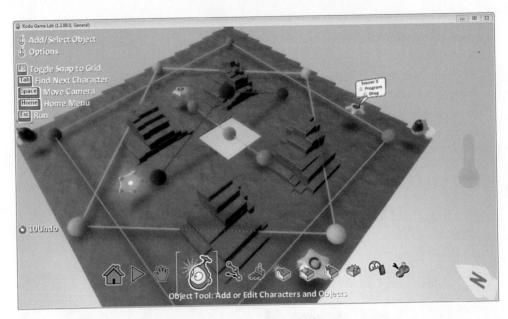

FIGURE 7.23   Giving the Smart Saucer a color because it's special.

Now that the game's target objects are created (as well as paths), it's time for a few remaining programming changes involving scoring, and the game will be ready for two players to go saucer hunting. Hey, that's a great name! I'm going to call this game *Saucer Hunt*.

Score Programming

Now that the game's objects are created and tested, it's time to go and fix the programming for the Player 1 and Player 2 Kodus. If you'll remember, I copied and pasted them into the Saucer Hunt game from the Chapter 5 game, which means they still have programming in them related to shooting at trees and rocks. Figure 7.24 shows White Kodu's programming.

You can leave the first two programming rows (1 and 2) alone. These are related to the movement and firing of missiles. It's Program Row 3 through Programming Row 5 that we need to fix, as follows:

1. I click the Tree tile in Programming Row 3 and change it to a Saucer (stored in the Bots I pie menu).

2. I also click the + to the right of the Saucer tile and select White as the color. This is because I'll be using Programming Row 3 to specify points earned for each missile hit on one of the path-following saucers.

   Figure 7.25 shows that I've completed Programming Row 3 by awarding 5 points to the White Kodu's score for each missile hit on a path-following (white) saucer.

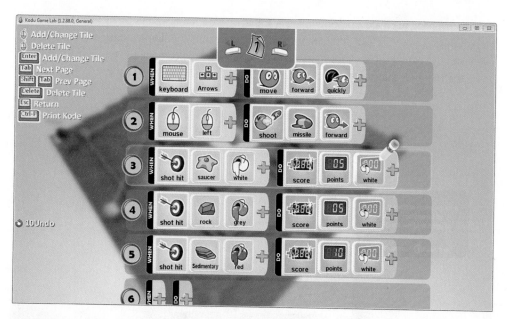

FIGURE 7.24   Program for the White Kodu.

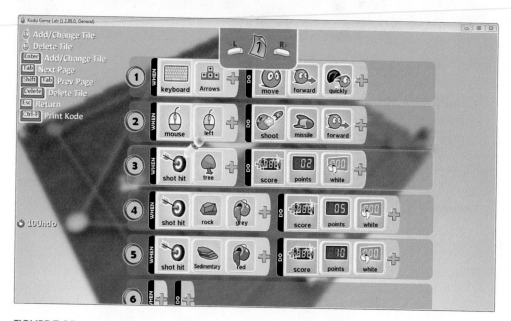

FIGURE 7.25   Scoring points for missile hits on path-following saucers.

3. I now need to create a programming row that awards points for missile hits on the red Smart Saucer. The Smart Saucer is harder to hit, so more points should be awarded to a player who can successfully hit it with a missile. Figure 7.26 shows the completed Programming Row 4 and the 20 points that are awarded to the White Kodu if it hits the Smart Saucer.

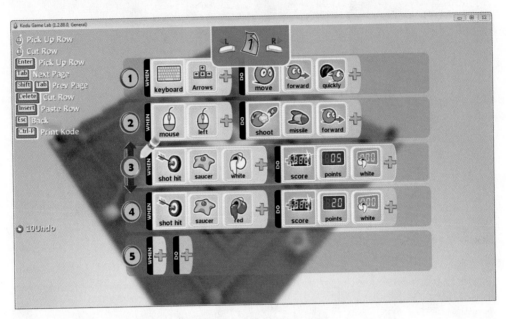

FIGURE 7.26 Scoring points for missile hits on the smart saucer.

4. Finally, I copy and paste Programming Row 3 and Programming Row 4 from the White Kodu into the Blue Kodu, making certain to change the color of the scoreboard that is awarded for hits on saucers. Figure 7.27 shows the updated Blue Kodu program.

And now it's time to play *Saucer Hunt*!

Figure 7.28 shows a game in progress. The Smart Saucer has already taken one hit by the White Kodu (awarding 20 points), and the Blue Kodu has scored two hits on the path-following saucers.

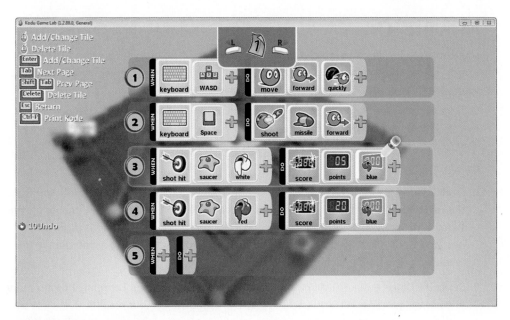

FIGURE 7.27   Program for the Blue Kodu.

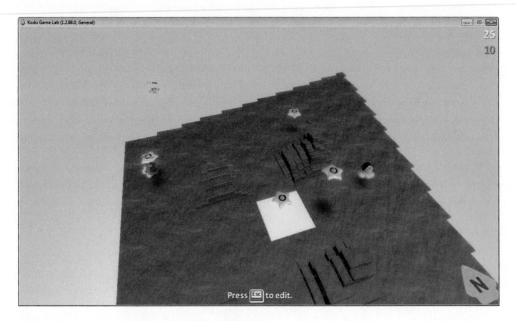

FIGURE 7.28   Player 1 versus Player 2 in *Saucer Hunt*.

Moving On

I hope that you had fun with this chapter. With an understanding of creating paths, using colors to assign paths and control scoring, and copying and pasting objects and their built-in programs, you've got some powerful tools that can help you make some super-fun games.

But let's not stop here. Before I end this chapter and send you on to Chapter 8, "Dangerous Targets: Programming Enemies That Fire Back," I've got some tweaks I want you to try on *Saucer Hunt* to see whether they add to (or take away from) the fun of the game.

Here's what I want you to do before moving on to Chapter 8:

1. Modify *Saucer Hunt* by removing the invisible wall that surrounds the borders of the world and the center hole. Select the Object tool, right-click anywhere on the terrain, and choose Change World Settings. Scroll down the list to the second option: Glass Walls. Click the green power button to turn it off and play the game. See what happens if your Kodu gets too close to the world's edges or the center hole.

2. Select the Object tool, right-click a Kodu, and select Change Settings. Experiment by increasing or decreasing the Max Hit Points of each player's Kodu character (but keep them equal to be fair). At what point does the game become more about hunting the other player first before shooting at the saucers? Keep in mind that when a player is destroyed by another player, it doesn't end the game; the saucers are still available for points. Does allowing the players to fire missiles and destroy the Kodus make the game more fun or take away from the fun?

3. Here's a tough one! See whether you can figure out how to have one player's missiles *add* hit points back to a saucer. Here's a hint: For the When box, use the Shot Hit and Saucer tiles, but do not specify a color. For the Do box, look for the Heal option in the Combat pie menu. Continue to add tiles that specify points to add health back, as well as to which object to apply the healing. The options are Me or It. Which do you think is the correct choice? After you've figured it out, award points to the healing player for each successful healing missile that hits.

When you finish this homework, click the Home Menu button and save your newly created world before selecting Exit to Main Menu. From the Main Menu, select Quit Kodu to close down Kodu Game Lab.

8

Dangerous Targets: Programming Enemies That Fire Back

In This Chapter

○ Targets That Fight Back

○ Saucers Go Boom

○ Game Over?

○ Return Fire

○ Moving On

Firing at targets that don't fight back has been a popular type of game for many years. Many of you probably won't be familiar with a very early video game called Asteroids, but this game placed the player in the middle of an asteroid swarm. The player had a limited-use shield and a laser cannon that fired individual shots for each press of the Fire button. It was addictive, and the meteors got bigger and faster as the game progressed. But the game's difficulty level could be tweaked by adding in a large and small flying saucer that could fire on the player. This really added to the danger! In this chapter, you learn how easy it is to add targets that fight back, and your players will enjoy the extra challenge.

Targets That Fight Back

I really hope that you're starting to develop some ideas of your own for games you want to create with Kodu Game Labs. You've learned a lot over the previous seven chapters, plenty to keep you busy building some interesting worlds and unusual terrain and then adding in some obstacles, targets, and a player or two.

In Chapter 7, "Difficult Targets to Hit: Increasing Game Difficulty and Path Following," you learned how to create a game that I hope you had fun playing with a friend. Not only were your missiles useful for hitting the saucers, but you might also have discovered that it helps to take a few shots at your opponent to draw attention away from the game. That's a solid strategy, especially in games like *Saucer Hunt*, where the game has a beginning and an end. *Saucer Hunt* had a few problems, however, that you may or may not have noticed:

○ First, the saucers were programmed to take hits but could never be fully destroyed. We need additional programming that lets an object monitor its health (hit points) and when it reaches 0, the object disappears in a poof or a big explosion.

○ Second, if you or your opponent is destroyed or falls off the world (either off the edge or into the hole in the center of the world), the game doesn't end. The other player can continue to shoot at the saucers and get the highest score possible.

○ And third, you can hit the saucers with your missiles, but they lack any missiles of their own to fire back at you.

This chapter addresses all three of these limitations. First, we're going to modify *Saucer Hunt* so that when you or your opponent hit a saucer too many times the saucer will be destroyed. You also learn how to give your game the capability to end itself when certain conditions are met. And the chapter ends with us ramping up the difficulty of the game by enabling the smart saucer to fire an occasional missile at you or your opponent.

So, let's get started. I won't be building the *Saucer Hunt* game from scratch, so refer back to Chapter 7 if you need to create it.

Saucers Go Boom

There is nothing more gratifying in a shoot-em-up game as taking out an enemy and seeing a big explosion on the screen. Well, that's what I want to add to the *Saucer Hunt* game in this section: a big explosion.

Go ahead and open up the *Saucer Hunt* game from Chapter 7. You should see something similar to what's shown in Figure 8.1.

> **NOTE**
> Just another reminder that as the book progresses, I'm not going to show you how to re-create all the special programming needed for every object that you've learned in previous chapters. For example, I showed you in Chapter 7 how to turn on the smart saucer's hit points so that you can see how much damage it has taken. I want to enable the visible hit points on all the saucers, so refer back to Chapter 7 if you need a reminder how to do that. (Hint: Right-click the object and browse through the Change Settings options.)

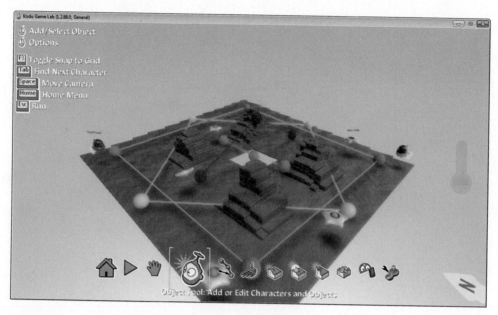

FIGURE 8.1 *Saucer Hunt* version 1.0 ready for an upgrade.

Before I start adding the programming required for a saucer to explode when its hit points reach 0, I need to make some tweaks to the game.

First, I want to enable all of the saucers and Kodus so that I can see how many hit points they have left. Figure 8.2 shows that I've turned on the Show Hit Points for all saucers as well as the two Kodus.

You might be thinking it would be more fun to *not* know how many hit points a saucer has remaining or how many your opponent has remaining. And you might be right. You won't know how a tweak like this affects your game until you actually play it a few times using both conditions: hit points on and hit points off.

I believe that knowing how many hit points you and your opponent have adds to the fun. As the smart saucer and your opponent fire missiles at you, you might lose track of your hit points. Using the Hit Points bar allows you to change your strategy should you find your hit points getting low. And if your opponent's hit points are low, you'll want to definitely consider rushing in and firing a few missiles to take the opposing Kodu out of the game.

But again, this is simply a tweak I want to turn on and test to see how it affects gameplay. If I find that knowing the number of hit points the saucers have left makes the game easier, I can turn the Hit Point bars off. I might also find that having to mentally track the number of hits my opponent has taken adds to the complexity of the game.

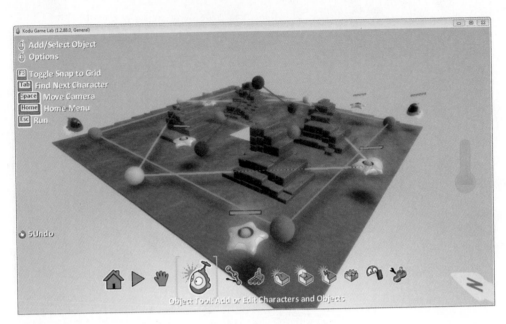

FIGURE 8.2 Hit points are displayed or all saucers and Kodus.

For now, though, let's turn them on for testing purposes. As you test your modifications to the game, you'll be able to see which saucers are close to 0 hit points and watch for the explosion. If you don't see the explosion, you'll know you need to take a better look at the underlying programming.

The following are six additional tweaks to the game that I want to make before I show you the programming required to explode a saucer when its hit points reach 0:

○ Set the two Kodus' missiles to do the same amount of damage. Right-click both Kodus, select Change Settings, and set Missile Damage to 5.

○ Set the four path-following saucers to have 50 hit points each. Once again, right-click each saucer, select Change Settings, and set the Max Hit Points option to 20. Four missile hits will destroy a path-following saucer.

○ Set the smart saucer to have 80 hit points.

○ Set both Kodus to have 100 hit points.

○ Set both Kodus to have their missile reload time equal to 0.5. This will affect how fast each player can fire missiles. The lower the number, the faster the missiles will fire when you press and hold the Fire button.

○ Set both Kodus to have their missile speed at 10. This will affect how fast the missiles speed across the screen. The higher the number, the faster the missile flies.

TIP

Be sure to save your work with a new version number, or feel free to give it a new name. I'm saving mine as *Saucer Hunt Extreme*.

Okay, after you've made the additional tweaks to the objects, it's now time to add the programming to create the explosions that are seen when a saucer's hit points reach 0.

I show you how to modify one of the four path-following saucers with the new programming. You need to add the same programming to the remaining path-following saucers and to the smart saucer. Remember that you can copy an entire programming row and paste it into the other objects' program.

First, I open up a path-following saucer's program listing, as shown in Figure 8.3.

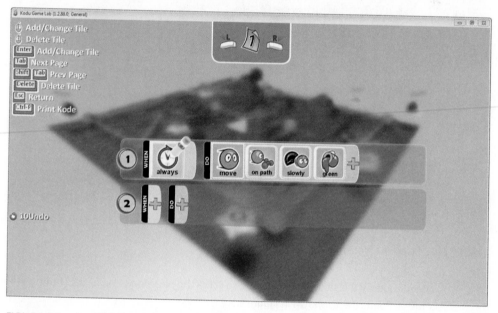

FIGURE 8.3   A path-following saucer's program.

As you can see, all this saucer is programmed to do is follow a path (in this case, the green path). There is no additional programming. If you've made the tweaks described earlier and set the path-following saucer's hit points to 20 and the missile damage to 5, what do you think will happen when you hit a path-following saucer four times?

If you said its hit points would reach 0 and it will explode, you are correct. But what if I want the saucer to do something interesting other than just explode when its hit points reach 0?

What's needed is some additional programming that tells the path-following saucer to monitor its hit points and do something unusual when that number reaches 0. I want something like this:

WHEN hit points = 0, DO stun saucer and then vanish.

To achieve this, follow these steps:

1. Click Programming Row 2's When tile and select the Health option, as shown in Figure 8.4.

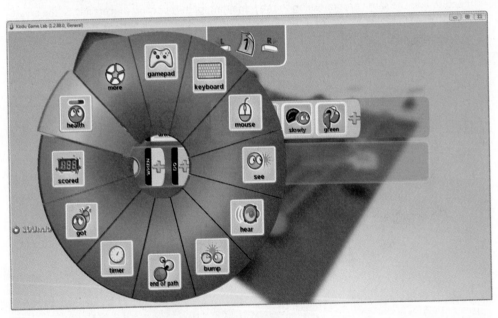

FIGURE 8.4 Select the Health option for the When tile.

2. You need to specify the value for the Health, so I click the plus sign (+) after the Health tile and select the 00 Points tile, as shown in Figure 8.5.

3. Now it's time to specify what happens when the saucer's hit points (health) reaches 0 points. So, tap the Do tile and select the Combat pie piece, as shown in Figure 8.6.

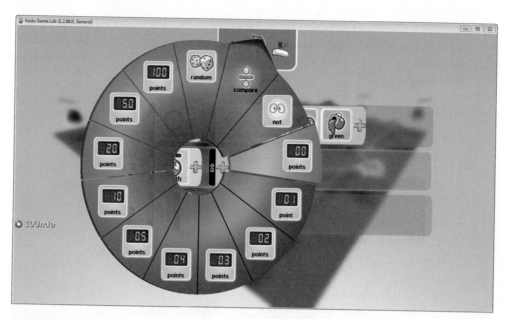

FIGURE 8.5   Specify a health of 00 points.

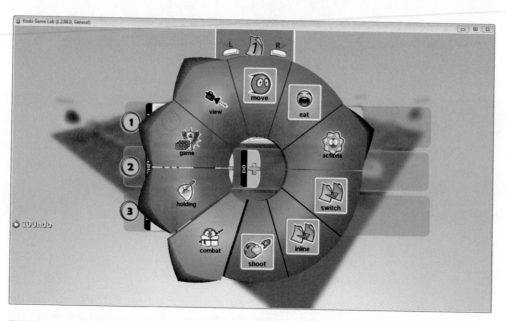

FIGURE 8.6   Select the Combat pie piece to view additional options.

4. When you select the Combat pie piece, a new pie circle opens, as shown in Figure 8.7. Pick the Stun option because it has a really cool sound effect that triggers just before the saucer disappears. (You could also pick the Vanish option, which would cause the saucer to disappear in the blink of an eye.)

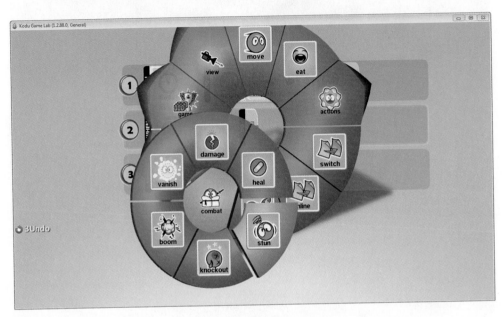

FIGURE 8.7   Choose the Stun option for an explosion.

> **NOTE**
> Take a careful look at the Combat pie piece again and you'll see an interesting option called Heal. Can you think of how a Combat option such as Heal could be used in a game? Imagine giving your opponent the capability to heal saucers instead of destroying them? One player tries to destroy while the other fires "healing" missiles. That might make for an interesting variation of *Saucer Hunt Extreme*.

5. Before you leave the program, be sure to right-click the programming row's number (in this case, 2) and select the Copy Row option shown in Figure 8.8.

6. Leave the current saucer's programming screen (tap the Esc button), and then right-click the other saucers, one at a time, and right-click the programming row's number and select Paste Row, as shown in Figure 8.9.

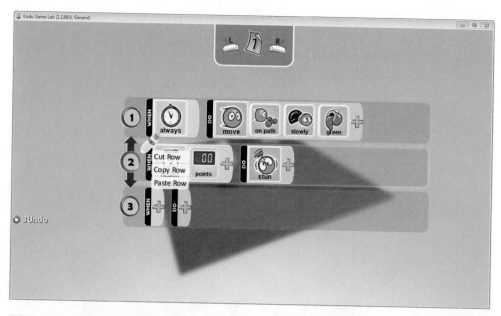

FIGURE 8.8 Copy your new program line.

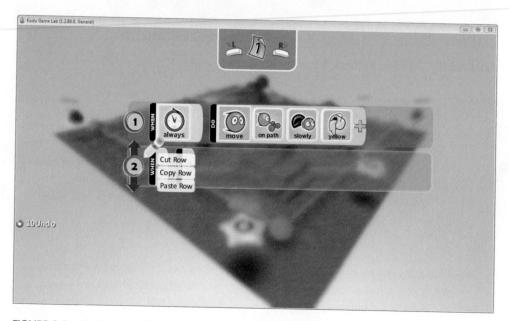

FIGURE 8.9 Paste a copied program line into all remaining saucers.

Now it's time to test the program to see if the saucers actually explode when their hit points reach 0.

As you can see in Figure 8.10, I've managed to rack up some points by destroying one path-following saucer completely. I've also scored some hits on my opponent's Kodu, and a few of the remaining saucers have been damaged (as their Hit Point bars show). The saucers also have a nice loud *stun* sound when they are destroyed. Yeah!

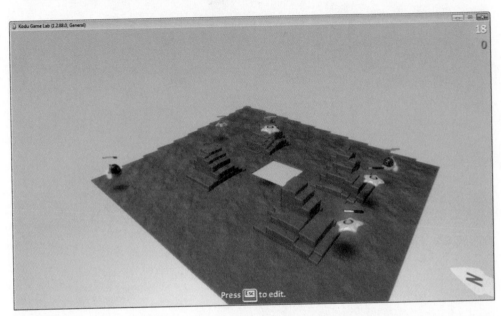

FIGURE 8.10   The updated game, complete with stunned (and exploding) saucers.

> **NOTE**
>
> During the test games, I figured out rather quickly that the smart saucer is just too fast and too smart to hit. Really, the only way to hit it with a missile is with a lucky shot. To make the game a little easier, I'll reduce the smart saucer's hit points and reduce its forward speed multiplier from 1.0 to .5. This will slow the smart saucer down just a little. It's still going to be hard to hit because it watches and listens for the Kodus, but the reduction in speed will decrease the game's difficulty.

Removing a saucer with an explosion is a nice special effect, but it's really more of a game-changing feature because with a saucer gone players will no longer be able to receive points for hitting it. The reduced number of targets means your opponent will likely be firing on the same saucers for points.

And because both Kodus can be damaged by missiles, there's always the chance you could eliminate your opponent from the game with enough missile hits. And this brings up the point of the next section of this chapter: ending a game.

Game Over?

There are a couple of ways I can choose to end *Saucer Hunt Extreme*:

❍ End the game when all saucers are destroyed and the winner is the player with the most points.

❍ Immediately end the game if one of the Kodu players is destroyed, awarding the win to the surviving player.

Both of these options change the style of the game slightly. With the first option, there is only a slight incentive to try and hit your opponent with missiles. Your opponent will be getting points by shooting and hitting saucers while you try to hit your opponent and ignore the saucers. Even if you end up destroying your opponent, should your opponent destroy enough saucers and gather enough points, you'll still lose the game.

The second option creates a game that encourages players to fire missiles at one another, ignoring the saucers completely; all saucers could be left on the screen, flying around, but if you successfully destroy your opponent, you win.

Neither of these is an ideal way to end the game to me. I want to reward players for shooting at the saucers, but I also want them avoiding the hazards and not falling off the playing field. And they should try to avoid missiles from the opposing player. I also don't want the game going on forever and ever; it needs to end in a reasonable amount of time.

Time. Hmm… now that's an idea. A time limit!

Let me show you how to put a time limit on *Saucer Hunt Extreme*, and then I'll show you some additional tweaks that can be made on the game.

First, adding a time limit to a game involves a little bit of programming trickery with Kodu Game Lab. Remember that all of Kodu Game Lab programming involves checking a condition (When) and performing an action (Do), and this programming is *always* done on an object in the game.

This means you need to add an object to the game that has the sole purpose of tracking time and determining when a certain amount of time has elapsed.

Figure 8.11 shows that I've dropped a small rock into the game. When I'm done programming the rock, I'm going to shrink it down to such a small size that it will be barely visible in the final game, but for now I'm leaving it a larger size so that I can easily find it and click it when I need to program it. I call this the *timer rock*.

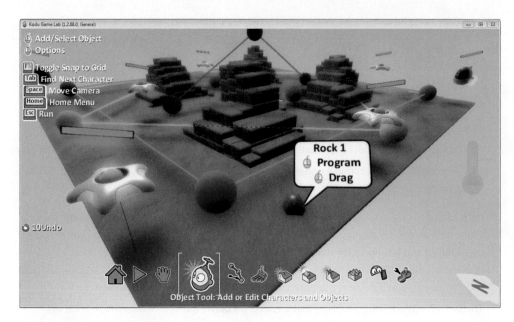

FIGURE 8.11   The timer rock.

Now for the trickery part. I want the timer to actually appear on the screen, and to do this I add a third scoreboard that will continually count up in 1-second increments. I make it yellow in color so that it's easy to spot:

1. I right-click the timer rock and select the Program option. The first When block I want to add is the Timer option shown in Figure 8.12.

2. The Timer tile requires me to specify how often something happens. So, I click the + to the right of the Timer tile. Figure 8.13 shows the options I then have available.

3. I want the Timer to do something every single second, so I select the 1 Second pie piece. (I could easily select 5 Seconds, for example, and whatever action I specify for the timer rock's Do block would then only happen every 5 seconds… 10, 15, 20, and so on.)

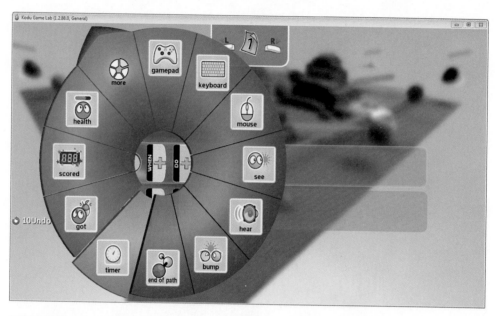

FIGURE 8.12 The Timer tile tracks how much time has elapsed.

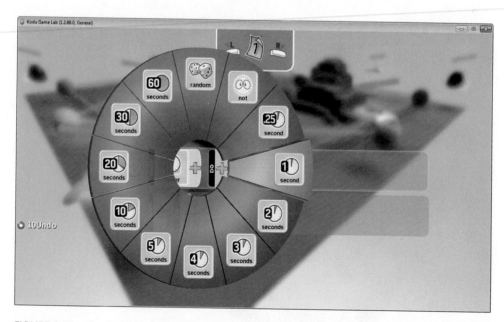

FIGURE 8.13 The Timer tile will wait a specified number of seconds.

4. I now need to specify exactly what happens every second the Timer counts up, so I click the Do block and first select the Game pie piece, as shown in Figure 8.14.

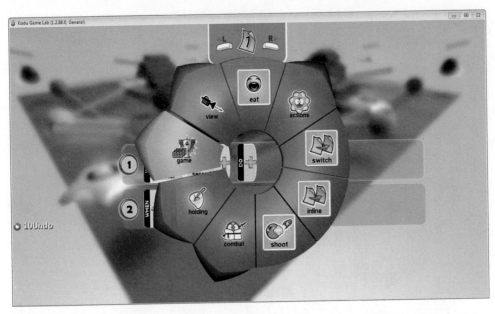

FIGURE 8.14 The Game pie piece allows for a new scoreboard to be added to the game.

Another pie circle appears as shown in Figure 8.15. I want the Score option (with the + sign).

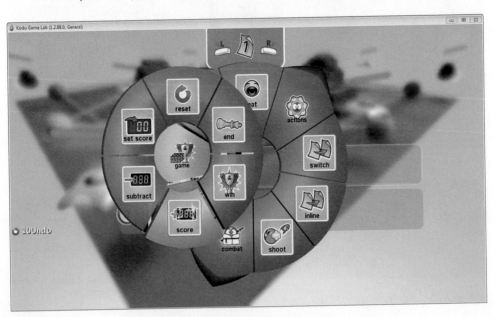

FIGURE 8.15 The new scoreboard serves as a timer that counts up.

5. I click the + to the right of the Score tile and select 01 Point, as shown in Figure 8.16.

FIGURE 8.16 Increment the scoreboard/timer by 1.

6. All that's left is to specify the color of the new Timer feature. I click the + to the right of the 01 Point tile and choose the Scores pie piece, which then allows me to select Yellow as the color of the scoreboard that will serve as the timer. You can see this in Figure 8.17.

Figure 8.18 shows the final programming for the timer rock's Programming Row 1.

Go ahead and play the game. You'll now see a new yellow score underneath the white and blue scoreboards. But this yellow scoreboard isn't keeping score; instead, it counts up in 1-second increments. Figure 8.19 shows the new Timer feature as it counts up in a game.

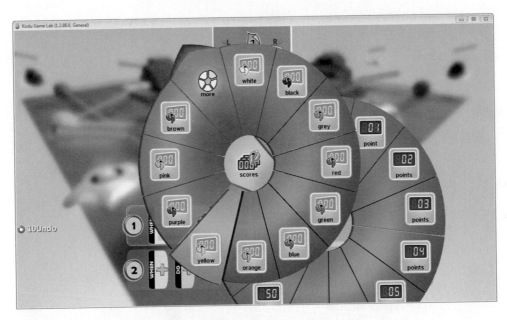

FIGURE 8.17 Select the timer color to be displayed.

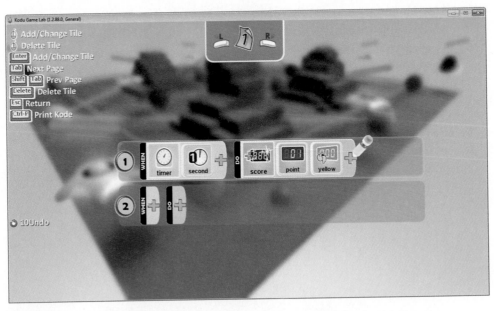

FIGURE 8.18 This bit of programming creates a yellow scoreboard that will act as a timer.

FIGURE 8.19   The timer is working and counting up in 1-second increments.

If I leave the timer rock as it is, the timer will just keep counting up forever, with no end in sight. What's needed now is some additional programming that tells the game when to end.

I think two minutes is long enough, don't you? Here's how I'll go about ending the game when 120 seconds have passed:

1. I reopen my timer rock's program.

2. I then click the When box in Programming Row 2 and select the Timer tile again, but this time I want to have an action occur at the 120 second mark.

   You might have noticed that there is no 120 second tile, but don't let that stop you. Kodu Game Lab offers a simple solution that involves nothing more than basic arithmetic. Notice in Figure 8.20 that there is a 60 Seconds tile.

3. I need the game to last 120 seconds, not 60, so what's needed is another 60 seconds, right? Well, all I have to do is click the + to the right of the 60 Seconds tile and add another 60 Seconds tile, as shown in Figure 8.21.

FIGURE 8.20 Choose the 60 Seconds tile.

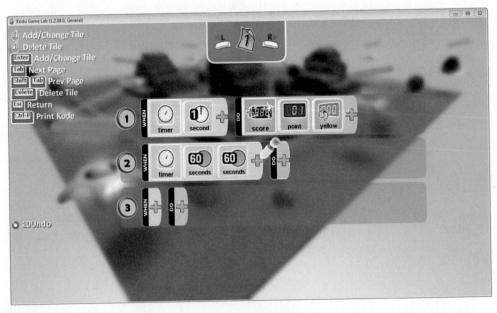

FIGURE 8.21 Add more time by adding additional time tiles.

You'll see some more examples later in the book that use this method of stacking time and points together to add them up. For now, though, all you need to know is that the timer rock will now perform some action when the timer reaches 120 seconds.

4. I then click Programming Row 2's Do box and select the Game pie piece, as shown in Figure 8.22. Another pie circle appears with options.

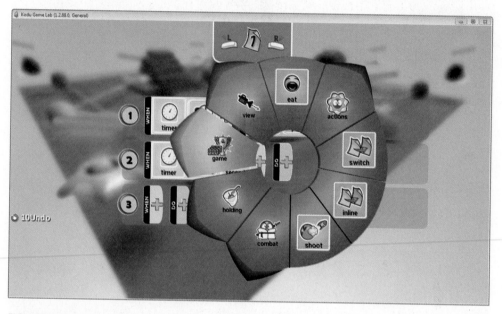

FIGURE 8.22 Select the Game pie piece to specify what happens after 120 seconds.

5. I have many options (including Reset and End), but I select the Win pie piece and finish out the timer rock's programming, as shown in Figure 8.23.

Go ahead and play the game. You'll see the yellow timer counting up, and when it hits 120, the game ends, as shown in Figure 8.24.

In the upper-right corner of the screen are the scores of the two players, allowing you to determine which player won the game.

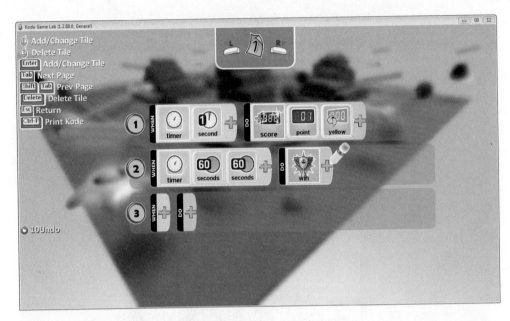

FIGURE 8.23   The Win option ends the game with the word "Winner."

FIGURE 8.24   We have a winner!

Return Fire

Before we leave *Saucer Hunt Extreme*, there's one more tweak I want to add to the game: I want to enable the smart saucer to fire a missile back at the players.

You saw in Chapter 7 how to give the two Kodus the capability to fire missiles at the saucers, so refer back to that chapter for the programming details. Here, I move quickly through the programming tiles required to enable the smart saucer to target the players.

First, Figure 8.25 shows the completed Programming Row 4. The rule works like this:

WHEN smart saucer sees Kodu (White or Blue) DO shoot missile

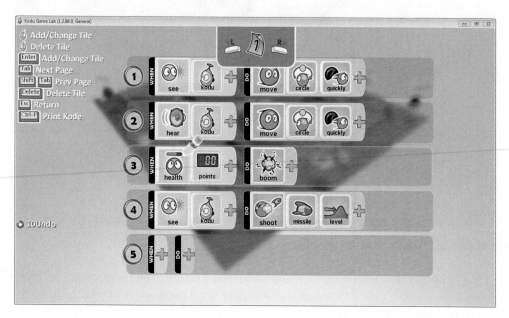

FIGURE 8.25 Now the smart saucer can fight back.

After testing this new bit of programming, I had to make a few tweaks to the game:

○ I reduced the smart saucer's missile damage to 5. (It was set to 50 by default, and it quickly defeated both Kodus in less than 10 seconds.)

○ I increased the missile loading time to 5.0. This gave the smart saucer a much slower firing rate.

○ I decreased the smart saucer's missile speed to 4.

○ I decreased the number of missiles the smart saucer could fire simultaneously to 2.

○ I moved the smart saucer's starting position to the center of the game field. Originally, it was much closer to the White Kodu, and the White Kodu always took an immediate missile hit when the game started. And the smart saucer's missile is heat seeking (once it's launched, that missile will hunt down whichever Kodu was fired upon); this will add some fun to the game, for sure.

Figure 8.26 shows these settings (in the smart saucer's changed settings list).

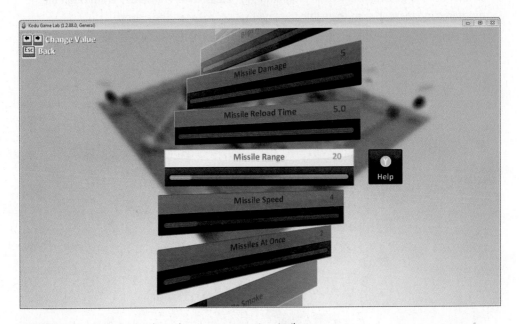

FIGURE 8.26 Tweaks made to the smart saucer's missiles.

As you saw throughout this chapter, creating a game requires constant testing and balancing. You'll often find yourself making a small change, testing the game, and then figuring out the change made the game better or worse.

The smart saucer, for example, was simply too powerful at the beginning of the game after I enabled its missiles. I had to modify the missile settings, slowing them down and reducing their power, until the game felt balanced.

Keep this in mind as you develop your own games. Always be on the lookout for how you can make the game better with one or two simple tweaks. Sometimes it'll take just one or two tweaks. At other times, you might have to revisit the game's rules completely and do some major rework on the programming. But programming with Kodu Game Lab is extremely fun, so you'll probably find as I have that any chance to tweak a game is simply another chance to have fun and maybe find a new tile or new game setting that you can incorporate into future games.

Moving On

Few things can make a game more fun than a smart opponent or an opponent that fires back. With this chapter, you learned how to create *smart* and *dangerous* opponents, and now you can give your games a bit more of a challenge because your players will need to be on guard.

Here's what I want you to do before moving on to Chapter 9, "Grab That Power Up: Using Pages for More Complex Programs:"

1. Modify *Saucer Hunt Extreme* so that if a player's missile hits the opposing player that player loses a point on the scoreboard. This will provide a little incentive for each player to occasionally take a missile shot at their opponent and not just at the saucers.

2. Many games offer a mix of speed versus firepower. A fast player might fire slower missiles, whereas a slow player might fire faster missiles or missiles that do more damage. Experiment by tweaking the Blue Kodu to fire faster missiles and move slower, and change the White Kodu to fire slow missiles but be able to move quickly around the playing field. Try to find a balance that is fair to both players.

3. You now know how to remove a saucer from the game with an explosion when its hit points reach 0. Modify the game by making both Kodus behave in the same manner. When a Kodu reaches 0 hit points, have it explode. There's a way to end the game when a player's object has its hit points reach 0. Can you figure out how to modify *Saucer Hunt Extreme* so that if a player's Kodu drops to 0 hit points the game ends?

When you finish this homework, click the Home Menu button and save your newly created world before selecting Exit to Main Menu. From the Main Menu, select Quit Kodu to close down Kodu Game Lab.

9

Grab That Power Up: Using Pages for More Complex Programs

Changing the Game Conditions

Good games should always have a beginning and an end. The beginning could be a race to collect items, or maybe an intro movie or animation (also called a *cut scene*) that sets up the game's story. The ending of a game could occur when time runs out or a player's health reaches zero. You'll see more examples in this book of openings and endings of games, but this chapter is all about what happens in the middle.

There are numerous examples of games that play the same all the way through, from beginning to end. Famous games such as *Space Invaders* or *Pac-Man* both have game screens that look the same at the beginning, middle, and ending of a game. The problem with games that stay the same from beginning to end is simple—they can get boring fast. But if you look carefully at *Space Invaders* and *Pac-Man*, there's usually something that changes, and it can be subtle or extremely obvious.

For *Space Invaders*, the player shoots at alien targets that march left and right across the screen. When the aliens reach the edge of the screen, they drop down a level, moving closer to the player. One strategy is to eliminate all the targets on the bottom row of the screen, giving the player more "room to breathe" along the bottom edge. But if that's all there was to the game, Space Invaders would have been a game that you just played until you got bored and walked away. Instead, the game designers introduced some changes into the game that were subtle at first, and then very obvious:

○ The more alien targets you eliminate, the faster the remaining aliens begin to move. The last alien target on the screen is lightning fast and can only be hit by a well-timed laser blast.

○ After clearing a wave of alien targets, a new screen fills with faster-moving and faster-shooting targets, and they start at a position closer to the bottom of the screen, and the player.

What these two game-changing conditions do is create a game that is impossible to play for long periods of time. Eventually, the targets are so fast, and fire at you so relentlessly, and begin their march so close to the bottom of the screen… well, you get the idea. The goal of *Space Invaders* is purely score-driven; get as high a score as you can before the game beats you.

Pac-Man also has a standard playing field: The labyrinth that *Pac-Man* moves around never changes. Neither does the quantity of enemies that chase you; it's always four. But the game developers of *Pac-Man* recognized that eating up the dots and running from the four enemy ghosts would get boring fast. So, they added their own game changers:

○ Players can eat four power dots to turn the tables and chase and "eat" the ghosts for extra points. This also returns the ghosts momentarily to a holding pen in the center of the screen.

○ Not only do the ghosts move faster as levels are cleared, but they also spend less time in the holding pen.

○ In later levels, the power dots are almost useless, turning the ghosts into targets for less than 2 seconds—not enough time for *Pac-Man* to eat them.

○ There are breaks provided to the players in the form of small animated movies of *Pac-Man* chasing the ghosts in humorous ways. These give players a chance to catch their breath, flex their hands, and prepare for the next (more difficult) wave.

Pac-Man was a phenomenal success (and it's still a popular game today). But I don't believe it would have been nearly as popular and fun if the game developers hadn't added in the game changers.

For a game like *Saucer Hunt Extreme*, which ends when time runs out or a player's health hits zero, game changers aren't always necessary. *Saucer Hunt Extreme* is a fast-paced game, but it's not meant to be played for hours and hours. It has an ending that cannot be avoided; either the time runs out on the players or someone loses all their health.

But what would happen if you removed the time limit, gave the players unlimited health (basically making them indestructible and invincible to missiles), and had an infinite number of saucers for the players to shoot? It might be fun for the first few minutes, but players would become bored

> **TIP**
>
> You will learn in Chapter 10, "The Cameras Are Rolling: Camera Controls for Solo and Multiplayer Games," how to reduce the amount of programming that's required when testing the same condition (a missile hitting a saucer, for example, to reduce the timer and score points) by using the When box's tiles only once. It's a trick that involves tucking a programming row underneath the one above it and using its When condition instead of re-creating the same When tiles.

That's Game Changer 1, but I've still got two game changers left to implement. These last two game changers, however, require me to use a new feature that you might not have encountered yet. That feature is called *pages*, and you're going to be amazed at how it can greatly improve the complexity and fun of your games.

Turn the Page

Before I show you how to use pages, let me show you where they're located. Open a Kodu's program (either Blue or White) and take a look at the very top of the screen. Figure 9.3 shows the Pages tool.

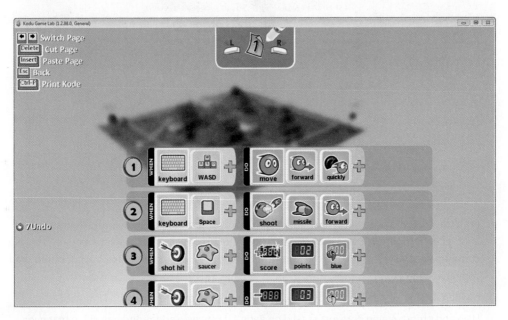

FIGURE 9.3   The Pages tool always tells you what page number you're programming.

In Figure 9.3, you can see that I'm on Page 1 of the Blue Kodu. (If you aren't sure which Kodu I'm looking at, look at Programming Row 3 in Figure 9.3 to see which scoreboard is getting the points for a missile hit.)

You can click the left (L) or right (R) buttons with the mouse, or you can use the L or R buttons on the D-Pad to move between pages. Keep clicking on the L or R buttons and you'll find that each object has a maximum of 12 pages. Try to click through to Page 13 and you'll find yourself returning to Page 1. There is no Page 13!

Another trick you need to know about before we get into a discussion on using pages is that when it comes to copying and pasting programming you can copy an entire page and paste it into another page, just as you can copy an entire programming row (like I did in the previous section to copy the timer modification program to the other Kodu) and paste it into another programming row.

Figure 9.4 shows what happens when I right-click Page 1.

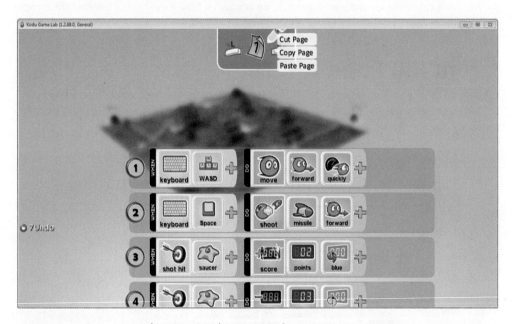

FIGURE 9.4 Cut, copy, and paste using the Pages tool.

I can use the Cut option to cut an entire page's worth of programming rows and then switch to another page, right-click, and choose the Paste option to put all those programming rows on the current page. Likewise, I can use the Copy option to leave a page's programming intact and then copy that page's programming rows to another page. This will come in handy shortly.

I switch to Page 2 of the Blue Kodu; you can see that it's completely blank in Figure 9.5.

I can add programming here just as I did on Page 1. I can even add programming so that every missile strike that Blue Kodu makes adds 100 points to the Blue scoreboard. Pretty nice for the blue player! But here's the catch: Unless some programming on Page 1 tells Kodu Game Lab to jump to Page 2, any programming on Page 2 might as well be invisible. It will never run and never affect the game.

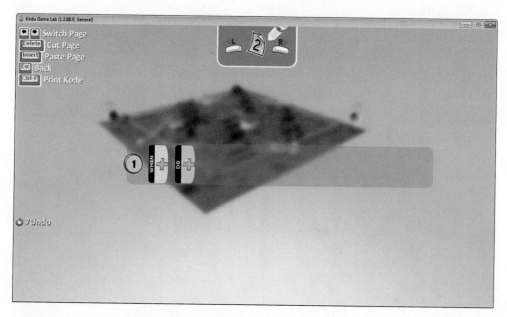

FIGURE 9.5   Not much is happening on Page 2. Yet.

CAUTION

Here's something you might find unusual if you experiment a bit. If you were to cut Page 1's programming and then paste it into Page 2, leaving Page 1 blank, everything in the game will still work… except for Blue Kodu. Kodu Game Lab always expects to start the game with programming on Page 1 of every object.

So there's your first tip when it comes to using pages: You always need to tell Page 1 to jump to Page 2, for example, if you want any programming on Page 2 to execute (run). Keep in mind, however, that you can skip pages; you can have programming on Page 1 that jumps to programming on Page 4 or Page 8. You don't have to move linearly from Page 1 to Page 2 to Page 3, and so on.

So now that you see how to move between pages and know how to cut, copy, and paste between pages, you're probably wondering why you'd ever want to use pages. I answer that question as I add another game changer: decreasing the smart saucer's speed as it takes damage.

Game Changer 2: Decrease Smart Saucer Speed

Take a look at Figure 9.6, which shows the current programming for the smart saucer.

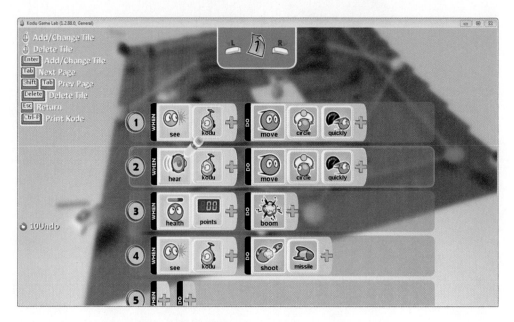

FIGURE 9.6 The smart saucer's programming.

I want to point out a few things to you about Page 1 of the smart saucer's programming. First, Programming Rows 1 and 2 both use the Quickly tile to define how fast the smart saucer circles a Kodu when it sees or hears that Kodu.

Second, Programming Row 3 causes the smart saucer to explode when its hit points reach zero.

Game Changer 2 is supposed to slow down the smart saucer when its hit points dip below a certain value. I've set the Max Hit Points of the smart saucer to 35, so I'm thinking it might be nice to reduce its speed a small amount when the hit points reach 25, and then reduce its speed even more when the hit points dip below 15.

Take a look again at the programming seen in Figure 9.6. Because I've defined the movement speed of the smart saucer in Program Rows 1 and 2 as Quickly, that's the speed that the smart saucer will fly…no matter how much damage it takes. Yes, I could add some programming in Programming Row 5 that says When Health equals 25, Move Slowly, as shown in Figure 9.7, but will it work?

Although the new programming row in Figure 9.7 looks like it will work, there's a problem. Programming Row 1 always sets the speed to Quickly. The same goes for Programming Row 2. When the smart saucer sees or hears a Kodu, it begins to circle the Kodu at a fast speed. Even when its hit points reach 25 and Programming Row 5 says to move Slowly, the speed is reset to Quickly as soon as a Kodu is seen or heard.

Test the game with the new programming seen in Figure 9.7. No matter how many times I hit the smart saucer, it remains at the same speed: fast.

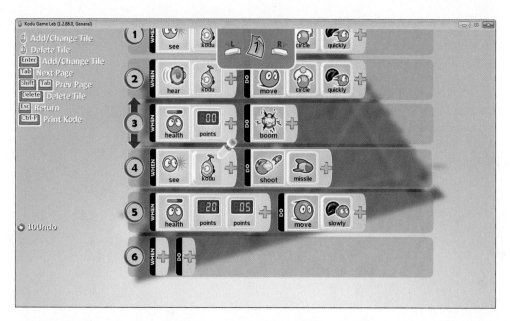

FIGURE 9.7 Modifying the program to try and slow down the saucer.

What's needed is the capability to change the Quickly speed specified in Program Rows 1 and 2. And guess what? I can do that with a new page.

First, I copy all of Page 1's programming by right-clicking the Page tool and choosing Copy. Next, I move to Page 2, right-click, and select the Paste option. As you can see in Figure 9.8, Page 2 has an identical copy of the programming from Page 1 (minus Programming Row 5, which I deleted because it doesn't work).

Let's pretend for a moment that the programming on Page 2 will automatically start running when the smart saucer's hit points reach 25. I haven't shown you how to make this happen yet, but let's create the programming that will slow the smart saucer down a bit before I show you how to actually use the Page 2 programming.

First, if the programming on Page 2 starts running, I need to change the saucer's speed. That's an easy fix. I'll remove the Quickly tiles from Program Rows 1 and 2 and replace them with Slowly. I don't have to delete or cut those tiles; if I left-click them, a pie menu appears like the one in Figure 9.9, allowing me to modify that tile and choose the Slowly tile.

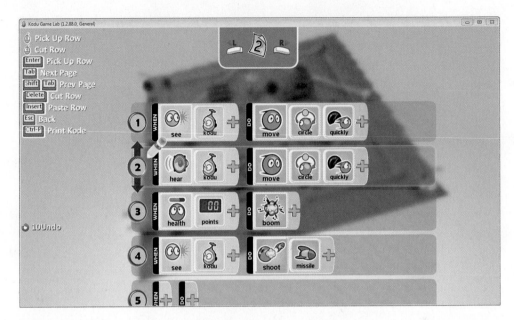

FIGURE 9.8   Page 2 contains identical programming copied from Page 1.

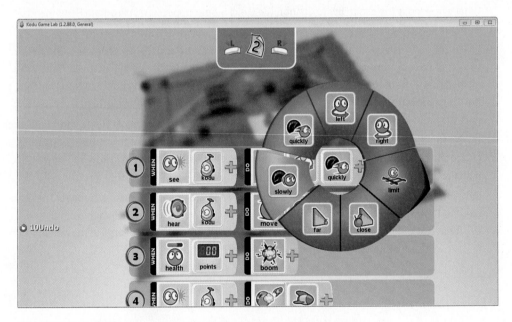

FIGURE 9.9   Left-click an existing tile to see possible replacements.

I'll do this for both Programming Rows 1 and 2. Figure 9.10 shows the modified programming. When the Page 2 programming is executed, the smart saucer circles slowly, as if its engines have been damaged.

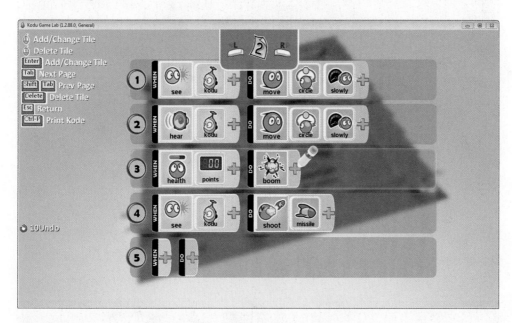

FIGURE 9.10 The smart saucer moves a bit slower when it's damaged.

Notice now that Programming Row 3 (on Page 2) still has the condition that when the hit points reach zero the smart saucer explodes. That would be fine, but I want the smart saucer to move even *slower* when it reaches 15 hit points. How do you think I can accomplish this?

If you said by copying the Page 2 programming (all of it) and pasting a copy into Page 3, you'd be right. Figure 9.11 shows Page 3 with identical programming found on Page 2.

Here's a little trick you might not yet have discovered. You can stack Slowly and Quickly tiles. They add together, so two Slowly tiles means the smart saucer is moving slower than if it had one Slowly tile. (A third Slowly tile can be added, but that's it… no more.)

If I click the plus sign (+) to the right of both the Slowly tiles in Program Rows 1 and 2, I can add a second Slowly tile to each. Figure 9.12 shows the additional tiles.

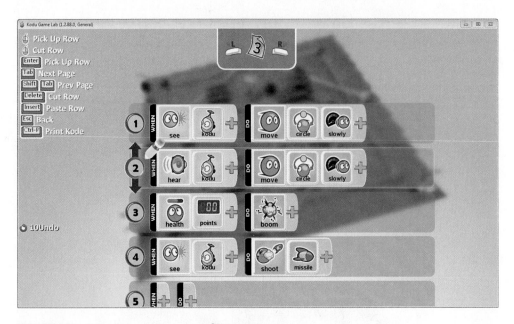

FIGURE 9.11 Page 3 is an exact copy of Page 2. For now.

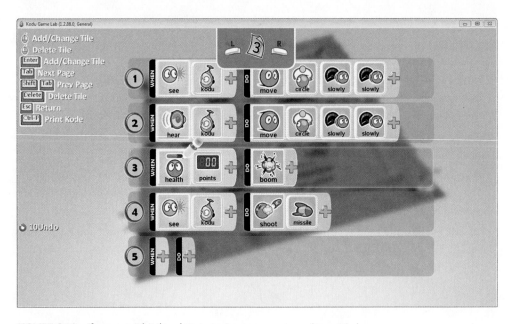

FIGURE 9.12 If you can't hit the slow smart saucer now, you're not trying.

Once again, I'm assuming that the Page 3 programming will run when the smart saucer's hit points dip to 15. But I haven't added the programming that allows for changing from Page 1 to Page 2 to Page 3. To do this, I return to Page 1, shown in Figure 9.13.

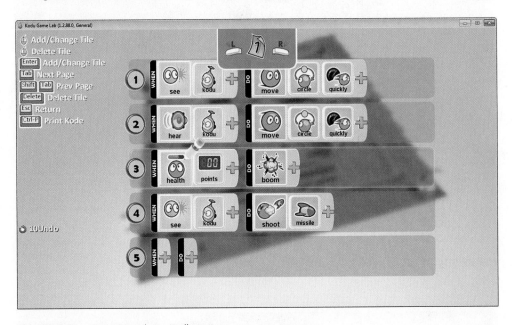

FIGURE 9.13   Page 1 is where it all starts.

Look at Programming Row 3. When the smart saucer's hit points reach zero, it explodes. But that's not what I want to happen. I want the smart saucer to slow down when its hit points reach 25. I want the programming on Page 2 to run.

And here's how I do it. First, I click the 00 Points tile and change it to 20, as shown in Figure 9.14.

If I stop there, I get a condition where the smart saucer will explode when its hit points reach 20. That's not good. I'll fix the exploding part in a moment, but I didn't see 25 as an option in the pie menu that appeared. How do I get to 25? Easy. I add 5. Figure 9.15 shows that I've tacked on a 5 Points tile in the When box: 20 plus 5 equals 25.

Just so you know, I could have added the 5 Points tile first, followed by the 20 Points tile. The order doesn't matter. If the number tiles are side by side, they're added together.

As it stands right now, I've still got a problem. The smart saucer will explode when its hit points reach 25, not 0. And now we reach the trick to move to other pages.

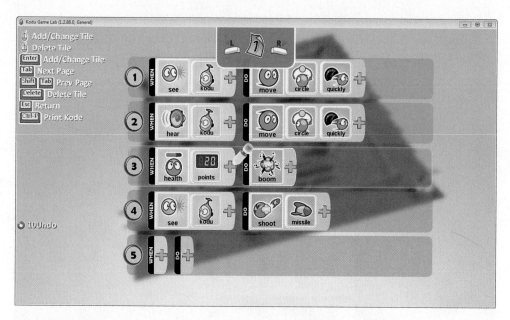

FIGURE 9.14 This will explode the smart saucer when it reaches 20 hit points.

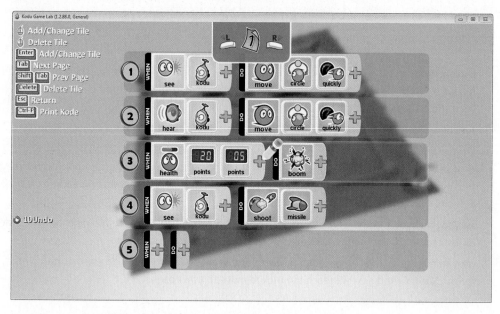

FIGURE 9.15 Number tiles add together when they're side by side.

First, I left-click the Boom tile shown in Figure 9.15 and a pie menu appears like the one in Figure 9.16.

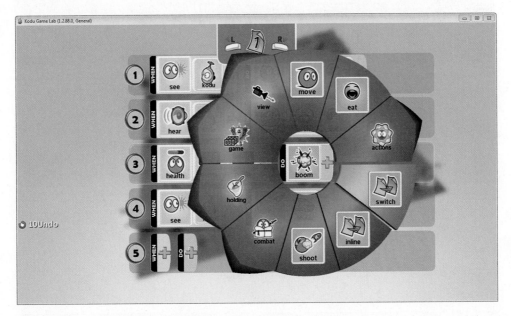

FIGURE 9.16   A new pie menu offers up some interesting options.

The tile I need is the Switch tile. After I select it, I click the + to the right of the Switch tile and choose the page number I want to jump to if the When condition is met. Figure 9.17 shows the new bit of programming.

Now let's look at Programming Row 3. When hit points equals 25 points, switch to Page 2. That's what I want.

Now, remember that when hit points equal 15, I want to switch to Page 3. I can go and modify Programming Row 3 on Page 2, but why don't I save a little time and just copy it from Page 1? Then, all I have to do is change the 20 Points tile to 10 Points, and the Page 2 tile to Page 3.

Figure 9.18 shows Page 2 and the new Programming Row 3.

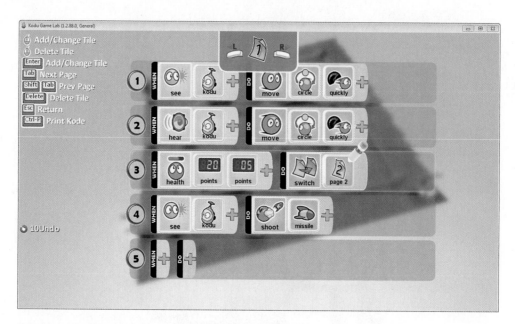

FIGURE 9.17   The Switch tile lets you move to other pages.

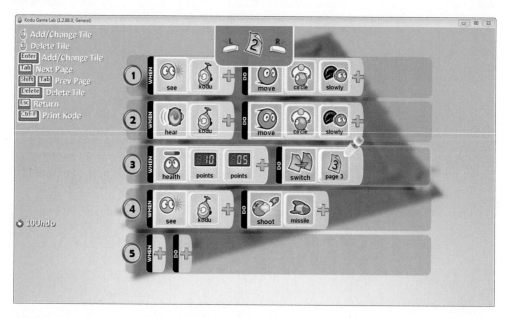

FIGURE 9.18   Page 2 has the new programming that will jump to Page 3.

I think you should be able to figure out what happens on Page 3. Figure 9.19 shows that Page 3 keeps the original Programming Row 3 that explodes the smart saucer when its hit points reach zero. But you could easily add a Page 4 that adds a third (and final) Slowly tile to the mix; you'd also need to modify the Page 3 Programming Row 3 so that it jumps to Page 4 when the Hit points reach 10 or 5 points.

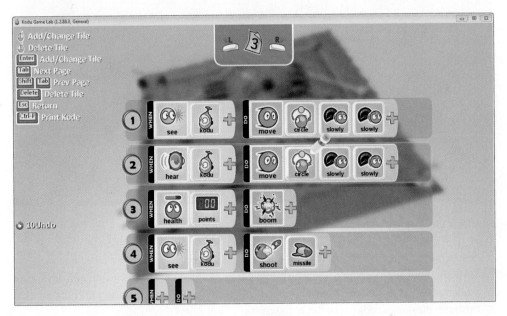

FIGURE 9.19 Page 3 removes the smart saucer from the game.

Keep in mind that all objects can have multiple pages. I've just modified the smart saucer, but I could do something similar with the path-following saucers, or something completely different. Think about it: I could add programming that enables them to fire missiles when their hit points reach 10 points. Think of it as giving them a brief fighting chance just before they go *boom*.

And now I've reached Game Changer 3. If you read it carefully, I think you might be able to figure out how to implement it. When a Kodu starts losing hit points, I want to allow players to nibble on health trees to regain some points. While they're eating on health trees, however, they can't fire missiles.

I think you should be able to figure this one out, but just in case, I go over the solution quickly in the next section.

Game Changer 3: Heal with Health Trees

This section shows you the new programming for the Blue Kodu. You add the exact same programming to the White Kodu. The first thing to do is to create four trees and put them between the four small mountains, as shown in Figure 9.20.

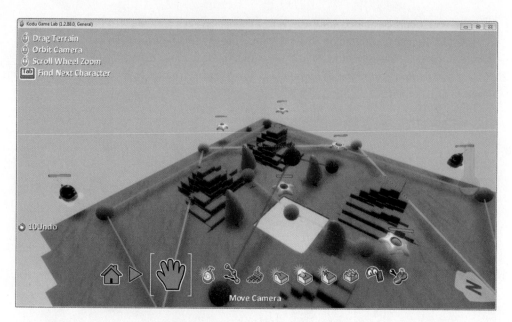

FIGURE 9.20   Add some health trees.

I could make the game more difficult by adding a single tree; Player 2 might be a bit more cautious about approaching a tree if he thinks Player 1 is going to try and fire on him while he is nibbling on the health tree. I'll leave that for testing and see whether reducing the number of trees frustrates players or adds to the fun of the game.

Now, I could add a simple bit of programming, as shown in Figure 9.21 that adds health to Kodu.

This would work, but there's a problem: The Kodu being healed can still fire missiles. I want to simulate the eating from the health tree by turning off the ability to fire missiles for 3 seconds. I can't do that from Page 1, so I have to jump to Page 2 to make this happen.

Figure 9.22 shows that I've changed the Heal tile to the Switch tile and pointed it to Page 2.

FIGURE 9.21   Bumping a tree puts hit points back on a Kodu.

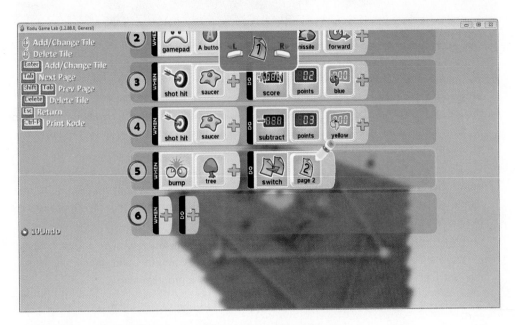

FIGURE 9.22   When a player bumps a tree, jump to Page 2.

What needs to happen when a player bumps a tree? Well, the player still needs to be able to move, but the player needs to lose the capability to fire missiles. I'll copy Programming Row 1 over to Page 2, as shown in Figure 9.23.

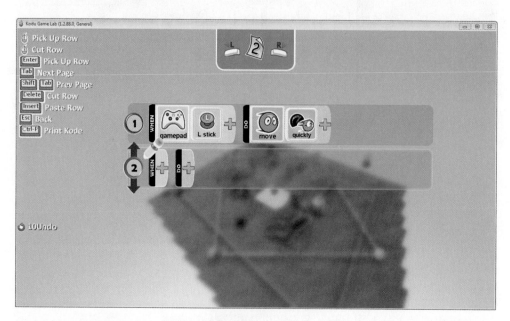

FIGURE 9.23   While on Page 2, Kodu still needs to be able to move.

The jump to Page 2 happens when Kodu bumps a tree, so I go ahead and add back in the programming required to heal Kodu for 3 points. You can see that in Figure 9.24. I've specified the Me tile just to make certain that only the Blue Kodu is healed when this tree bump occurs. The Me tile isn't required here, but it's still helpful because it lets you know that you're healing Kodu instead of the object it bumped. (Yes, trees have hit points, too.)

I've also added the Once tile. If I don't do this, Kodu's hit points will continue to be healed by 5 points over and over again while the 3-second period is occurring. This happens fast, so one tree nibble will heal Kodu up to full health. The way to stop this is to add the Once tile. This causes the healing of 5 points to only occur once per tree bump.

What's left? Well, we need to stay on this screen for 3 seconds before returning to Page 1 (where missiles will be reenabled). We can add a simple Timer tile to count to 3, and when it's done use the Switch tile to jump back to Page 1. Figure 9.25 shows the programming.

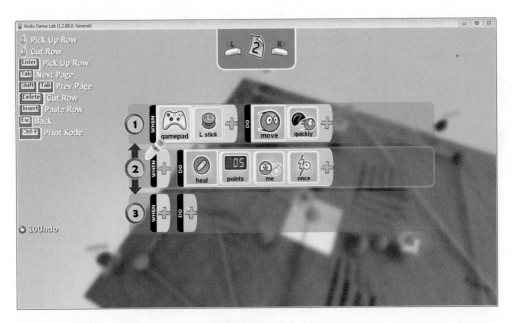

FIGURE 9.24   Heal Kodu for 5 points, but only do it once per bump.

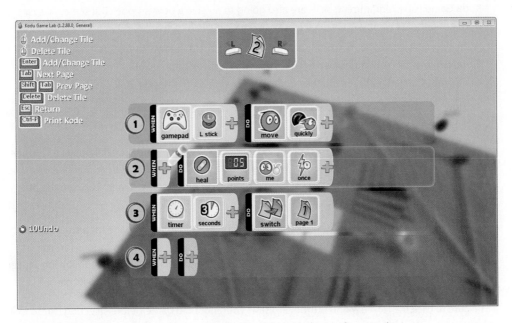

FIGURE 9.25   Wait for 3 seconds (no missiles) and then Kodu can fire missiles.

Now I just need to test it again and… it works. When Kodu bumps a tree, he begins to heal and he can't fire missiles. Just 3 seconds later, he can fire missiles again. And he only heals once per tree bump. Perfect!

> **TIP**
>
> Did you know you can make objects such as trees and rocks invulnerable? Most objects have a certain number of hit points, so they can eventually be destroyed. One strategy in this game might be to destroy all the trees. You'll have to run some tests to see whether that makes the game more fun… or takes away from the fun.

You're going to see a lot more examples using pages in later chapters. But for now, you're probably starting to see some of the benefits that pages bring. Imagine creating a game that changes tactics at certain times, or when players reach certain objectives or landmarks.

Moving On

I included "Grab That Power Up!" in this chapter's title for a few reasons. One, with pages, your games are really going to get a power boost. Second, after you've mastered using pages, your Kodu Game Lab programming skills are also going to receive a power boost. But there's also a third option that I want you to investigate now that you've had some hands-on time with pages.

In many games, there are items called *power-ups* that provide temporary boosts in speed, firepower, health, or all three. Using what you know from all the previous chapters, I've got a few challenges that you might like to take on before moving on to Chapter 10:

1. How might you modify *Saucer Hunt Extreme* so that players might get a speed boost when they nibble on a health tree?

2. What kinds of objects could you add to the game that would provide special powers? Consider a rock that, when bumped, changes a player's Kodu from firing missiles to firing blip balls. (Blip balls fire very fast, and even at low damage, getting hit by 10 or 20 of them can ruin the other player's day.)

3. You've seen how to use the Timer block to hold a player on a certain page for a small amount of time. How would you use the Timer tile to disable the smart saucer's weapons for five seconds when it's hit by a missile? Could you figure out how to modify a path-following saucer so that it seeks out a tree when it's health dips below 10 and then it returns to its path?

Be sure to click the Home Menu button and save your modified game before selecting Exit to Main Menu. From the Main Menu, select Quit Kodu to close down Kodu Game Lab.

The Cameras Are Rolling: Camera Controls for Solo and Multiplayer Games

In This Chapter

○ It's All About Your Point of View

○ Strange World

○ Fixed Position Camera Mode

○ Fixed Offset Camera Mode

○ Free Camera Mode

○ In-Game Camera Changes

It's All About Your Point of View

We take a break from game design in this short chapter to introduce you to a feature that you might not have thought about yet when it comes to the games you want to create: point of view, or POV.

POV refers to how the player sees a game. If you're playing *Flight Simulator*, for example, the best way to experience that software is from the cockpit, sitting in the pilot's seat and seeing things exactly as a real pilot would see when looking out an airplane's windows. Your POV is from the pilot's seat. But even if the software could enable you to fly the plane as if you were sitting on a wing or the tail of the aircraft, would you really want to do that?

○ **First-person view:** Sitting in the pilot's seat and seeing what a real pilot sees is called *first-person view*. You're seeing with your own eyes the perspective you would see if you were sitting in the pilot's seat of a real aircraft. This means you can't see the bottom of the airplane (unless the airplane is made of glass). It also means you can't see the runway behind you that is disappearing fast as you take off.

First-person shooters (FPS) are popular games. You run and shoot as if you were standing in the game world, weapon in hand. But FPS games aren't the only game in town, so to speak.

○ **Bird's eye view:** Long before first-person view was a popular view for video games, the standard was the simple bird's eye view, which placed you high above the game world, allowing you to see every enemy, every obstacle, and every aspect of the game. Kodu Game Lab enables you to create games where the game world (the playing field) is fixed and doesn't move. You can also set the distance from the surface of the game world that the player will view the game: very close, down in the action, or high above, where you can see what's coming around the corner.

○ **Above and over-the-shoulder view:** There's another type of view, too, called above and over-the-shoulder. It's not the same as first-person view, but it does allow the player to watch as the game world moves around as the position of the player moves. As you direct Rover or Kodu, for example, the surrounding world will move left, right, or away while Rover or Kodu stay in the same spot on the screen. (This will all become clear shortly when I show you how to test the various views.)

Experimenting with camera modes in Kodu Game Lab is fun. You can do some really interesting things, such as start a game showing one location on your world as the view races to the starting point of the game. (This could be useful for a large world where you want to give the player an idea of just how big the game play area really is.)

I walk you through all three camera modes shortly (Fixed Position, Fixed Offset, and Free), but first I need you to create a new world that will help you better understand how these three modes work.

Strange World

If you've been experimenting with Kodu Game Lab, I really hope you've had some fun with the world building tools. You can create terrain that's wild, silly, or dangerous... or all three at once.

For this chapter, however, I need you to create something fairly specific so that you can see how the three camera modes work. You can obviously create any type of world you want, but Figure 10.1 shows the one I am using.

I've used a different color terrain to create connections between the letters. After I drop Kodu on the game world, I can move him around the world using these connectors.

And there's my first step: dropping in Kodu and programming him for simple movement. Figure 10.2 shows that I've placed Kodu in the upper-left corner of the W.

FIGURE 10.1   This is a place I like to call *Weird World*.

FIGURE 10.2   Kodu's starting point is in the W.

Now I need to give Kodu just enough programming to control his movement around *Weird World* with the Left Joystick. Figure 10.3 shows the program. At this point in the book, you should be able to locate the proper pieces of the program, but refer back to the earlier chapters if you need help with programming movement.

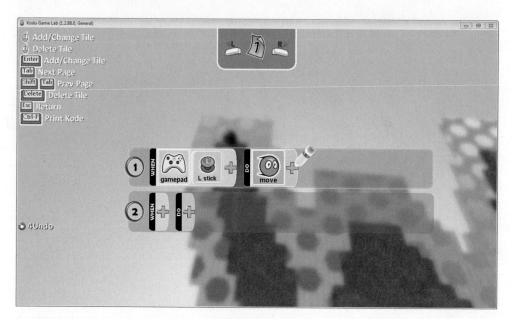

FIGURE 10.3   Movement programming for Kodu.

Before I take Kodu for a spin, I need to define a POV for this game.

> **NOTE**
>
> I'm not going to enhance this game with targets and missile firing and scoring and other features that you should be familiar with at this point, but feel free to modify this world (or your world) and create a completely new game after you finish with this chapter.

Camera Modes

Three different options are available for your games when it comes to the location of the camera. In the following sections, you learn how each of the three options works and how to implement them in your own games. Ultimately, you'll want to spend a little time using each of the three methods so that you'll understand when one method works better over the others.

Fixed Position

Fixed Position is probably the easiest of the three camera modes to use, and it's also the default. With Fixed Position, you're locking the camera in place, and as players move around the game world, the camera stays put. Here are the steps needed to implement Fixed Position camera mode in your own games:

1. Select the Object tool.

2. Right-click anywhere on the world, except for on Kodu, and select Change World Settings, as shown in Figure 10.4.

FIGURE 10.4   You can find Camera Mode under the Change World Settings menu option.

3. Scroll down the list until you find the Camera Mode option shown in Figure 10.5. Fixed Offset is currently selected in Figure 10.5, but you might see a different option selected.

4. Start with the option on the far left: Fixed Position. Click the small dot underneath the icon of the video camera with the anchor inside it. The title of the option should change to Camera Mode: Fixed Position, as shown in Figure 10.6.

   With Fixed Position, the game is played with the view locked. In essence, the game's camera is pointed at a specific point in the game world and stays fixed there as long as the game is running.

FIGURE 10.5 Find the Camera Mode option in the scrolling list.

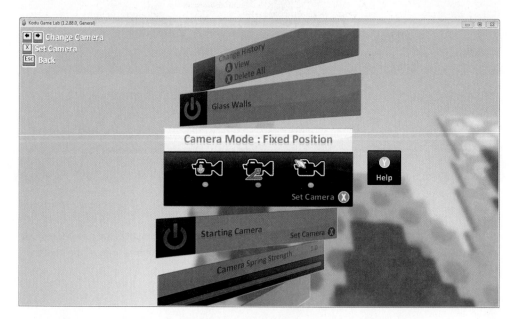

FIGURE 10.6 Change the Camera Mode to Fixed Position.

5. Press the Play button and play this game by driving Kodu around. First, though, look carefully at Figure 10.7 and notice how much of the W is visible and where Kodu is located.

FIGURE 10.7 The W is visible and centered on the screen.

I want you to notice the location of Kodu and how the W is centered on the screen because after I start playing the game an interesting thing is going to happen.

To move Kodu to the E, I need to drive him to the lower-right corner of the W as seen in Figure 10.8, so Kodu can cross the connector I created between letters. But guess what? He's gone! What happened?

FIGURE 10.8 Kodu cannot move any farther to the right to explore *Weird World*.

Because I have set Camera Mode to Fixed Position, it stays looking at the very center of the W. I set that center point of W as the point where the camera will stay locked, which I show you how to do shortly. For now, though, try to run the game yourself and verify that Kodu can continue to move off the screen and into unknown territory.

You might be thinking this is a real problem, but consider for a moment that the Fixed Position camera mode can be useful. If you create a game world that can fit entirely on a single screen, you might not have need for the other two camera modes.

Before I show you how to create the point that the camera locks to, notice that while driving Kodu (or whatever character you are using) that the camera doesn't stay focused on Kodu like it might have in other Kodu games you've played. In Fixed Position camera mode, I can drive Kodu all over that W, and nothing but Kodu moves; the W stays locked in place because the camera is holding the point I set directly in the center of the screen.

But that's easy to change. Suppose that I want to lock the camera somewhere between the W and E so that I can at least watch Kodu cross the connector from W to E. Here's how to do so:

1. Go to the Change World Settings list (shown in Figure 10.5) and select the Camera Mode option.

2. Verify that Fixed Position is still the selected camera mode.

3. Click the Set Camera option (or press X on the D-Pad).

4. When the scrolling list disappears, drag the world left or right (or rotate it), as shown in Figure 10.9.

Figure 10.9 Drag and rotate the world so the camera lock point is centered.

5. Drag the world so that the point where you want to lock the camera is as close to the center of the screen as possible.

   Figure 10.9 shows that I've put the empty space between the W and the E in the center of the screen.

6. When satisfied with the camera lock position, press Enter (or press A on the D-Pad).

I've left Kodu in the upper-left corner of the W, so notice what happened when I started the game again in Figure 10.10.

FIGURE 10.10 The camera is looking between the W and the E.

First, where is Kodu? Well, he's right where I left him: in the upper-left corner of the W. But he's offscreen! Yes, that could be a problem, but for now I know enough of the landscape (it's just a big W, right?) to get him from his current location to the lower-right corner of the W where the connector is located.

Figure 10.11 shows that I've managed to drive him over the connector between W and E and then over the connector between E and I. The camera is still locked on the empty space between the W and E, preventing Kodu (and me) from moving forward in the game. (I show you later in the chapter how to get around this issue.)

That's the Fixed Position camera mode. Fortunately, it's not the only camera mode, so you'll be able to design bigger games with much larger worlds to explore. To explore a larger world, however, you need to know about the other two options: Fixed Offset and Free.

FIGURE 10.11 Kodu is barely visible on the I part of *Weird World*.

Fixed Offset

With the Fixed Position camera mode, the game's playing field is locked in place. Any player controlling Kodu or Rover or any other object has the edges of the screen as the boundaries for the game.

But let's change the Weird World game up a little bit. Go back to the Change World Settings list (see Figure 10.5) and select the Fixed Offset option shown in Figure 10.12. It's got an icon of a video camera with a red angle-pointer in it.

Now I'll take Kodu for a spin, as you can see in Figure 10.13.

So far, so good. Figure 10.13 shows Kodu crossing the W and heading to the E. Let me keep driving him and see where this goes. Take a look at Figure 10.14 and you see that I've got him heading down the I toward the connector leading to the R.

Have you noticed anything interesting about the POV? Play the game again and notice this: Kodu always stays in the center of the screen. He's become the camera's lock point. Cool!

Start the game again and maybe you'll notice something else unusual: It doesn't matter where you set the camera's lock point; it always starts on Kodu.

Fixed Offset forces the camera to follow Kodu as he explores *Weird World*. The entire world moves onscreen, but Kodu stays right in the center of the screen.

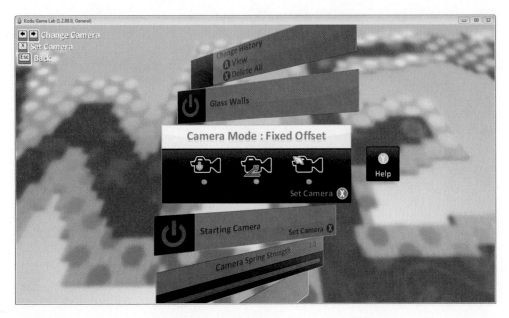

FIGURE 10.12 Select the Fixed Offset camera mode.

FIGURE 10.13 Taking Kodu for a spin around *Weird World*.

FIGURE 10.14   Kodu's almost to the end of *Weird World*.

CAUTION

What happens if you place a second player's Kodu on the D on *Weird World*? Try it and see. Did you see what happens? The camera starts halfway between Player 1 and Player 2, and unless the players are very good at navigating blindly, it will be extremely frustrating for them because the world will not move toward either player until they are roughly in the same area of the screen. This is why creating two-player games can be tricky, especially when it comes to setting a camera mode. You'll have to experiment with placing players and setting camera modes until you find the right mode that works.

Fixed Offset is perfect for single-player games where you want the player to be the center of attention. It's also very useful for side-scrollers like Microsoft's Splosion Man (http://www.splosionman.com), where the player will be constrained to moving in one or two directions (east or west, for example) and the camera will follow players as they move about the game world.

But Fixed Offset can also be dangerous to a player, especially if a missile-firing enemy is just offscreen and not visible. The player might not see the enemy, but the enemy probably sees the player.

One solution to this is to give the player a fast look at the playing field. And by fast, I mean *fast*. You can do this by defining a starting position for the camera when the Play button is pressed and programming in a delay of 10 seconds by adding WHEN Timer 10 Seconds DO Switch Page 2. Page

2 would then contain the programming that starts the game. When the game begins, the game simply sits waiting for 10 seconds, allowing the player to get a quick look at the game world. When the 10 seconds are up, because Kodu (or another object) has game controller or keyboard controls, the camera zooms in on the player-controlled object.

When the Play button is pressed, the starting position of the camera is onscreen for a fraction of a second before it speeds across the game world to the position of Kodu (or your player's object).

To set the camera's starting position, just follow these steps:

1. Drag or rotate your world so that the point where you want the game's camera to show at the start of the game is centered.

   Figure 10.15 shows that I selected the curved path of the D in the Weird World map.

FIGURE 10.15   Select the camera's starting position when the Play button is first pressed.

2. Go back to the Change World Settings list and scroll down just below the Camera Modes option to the Starting Camera option shown in Figure 10.16.

3. Turn it on (if it's not active) by tapping the icon to the left of the text; the power button turns green to let you know it's active.

   If you're using a mouse/keyboard, the camera's starting position is locked automatically just by scrolling to the Starting Camera option. That's it. But if you're using the D-Pad, you can tap the X button to change it again.

4. Press the Play button.

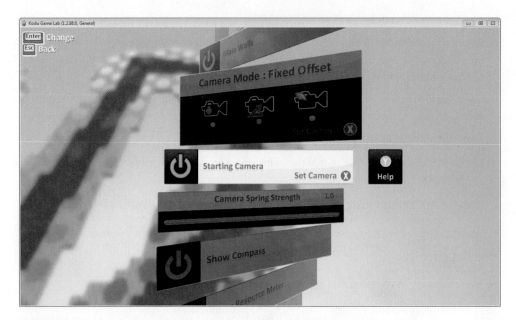

FIGURE 10.16   Use Starting Camera to lock in the game's starting point.

Did the camera fly from starting point to Kodu's position? I think it's a little too fast, but it might be just enough to give your player a hint of what's to come in the game.

> **NOTE**
> When you press Escape to end a game, the camera automatically returns you to the Starting Camera position you set.

That's the Fixed Offset option. It is so useful for single-player games, but there's one final option you need to know about to make the best POV choice for your future games.

Free

The third and final camera mode available to you is the Free option shown in Figure 10.17. It's got an icon of a video camera with a wing inside of it.

Go ahead and change the *Weird World* game's camera mode to Free and press the Play button. Figure 10.18 shows that, at first, the world zooms out so that you can see the entire game world.

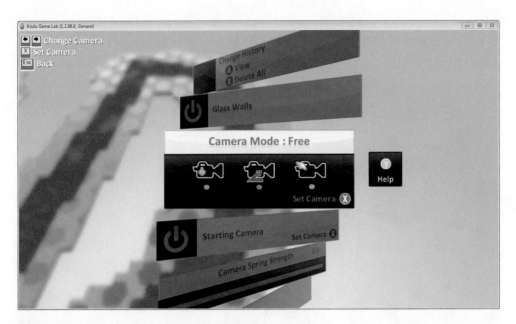

FIGURE 10.17   The Free camera mode option.

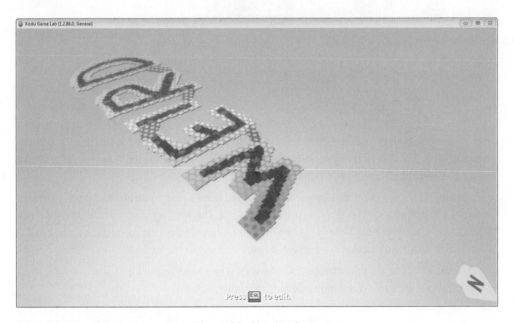

FIGURE 10.18   The entire game world is visible, but details are tiny.

Fortunately, the Free camera mode supports zooming and rotating, so I can zoom in on Kodu, zoom out, and rotate. Figure 10.19 shows that I've zoomed in on Kodu as he's crossing the connector over to E.

FIGURE 10.19   Zooming in on your world is easy in Free camera mode.

What happens if I keep zooming in? Try it.

Whoa! First-person view.

Figure 10.20 shows what happens when I zoom in far enough: I've become Kodu!

This works for both mouse/keyboard and D-Pad users. Mouse users need to use the scroll button on top of their mouse to zoom in, and D-Pad users press and hold the Right button until they're fully zoomed in and looking out in first-person view.

Free camera mode is great for players wanting to see what's waiting up ahead. To see all the details, though, you sometimes have to zoom way out. This means missing smaller details. Until Kodu comes up with a portable flying camera that he can send out on spy missions, you'll just have to drive him to places you want to explore.

You're almost done with this chapter, but there's still one more useful bit of programming info I want to share with you: changing camera mode during a game.

FIGURE 10.20 First-person view lets me see the world as Kodu sees it.

In-Game Camera Changes

As you start developing your own games (and keep in mind that we've still got quite a few chapters ahead of us with all kinds of fun techniques), you might find yourself needing to change the way the camera works. Now, you're not going to be able to move from Fixed Position to Fixed Offset to Free and back again. After all, you pick your camera mode when you're designing the game, and that's what you're stuck with. Sort of.

Let's return to *Weird World* and drop a new object at the bottom corner of the W. I've placed a coin, but you can place a star or coin or whatever object you like from the collection shown in Figure 10.21.

Figure 10.22 shows that I've dropped a star and enlarged it to be more visible on the playing field.

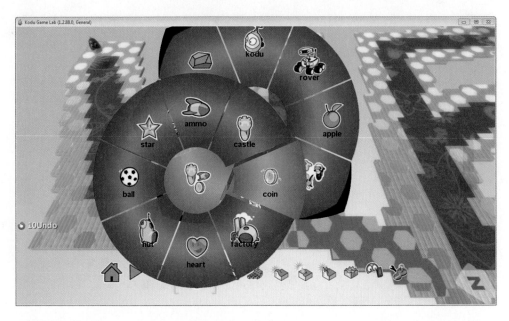

FIGURE 10.21   Drop a small treasure for Kodu to find.

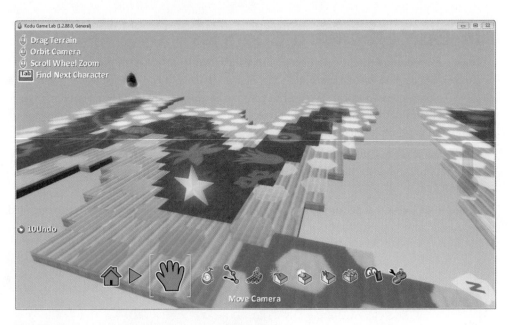

FIGURE 10.22   Kodu needs to find and grab the star.

I need to program Kodu to grab and hold on to the star when he bumps it. So, I open up Kodu's programming and add the tiles you see in Figure 10.23 to Programming Row 2.

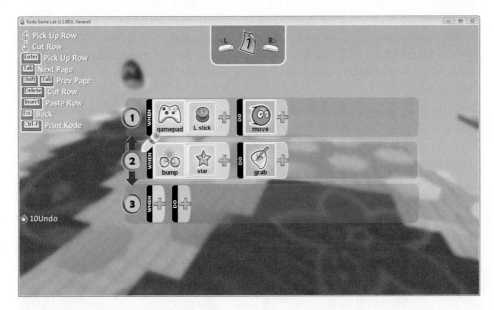

FIGURE 10.23   Programming for Kodu to grab and hold on to the star.

In the When box, select the Bump and the Star tiles, and add the Grab tile to the Do box.

Go ahead and set the camera mode for the game back to Fixed Offset and play the game. Go and grab the star. Figure 10.24 shows that after Kodu touches (or bumps) the star, the star appears in front and slightly above him.

FIGURE 10.24   We have a winner!

As he moves around, the star moves with him. The camera mode also stays at Fixed Offset. But I can change that (and so can you). First, I reopen Kodu's program. What I want to do is change the POV of Kodu from fixed offset to first person when he grabs the star. I've already programmed what happens when he bumps the star (see Figure 10.23), but here's a new programming trick for you.

Notice that Programming Row 3 sits right under Programming Row 2. This means that any programming I place in 3 is always being checked (When) for a condition that will trigger the action (Do). But if I click the 3 and hold down the mouse button while dragging to the right, Programming Row 3 moves to the right, as shown in Figure 10.25.

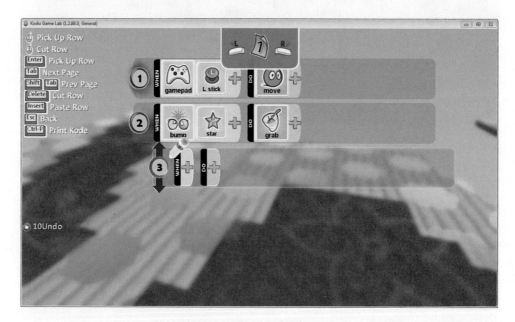

FIGURE 10.25   Tucking Programming Row 3 underneath 2.

You can view this in a couple of ways. One is that 3 is now a child of 2. Programming Row 2 is the parent of 3, and any programming found in 3's condition will be checked *only* if 2 is triggered.

Another way to think about Programming Row 3 is that it is dependent upon 2's condition being met. Did Kodu bump the star? No? Then Programming Row 3's program is never checked. Did Kodu bump the star this time? Yes? Okay, then check to see whether 3's When condition is true.

The programming for Programming Row 3 changes the camera view to first person when the star is bumped. Because 2 is already checking for that condition and the programming in 3 will run only if 2's condition is true, I don't need to program 3's When box. Instead, I just click the Do box, as shown in Figure 10.26, and select the View pie piece.

A new pie menu opens, and I select the 1st Person tile, as shown in Figure 10.27. Notice that I could have selected the Follow tile, which mimics the Fixed Offset camera mode. You can also select the Ignore tile to take the camera off of an object (such as Kodu) and force it to follow another object (as shown in an example later in this book).

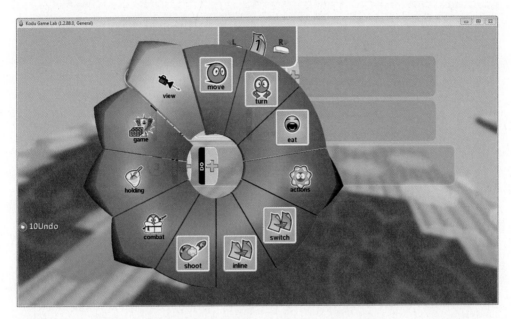

FIGURE 10.26   Select the View pie piece for Programming Row 3's Do box.

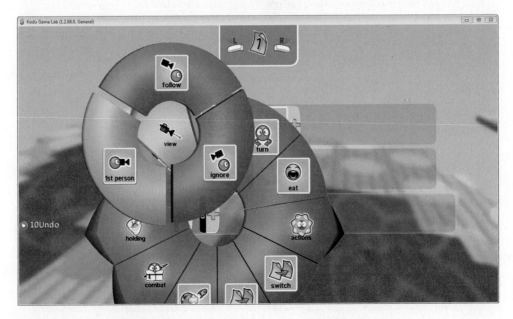

FIGURE 10.27   Select the 1st Person tile to change camera view to Kodu's view.

Kodu's updated program now looks like the one in Figure 10.28.

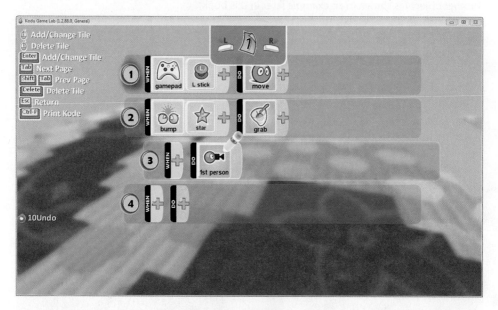

FIGURE 10.28   The new Kodu program changes the Camera Mode when the star is bumped.

Now go play the game, bump the star, and see what happens. Figure 10.29 shows that my view has changed to first-person view and I've got the star floating in front of me. Woo hoo!

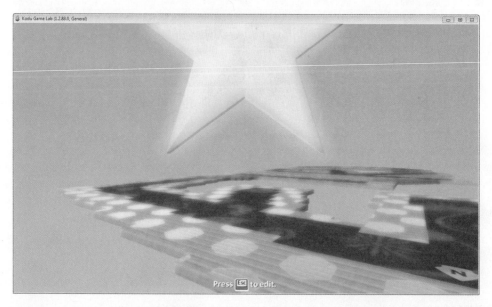

FIGURE 10.29   The view automatically changes to First Person once the start is bumped.

You can move between First Person (which is a form of Free camera mode—you're zoomed in all the way) and Fixed Offset by using the View pie piece in your programming and selecting the 1st Person or Follow tiles as needed.

Getting good with the various camera modes will increase your Kodu Game Lab skills and make your own games much more interesting and fun to play. Spend some time working with all the camera modes until you're comfortable with how they work. Your familiarity with the modes will pay off later when you're creating advanced games that can move back and forth between first-person and other views.

Moving On

Have the various camera views given you any ideas for your own games? It just makes sense that some games will work better with a fixed view, and other games will be more fun with a camera that follows the player. And the Free camera mode is sure to open up some interesting game possibilities for you with the capability to rotate, zoom, and see the world in first-person view. As with everything you learn about Kodu Game Lab, let your imagination and creativity run loose and see what you can create.

Before you begin Chapter 11, "Good Game Design, Part 1: Tips and Tricks for Better Game Programming," here are a few tweaks for you to try:

1. Using what you learned in this chapter about pages, try to modify Weird World so that when Kodu grabs the star, he gets some bonus powers, such as missile firing and a scoreboard.

2. Either modify *Weird World* or create your own game so that crossing certain boundaries changes the camera view. You could use a condition such as Kodu seeing a castle, or Kodu hearing a saucer to trigger a change from fixed offset to first-person view or vice versa. Experiment with the programming to see what pie pieces allow you access to the View pie piece.

3. You'll learn later in this book about the Ignore pie piece that can take the camera off of a player object. But that doesn't mean you can't try your own hand at figuring out how the Ignore tile works. Try adding another object on the screen (such as a saucer) to see what it takes to have the camera follow that object either on a path or randomly. Be sure to program in a When-Do condition that sends the camera back to the player.

When you finish with the homework, click the Home Menu button and save any work you've done before selecting Exit to Main Menu. On the Main Menu, select Quit Kodu to close down Kodu Game Lab.

Good Game Design, Part 1: Tips and Tricks for Better Game Programming

In This Chapter

○ Better Game Programming

○ World Design: Tips and Tricks

○ Game Management: Tips and Tricks

○ Object Programming: Tips and Tricks

Creating games with Kodu Game Lab is fun. As a matter of fact, I often find that designing and programming games is much more fun than playing them. Don't get me wrong...I love to play games. But there's just something really cool and fun about creating a game from scratch with Kodu Game Lab that no one has ever seen or played before.

One of the cool things that you're going to discover about programming games is that there's always something new to learn. You might see a new programming technique for controlling an enemy target while viewing someone else's game programming. You might find a feature tucked deep in a pie menu that you finally have an opportunity to use in a program. Or you might also find a new style of game that you've never tried before.

Kodu Game Lab has plenty of hidden options to explore and use, and just as students of music, art, and literature study the masters, there are also plenty of games designed by other Kodu programmers for you to download and examine to see how the magic was done.

This chapter is all about tips and tricks for improving your game design. It's by no means complete, but the advice provided can help you gain proficiency with Kodu Game Lab and get that dream game in your head out into the real world for others to play.

This chapter consists of three main sections. The first section suggests ways to build your game's world before you populate it with objects, obstacles, targets, and traps.

The second section helps you track your progress as you build games. After all, although programming is fun, it can sometimes get confusing with all the changes and updates and new objects you add to a game. You need to establish a method for managing your games as they develop, so don't skip this section.

The third section offers some advice about programming the objects that inhabit your game world. This advice will prove especially useful during the numerous tests that you'll run on your game before sharing it with the world.

By the way, I've broken up the tips and advice information into three chapters, so you'll find even more help a bit later in Chapter 15, "Good Game Design, Part 2: More Tips and Tricks for Great Games," and Chapter 19, "Good Game Design, Part 3: Giving Players a Great Experience."

World Design: Tips and Tricks

Take a look at Figure 11.1. Welcome to *MegaLand*!

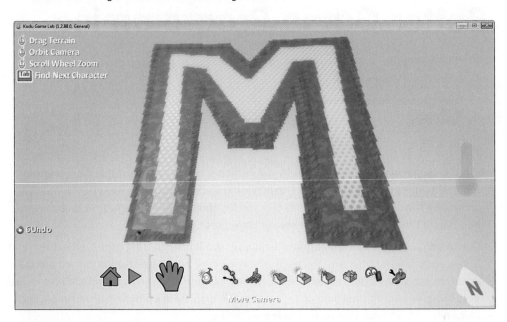

FIGURE 11.1 *MegaLand* isn't huge. It's H-U-G-E!

Do you see Kodu? Look closely. He's in the lower-left corner of the *M*. I won't blame you if you didn't see him at first. He's a bit hard to spot because the game world I've created is so big. But that doesn't matter. It's time to program a game.

I want to program a little seek-n-find game, where Kodu needs to find certain objects such as stars or coins to turn on various weapons, so that he can fire at enemies for points. Yeah, that sounds fun. I can make it so that when he grabs a star he can fire missiles, and if he grabs a coin, he can fire blip balls.

Probably a good place to start is to drop a coin on the map and program him to go touch it. I already know how to program to test when he bumps into an object (refer back to Chapter 10, "The Cameras Are Rolling: Camera Controls for Solo and Multiplayer Games.") Figure 11.2 shows both the simple bit of programming that tests for when Kodu bumps into a coin and the movement programming. (I'm using a game controller.)

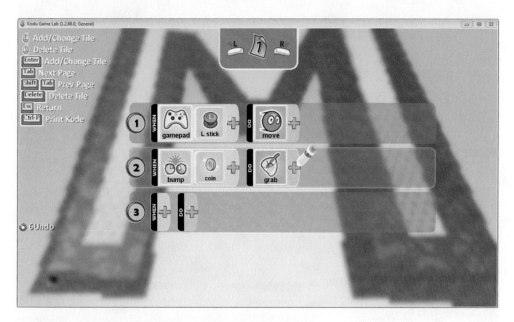

FIGURE 11.2   Enabling Kodu to move around and grab a coin.

Okay, now it's time to place a coin. I think I'll drop one in the lower-right corner of the *M*, on the opposite side of the world. Figure 11.3 shows the coin. Do you see it? It's right… there. (You might want to squint.)

Now it's time to test the Grab tile to see whether Kodu actually grabs and holds on to it. I just press Play and start driving Kodu with the Left Joystick.

Wow, this is taking a long time. I timed it, and it actually took me about 52 seconds to reach the coin. That's not good. Maybe I should have just put the coin a bit closer to Kodu. Yeah, let me try that. Figure 11.4 shows that I've moved the coin much closer.

Now let me test to see whether Kodu can bump and grab the coin. Oh, yeah! And it didn't take long either.

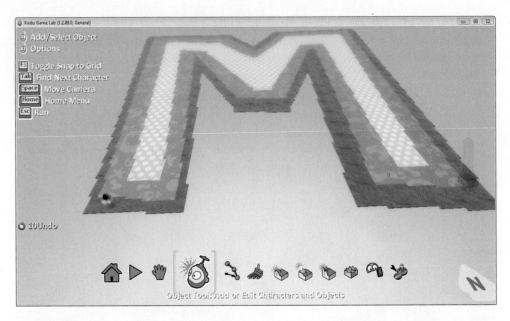

FIGURE 11.3   There's the coin… way over there.

FIGURE 11.4   I'll just move the coin a little closer to Kodu.

I have a feeling you picked up on the point of this little example. When you're designing your game world, why not start small? I know I'm in for a lot of testing: bump the coin, grab the coin, fire blip balls, and so on. So rather than create this huge game world that I'll have to navigate when I test my game (and drag and zoom around while I'm placing objects and other items), why don't I create a miniature version first, like the one shown in Figure 11.5? Welcome to *MiniLand*.

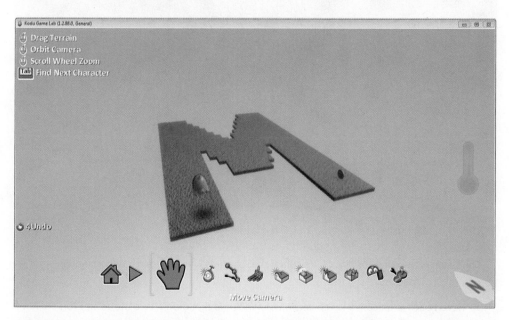

FIGURE 11.5   A smaller world still lets me test all the game's programming.

As you can see, this new version still lets me test the movement controls and get to the coin much faster. Later, when I'm happy with the game's objects and how the programming works, I can then set about increasing the size of my game world.

And speaking of increasing the size of the game world, have you had any difficulties fine-tuning your terrain? Have you tried to build a wall and had it look more like a small anthill? Do you wish you had a bit more control over where terrain is placed and in what quantity? I do too.

Take a look at *MiniWorld* in Figure 11.6. I've tried to create a castle where I'd like Kodu to take the coin. It's not pretty.

I switched the terrain color to the gray brick, and I then used Up/Down: Create Hills or Valleys to grow the brick upward to simulate a castle. I guess it would work, but I can do better. Let me show you.

FIGURE 11.6   *My castle doesn't really look like a castle.*

The secret is reducing the size of the cursor that controls where terrain is added (and in what quantity), as follows:

1. Revert back to an earlier saved version of *MiniWorld* that didn't have the castle. You did have an earlier version, didn't you? (If not, you're going to want to read the next section on game management.)

2. After reloading *MiniWorld*, zoom in on the corner of the M where I want to place my castle. Figure 11.7 shows just the spot.

3. Select the color/style that you want to use for your castle. You know, castles are always dark gray and gloomy, aren't they? Let's break the rules. I'm going with an eye-catching red, but you pick what you like.

4. When a painter wants to paint the tiny details on a piece of canvas, she doesn't reach for the largest brush, does she? Nope. She picks a small brush, with a thin, tiny set of bristles so that she can apply the paint in small amounts. And that's what I'm going to do here. Figure 11.8 shows the size of the brush I'm working with currently.

   It's square (because I'm going to paint a castle, I use the square-shaped brush because I plan to add bricks that are square shaped, but I could easily use a round brush head) and very large. I need to shrink it down.

FIGURE 11.7 This looks like a good place to put a well-designed castle.

FIGURE 11.8 I can't paint with a brush that size. It's too big!

5. On the keyboard, use the left arrow key to shrink the paintbrush size. (The right arrow key increases the size.) As you can see in Figure 11.9, the size of the paintbrush has been reduced to the smallest size possible.

FIGURE 11.9   Now you can paint bricks using the smallest brush possible.

With the small paintbrush, you can now paint individual blocks (or bricks), as shown in Figure 11.10. Notice that individual blocks can be placed exactly where you want them, allowing you to draw in the shape of a castle with a single entrance at the front.

I know; it doesn't look like a castle yet, but hang on. Zoom out a bit so that you can see a bit more of the surrounding terrain, and switch now to the **Up/Down** tool, which will let you grow the terrain. Just as with the paintbrush, you can use the left/right arrows on the keyboard to increase the size of the affected area that will move up (or down) when you hold down the mouse button over certain terrain.

You've got to be careful here that you don't select a block of grass. Figure 11.11 shows the cursor hovering over a single block of the castle. It will glow, helping you to easily find it.

FIGURE 11.10   The individual blocks that make up the walls of my castle.

FIGURE 11.11   Place the Up/Down tool on a single block of terrain.

Now, when you hold down the mouse button, up grows part of the castle wall. Figure 11.12 shows a single block elevated up to a height of six blocks. (You might find this difficult to tell from Figure 11.12, but it's definitely six blocks high.)

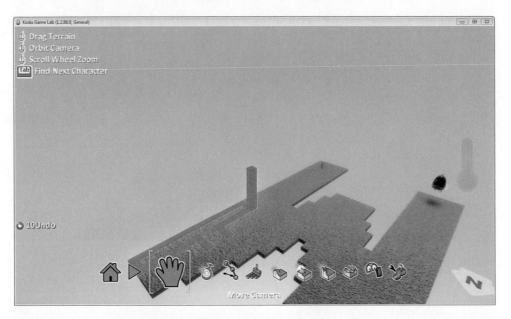

FIGURE 11.12   The castle has a very tall wall, but only in one place.

All that's left is to grow the rest of the castle. And keep in mind that the Up/Down tool has a number of options available, such as the Magic Brush that will apply the same change to all terrain of an identical color. Instead of building up the castle brick by brick, simply switch to the Magic Brush and drag the walls up all at once, and then apply some single brick touches and new colors here and there. Figure 11.13 shows the castle.

It takes practice to use the paintbrush and the terrain editing tools. Sometimes it can get a little frustrating when the terrain doesn't behave, but if you need detail in your world (like the walls of my castle), you want to spend some time using the tiny paintbrush.

Given enough time, I could add a drawbridge, some windows, and even a moat. (You learn how to add water effects in Chapter 13, "World Design: Creating Environmental Special Effects.")

You learn some more tips about world design in Chapter 15, but now let's change gears and think about game management—keeping track of your work, your programs, and your changes and updates.

FIGURE 11.13   *MiniWorld*'s Castle of Coins.

Game Management: Tips and Tricks

You learned early in this book how to save your work and your games, and I mentioned that you can use the version number to help keep track of it all, but even a game name and version number aren't always that helpful.

Take a look at Figure 11.14 and you'll see the Game Save screen that I filled out for version 2 of *MiniWorld*.

If you're wondering what happened to version 1, I can tell you that it's safe and sound. Version 1 contains just the terrain in the shape of the letter M along with Kodu and the coin. Why have I decided to increase the version number to 2 rather than simply save it as version 1 again?

Take a look back at Figure 11.13, which shows my castle. I like the castle, but I'm starting to think that instead of a castle it might be nice to completely delete the castle and have Kodu take the coin to Rover instead.

If I were to just save the castle version of the game (overwriting the version without the castle) without incrementing the version number, I would have to go back and erase the castle. It wouldn't take a lot of time, but it would slow me down a bit. But I don't have to erase the castle; I can just reload *MiniWorld* version 1 and start from there.

When programming your games, it's always a good idea to save your game after every major change. Did you just add a saucer to the game? Save a new version of the game. Did you just move the castle from the right to the left? Save a new version.

FIGURE 11.14   The Game Save screen is extremely helpful in managing your game.

All these saved versions of your game don't really take up a lot of hard drive space, and each of them is a potential time-saver to you should you change your mind about a new game element.

But just giving them version numbers often isn't enough to help you distinguish between the various versions of your game. That's where the Description field really becomes useful.

Take a look at Figure 11.15 and see what I've done there.

You don't have to type up the same level of detail that I've done, but it certainly won't hurt. A good recommendation is to add comments in the Description field that describe what didn't change between this version and the previous version and what *did* change. Just remember to strip out these notes before you upload your final version of the game for others to play (see Chapter 18, "Join the Community: Online Help and Sharing Games").

So, I've got the "Existing" part of the description that just so happens to match the description of *MiniWorld* version 1. But the "New" part of the description contains what I've added since version 1: the red castle.

I can click the Save button now and save the description, but I want to point you to one more useful item. In the lower-left corner of the Save Screen, you'll see the Tags button. Tap on the Tags button to display a list like the one in Figure 11.16.

When you finish with the game, don't you want to share it with other players? Well, the Tags button lets you select one or more descriptive words that describe the type of game you are creating. Is it an action game or a shooter? Is it still a work-in-progress (you haven't finished it yet) or is it all polished and you're now ready to move on to the next game? Is it more suited for a mouse/keyboard user or a D-Pad or both?

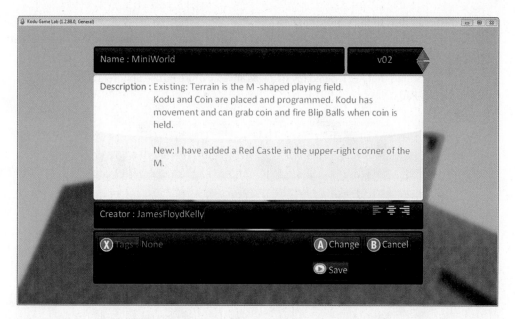

FIGURE 11.15   Use the Description field to refresh your memory about a game version.

FIGURE 11.16   Use the Tags button to help describe your game to potential players.

Click the boxes next to the words that describe your game, select as many as you need to accurately describe your game, and don't forget to select whether it's a keyboard/mouse or D-Pad game.

Figure 11.17 shows that I've labeled my game as an Adventure Puzzle Shooter for the Xbox Controller (D-Pad).

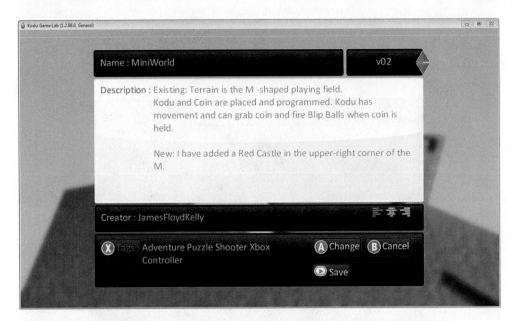

FIGURE 11.17   Tags you select will be visible to players searching for unique games.

You'll discover more about the benefits of tags when I introduce you to sharing games in Chapter 18. But for now, just try to get in the habit of providing a set of tags for all games you design. The tags you select remain as you increase the version number of your game, so you only have to pick them one time.

After saving your game, you can continue working and updating and testing. If you need to return to a previous saved version of your game, however, just go to the Home Menu and select Load World. Tap My Worlds to view all your saved games. As you can see in Figure 11.18, you can scroll through the various versions you have saved and view the text you typed into the Description field at the bottom.

Good use of the version number, tags, and the Description field will ensure that you'll always be able to find the game you want to open and work on (or play). Get in a habit of always updating the Description field, and you'll find over time that as you move from Game A to Game B and back to Game A that you can jump more quickly back into a game's development and be familiar with the current version and its programming.

FIGURE 11.18   Use the version number and description to find the saved version you need.

> **TIP**
>
> You can also use the Description field for notes to yourself about how to improve a game, or notes about what you want to accomplish next. If you leave your game development for a week or longer, you might find it useful to come back and read in the Description field something like "Next I want to add programming to the castle so that when Kodu bumps it the coin is vanished and Kodu gains an increase in his movement speed."

Object Programming: Tips and Tricks

Staying with the *MiniWorld* game, this section shows you a few tricks that might come in handy when you're working with non-player-controlled objects.

First, let's test the game by giving Kodu something to shoot at after he's got the coin. If you remember, when he grabs the coin, he gets the ability to shoot blip balls. Let's create an enemy target that keeps coming back until the coin is delivered to the castle.

You've already learned in earlier chapters how to add target objects and configure their speed, hit points, and other characteristics. But after you've destroyed that object, it's gone for good.

But there is a way to configure an object, one that enables you to reuse the object over and over again. It's called a *creatable*, and this is how it works:

1. I add the Sputnik object shown in Figure 11.19.

FIGURE 11.19 Drop in the Sputnik object anywhere you like.

2. Before I turn Sputnik into a creatable, I set some of its characteristics by right-clicking and clicking Change Settings.

3. This opens up the scrolling list of options, and the first one I tweak is Max Hit Points, as shown in Figure 11.20. I drag it down to 5 Hit Points.

TIP

I pause here to offer a tip that will help during testing. Later in the game, I'll increase the hit points on Sputnik to see how it affects the game play. But for now, I've decreased the hit points to 5 because I'm more concerned right now about testing Kodu's firing ability and the ability to create new Sputniks (called *respawning*). If Kodu's blip balls each do damage of 2 points and Sputnik has 100 hit points, it'll take 50 hits to destroy a Sputnik, and then (I hope) a new Sputnik will appear. I'd rather not spend all my time shooting at Sputnik; I just want to confirm that the blip balls can destroy it and that when it's destroyed a new one appears.

So here's the tip: Lowering your enemy targets' hit points will help during testing by not requiring you to shoot at the targets for long periods of time. (I could also increase the damage done by Kodu's blip balls to 50, 100, or even 500; that'll speed up the destruction.)

So, after I set Sputnik's max hit points, I need to go create its programming.

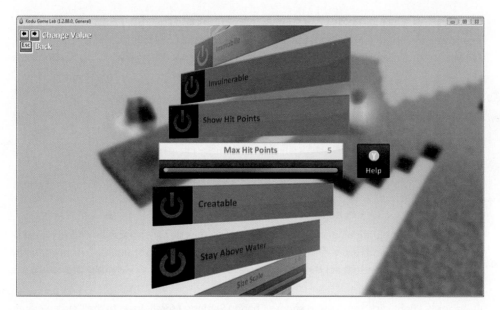

FIGURE 11.20   Set Sputnik's maximum hit points.

Figure 11.21 shows the basic program I created for Sputnik. When it sees or hears Kodu nearby, it runs away fast. (Refer to the earlier chapters for help with programming objects to run away when they see or hear a player.) Note that you can use either the See or Hear option; you don't have to use both. I'm providing both here so that you can see that they work basically the same.

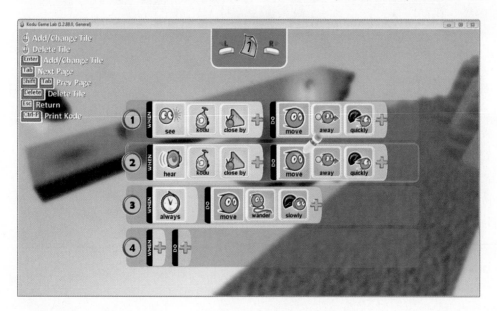

FIGURE 11.21   Program Sputnik to run from Kodu if it sees or hears him.

As you can see in Figure 11.21, when Sputnik sees or hears Kodu nearby, it moves away quickly. Again, you don't have to have both the See and Hear rows; just one will do. The WHEN Always – DO Move Wander Slowly ensures that Sputnik never gets trapped in a corner as Kodu approaches.

> **NOTE**
>
> Objects have two ranges related to seeing and hearing: Close By Range and Far Away Range. You can find these settings by right-clicking an object and selecting Change Settings. Scroll down the list and drag the bars left or right to fine-tune an object's ability to see and hear. Set these two options to the same value to avoid confusing objects with a "dead zone" area between Close By and Far Away where an object will be considered invisible.

After testing this programming, I can verify that Sputnik runs slowly at first (when Kodu is near but not facing Sputnik), and runs very fast when Kodu becomes visible to Sputnik. Now I need to turn Sputnik into a creatable so that I can constantly respawn a new Sputnik when the previous one is destroyed.

Once again, I right-click Sputnik and choose Change Settings. I scroll down to the Creatable option shown in Figure 11.22 and turn it on by clicking the power icon to the right; when it turns green, I've turned Sputnik into a creatable.

FIGURE 11.22 Convert Sputnik into a creatable.

Go ahead and play the game after you turn Sputnik into a creatable. Uh oh, Sputnik disappeared!

Here's the secret about creatables: they must be "created" by something. This something can be a timer, an inanimate object like a rock, or even another enemy object. What's needed is a bit of programming that drops a creatable on the screen.

Take a look at Figure 11.23 and you'll see that I've dropped a tree onto the game world.

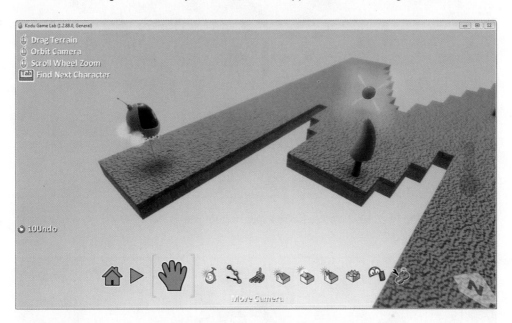

FIGURE 11.23   Drop an object on the screen that will spawn creatables.

That tree is going to create the first Sputnik object. The Sputnik creatable cannot create itself, so I have the tree do it using the program you see in Figure 11.24.

As you can see, I've set it so that when the timer reaches 1 second (the timer starts counting when the game starts), it needs to do something. What does it need to do? It needs to add the Sputnik creatable just once. To make this happen, I click the Do box and select the Actions pie slice; this opens a new pie menu that offers up the Create tile shown in Figure 11.25.

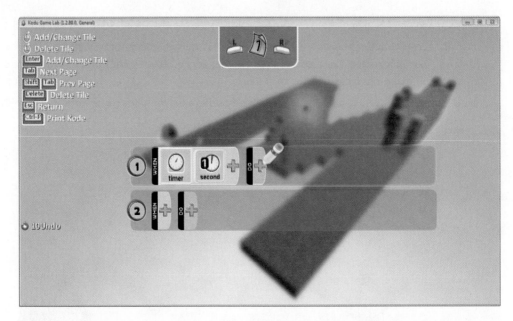

FIGURE 11.24   The Tree object creates the first Sputnik creatable.

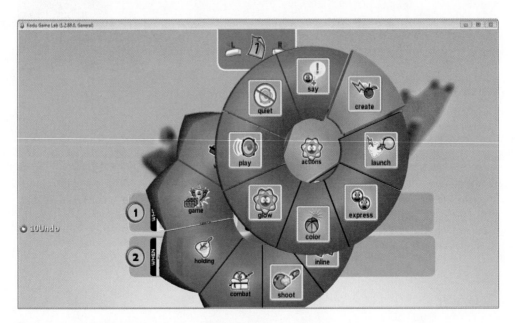

FIGURE 11.25   Select the Create pie piece to add to the Do box.

Now I need to specify what to create. Earlier you saw me create a creatable called Sputnik. That's the only creatable I've made so far, but you can create as many creatables as you like by clicking the plus sign (+) next to the Create tile and selecting the Creatables pie piece, shown in Figure 11.26.

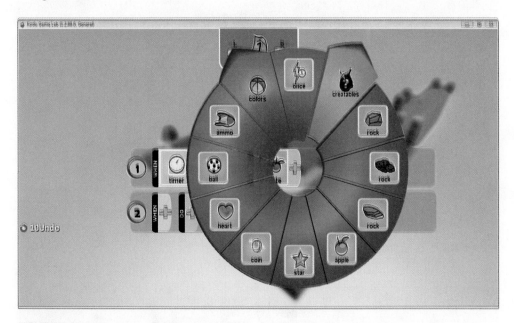

FIGURE 11.26 Select the Creatables pie piece.

After clicking the Creatables pie piece, you'll see a new pie menu appear that displays all the creatables you've made. Figure 11.27 shows the single Sputnik creatable, so I'll click that one.

After the Sputnik tile is added to the program, I click + to the right of it and select the Once tile that appears. Figure 11.28 shows the tree's now completed program.

Now there's just one more bit of programming to do. Remember, when Sputnik is destroyed, I want a new Sputnik to appear. This new Sputnik will have the same programming as the one before it, so it will run away from Kodu. To make this happen, I need to go back to the Sputnik creatable still sitting on my game world (the one that disappears when the game begins) and right-click it to open its program.

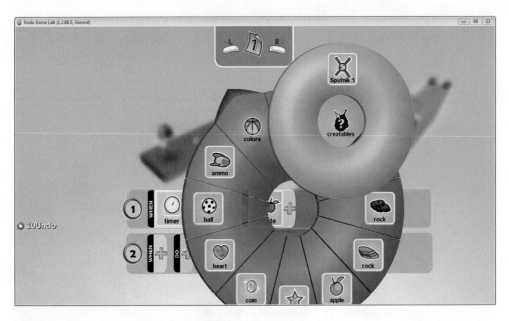

FIGURE 11.27 Select the Sputnik creatable.

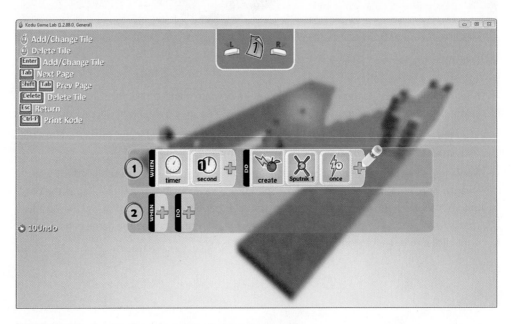

FIGURE 11.28 The tree launches a single Sputnik creatable.

Figure 11.29 shows the programming that I've added in Programming Row 3. It's pretty easy to figure out: When Sputnik's hit points reach zero, create a new Sputnik. (You just learned how to use the Create tile that gives you access to the creatables you've made in the tree's program.) Or, another option is to let the tree create a new Sputnik when it no longer sees the old Sputnik. Use WHEN See Sputnik Not – DO Create Sputnik.

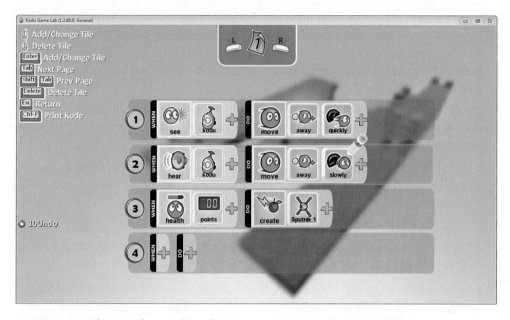

FIGURE 11.29   The Sputnik creatable will create a new Sputnik when its hit points run out.

Now play the game. When it starts, the tree creates a Sputnik that runs from you. Go grab the coin, get the blip ball function, and take some shots at Sputnik. When you destroy the Sputnik, another one should appear in its place and try to run from you.

> **NOTE**
>
> Because *MiniWorld* is so small, Sputnik does not have many places to run. Remember, when I expand the world later, turning it into *MegaWorld*, the Sputnik creatables will have plenty of places to run and hide.

Creatables are a great tool for giving your game recurring enemies. Not every game needs enemies that constantly respawn, but if you're developing a shooter game and want to have objects that aren't destroyed permanently, the Creatable feature is what you need. Creatables are also a great way to keep the size of your games manageable, because you only need to have them on the game world when they are needed and can vanish them when they are no longer needed.

Moving On

You'll find a lot more tips and tricks throughout the remainder of this book, especially in Chapter 15 and Chapter 19. Up next, however, we get you back into the design of a new game. Chapter 10 and Chapter 11 have taught you a lot of new techniques to add to those you learned in previous chapters, so now it's time to put everything you've learned so far into action and combine your existing skills with some new ones. Throughout the remainder of this book, I spend less and less time showing you how to program objects using tiles you're already familiar with. If you get stuck, you can use the index or just reread a previous chapter that covers the programming task you're stuck on. This frees me up to introduce you to more of Kodu Game Lab's features that you haven't seen yet.

You get a break on the homework in this chapter. You've learned a lot as we approach the halfway point of the book, so just take some time and have some fun doing what *you* want to do. But here are some suggestions if you need a good challenge:

1. Return to the *Saucer Hunt Extreme* game and turn the smart saucer into a creatable. How long can you and your opponent survive if you turn all the path-following saucers into smart saucers?

2. Try to use the world-building tools to re-create a familiar room (maybe your bedroom or your classroom). Add elements such as bookshelves or chairs or rugs. Get creative. It'll give you good practice designing worlds at the macro (large) level and the micro (small) level.

3. In anticipation of the next chapter, start thinking about games that don't involve shooting targets. You've already seen how to grab objects such as a coin or star, so what would it take to create a game where players race to grab objects? What kind of programming is required to ask permission from another object (such as a saucer) before taking a coin or star?

Be sure to click to the Home Menu and save any work you've done before selecting Exit to Main Menu. Don't forget to add some additional information to the Description field.

12

Adding Conversations and In-Game Instructions

Until now, almost all the games created in this book have involved one or more objects shooting missiles or blips at other targets. Kodu Game Lab is certainly useful for creating games that require good hand-eye coordination and a fast finger on the firing trigger. But not every game has to have an element of destruction. Some of the best games out there don't keep score and don't require you to fire on enemy targets. In this chapter, you learn another method for bringing two objects together, and it doesn't involve shooting missiles or blips. Let's just say that sometimes you've just got to talk things over. And while you're learning some new programming tricks, you also learn how to help the players of your game by providing some instructions; never underestimate the value of providing some help to players, even if it's just telling them the goal of the game and maybe what certain buttons do when pressed.

Add Fun Sounds to an Object

If you've been playing your games as you program them, you're certain to have heard some strange sounds from Kodu, Rover, and many other objects. You might not speak their language, but you can definitely hear them talking, especially when they bump into things.

In this chapter, you learn how to enable these objects to communicate with one another, but in a language you can understand as well. Before that, however, let's take a look at a few programming tiles that you can use to give your objects some humorous sound effects.

Take a look at Figure 12.1. I've placed Kodu on a single block of terrain along with a tree and opened up Kodu's program.

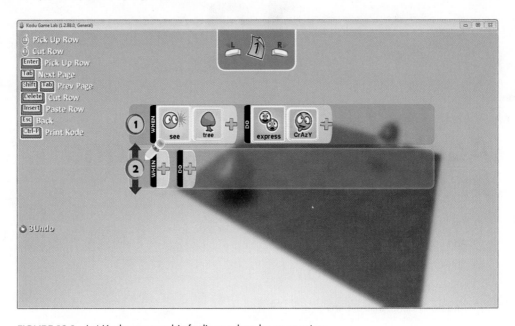

FIGURE 12.1   Let Kodu express his feelings when he sees a tree.

Here are the simple steps for re-creating the program seen in Figure 12.1:

1. Select the See tile first and then the Tree tile for the When box.

2. Click on the Do box and select the Actions pie slice from the pie menu.

3. Choose the Express pie slice.

4. Click the plus sign (+) to the right of the Express tile and select from a number of expressions, all shown in Figure 12.2.

Each emotion has its own sound effect, so experiment with each and listen closely. You can use these sound effects as cues to your players when they reach certain goals, see or hear special objects, or when they bump into other objects.

You can also program sound effects to trigger after a specified time has elapsed. Figure 12.3 shows that I've modified Programming Row 1 and added Programming Row 2, which triggers after five seconds has elapsed from when the game starts. Kodu first shows how happy he is at finding the tree, and then 15 seconds later a ring of flowers appears around his head.

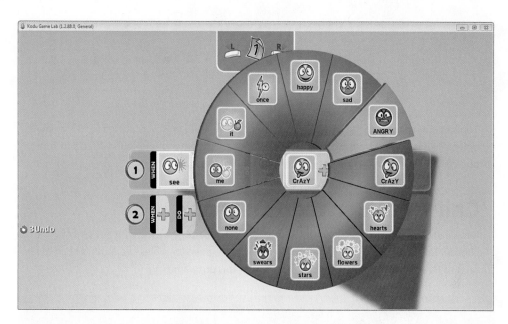

FIGURE 12.2   You have many different emotion options to give to Kodu for when he sees a tree.

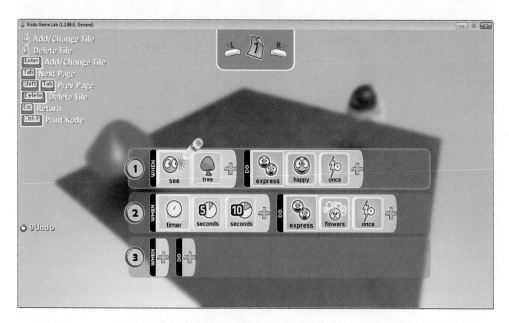

FIGURE 12.3   Use the Timer tile to delay certain emotions.

> **TIP**
> Notice that I've used the Once tile after each emotion so that Kodu doesn't keep making the sound over and over and over.

You can add sound effects to both moving objects (like Kodu or Rover) as well as to inanimate objects like rocks and trees. So, seriously consider adding some simple sound effects to your objects as you polish the final versions of your own games.

Chit-Chat Between Objects

Kodu can certainly make some funny sounds, but he can also converse with any object you choose. Take a look at Figure 12.4 and you'll see some speech bubbles over Kodu's head as he talks to Rover. In a moment, you learn how to add this programming.

FIGURE 12.4   I move the coin a little closer to Kodu.

The text bubble over Kodu's head doesn't last long…about three seconds. But using some simple programming that I'm about to show you, you can program in a conversation between two or more objects easily. Here's a brief overview, and then I'll get into the details:

1. In the When box, program in the condition that will trigger the text bubble.

2. In the Do box, add the Say tile and provide the text.

3. Repeat steps 1 and 2 using a Timer tile so that your objects aren't all speaking at once.

Let's take a look at how to program a simple two-way conversation between Kodu and Rover. First, I want to write down the conversation so that I can more easily program in what each will say and when. Here's an example:

Kodu: Have you seen a tree around here? (3 seconds)

Pause 1 second

Rover: No. Have you? (3 seconds)

Pause 1 second

Kodu: You might want to look behind you! (3 seconds)

Pause 1 second

Rover: I'm not falling for that trick.

Now let me show you how easy it is to program this conversation. First, let's start with Kodu's program. To create his first bit of dialogue, just follow these steps:

1. In the When box, add the See tile first and then the Rover tile second, as shown in Figure 12.5. (You can find Rover in the Bots II pie slice.)

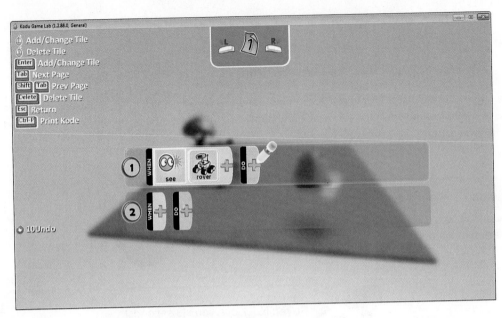

FIGURE 12.5 Kodu won't start talking until he sees Rover.

2. In the Do box, select the Actions pie slice, and then choose the Say tile shown in Figure 12.6.

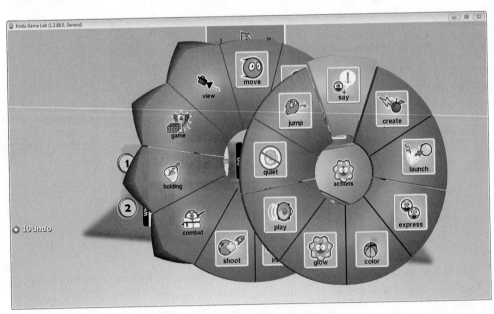

FIGURE 12.6 The Say tile is where a conversation starts (and ends).

After you select the Say tile, a window opens like the one shown in Figure 12.7.

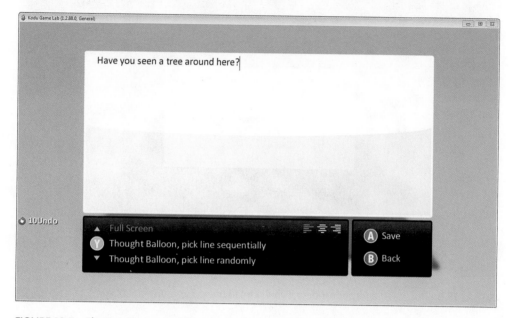

FIGURE 12.7 The Say tile opens this screen, where you type words an object will speak.

3. I'll type in the first bit of the conversation between Kodu and Rover: Have you seen a tree around here?

At the bottom of this screen, you have three options:

○ Full Screen

○ Thought Balloon, Pick Line Sequentially

○ Thought Balloon, Pick Line Randomly

If you choose the Full Screen option, instead of a small text bubble appearing over an object's head, the text is displayed much larger, as shown in Figure 12.8. This is useful if you have a large amount of text you want Kodu or the other object to speak.

Clicking Continue (or pressing the A button) closes the text box.

If you choose the second option (Thought Balloon, Pick Line Sequentially), any text typed into the window is displayed as shown in Figure 12.7, one line at a time. Kodu speaks anything typed on the top line first, followed by any test on the second line, and so on. Each line is displayed in a small text bubble until all lines have been finished.

FIGURE 12.8 You need a larger window if you want to use a large amount of text.

CAUTION

If you don't tack on a Once tile at the end, the conversation will start again. Also, the more lines you type here, the more text bubbles will have to be displayed. Keep this in mind as you program in a back-and-forth conversation between two objects using the Timer tile. If Kodu isn't done speaking before Rover is programmed to start his dialogue, both text bubbles will appear onscreen, possibly confusing a player. Test the timing until you get it just right.

The third option (Thought Balloon, Pick Line Randomly) picks one line at random.

No matter which of the Thought Balloon options you choose, remember to place a Once tile after the Say tile so that Kodu ends the conversation.

Those are the three steps for adding in text you want a character to speak. You simply repeat this bit of programming by adding in more Say tiles to simulate a conversation.

Now, after I've programmed in Kodu's opening question, it's time for Rover to respond. I'll go ahead and open Rover's program and, as you can see in Figure 12.9, it's the same programming as I gave to Kodu, but for the Say tile I entered in the text No. Have you?

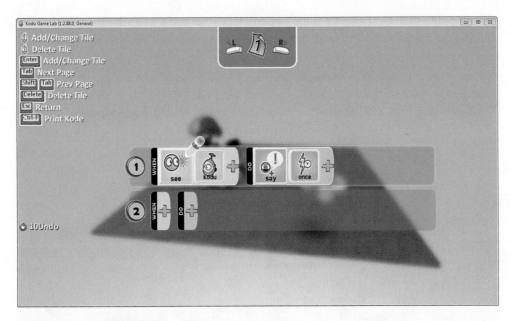

FIGURE 12.9   Adding in Rover's response to Kodu's question.

I want to test this conversation so far, so I click the Play button. Figure 12.10 shows what happens.

FIGURE 12.10   Everyone wants to talk at once.

Both Kodu and Rover attempt to talk at the same time—not good. What we need is some additional programming to time the responses so that it looks like a real back-and-forth conversation.

Kodu starts talking when he first sees Rover. I need Rover to wait until Kodu is finished... about three seconds, but I'll make it four seconds to be safe. Figure 12.11 shows the additional programming I added. Don't worry; I know it looks a little confusing, but I'll explain how it works.

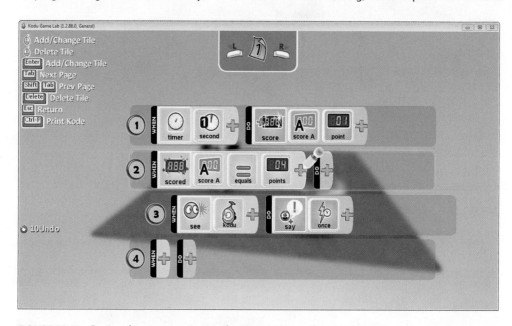

FIGURE 12.11   Pacing the conversation so that Rover responds to Kodu's question.

Here are the steps involved (explained in detail in a moment):

1. Create a new scoreboard that increments by a single point every second.

2. Create a condition that checks the value of the new scoreboard. When the score equals a certain value, the Say tile below that programming row executes.

3. Repeat steps 1 and 2 for each bit of the back-and-forth conversation.

Now here's the more detailed explanation for how it works.

First, drop in a Timer block and add the 1 Second tile in the When box.

In the Do box, you select the +Score tile. Then, click the + to the right of the +Score tile and a pie menu will appear showing various points, as shown in Figure 12.12. Don't choose any points; instead, select the Scores pie slice.

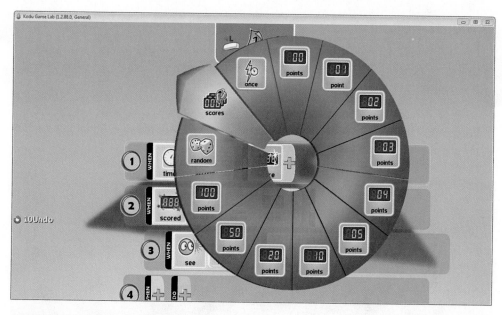

FIGURE 12.12   Select the Scores pie slice.

When you click the Scores pie slice, another pie menu appears, like the one in Figure 12.13, showing all the colored scoreboards. The colored scoreboards actually put a number on the screen, and that's not what I want.

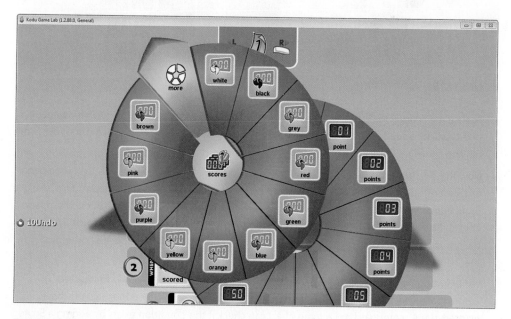

FIGURE 12.13   You don't want to select a colored scoreboard.

> **TIP**
> You've already learned how to use a scoreboard to display a timer for a game. You used a colored scoreboard because you wanted the timer to appear on the screen. If you don't want the number to display onscreen, you need a different kind of scoreboard.

Instead of selecting a colored scoreboard, I click the More pie slice shown in Figure 12.13, and this time I get access to the lettered scoreboards shown in Figure 12.14.

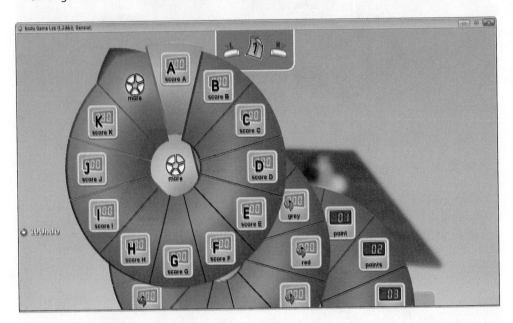

FIGURE 12.14 Use the lettered scoreboard to track the time elapsed.

I chose the Score A tile, but any letter will work. All that's needed now is to specify how many points will be added to the A scoreboard, and I do that by clicking the + to the right of the Score A tile and choosing the 1 Point tile, as shown in Figure 12.15.

Now that I've got a method for tracking how many seconds have elapsed since the game began, I can start programming the order of the conversation. Remember, when the game starts, the game timer equals 0 and Kodu asks, "Have you seen a tree around here?" This text bubble disappears after three seconds, and I want to wait one additional second before Kodu responds. This means the game timer will equal four seconds when I want Kodu to speak. So, how do I program Kodu so that he begins talking after four seconds have elapsed?

Well, I know I need to check the A scoreboard to see whether it has reached four points. Remember, every second adds one point to the A scoreboard. So, when four seconds have elapsed, the A scoreboard has a score of 4. I can check if this condition exists by adding a Scored tile to the When box and specifying the A scoreboard, as shown in Figure 12.16.

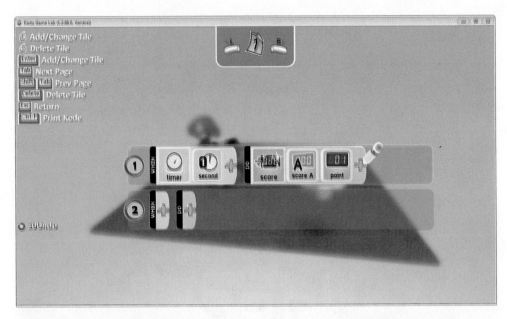

FIGURE 12.15   Programming that increments the A scoreboard by one point each second.

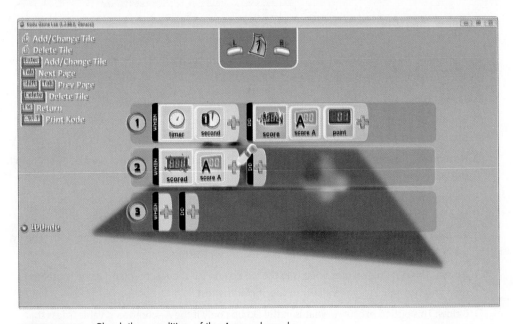

FIGURE 12.16   Check the condition of the A scoreboard.

I'm not done yet. Although I've specified in the When box that I want to examine the A scoreboard, I haven't specified exactly what I want to check, and that is that the A scoreboard equals 4 points.

If I click the + to the right of the Score A tile, I find this interesting tile labeled Compare, as shown in Figure 12.17.

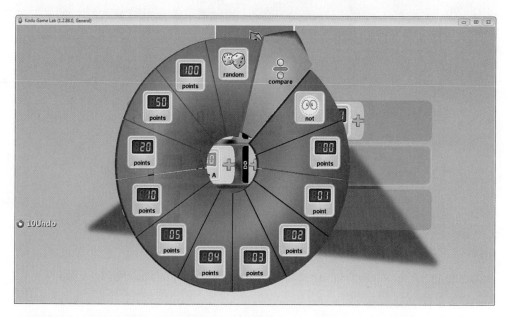

FIGURE 12.17   The Compare pie slice is very powerful.

This Compare pie slice is one amazingly powerful tool that you'll find yourself using over and over. Click it and you'll see the pie slices shown in Figure 12.18.

You have six options available here:

○ **Equals**: This option checks to see whether the A scoreboard matches a specific value. If it's a match, the When box executes whatever is in the Do box.

○ **NotEquals**: This option executes what is in the Do box only if the A scoreboard does *not* match the value you specify for the test.

○ **>= (greater than or equal to)**: This option executes what is in the Do box only if the A scoreboard value is greater than or equal to the value you specify for the test.

○ **<= (less than or equal to)**: This option executes what is in the Do box only if the A scoreboard value is less than or equal to the value you specify for the test.

○ **Above**: This option executes what is in the Do box only if the A scoreboard value is greater than (but not equal to) the value you specify for the test.

○ **Below**: This option executes what is in the Do box only if the A scoreboard value is less than (but not equal to) the value you specify for the test.

These six options might be confusing at first, so let me show you two of them in action; you'll then begin to find that the Compare options make sense.

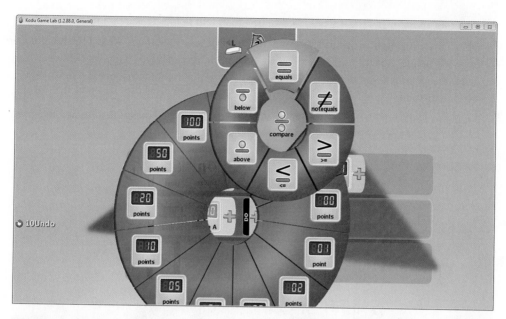

FIGURE 12.18 You can check six conditions using the Compare options.

Let me start with the Equals option. I add the Equals tile and follow it with a 4 Points tile, as shown in Figure 12.19.

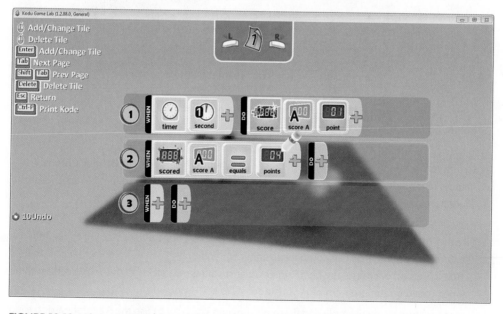

FIGURE 12.19 The condition to test the A scoreboard uses the Equals tile.

Read this left to right: If the A scoreboard value equals four points do something.

What if it the A scoreboard equals three points? What happens? Nothing. What if the A scoreboard equals 10 points? Again… nothing. Whatever I choose to program next happens only when the A scoreboard equals four points. And you already know what I want to happen: I want Rover to respond to Kodu.

But before I add in Rover's response, let's go back and change the Equals tile to something else. Figure 12.20 shows that I've changed it to the Below tile.

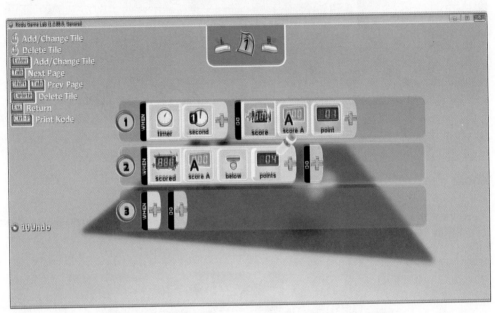

FIGURE 12.20 What happens if the A scoreboard value is below four points?

Now let's read Programming Row 2 left to right again: When the A scoreboard value is below four points, do something.

What happens if the A scoreboard value is two points? Is 2 below 4? Yes. So, whatever I choose to program underneath Programming Row 2 will execute. What happens if the A scoreboard value is four points? Is 4 below 4? Nope. Four equals four, so the programming I add underneath Programming Row 2 would not execute.

I could easily change the Below tile to the Above tile and have the When condition check to see whether the A scoreboard value is higher than four points. I hope you're starting to see that using the Compare options you can compare a variety of conditions, such as an object hit points, its actual score, and of course, the game timer, against values you pick and then have certain things happen based on the programming you add in a Do box. Cool, huh?

I want to return to my example and finish up showing you how to use the A scoreboard to trigger Rover's first response ("No. Have you?") and the rest of the conversation. Figure 12.21 shows that I've added in the programming for Rover's first response to Programming Row 3 and set Programming Row 3 to execute only if the condition in Programming Row 2 is true. (You drag the row to the right so that it sits just under and to the right of the programming row above it.)

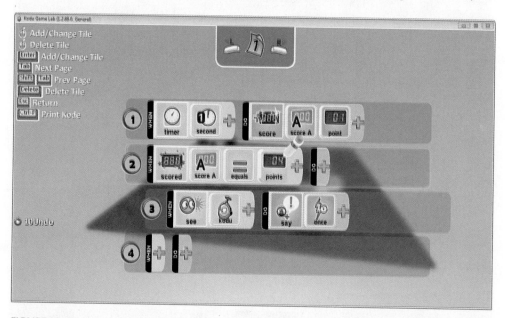

FIGURE 12.21   Rover will respond to Kodu's question when the A scoreboard equals four.

I already know that after Rover responds "No. Have you?" that Kodu will speak again. How many seconds will have elapsed? If Rover starts speaking at four seconds and his text bubble disappears after three seconds, that brings the game timer up to seven seconds. I want a slight pause between Rover and Kodu, so I add one more second of silence. This means that Kodu will say "You might want to look behind you!" when the game timer equals eight points (seconds).

Figure 12.22 shows the new programming I've added to Kodu to let him speak to Rover again.

After Kodu responds, Rover has one more response that occurs when the game timer reaches 12 seconds. (Kodu responds at 8 seconds, waits 3 for the text bubble to disappear, and then 1 additional second of silence equals 12 seconds.)

Figure 12.23 shows the final bit of programming that I've added to Rover to let him finish up the conversation.

TIP

If you click the + to the right of the Once tile after each Say tile, you can specify the color that will surround the text bubble.

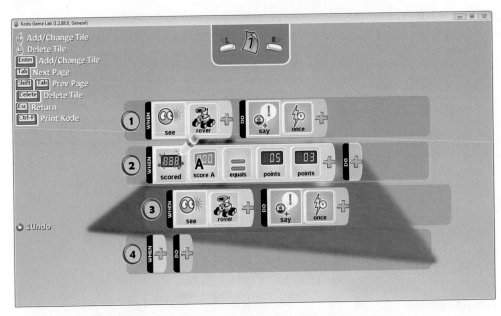

FIGURE 12.22   Kodu speaks again, but this time after eight seconds have elapsed.

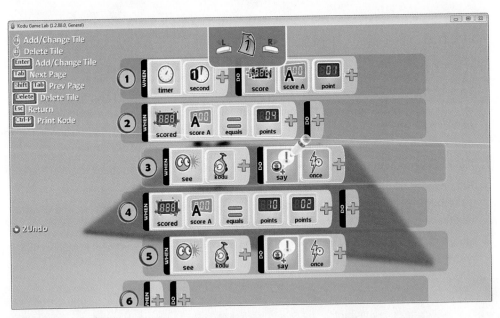

FIGURE 12.23   One final comparison to see whether the A scoreboard equals 12 points.

After the conversation is over, I can easily add another programming row like the one in Figure 12.24 to move the game forward and jump to Page 2, where the game's action begins.

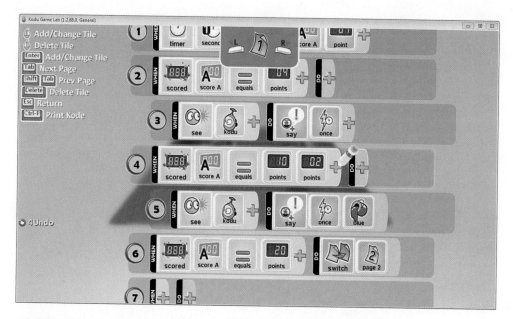

FIGURE 12.24   Use the A scoreboard to trigger many different events in a game.

You'll see more uses of the game timer and the Compare options later in the book, but what I want you to take from this section is how to structure a simple conversation between two objects. And with some additional programming, you can easily bring a third object into the conversation.

Now that you understand how to give objects a way to speak onscreen, you might wonder how you can use this feature. In Chapter 22, "Sample Game 3: On a Mission," you learn how to program *The Dune Treasure*, a game that sends Kodu on a dangerous treasure hunt. Kodu needs to obtain clues from friends and fight enemies as he searches for a valuable treasure. Conversation plays a big part in this game, and you'll find in your own games that sometimes it's fun to slow the action down a bit and let two friends (or even two enemies) have a little chat.

Nontimed Conversations

As an alternative to creating conversations that are based on the Timer, you have another option when creating conversations between objects.

Take a look at Figure 12.25 and you'll see Kodu and Rover on opposite sides of a small piece of terrain.

Rover has something he wants to say to Kodu, but until Kodu greets him with special code word, Rover keeps silent. To make this happen, I've added a little bit of programming to Kodu that you can see in Figure 12.26.

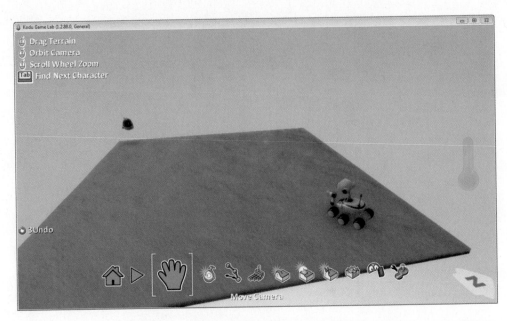

FIGURE 12.25 Rover would like to speak to Kodu when Kodu approaches.

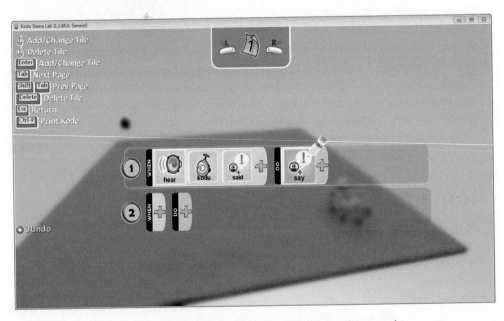

FIGURE 12.26 You can program an object to listen for certain sounds or words.

Here you can see a simple WHEN-DO situation:

WHEN Kodu says (X), DO say (Y).

Figure 12.27 shows the Said tile opened.

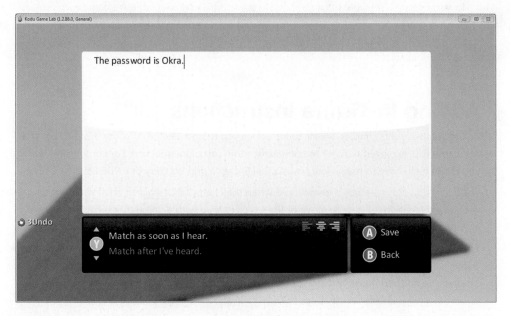

FIGURE 12.27 Put game instructions and explanations of controls in the Description field.

The text "The password is Okra" is what Rover will be listening for before responding. Notice the two options at the bottom of the screen: Match As Soon As I Hear and Match After I've Heard. If you use the Match As Soon As I Hear selection, Rover immediately recognizes a match if Kodu says "The password is Okra." For a more realistic response, select the other option, Match After I've Heard. This lets Kodu say the phrase and then Rover respond with a bit of information.

Using the Hear option, you can program objects to listen for words or phrases using the Said tile or you can listen for specific sounds. (I cover programming sound effects in Chapter 14, "Games Should Be Heard: Programming Music and Sound Effects.") Using this method, you can program any assortment of objects that can respond to specific words, phrases, or sounds, no matter the order in which the players may approach the objects.

TIP

In addition to using the Said tile to listen for specific sounds or words, you might also be interested in a more advanced option that uses tags and can save you some typing. So, for the preceding example, you would program Kodu to use a Say tile and enter the following text:

The password is Okra <tag password>. What you've done here is create a shortcut that references the phrase "The password is Okra" and assigns this phrase a tag's name. Then, with Rover's Said tile, instead of typing out "The password is Okra" that he's waiting to hear, you simply type <tag password>. Using this method, you can assign a tag to every statement you want an object (such as the player's Kodu) to speak and then use that tag's name with other objects to trigger conversations or actions when the tag's name is heard. Easy! Remember, <, then tag, then a shortcut name, followed by the closing >.

Adding In-Game Instructions

Before you leave this chapter, I want to introduce you to one new bit of game design. I bet that any game you've played before has come with some sort of instructions. For complicated games, you might even have to read a lengthy manual (either a printed copy or a PDF file).

You'll find that players enjoy a game more when they know what's going on. If you create a game with no explanation for how to move or fire, you'll end up with a game that is frustrating for anyone who plays it.

You don't have to be a professional writer to give your game players some good instructions. Kodu Game Lab makes it extremely easy to give players some instruction before they begin playing. After you've finished programming your game and you're happy with how everything works, select the Save Game option that opens the screen shown in Figure 12.28.

FIGURE 12.28 Put game instructions and explanations of controls in the Description field.

Delete any text from the Description field that you might have used to help you debug or document the various versions of your game. In its place, type in a brief description of the game's goal along with explanations about the controls. As you can see, I've included the goal (Kodu needs to have a talk with Rover), explained that the game requires a game controller, and that the player steers Kodu with the left joystick and fires missiles at obstacles with button A.

> **TIP**
>
> Did you know you can include graphics in your game's Description such as a small picture of the A button? Use the < and > brackets for this in your description, and inside the brackets is where you place the special image name. For example, in the description you could type Press <A Button> to Fire Missiles, and in place of the <A Button> a small graphic will be inserted showing the actual A button. Cool! Other options include B and X buttons as well as Left Stick and Right Stick.

Now you just have to configure the game so that when it starts, the instructions display onscreen, as shown in Figure 12.29.

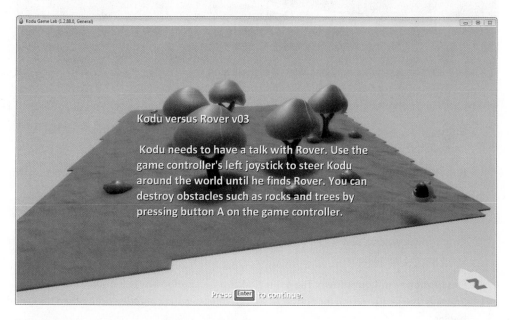

FIGURE 12.29   My instructions appear onscreen.

To program your game to display instructions when the game begins, follow these steps:

1. Select the Object tool.

2. Right-click an empty spot of terrain and choose Change World Settings.

3. Scroll down the list to the Start Game With: option, shown in Figure 12.30, and choose an option.

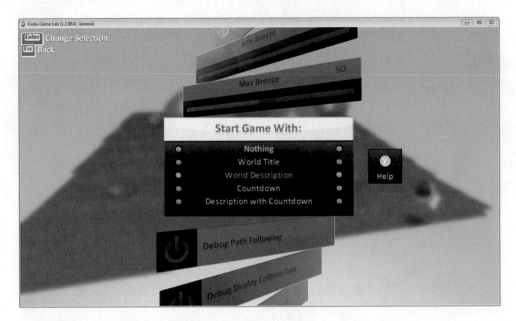

FIGURE 12.30   Choose what appears when the game starts.

You have five options here:

○ **Nothing**: When a player begins the game, no text appears onscreen, and the game begins immediately.

○ **World Title**: Only the name of the game appears; pressing Return (or button A) starts the game.

○ **World Description**: Both the game title and any text you entered in the Description box display. Pressing Return (or button A) starts the game.

○ **Countdown**: When a player presses the Play button, a timer begins a three-second countdown, and then the game begins.

○ **Description with Countdown**: The game title and Description box text display onscreen. Pressing the Return button (or button A) starts a three-second countdown, and then the game begins.

Pick the option that works best for you. (I prefer the Description with Countdown, but you can use any option you want for your games.)

Moving On

You have a lot more to learn about integrating conversations into your own games. For instance, after a conversation ends, you might want to program Rover to go visit a special mountain and have Kodu follow him. You can also use the Say tile to give your players instructions as they play the game. Think about Kodu approaching Rover and having Rover programmed to tell Kodu that he's been upgraded with missiles so that he can go save the town from the menacing saucers. Rover might need to tell Kodu what button fires the missiles, or maybe Kodu needs to provide a magic word to a castle's gatekeeper to enter. You've got plenty of possibilities, so spend some time playing around with the Say tile and see what you can do with it in your own games.

Also, now that you've learned how the Compare options work, I want to give you some homework before you move on to Chapter 13, "World Design: Creating Environmental Special Effects." So, give these some thought and see whether you can figure out how to make them happen:

1. How might you use a lettered scoreboard to track the number of stars or apples that Kodu has bumped or collected? Think about how this could be useful in a seek-and-find game where players must find 3 apples and have more than 50 hit points left. What Compare options would you use to ensure that each player has the correct number of items before moving forward in a game?

2. Use the Compare options to make changes in one of your previous shooter-type games. How would you go about increasing the speed of an enemy target as a game progresses? (You learned one method in the *Saucer Hunt Extreme* game that looks directly at the health of an object and slows it down as it is damaged, but now you've got the Compare options available and so can access a lettered scoreboard.)

3. You've seen how to time conversations based on a hidden scoreboard (A scoreboard). Can you think of another way of using the Compare options with the value of the A scoreboard to affect game play? (Hint: Instead of triggering conversations based on the A scoreboard value, imagine giving players special powers/features that turn on and off at certain times in a game.)

Be sure to click the Home Menu button and save any work you've done before selecting Exit to Main Menu. Don't forget to add some additional information to the Description field.

13

World Design: Creating Environmental Special Effects

In This Chapter

○ Your World's Terrain and Sky Color Effects

○ Do You Need a Breeze or a Hurricane?

○ Lakes and Rivers

○ Objects and Water

Let's continue our look at designing a game world, which we began in Chapter 6, "Build Your Own World: Moving Mountains and Painting Terrain." You have so far learned how to add terrain, change its color and texture, and even how to grow and shrink mountains and build walls. But you have plenty more to learn about when it comes to giving a game some fun and interesting sites to see. In this chapter, you learn how to use some visual settings to give your world a slightly different look and you get some hands-on experience with adding water effects.

Your World's Terrain and Sky Color Effects

Whether you have an idea for a game already well developed in your head or already created in Kodu Game Lab, you can add some interesting world effects to the overall look of the game, and they involve absolutely no programming.

You access these world effects by clicking the Change World Settings button on the toolbar shown in Figure 13.1.

FIGURE 13.1   The Change World Settings button.

The Change World Settings options appear on a familiar-looking scrolling list. Figure 13.2 shows that I scrolled down the list using my mouse's center wheel and stopped on the Sky feature.

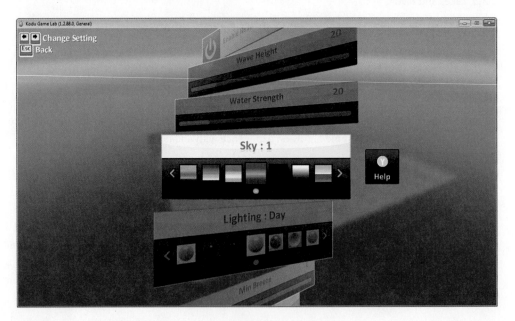

FIGURE 13.2   Select the Sky option to make some color changes.

Under the Sky option, you'll find 21 different color schemes that you can apply to your game world's sky. These colors range from absolute black to baby blue, but it's the color schemes that we don't see in our real world that can really help make an eye-catching game.

Figure 13.3 shows my selection of an alien landscape and horizon for Rover to explore.

FIGURE 13.3   What strange planet has Rover landed on with that sky?

I made the color selection for land and sky before I started programming the game, but I could easily have modified the sky color (and the color of the terrain using the Magic Brush) after I programmed the game. As a matter of fact, I highly encourage you to experiment with changing the sky and terrain colors to find a combination that adds to the uniqueness of your own games.

TIP

When you make a change to the Sky color scheme, the change is made instantly and the Change World Settings option disappears, letting you view the results immediately. This makes it very easy to change the color, look at the results, and decide whether you like it. You can move through all 21 options quickly to find the best sky color for your games.

Watch how fast I can change this world from an alien landscape to an Earth-based desert. I'll first change the sky color to option 7. Figure 13.4 shows the new sky. Just looking at it is making me a little thirsty.

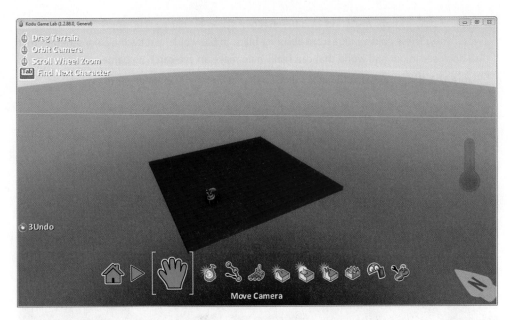

FIGURE 13.4 The sky changes from alien to something closer to home.

Next, I'll find a terrain color that works well with that sky color and makes me think of a sandy desert. I think I found the right match. Does Figure 13.5 make you think of a sandy desert?

FIGURE 13.5 Rover has been dropped in the desert to find a hidden tomb.

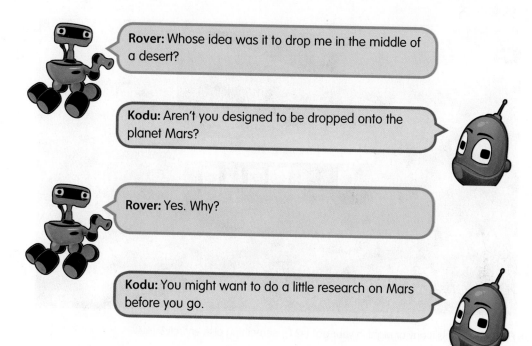

Rover: Whose idea was it to drop me in the middle of a desert?

Kodu: Aren't you designed to be dropped onto the planet Mars?

Rover: Yes. Why?

Kodu: You might want to do a little research on Mars before you go.

I don't know about you, but the color of this sky and the terrain color definitely has me thinking about a new game called *The Dune Treasure*. (As a matter of fact, I show you how to program *The Dune Treasure* in Chapter 22, "Sample Game 3: On a Mission," so don't think this sky color and terrain won't be used.)

Now that I've got my sky and terrain colors picked out, I can make one additional setting to set the mood. Return to the Change World Settings scrolling list, and look just below the Sky options, and you'll see the Lighting option box shown in Figure 13.6.

Once again, you have some options that can completely change how your game world looks. There are eight options, including Day, Night, Mars, Dark, and even one called Dream. Each of these options applies a slightly different lighting effect on the surface of the terrain.

For example, in Figure 13.7, I've applied the Mars effect. Notice how the terrain now blends a bit better with the orange-yellow sky as compared to the terrain in Figure 13.5.

FIGURE 13.6   Is it day or night in your game? Or something else entirely?

FIGURE 13.7   Lighting effects provide even more options for coloring your world.

With various combinations of the terrain color, the Sky options, and the Lighting effects, you can create some amazing landscapes. Just take a look at Figure 13.8; I've used Terrain 17, Sky 2 (pitch black), and Lighting: Space to simulate Rover on the moon, complete with craters.

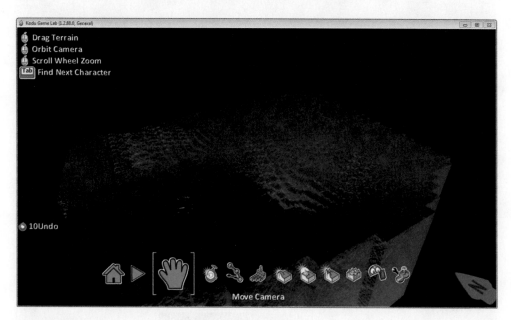

FIGURE 13.8 Breaking News: Rover lands on the moon!

After you've found a combination of terrain, sky color, and lighting effects that you enjoy, you can set about creating a game that fits with that visual theme. The other option is to design your game first and then find a combination of colors and effects that makes your existing game visually appealing, or at least eye-catching enough to make someone want to play it.

Do You Need a Breeze or a Hurricane?

Let me return to the desert that Rover is currently preparing to explore. In a desert, Rover is sure to want some shade, so he's going to keep his eyes open for some trees. Fortunately for him, I can provide those to him by simply dropping the cluster of trees shown in Figure 13.9.

You can't see it in Figure 13.9, but those trees are gently swaying side to side as a soft breeze rustles their leaves. This breeze is random and can change over time, moving from no breeze at all to a good gust.

I'd like to have some fun with Rover and put him inside a nice strong desert windstorm. And to do that, I return to the Change World Settings button and scroll down the list of options until I get to the Min Breeze effect shown in Figure 13.10.

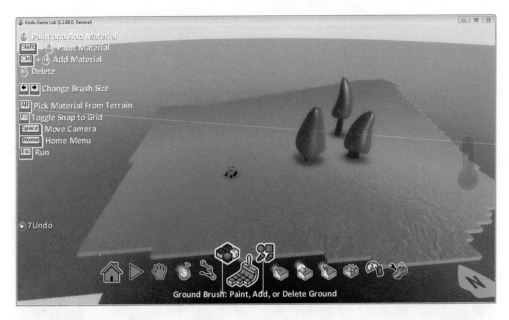

FIGURE 13.9 Adding some shade for Rover.

FIGURE 13.10 The Min Breeze effect.

The Min Breeze effect is a drag bar that can move all the way to the left to a setting of 0, which means no breeze at all. If the drag bar is moved all to the way to the right to a setting of 100, a strong wind will continually rip across the surface of the desert. I set it to 50 and then scroll down to the option below it called Max Breeze, shown in Figure 13.11.

FIGURE 13.11   The Max Breeze effect.

The Max Breeze effect is another drag bar, moving from 0 to 100. If you experiment with the Min Breeze and Max Breeze drag bars, you'll find that they are linked; if you drag the Max Breeze value to 10, the Min Breeze value will automatically move to 10 if you had it set at a higher value.

CAUTION

You cannot have a Min Breeze of 20 and a Max Breeze of 10. The Min Breeze value will always be lower than or equal to the Max Breeze value.

As I said, I want to have some fun with Rover, so I'll set the Max Breeze to 100. After I do so, it's time to check those trees. You'll have to either take my word for it or make the settings yourself, but those trees are really dancing.

NOTE

The speed of the wind really has no effect on game play; it's more a matter of providing another visual should your game have any trees in it. Still, it's a nice visual effect that can make a game look more visually appealing.

Lakes and Rivers

If you've done any exploring on your own of Kodu Game Lab, you might have already discovered that in addition to solid terrain you can also add water to your game world. But if you've not yet noticed or clicked the Water Tool shown selected in Figure 13.12, let me point you to it and show you how it works.

FIGURE 13.12 The Water Tool lets you add water to your game just as you add terrain.

Now, the first thing you want to know about the Water Tool is this: When you add water, it expands at an even level. So, if you try to add water to a flat world, the entire world will be covered with a layer of water.

Don't believe me? Try it. Figure 13.13 shows what happens when I select the Water Tool and left-click once anywhere on the flat terrain. (Don't hold the left mouse button down; I show you why in a moment.)

Fortunately, I can click right-click the water and remove it instantly.

When you click the Water Tool, you'll see the Water Color Selection icon above and to the right that allows you to select the shade of the water. The default option is Clear, but you can click the Water Color Selection icon and choose from Green, Orange, or Black, and a few more. (Option 7 looks more like Lava, so imagine what kind of game you could make with that.) Any water you add to your game will then have that color shade applied to it. Just take a look at Figure 13.14 and notice the murky, oily water that has spilled in the area. Yuck!

FIGURE 13.13 This desert just had a flood.

FIGURE 13.14 Choose your water color carefully.

Adding water to your games is as easy as selecting the Water Tool and left-clicking until you're happy with the level of the water. But don't hold down on the left mouse button too long, or you might find your game world completely submerged. Poor Rover better be wearing scuba gear in Figure 13.15.

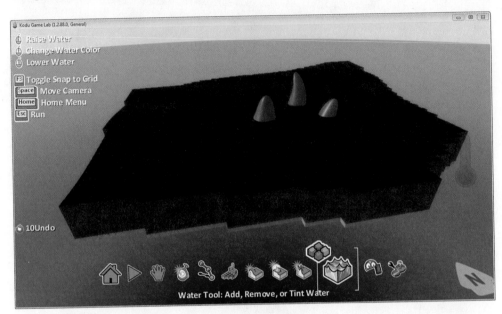

FIGURE 13.15   Do you prefer the shallow end or the deep end of a pool?

If you find that you've added too much water, just hold down on the right mouse button until you're happy with the water level.

Water in Kodu Game Lab behaves similarly to water in the real world. If you dig a small hole in the ground and pour in enough water, the water will form a small lake (a *very* small lake). In Kodu Game Lab, you create your own lakes using a similar method.

First, I need enough "soil" to actually be able to dig a hole. But that hole must not go completely through your game world, as shown in Figure 13.16. If you remove all the terrain to create a hole, there's nothing underneath to hold the water.

Fortunately, it's easy to increase the depth of my terrain so that I actually have some terrain in which to dig a hole that doesn't go completely through my world, as follows:

1. I start by selecting the Up/Down tool shown in Figure 13.17.

2. I then need to click the Brush Shape icon that appears above and to the right of the Up/Down tool. (You can see this Brush Shape icon in Figure 13.17).

FIGURE 13.16   Don't remove too much terrain; otherwise, the water will drain away.

FIGURE 13.17   Select the Up/Down tool to increase the thickness of your terrain.

3. From the Brush Shape options, I choose the Magic Brush shown in Figure 13.18.

FIGURE 13.18   Choose the Magic Brush from the Brush Shape options.

4. Now I'll move the mouse pointer (or game controller cursor) over any part of the terrain. The terrain should begin to flash to let you know that all the terrain is currently selected. All that's left to do now is hold down the left mouse button and watch as the terrain increases in thickness.

Figure 13.19 shows that I've added a good bit of "sand" underneath my desert.

> **NOTE**
>
> I've changed the Sky color temporarily so that you can more easily see how much thickness has been added to the desert terrain.

Now it's time to add a small pool of water to my desert oasis, and for that I'll once again use the Up/Down tool. This time, however, I want to remove terrain:

1. I again select the Up/Down tool, and then change the Brush Shape from Magic Brush to the Medium Round Brush, as shown in Figure 13.20.

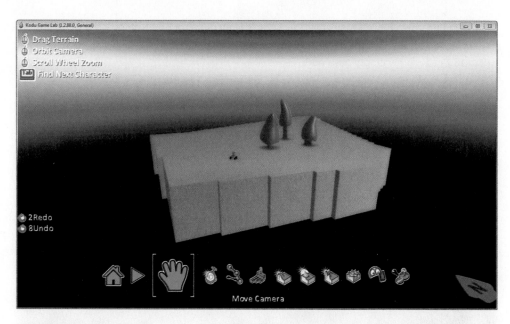

FIGURE 13.19   My desert now has enough thickness to dig a nice hole.

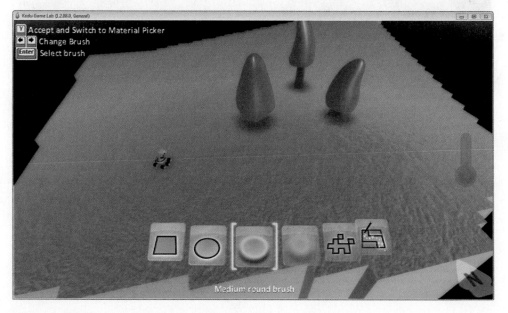

FIGURE 13.20   Use a round brush to create a small lake or pool.

2. Holding down the left mouse button, I drag the medium round brush over the terrain between the trees until a suitable amount of terrain has been dug out and a small hole created. Figure 13.21 shows my empty oasis pool.

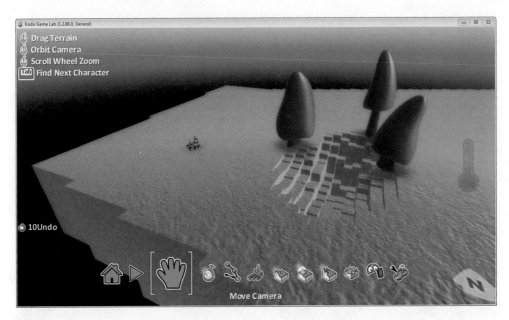

FIGURE 13.21 An empty oasis, ready to be filled with some water.

3. Now I just need to select the Water Tool and fill the hole. Figure 13.22 shows that I've filled it with a nice bit of rippling green water.

And that's how you create a small or big lake. But what about a river? Well, think of a river as a lake that just keeps moving across your terrain. It can be shallow or deep, and also requires that you use the Up/Down tool (along with a round or square brush shape).

Figure 13.23 shows that I've created an S-shaped river behind Rover by pressing and holding down the right mouse button while the Up/Down tool is selected.

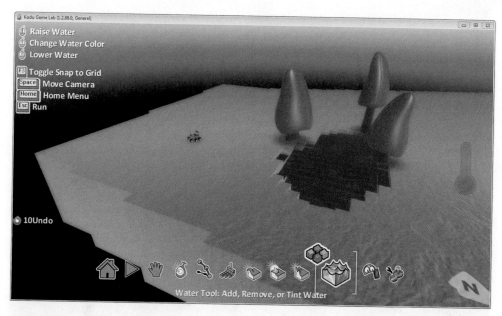

FIGURE 13.22 Finally, some water for Rover!

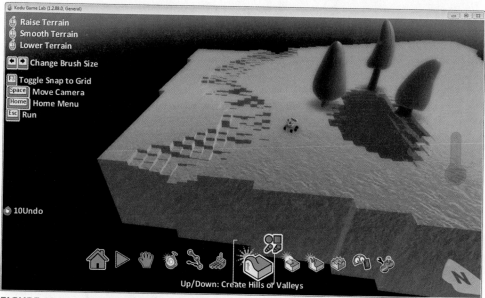

FIGURE 13.23 An empty riverbed running through the desert. What a sight!

I'm satisfied with the path of my soon-to-be river, so all that's left is to add some water with the Water Tool. Figure 13.24 shows the now-full river.

FIGURE 13.24   Rover has his choice between a river and a lake.

Rover: That's weird. The water in the river isn't draining away. It must be the glass walls.

Kodu: Actually, the water will stay in place even if the Glass Walls option in the Change World Settings scrolling list is turned off.

Rover: That's too bad. It would be a fast way to drain a pool, wouldn't it?

Objects and Water

Experiment with any lakes and rivers you create; you'll quickly find that if a lake or river is too deep players cannot escape if they fall in. Rover can easily cross the shallow river to the other side, as shown in Figure 13.25, but if he gets in the small oasis pool, he's not getting out.

FIGURE 13.25 Water can be safe to cross if it's not too deep.

But you might find other aspects to water interesting. First, objects can detect water. Here's a simple set of steps for determining whether a player is in the water (versus being on dry land):

1. Right-click the player-controlled object (such as Rover) and choose Program.

2. Click the When box and select the More pie slice, shown in Figure 13.26.

3. Select the On Water tile, shown in Figure 13.27.

The On Water tile enables you to trigger certain actions or events when an object touches water. In this instance, I could give Rover the capability to use his scanner when he's on solid ground, and make him switch to using his laser beam while he's in the water. Figure 13.28 shows the simple programming I could add to take away his scanning ability while he's wet.

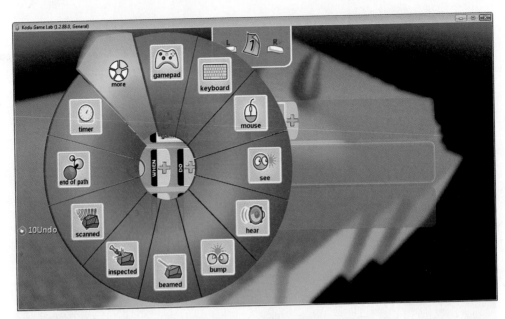

FIGURE 13.26 Program Rover to detect when he's on (or in) water.

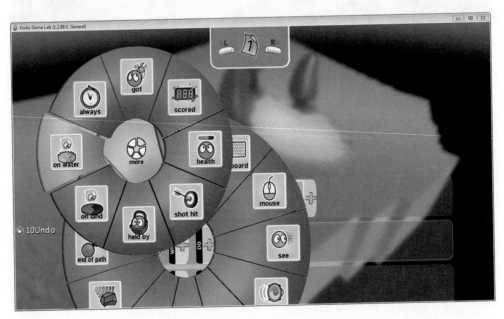

FIGURE 13.27 The On Water tile checks to see whether an object is touching water.

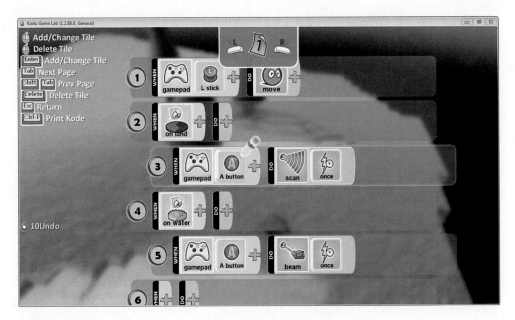

FIGURE 13.28 No more scanning until you get yourself dried off.

There's a matching On Land tile as well. So if you create a game that has both water and terrain, you'll always be able to add additional programming for special conditions where an object can either be on dry land or swimming around.

Moving On

So now you've seen how to use and modify water, wind, sky color, and lighting in your own games. Three of these are mainly used just for changing the look of your game, but you can add water to a game for a variety of reasons: obstacles, places to visit to obtain items or special powers, and even as the primary location for a game, such as a race over water. If you dig around inside the Object tool, you'll find a number of objects that are made just for water, including the Fish, Turtle, and Ship objects. You can program some of these objects to also function on dry land, but not all of them. Find and drop a Ship object on the land, and see what happens when you try to program it to move with the mouse or game controller.

Before you leave this chapter, I want to challenge you to spend a little time investigating Kodu Game Lab on your own. You've now moved into the second half of the book, and I am going to start giving you some things to try to locate on your own that I'll be introducing in later chapters. So, let's start with the following:

1. You learned how to create paths back in Chapter 8, "Dangerous Targets: Programming Enemies That Fire Back," using the Path tool. With the Path tool, an object can be programmed to follow

a path you assign to it. In some games, you might need an object to only move on a path in one direction. Using the Path Tool, create a few paths and see whether you can figure out how to assign a direction for that path. (Hint: You'll want to experiment with right-clicking somewhere on that path to find a hidden Change Direction feature.)

2. If you've been playing the games you've been programming with Kodu Game Lab, you've probably heard plenty of sound effects, but did you know that you can also program music into your games? Using the Object tool, try and find the tiles you would need to add some background music as Kodu or Rover move around in a game. (Hint: Be on the lookout for a Play tile, hidden in the Actions pie slice.)

3. Certain characters can hover or fly (like Kodu), which means they'll float over any water surface you create. But if you right-click Kodu (or another object) and choose Change Settings, scroll down the list, and turn off the Stay Above Water option, you can create an underwater game where Kodu can swim and interact with other underwater objects. Give it a try.

Be sure to return to the Home Menu button and save any work you've done before selecting Exit to Main Menu. Don't forget to add some additional information to the Description field.

Games Should Be Heard: Programming Music and Sound Effects

In This Chapter

○ Add a Music Soundtrack

○ Program Background Noise for Your World

○ Adding Sound Effects

○ Using Sound Effects for Player Conditions

Games created with Kodu Game Lab have some amazing visual effects. Missiles flying across the terrain, flying saucers, trees swaying in the breeze, and even Kodu and Rover can't sit still for too long. And there are also some great sound effects. You've heard the sounds of missiles being launched, targets exploding, and the funny sounds from Kodu as he talks to his friends (and enemies). These are the built-in sound effects that are assigned to objects and actions. But did you know you can add even more sound effects and assign them to specific actions that a player makes? You can add a sound to alert players when their hit points are draining away, and you can add sounds when a player picks up an object, such as a coin. There are silly sounds, and exploding sounds, and dozens more. And those are just sound effects. In this chapter, you also learn how to add music to your games and change that music in the game to reflect what's happening onscreen: fast music for action and maybe some slower music for less-intense game play.

Adding a Game Music Soundtrack

This chapter begins by showing you one of the easiest and best ways to give your game an extra bit of kick: music. Everyone loves music, and when you're playing a game, the soundtrack playing in the background can really entertain and inspire a player.

When it comes to music, the soundtrack you add needs to match the type of game you're offering to your players. Would you want to play a fast shoot-em-up game with a slow song playing in the background? Probably not. And when you're playing a game where you need to pay attention to a text bubble or a tricky puzzle, you might not want a loud, speedy song to distract you from thinking.

Kodu Game Lab has a lot of different music that can be played in your game. And you're not limited to just one style of music, either. You can easily change the background music during the actual game. If you have a game that changes speed (such as finding a bunch of stars or coins and then having to fight some bad guys to get to them), you could have a slower song playing at first and have it change to a faster-paced song when the fighting starts.

I show you how to do this later in the chapter, but right now I want you to take a listen to all the different styles of music that are available in Kodu Game Lab. To do this, I want you to add Kodu to a new game world and program him as shown in Figure 14.1.

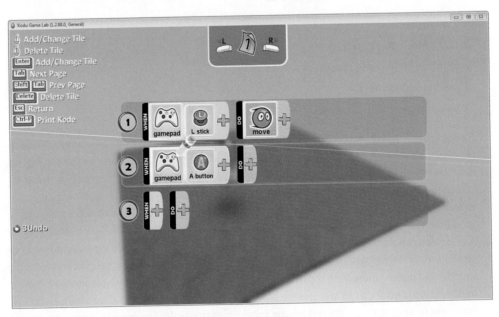

FIGURE 14.1   A simple program for Kodu to hear some music.

1. Add the basic programming to move Kodu around on the screen. I use this later when I introduce you to sound effects, so you might as well go ahead and add movement control for a game controller or mouse/keyboard combo.

2. Add a bit of programming that will let you press the left mouse button or button A on a game controller.

As you can see in Figure 14.1, I'll be using the game controller's left joystick for movement control and button A to control sound effects a bit later.

Now I want you to add an Always tile to Programming Row 3. Click the When box, then select the More pie slice, and then choose the Always pie slice shown in Figure 14.2.

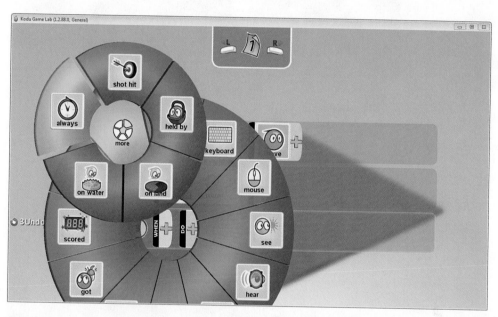

FIGURE 14.2   The Always tile will be used to assign a game soundtrack.

> **NOTE**
>
> You might be wondering whether the Always tile is even necessary. If you leave the When box blank, any programming you add to the Do box will always be executed (unless the Do row is indented beneath an existing programming row; in that case, it will be executed only if the condition in the row above is executed). It's good programming technique, however, to add the Always tile. It helps you remember that the programming in the Do box will always be executed during a game. But should you see some programming in the Do box with nothing in its matching When box, it has the same effect as if an Always tile were placed there.

Now it's time to select a style of music for the game's soundtrack. Click the Do button, then select the Actions pie slice, and then click on the Play tile shown in Figure 14.3.

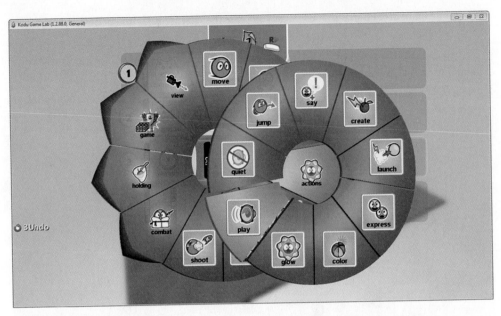

FIGURE 14.3 The Play tile is what assigns music and sound effects to be played.

Click the plus sign (**+**) to the right of the Play tile and you'll see a pie menu appear like the one in Figure 14.4.

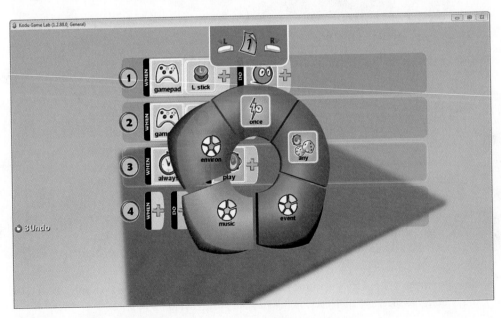

FIGURE 14.4 This pie menu offers music and sound effects by category.

Music and sound effects are kept separate here. The Event pie slice is where you'll find sound effects, and we return to that category a bit later. For now, let's focus on the Music pie slice shown in Figure 14.4. This is where both slow and fast-paced music can be found, so go ahead and click that pie slice and you'll see additional categories appear, as shown in Figure 14.5.

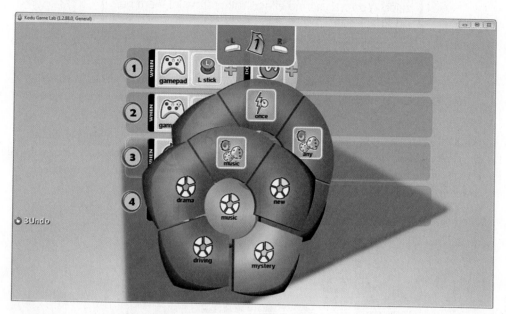

FIGURE 14.5   Music is divided up into four categories.

Rover: I also see some tiles that have dice in them. What are those?

Kodu: Those tiles can be selected to have random music or sound effects played.

Rover: That sounds like it would make a lot of noise!

Kodu: The random tile might be useful for music, but I agree that using it to play random sound effects might get annoying to players. It's probably best to always select a game's sound effects rather than let them be selected randomly.

There are four categories of music: New, Mystery, Driving, and Drama. The music found in the Mystery and Drama categories tends to be a little slower and quieter; the music in the New and Driving categories is definitely faster and, at times, louder.

I click the Drama pie slice to see what's inside. Figure 14.6 shows me that I have two options: Drama A and Drama B. I can listen to Drama A by moving the mouse pointer or cursor over its pie slice. If I move the mouse pointer over Drama B, the Drama A music stops playing and I begin to hear the Drama B music.

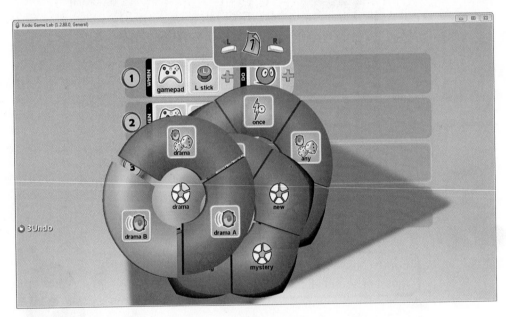

FIGURE 14.6   Move your mouse pointer or cursor over a music tile to hear it played.

By playing the music (or sound effect) when you move the mouse pointer or cursor over the pie slice, you can hear the music or effect without actually selecting it and adding it to the program.

I want something with a faster pace, so I go back to the New pie slice and see what's in there. Figure 14.7 shows that there are seven different pieces of music plus the Omni pie slice that randomly moves between all seven of these music selections.

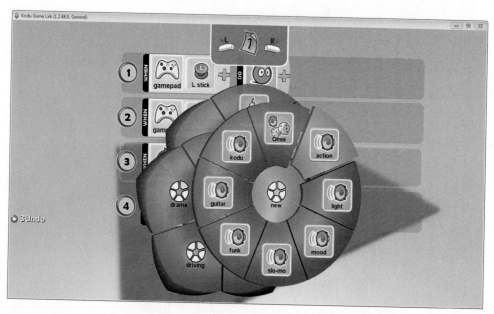

FIGURE 14.7   The New music category has seven fast-paced soundtracks available.

I encourage you to listen to each of them so you'll know what each music style sounds like. After you're done, go and listen to the Mystery, Driving, and Drama categories as well. The Music category has 15 different styles of music in all, so I'm confident you'll find something that sounds good and matches the style of your game. For me, I like the sound of Action, and I've added it to my program, as shown in Figure 14.8.

CAUTION

I've added the soundtrack to Kodu's programming, but I could easily have added it to any other object in my final game. Don't get carried away adding a unique musical soundtrack to every object, however. All music that is programmed with the Always tile will start up when the game begins, so if you've got Kodu programmed for one song, Rover programmed for a different song, and maybe a saucer programmed for another unique song, your game is going to be loud and probably obnoxious to players. Pick one song and stick with it or change the song later in the game. And remember, if a character is removed from the game (such as a saucer being destroyed by missiles), its music will stop when that character vanishes. If you want music to always be playing, consider adding that song to something like an invulnerable rock or tree that cannot be destroyed. (You learn how to do this later in the chapter.)

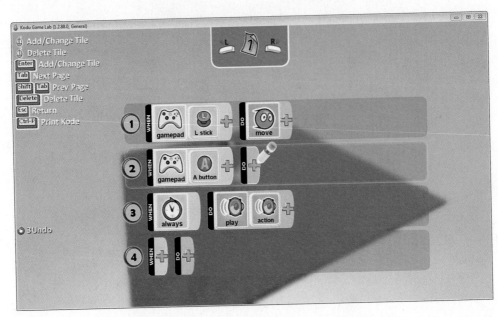

FIGURE 14.8   Kodu has his own musical soundtrack playing in the background.

Programming Background Noise for Your World

A variety of music is available in Kodu Game Lab, but you're not required to include it in your games. I've played games that have no music in them at all, but they do offer up some background sounds that still add to the quality of the game.

Imagine for a moment that you've created a two-player game with Kodu fighting Cycle. I've created a small world shown in Figure 14.9 where I've placed Kodu and Cycle.

Kodu and Cycle will chase each other around the field, trying to hit each other with missiles. Kodu and Cycle both have 100 hit points each, and missiles will do five points of damage when they hit. Both Kodu and Cycle will have their health bar displayed over their heads.

I add sound effects later in this chapter that give both players audible clues about special in-game items that appear. Because I don't want players to miss these sounds, I select music to be played, but I have some sounds playing in the background. I make my selections from the Environ pie slice, shown back in Figure 14.4.

I once again open up Kodu's program and remove the Action music tile and replace it with one of the Environ options shown in Figure 14.10.

As you can see in Figure 14.10, I have five options: Mars, Meadow, City, Forest, and Ocean. Move your mouse pointer or cursor over these and listen carefully. They're not loud, but they can give your game a subtle background sound rather than nothing at all.

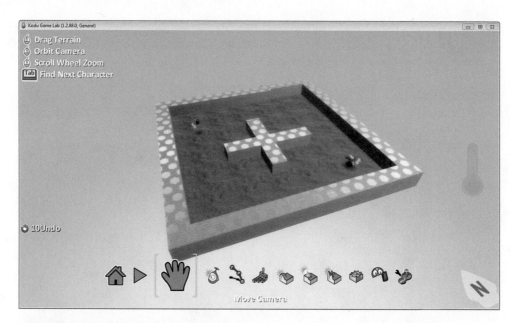

FIGURE 14.9   Let's get ready to rumble!

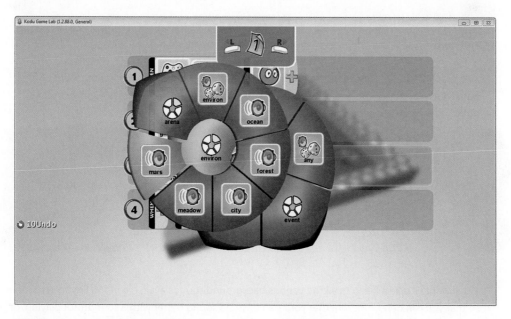

FIGURE 14.10   The Environ pie slice offers up background sounds that aren't as distracting.

The background sounds that I'm interested in, however, can be found in the Arena pie slice shown in Figure 14.11. Click it and you'll see seven unique background sounds (Arena A through Arena G) plus the Random Arena tile (with the dice).

FIGURE 14.11   Add some cheering to your game with the Arena sounds.

I like all of them, so I choose the Random Arena tile that will randomly change throughout the game and play any of the seven Arena sound effect tiles. Figure 14.12 shows that I've updated Kodu's program to use the Random Arena tile.

> **NOTE**
>
> Later in the chapter, you learn how to add sound effects. Sound effects, when played, do not stop the background music from playing. Because I've assigned the background sound to the Always tile in Kodu's program, that background sound will continue to play. The exception to this rule is if I should move to a different page (such as Page 2) where I use a different Always tile to specify different music.

You'll want to take a listen to all the various background sounds available in the Environ pie menu so that you can determine whether your game would sound better with a soundtrack playing, or just a simple repeating background sound.

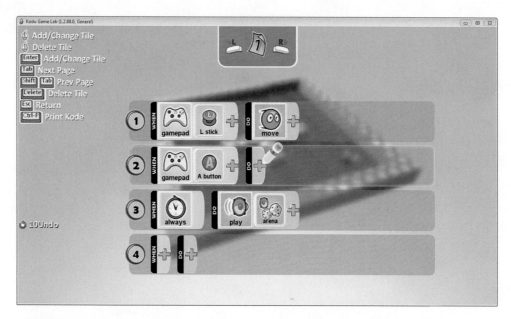

FIGURE 14.12   Kodu's program is updated to have cheering fans in the background.

Adding Sound Effects

As I continue to develop this game, I've given Cycle and Kodu the capability to fire missiles. When I press the Play button to test my game, I can steer Kodu with the game controller and Cycle with the WASD keys. Both can fire missiles at one another. And I can hear the crowd cheering in the background. So far, so good!

I added the walls in the center of the field so that Kodu and Cycle can't just shoot directly at one another. They'll have to maneuver around and try to get in a shot on their opponent. The game ends when one of the player's hit points reach zero. You can see the additional programming for this in Figure 14.13 for Cycle. (I've also added the same programming to Kodu.)

By itself, the game is sort of fun. But I think it can be made better by adding some special items to the game that appear at random points in time. I add a few trees and rocks scattered around the game world, and I'll use one of these objects to control a hidden timer that counts up in one-second increments when the game begins. (You can refer back to Chapter 8, "Dangerous Targets: Programming Enemies That Fire Back," for the steps used to create a timer/scoreboard.)

Figure 14.14 shows the programming I've added to one of the trees that will use the A Score tile. Every second that ticks by, the A scoreboard increases by one point. I'll use this to schedule some surprises in the game at random times.

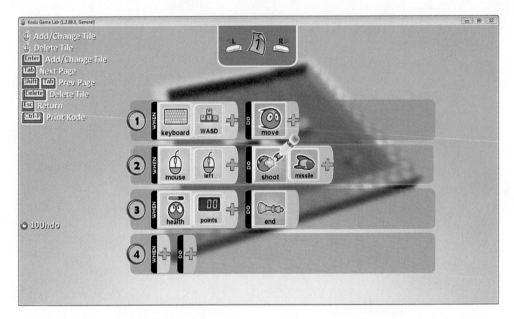

FIGURE 14.13 The game ends when Kodu's or Cycle's hit points reach zero.

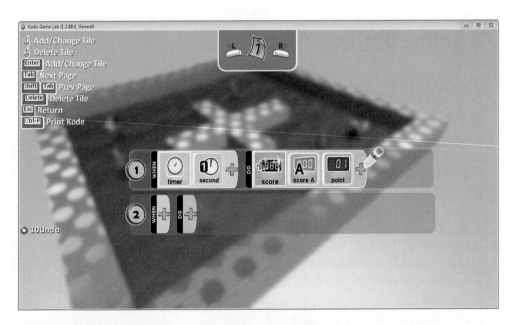

FIGURE 14.14 Configuring a hidden timer to allow for in-game surprises.

Now it's time to add one of those surprises. I've placed four trees on the map, and each tree will release a special item at a random time in the game. But before I do this, I need to make a creatable. As you might remember from Chapter 11, "Good Game Design, Part I: Tips and Tricks for Better Game Programming," *creatables* are objects that can be spawned (created) in a game over and over again. Every creatable has identical characteristics such as hit points or speed.

In this case, I want to create a special healing apple that will be created by two of the trees at random times. I want one to appear every 10 to 15 seconds, and I use the hidden A scoreboard to trigger the appearances of the healing apples.

But first, I need to create the healing apple creatable. I do this by first using the Object tool to drop an apple on the terrain and then right-clicking the apple to add its program (see Figure 14.15).

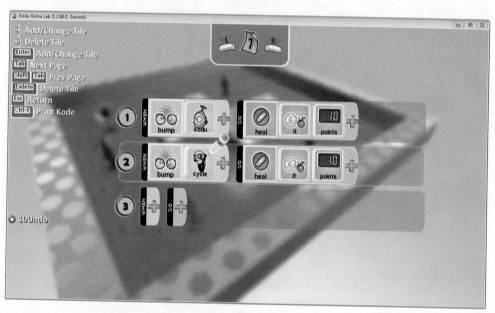

FIGURE 14.15   The healing apple program adds up to 10 hit points when collected.

As you can see in Figure 14.15, I specified that Kodu bumping the apple heals Kodu for 10 points. I copied Programming Row 1 into Programming Row 2 and changed the Kodu tile to the Cycle tile. That's all the programming needed for the healing apple, but I still need to make it a creatable. To do that, I right-click the apple, select Change Settings, and then turn on the Creatable option in the scrolling list by clicking its Power button (which turns green when turned on).

> **TIP**
>
> You can find the Heal tile in the Combat pie menu. Just click the Do box, then click on Combat, and you'll see the Heal tile available in the pie menu that appears.

Remember that a creatable will not be visible on the screen when you start the game. Instead, the creatable object will disappear, and only copies of it will show up when you program them to be created. To do this, I've opened up a tree object and added the program you see in Figure 14.16.

> **NOTE**
> If you're wondering when I'll be getting to the sound effects, I'm close. Just be patient for a few more programming steps.

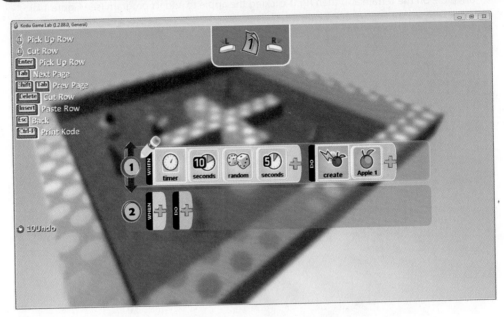

FIGURE 14.16 Program a tree to drop a healing apple every 10 to 15 seconds.

Take a look at Figure 14.16 again and let me explain the tiles. First, the When box simply says "When the timer has counted 10 plus 1–5 (random) seconds," I am specifying, by placing the Random tile after the 10 Seconds tile, that whatever amount follows the Random tile will be added to the 10 Seconds tile. The Random tile generates a value of 0, 1, 2, 3, 4, or 5, and then adds that to 10. So, this bit of programming allows me to specify a random amount of time passing of 10 to 15 seconds.

The Do box simply uses the Create tile (which you learned about in Chapter 11, to drop in my healing apple creatable (called Apple 1 here).

But I don't just want the healing apple to appear. I want a clear and obvious sound effect to be triggered to let the players know that a special item has appeared. To do this, I add some more programming to the tree object so that a sound effect is triggered when the healing apple is created.

Figure 14.17 shows this additional programming; notice that I've ignored the When box because I've indented Programming Row 2 underneath Programming Row 1. When the apple is created, the Play tile plays the Pow tile. (I've added the Once tile just to be specific, but by default the Pow tile will play only one time for every apple drop.)

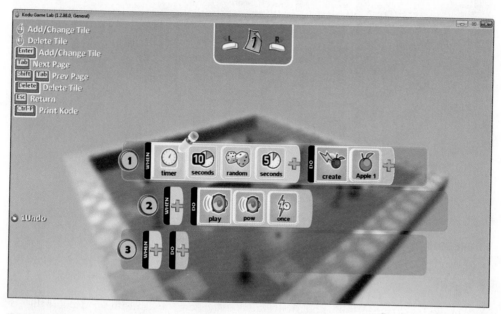

FIGURE 14.17 An easy-to-recognize sound will be heard when a healing apple appears.

I chose the Pow sound, but you can choose any sound you want. Just make certain that it's a sound that will be obvious to the players who might be concentrating on avoiding and shooting at their opponent, and not paying attention to dropped apples!

Before I move on to the next section and show you another use for sound effects, let me show you the final bit of programming that's required for Kodu (and Cycle) to obtain the health benefits of picking up a healing apple.

Take a look at Figure 14.18 and Programming Rows 5 and 6. (You need to copy these rows to the Cycle's program, as well.)

Programming Row 5 controls what happens when Kodu bumps into an apple: He grabs it. Easy enough! Programming Row 6, however, shows what happens to that apple. I want it to disappear (as if Kodu ate the apple) and not have Kodu carrying it around, so I've added a When box that says "When Kodu gets the apple," and the Do box has the Vanish tile and the It tile to make the apple disappear.

Try it out! Fire a missile at Kodu, and then wait 10 to 15 seconds for a healing apple to appear (and for the sound effect you programmed). Steer Kodu to the apple and watch the apple disappear at the same time as Kodu's health bar increases a bit.

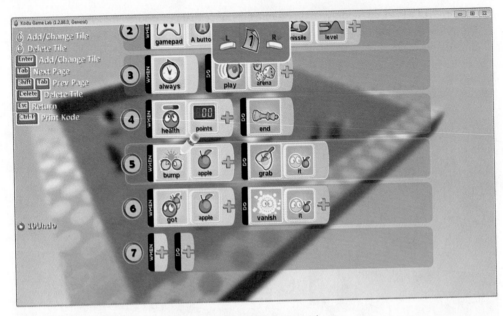

FIGURE 14.18 When an apple is bumped (picked up), it vanishes.

TIP

Why didn't I just indent the Do box from Programming Row 6 underneath 5 and ignore the Got tile? Try it! If you don't specify what Kodu "got," the only option for the Do box's Vanish tile is Me (meaning Kodu… and the game ends because when Kodu vanishes, his hit points drop to zero).

Remember to copy Programming Rows 5 and 6 to Cycle so that when Cycle bumps an apple, it receives the 10 healing points and makes the apple vanish at the same time.

NOTE

I created only a healing apple for this demo game. If you want, create additional in-game items that can help (or hurt) players who pick them up. You could easily add a bit of risk to the game by popping up a hurtful apple (that looks like the healing apple) that removes hit points. Players must decide if it's worth the risk to grab an apple; they won't know if it's a healing or hurtful apple.

Using Sound Effects for Player Conditions

Before this chapter ends, let's consider another possible use for sound effects that can provide players with audible feedback (as opposed to visual feedback) as they play your game.

Would you like to make your players' hearts race a little bit when their hit points drop below a certain value? Here's how you can use sound effects that are triggered based on conditions in the game (such as time elapsed, hit points remaining, or whether a player is crossing a dangerous territory such as water or a certain color of terrain).

Let's start with adding some additional programming to Kodu. Figure 14.19 shows that I've added Programming Row 7, which monitors Kodu's hit points.

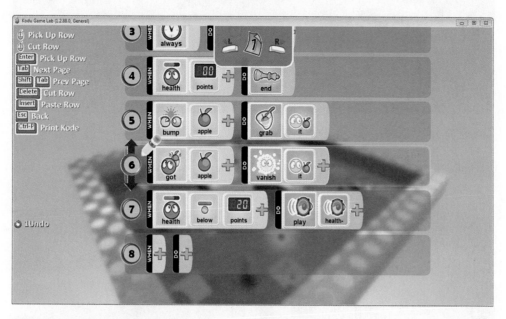

FIGURE 14.19   When Kodu's hit points reach 20, sound an alarm.

Here, I've added the Play tile. When I click the plus sign (+) to the right of the Play tile and select the Event pie menu, I then select the Arcade pie slice, and then the Health- (minus) tile. This sound effect sounds ominous (a downward zooming sound) that lets players know they need to find a healing apple or try a little harder to avoid their opponent.

Here's another example of using sound effects to alert players to danger. Figure 14.20 shows that I've added patches of dangerous hot coals to the playing field in many locations. You'll also see that as Kodu rolls over the hot coals, his hit points are dropping fast.

FIGURE 14.20 It's not a good idea to roll over hot coals.

Figure 14.21 shows Programming Row 8, which I added to apply damage to Kodu when he rolls over the hot coals.

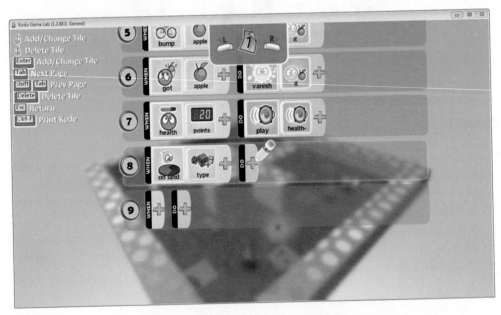

FIGURE 14.21 This programming row checks what type of terrain Kodu is rolling over.

To create this bit of programming, do the following:

1. Click the When box and click the More pie menu.

2. Choose the On Land tile.

3. Click the + to the right of the On Land tile and click the Types option, shown in Figure 14.22.

FIGURE 14.22 The Types option lets you specify the type of terrain.

4. All the various types of terrain will appear; I'll choose the one I selected to represent the hot coals.

5. Indent Programming Row 9 under Row 8, and for the When box, add the Timer tile and the 0.25 Seconds tile, as shown in Figure 14.23.

6. For the Do box, click the Combat pie slice and select the Damage tile.

7. Click the + to the right of the Damage tile and select a suitable amount of damage that will occur every second Kodu sits on the hot coals (I picked 2 points), as shown in Figure 14.24.

If you're wondering why I specified that damage would occur every 0.25 seconds, it's because some computers run faster than others, and while Kodu is sitting on hot coals, more damage can occur in a shorter time period on a faster computer. With this damage rate (2 points per 0.25 seconds), the game remains fair no matter what speed the computer the game is running on.

Test the game. Roll Kodu over some hot coals and watch his health bar.

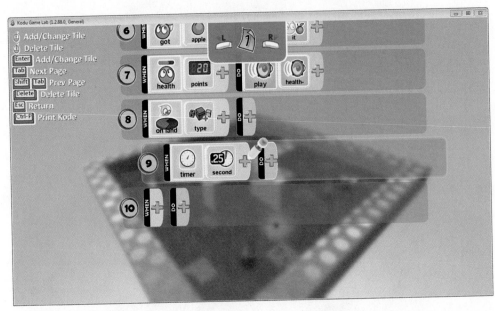

FIGURE 14.23   Programming the When box to perform an action every 0.25 seconds.

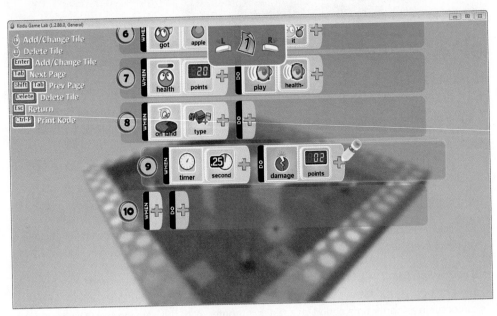

FIGURE 14.24   Every 0.25 seconds Kodu is on the coals, 2 points of damage occur.

Now, the damage that is applied by rolling over the hot coals already produces its own sound effect, but it is subtle and can easily be missed during the heat of battle. I want to add a sound effect that is clear and unmistakable. Figure 14.25 shows that I've also indented Programming Row 10 under Programming Row 8 and am using the Play tile to trigger the Shield- (minus) tile. Test it out. You'll definitely know something's wrong when you hear that Shield- sound effect triggered!

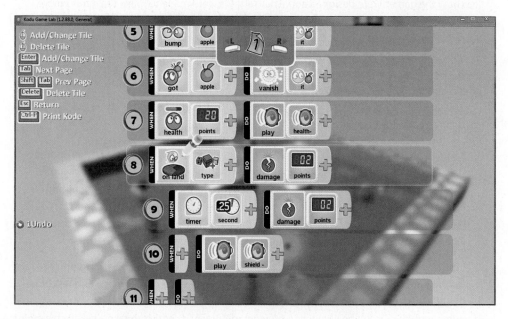

FIGURE 14.25   This alarm will remind the player to get off the hot coals!

As you've seen, sound effects and music can prove very useful when you're programming a game. You can do all sorts of things with them:

○ Trigger a sound effect when the game timer is close to zero. (Time is running out!)

○ Use a sound effect to alert players when a game's goal has changed (such as moving from finding a coin to having to fight some bad guys).

○ Program certain music to play only when specific conditions exist (happy music when Kodu is at full health and sad music when Kodu's hit points are running out).

○ Assign one sound effect to a beneficial item (such as a healing apple) and a different sound effect to a harmful item (such as a hurtful apple). Good players can figure out the change in sound to help them pick up only beneficial items.

○ Assign a different style of music to each player and have only the music of the highest-scoring player being played in the background; as scores change, so will the music.

Moving On

At the end of this book, you'll find four sample games documented. You'll also get some insight into how the games were designed and what settings were made to make the games more enjoyable. But I won't be able to show you every pie menu and every little setting that is selected, and that includes music and sound effects. Instead, I hope you've followed along in this chapter and discovered just how easy it is to add music and sound effects to your own games. When you reach the four sample games, you should be able to easily figure out how and why certain sound effects and music should be picked and added to a game.

Now, before you continue on to the next chapter, I've got a few special challenges for you that involve the hot coals and healing apples game you saw in this chapter:

1. Kodu and Cycle are equal in speed, missile damage, and hit points. Try to change up these settings so that each player has a unique power that the other player lacks. For example, consider making Cycle move faster than Kodu but reduce either the damage of his missiles or his hit points. Likewise, you can decrease Kodu's speed, increase his hit points, and make his missiles extremely dangerous by increasing the damage they deal. The goal is to create a game where each player will develop a unique strategy for winning.

2. I showed you how to create a healing apple. Now create the hurtful apple. Program the trees to give out both types of apples at the same pace (remove the randomness) and test how this affects game play. Do players avoid the apples completely? If so, consider increasing the number of hit points a healing apple provides; definitely incentive to take a risk if a player is low on hit points! Another option is to create the bad apple, a big, black apple that, when picked up, damages BOTH players. It's a nice little twist to the game that can benefit a player who might have a lot more hit points than her opponent.

3. Experiment with using new pages to change the music. You've seen how easy it is to copy the programming from one page to another, so all you need to do is add a new programming row that checks a condition (hit points less than 10?) and then switches to a different page with music. You can switch back to Page 1 when the hit points go above a certain level (hit points greater than 40) and the music changes back to the original tune.

Be sure to return to the Home Menu button and save any work you've done before selecting Exit to Main Menu. Don't forget to add some additional information to the Description field.

15

Good Game Design, Part 2: More Tips and Tricks for Great Games

In This Chapter

○ Better Game Programming

○ More World Design Tips and Tricks

○ More Game Management Tips and Tricks

○ More Object Programming Tips and Tricks

Earlier in the book, I broke Chapter 11, "Good Game Design, Part 1: Tips and Tricks for Better Game Programming," into three sections, with each section covering some tricks and tips related to world design, game management, and programming. In this chapter, I offer you some more information related to those three categories.

Better Game Programming

This chapter is all about tips and tricks for improving your game design. It's by no means complete, but hopefully you'll find some advice that will help you gain proficiency with Kodu Game Lab and get that dream game in your head out in the real world for others to play.

I'm breaking this chapter into three sections. The first section suggests ways to build your game's world before you populate it with objects, obstacles, targets, and traps.

In the second section, you learn how to track your progress as you build games; although programming is fun, it can sometimes get confusing with all the changes and updates and new objects you add to a game. You need to establish a method for managing your games as they develop, so don't skip this section.

Finally, the third section offers some advice about programming the objects that inhabit your game world. You'll find this advice especially useful during the numerous tests that you'll run on your game before sharing it with the world.

By the way, I've broken up the tips and advice information into three chapters (11, 15, and 19), so you'll find even more help a bit later in Chapter 19, "Good Game Design, Part 3: Giving Players a Great Experience."

More World Design Tips and Tricks

You've probably become quite confident in your world-building abilities at this point. If you've been following along with the examples in this book, you've had a chance to use all the various tools to add, raise, lower, and smooth the terrain. You've probably discovered some shortcuts and tricks of your own that have helped you create some unique and eye-catching worlds.

In this section, I offer just a couple of ideas about how you can create two fun and different game worlds for your games. I show you how I set them up and modify them, and then I leave it to you to further tweak them to fit the needs of your own games.

The Maze

Let's start a layout that's always fun: a maze. Take a look at Figure 15.1. It's got an unusual mix of terrain consisting of squares of different colors.

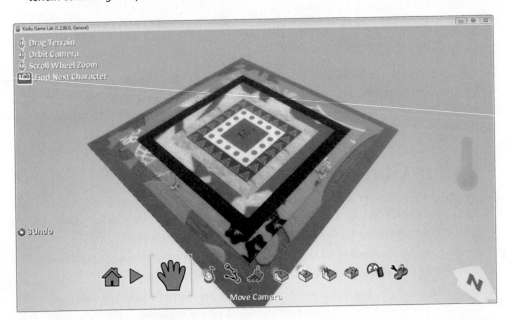

FIGURE 15.1 Time to build a maze.

To start my maze, I started with a large square of green terrain. Next, I changed the color and shrank the brush size just a bit using the Left arrow key. Remember, you can increase the size of the brush you are using to apply terrain by tapping the right arrow key and shrink it using the left arrow key. I continued in this manner, adding a slightly smaller square on top of the previous square until I ended up with 10 different terrain colors.

I raise every other color so that I get the series of walls shown in Figure 15.2. I'm using the Up/Down tool to do this.

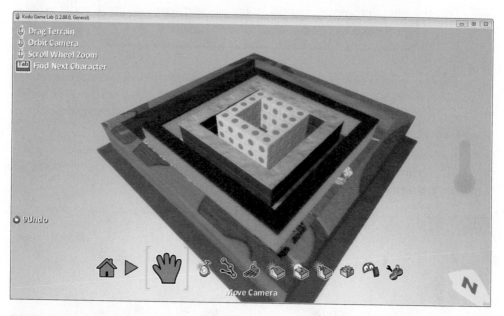

FIGURE 15.2   Raise walls to create the beginnings of a maze.

Rover: Why is the programmer using all these different colors for walls?

Kodu: I'm guessing that it might be difficult to see the various heights of the walls if they were all the same color.

Rover: But isn't that what makes a maze more challenging?

Kodu: Yes, it makes a maze more challenging to solve, but not necessarily to create. Using the different colors makes it easier to see all the different doors and pathways as the maze is being designed.

The player starts in the center of the maze and works outward to the exit. I need to remove portions of the walls to create doorways that will allow a player to move from the center of the maze, and to do this I once again use the Up/Down tool, but I shrink the brush size down so that I'm erasing only a small amount of each wall.

I also add tricks to the maze by growing portions of the nonwalls. These will create dead ends that players will encounter if they go the wrong direction. Figure 15.3 shows that I've added a series of doors and dead ends throughout my maze to make it more tricky.

FIGURE 15.3   Doors and dead ends are what make a maze fun.

All that's left now is to use the Magic Brush to change the color of the maze so the walls and floor match; this makes it much more tricky to navigate.

> **TIP**
>
> Remember to use the Alt button on the keyboard to pick an existing color so that you can apply it to other terrain.

Figure 15.4 shows that I've modified the maze so that it is all the same color/texture and the center of the maze matches the outer grassy ring.

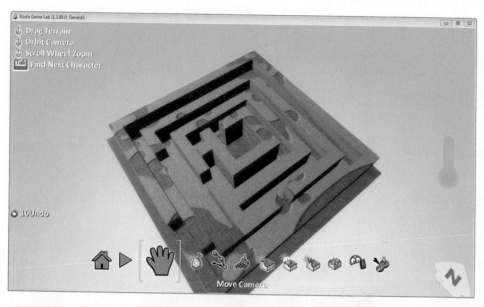

FIGURE 15.4   Coloring the maze a unique color, distinct from the surrounding terrain.

You can tweak the maze a little more by using the Up/Down tool to get all the walls the same height. I've only created a very small maze here, but given enough time, you could make one very large maze that could take hours to solve.

What are some other fun things you can do with a maze game? Here are some suggestions:

○ Instruct the player to zoom in so the game is in first-person perspective, and you've got a maze that will feel like the player is actually part of the game. (With the game controller, the player can squeeze and hold the right trigger to zoom in until the view changes to first person. If the player is using a mouse, the mouse wheel can be used to zoom in to first-person view.)

○ If your maze is large enough and has enough places to hide, you can place some enemies that might shoot at the player and steal away some hit points.

○ Place objects in doorways that will only disappear if you present them with the correct object: a star, coin, or a magic apple. Hide these objects throughout the maze, but be sure to test your game often to make certain players can get to the special objects.

The Stadium

Here's a fun game world for you. How about dropping your games into a full-fledged stadium, complete with robot fans? You'll want a grass playing field, of course, and plenty of seating for all the fans to view the game. It's put together like the maze, but with a few differences. Here's how you can do it.

First, I define the playing area and separate it from the stands. Figure 15.5 shows that I've added more grassy terrain as well as the side for the stands. (You can easily add another set of stands on the opposite side, or all four sides.)

> **TIP**
>
> It's often easier to lay out a game world by looking at it from straight above, or what's called the *bird's eye view*. Use the Move Camera tool to rotate your world so that you're looking at it from above, as shown in Figure 15.5.

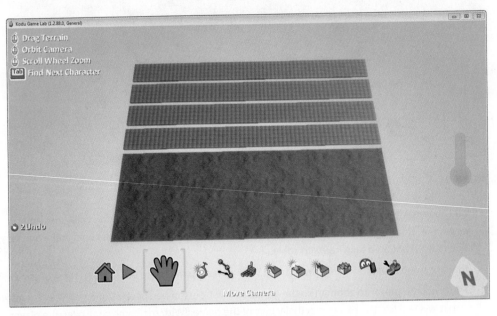

FIGURE 15.5   My stadium is all laid out with grass and stand locations.

Once again, using the Up/Down tool and the Magic Brush shape, I can raise the stands so that the tallest is in back and the shortest is in front (nearest the grass playing field).

Figure 15.6 shows that I've staggered my stands so that they mimic the seating you'd see at a stadium.

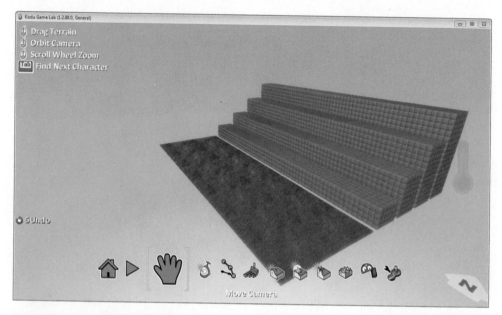

FIGURE 15.6   Seating for all the game fans.

Finally, I'll add some extra elements to complete the stadium look. Figure 15.7 shows that I've added a few thin chalk lines on the field, as well as a nice big scoreboard. Oh, and I added dozens of adoring fans who have showed up to cheer on the big game.

> **TIP**
>
> Place a few unique objects such as Kodu, Saucer, Cycle, and Rover, and then use the Copy and Paste feature to spread them around the stands. You can even go back and modify their color for a more diverse looking crowd.

That's a very simple stadium, but you can easily increase it in size depending on the game field you need. Place stands on all four sides, two sides, or maybe even in the middle (for a racetrack, for example).

> **CAUTION**
>
> Take a look at Figure 15.7 and you'll notice a temperature gauge that runs along the right side of the screen. As you add objects to a game, the gauge will fill up. This indicates how much processing power your game is taking to actually run. If it gets too full, your game will run sluggish or not at all. In Figure 15.7 it's a bit high because I've added in all those fans. I can reduce the gauge a bit by removing fans.

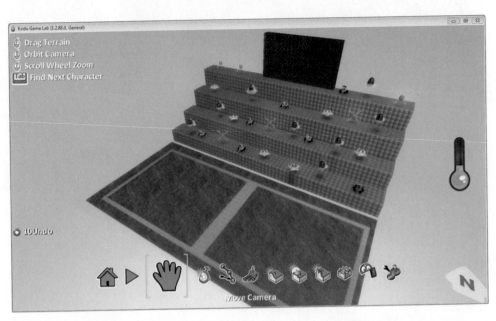

FIGURE 15.7   The finished stadium is now ready for a game to be added.

What else can you do with a stadium? Here are some suggestions:

○ Have some fun. Program one of the fans in the stands to occasionally make a dash around the field. You'll need to program a timer in (or use some programming that randomly picks a time) and a path for the fan to follow. You might see some interesting things happen when a fan runs on the field in the middle of a game!

○ Do you have a favorite sport? Try re-creating that sport field in Kodu Game Lab. Football, soccer, baseball, and many more game fields can all be duplicated. You might not be able to program the actual rules of these games in Kodu Game Lab, but it can be fun to try and create games that will work well when played on a particular field.

Your game worlds will only get more fun and crazy as you gain experience using all the terrain editing tools. Later, in Chapter 18, "Join the Community: Online Help and Sharing Games," I show you where you can go for even more inspiration and ideas to improve your game worlds.

More Game Management Tips and Tricks

Back in Chapter 11, I explained to you how providing a good name and description would be helpful to you in keeping the various versions of your game design organized.

Rover: Why not just have one game file and keep saving to it after you make changes?

Kodu: What happens if you make 20 changes and then realize that the fifth or sixth change needs to be undone? That would require a lot of Undo actions!

Rover: Okay, I see your point. But won't saving all these different versions of your game take up a lot of space on the computer?

Kodu: Not at all. These files are small, and you could have a dozen versions of a game and still need less than 2MB of storage space.

One of the best habits you can develop as a Kodu Game Lab programmer is to save new versions of your developing game as the game increases in complexity. For example, here's a progression of a game, *Maze of Mischief*, and how each of its versions differs:

○ **Maze of Mischief 1.0**: Basic terrain placed and Kodu added with steering controls.

○ **Maze of Mischief 2.0**: Added maze north of Kodu's position. No doors or dead ends added yet.

○ **Maze of Mischief 3.0**: First placement of doors and dead ends added. Player testing proved too easy to navigate maze.

○ **Maze of Mischief 4.0**: Removed dead ends and left doors. Added programming for timer countdown.

○ **Maze of Mischief 5.0**: Changed placement of dead ends. Player testing proved much more challenging and fun.

○ **Maze of Mischief 6.0**: Added a single enemy character that listens for Kodu and moves to his position. Testing sensitivity of hearing.

As you can see, each of the saved versions adds only one or two new elements (objects, terrain, programming, and so on). Should I find that I don't like the placement of the new dead ends in version 5.0, I can open up version 4.0 and start over with testing different locations for dead ends.

> ### CAUTION
>
> If you follow this method, it's quite possible you can end up with 10, 15, or even 30 versions of a game you're developing. It all depends on the complexity of the game and how many versions you want to save. Obviously, the earlier versions will be less complex and have fewer settings and programming to modify, but later versions can get quite complicated, with dozens of objects that all have their own programming (and possibly multiple pages).

As the versions of a game start increasing, you might find at times that you can't remember what value you assigned when a target is hit by a missile or how much time you added to a timer block for it to test for releasing a creatable. You can go and right-click an object, hunt for the page or tile you need, and find the information you lack, but you might also have to spend some time clicking and clicking and clicking... especially if you're having to hunt for differences between versions. Did version 2.0 have Kodu doing two points of damage to that saucer? Did I increase that damage to three points in version 3.0?

When these kinds of problems start popping up, Kodu Game Labs has a really cool feature built in that can help you quickly navigate your game's programming without all the click-click-clicking. Here's how it works:

1. Open up a version of your game.

2. Click the Home Menu button.

3. Select the Print Kode For Level option shown in Figure 15.8.

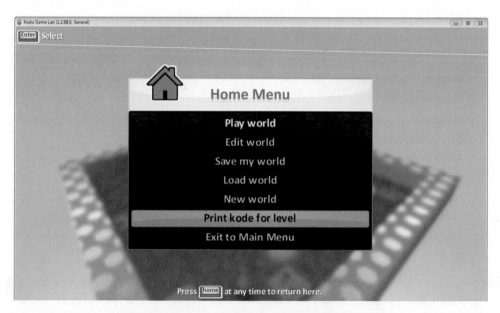

FIGURE 15.8 The Print Kode For Level option found on the Home Menu.

> **NOTE**
> The Print Kode For Level option requires a printer to be configured for the computer you are using.

Your printer will start spinning and out will come something that looks like the output shown in Figure 15.9.

```
TITLE : Saucer Hunt Extreme v02
CREATOR : JamesFloydKelly
DESCRIPTION :
Date : 1/14/2013 6:39 PM
========

Kodu 1
  Page 1
    1   When keyboard WASD -- Do move forward quickly
    2   When keyboard Space -- Do shoot missile forward
    3   When shot hit saucer -- Do score 2 points blue

Kodu 2
  Page 1
    1   When keyboard Arrows -- Do move forward quickly
    2   When mouse left -- Do shoot missile forward
    3   When shot hit saucer -- Do score 2 points white

Saucer 1
  Page 1
    1   When always -- Do move on path slowly yellow
    2   When health 0 points -- Do boom
```

FIGURE 15.9   A text breakdown of your game's programming.

As you can see, your program name and version number are included in the printout, along with the current date. Each object (Kodu 1, Kodu 2, Saucer 1, Saucer 2, and so on) will have its programming explained using the simple When/Do format, and each page of an object will be listed. Figure 15.9 shows an extremely simple Kode listing for version 2.0 of *Saucer Hunt Extreme*. Take a look at Figure 15.10 and you'll see a snippet of the Kode for a much more advanced game, *Mars Rover: Discovery*.

This printout was 11 pages long, and the Rover object alone used 9 of the maximum 12 pages! Kode also exists for the various rocks that Rover inspects in the game, as well as the Sputnik option that scans the terrain before the game begins.

```
TITLE : Mars Rover: Discovery
CREATOR : mblackmore
DESCRIPTION : Your mission is to search out sedimentary rocks and drill them to score BIG points. Laser rock:

Choose your route, avoid hazards, and explore the terrain.

How high can you score in 90 seconds?

Date : 1/14/2013 6:42 PM
========

Rover 1
  Page 1
    1   When scored orange equals 2 points -- Do follow
    2   When scored orange 0 points -- Do switch page 11
    3   When scored grey above 0 points -- Do switch page 5
    4   When on land type 17 not -- Do inline page 3
    5     When keyboard Up -- Do move north slowly slowly slowly
    6     When gamepad L stick up -- Do move north slowly slowly slowly
    7     When keyboard Down -- Do move south slowly slowly slowly
    8     When gamepad L stick down -- Do move south slowly slowly slowly
    9     When always -- Do move east slowly slowly slowly
   10   When on land type 17 -- Do
   11     When keyboard Up -- Do move north slowly
   12     When gamepad L stick up -- Do move north slowly
   13     When keyboard Down -- Do move south slowly
   14     When gamepad L stick down -- Do move south slowly
   15     When always -- Do move east slowly
   16   When gamepad B button -- Do beam
   17   When keyboard B -- Do beam
   18   When bump Sedimentary -- Do
   19     When always -- Do set score 1 point yellow
   20     When always -- Do switch page 12
   21   When bump Igneous -- Do
   22     When always -- Do set score 1 point yellow
   23     When always -- Do switch page 12
   24   When beamed Sedimentary -- Do score 50 points white once
   25     When always -- Do play points
   26   When beamed Igneous -- Do score 20 points white once
   27     When always -- Do play points
   28   When gamepad Y button -- Do say
          say verb text
          Press <X> to Inspect and <B> to Beam.
   29   When gamepad A button -- Do say
          say verb text
          Press <X> to Inspect and <B> to Beam.
   30   When gamepad R stick -- Do say
          say verb text
          Use <LS> to steer.
  Page 3
    1   When scored black below 2 points -- Do score black 1 point
    2   When scored black equals 1 point -- Do say
          say verb text
          Watch out! Sand makes me go slow.
    3   When scored black equals 2 points -- Do
    4     When timer seconds second -- Do set score black 0 points
  Page 5
```

FIGURE 15.10 A bit of Kode from the *Mars Rover: Discovery* game.

TIP

If you want to play *Mars Rover: Discovery* (created by MBlackmore), open up the Home Menu, click Load World, and click the Lessons button. The *Mars Rover: Discovery* game is one of three games you can dig into to see some examples of excellent game design. (The other two are *Mars Rover: The Expedition* and *Mars Rover: Set the Course.*)

The printouts are also a great place for you to write game information such as missile damage or hit points. The world settings are not included in the Kode printout, and neither are the object settings (accessed by right-clicking an object and selecting Change Settings).

Often when I'm creating a game, I crank the damage of a missile way up or way down; this helps when testing. Sometimes I don't want to hit an enemy target with 100 hit points 20 times, with each missile doing 5 hit points worth of damage. Sometimes I just want to test what happens after the object is destroyed. In that case, I set the missile damage to 50 or 100; the Kode sheet is the ideal place to write this down so that I don't forget later to change it back to a more reasonable value in a later version of the game.

Use the Kode printouts to keep track of the changes between versions. Rather than having to open up each version to inspect the objects' programming, you can more quickly flip to the page you need and find out the details of the programming. And if you've added in the important world settings (such as whether glass walls is on or off) and object settings (hit points, for example), these sheets become even more helpful to you.

More Object Programming Tips and Tricks

You learned about using creatables back in Chapter 11, and I want to continue the discussion on this useful and important programming tool and introduce you to another programming trick. To help with this discussion, I open up version 3.0 of my *MiniWorld* game that I wrote about back in Chapter 11. Figure 15.11 shows *MiniWorld*, complete with Kodu, castle, tree, coin, and a Sputnik creatable that is created by the tree.

FIGURE 15.11   Return to *MiniWorld* (Sounds like a movie title!)

I keep this game very simple. Kodu has six goals for this game:

1. Grab the first coin to enable blip firing.

2. Take the coin to the castle gatekeeper.

3. Destroy Sputnik and release Cycle and coin.

4. Obtain a second coin.

5. Destroy Cycle.

6. Take the second coin to the castle, pay the gatekeeper, and enter the Castle.

You should be familiar enough with Kodu Game Lab programming to figure out most of these steps. The catch here is that a smart player might try and skip the step of destroying Cycle and just pick up the second coin to take it to the gatekeeper. The gatekeeper will only disappear and let Kodu into the castle after both coins are paid and Cycle is gone for good. But remember, Kodu loses the capability to fire when he's not holding a coin, so if a player tries this, it's Game Over!

You've already learned how to detect when Kodu bumps an object such as the coin, and you learned in Chapter 11 how to program Kodu to pick up the coin and hold it as he moves around.

Now let's add the gatekeeper who will take the coins that Kodu delivers. Figure 15.12 shows that I've added the burly and strong Cannon. He's not letting anyone by until they've paid two gold coins and Cycle is gone.

FIGURE 15.12 Cannon guards the castle's entrance.

Figure 15.13 shows Kodu's program that was created back in Chapter 11, but with the newly modified Programming Row 5 that simply detects when Kodu bumps Cannon. When that happens, the Do box contains one tile: Give. You can find the Give tile by clicking the Do box and then clicking the Holding pie slice that appears. Kodu can grab, drop, or give. In this instance, I want him to give the coin to Cannon.

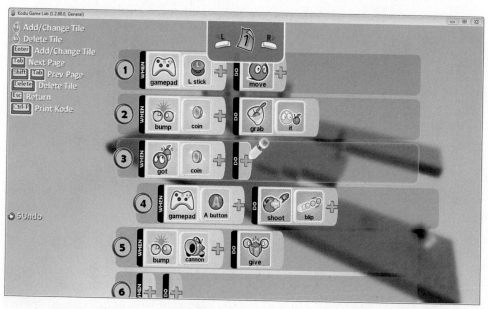

FIGURE 15.13   Program Kodu to give the coin to Cannon.

With the Give command, Cannon will actually take possession of the coin, and the coin will appear to float above his head. Now I need to add some programming that will let Cannon pocket the coin and wait for the next payment, or disappear completely.

> **NOTE**
>
> I have not added any programming that penalizes the player for firing on the gatekeeper (cannon). For a game that depends on a friendly character staying alive, you should issue both a warning (in the instructions) not to shoot at friendlies as well as program in a penalty should the player do so. Either way, if the player ends up destroying a friendly, the game will need to be restarted.

Figure 15.14 shows four programming rows that help control these actions.

1. Programming Row 1 vanishes a coin when Cannon gets one.

2. Programming Row 2 does 50 points of damage to Cannon for every coin obtained.

3. Programming Row 3 checks to see whether Cannon has only 5 hit points left. (Cannon starts out with 105 hit points.)

4. Programming Row 4 is indented under Programming Row 3 and is executed only if Cannon has 5 hit points left. If this is true, the B scoreboard is also checked to see whether it equals a value of 1 and, if so, Cannon disappears.

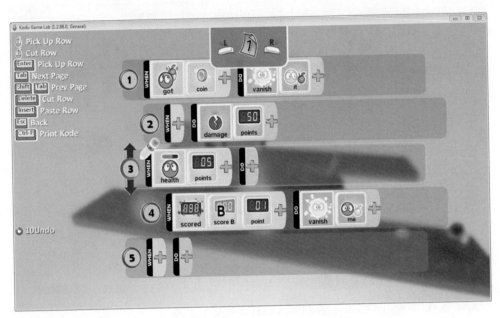

FIGURE 15.14 Program Cannon to take the coins and vanish.

> **TIP**
> When a game starts, the hidden B scoreboard automatically starts with a value of 0. When Cycle is destroyed, the B scoreboard is incremented by one point, and the B score holds a value of 1.

After testing the program to make certain this works (Kodu gives the coin to Cannon, coin disappears), it's time to return to that Sputnik creatable and program it to drop Cycle when it explodes.

In the original MiniWorld from Chapter 11, I had the Sputnik creatable programmed to create another Sputnik creatable when it was destroyed. I want to change that. As you see, a creatable can call other creatables, so I just drop a Cycle object onto the game world and make it a creatable. Figure 15.15 shows the original program. Notice Programming Row 3 that creates a new Sputnik when the current Sputnik is destroyed (hit points equal 0).

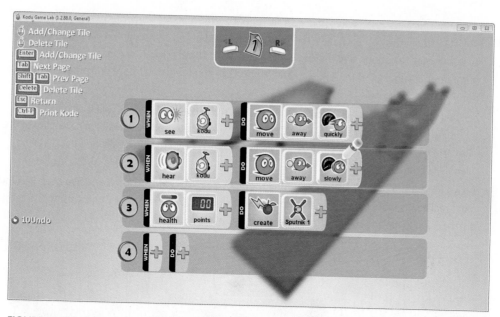

FIGURE 15.15   Sputnik creates another Sputnik when it is destroyed.

Now I'll change that so that Sputnik drops a Coin creatable and a Cycle creatable, as shown in Figure 15.16.

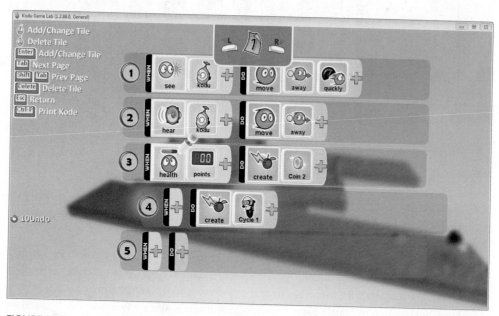

FIGURE 15.16   Now Sputnik drops a Cycle creatable and a Coin creatable when it is destroyed.

You might be wondering why I had Sputnik drop a Cycle creatable and not just a plain Cycle object? Later in this game, I have all sorts of uses for Cycles and coins; they'll be used to gain access to other locations, and making Cycle and the coin both creatables means I won't have to program them again. But the Cycle creatable and Coin creatable don't have any programming, right?

Not yet! But they will. You see, Kodu cannot deliver the second coin until Cycle is also destroyed. If Kodu tries to deliver the second coin, Cannon will take it, but Kodu will lose the capability to fire blips and will be unable to destroy Cycle. That means no entry into the castle, and the game is over.

Take a look at the programming I've added to the Cycle creatable in Figure 15.17. Do keep in mind that I really only need either Row 1 or Row 2, and not both. Cycle can see and hear using the same distances, so these two rows perform the same action.

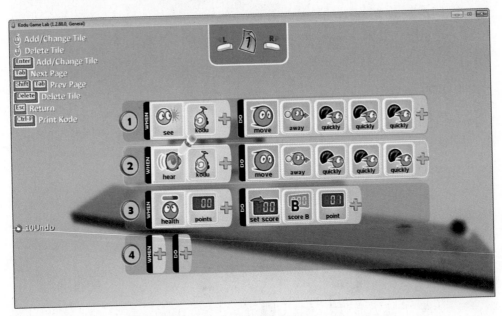

FIGURE 15.17   The Cycle creatable will run from Kodu.

Not only is Cycle programmed to evade Kodu, but when he is destroyed, he is programmed to set the B scoreboard to a value of 1. This B scoreboard is going to be useful to Cannon for deciding whether Kodu has completed his tasks in the proper order.

Now let's return to Cannon's programming. Refer back to Figure 15.15 and you'll notice something unusual. Cannon will disappear only when the B scoreboard has a value of 1 and when Cannon's hit points are equal to 5. If Cannon has to deliver two coins, he'll take 100 damage (50 per coin). So to keep him blocking the castle gates, I need to go and set his Max Hit Points to 105. You can see this in Figure 15.18. Just right-click Cannon, choose Change Settings, and scroll down the list until you reach the Max Hit Points option.

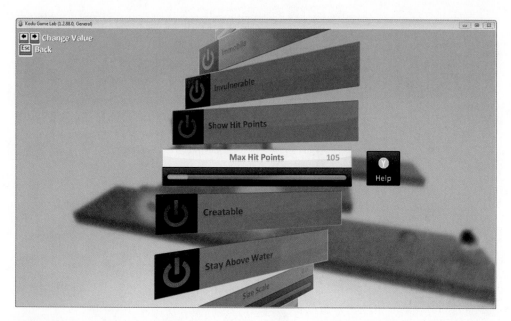

FIGURE 15.18   Set Cannon's hit points to 105.

Why didn't I set his hit points to 100? Well, if a player delivers two coins to Cannon before destroying Cycle, Cannon will still disappear in a poof because all of his hit points are gone. By increasing it to 105, I leave him with just enough hit points to continue his gatekeeper duties and prevent Kodu from entering the castle.

You might also find during testing that you can sometimes push and nudge other objects. This is also the case with Cannon. I found that every time I gave him a coin, he backed up a little bit. I want him to stand his ground, so I return to the Change Settings options for Cannon and turn the Immobile option to On, as shown in Figure 15.19.

And that's it. My *MiniWorld* game has been configured with a simple gatekeeper feature. Once I expand the world a bit, Cycle will have a lot more room to run, the castle will have a back gate that allows me to move Kodu onto a new portion of a larger world, and I can add more challenges that require the player to be fast on the fire button and be able to hunt out special objects.

> **TIP**
>
> By the way, you can easily tweak the gatekeeper job by adding more objects that must be delivered. By using hidden scoreboards like I did with the B scoreboard, you can control the order that players must perform certain actions. Just remember to increase the hit points of your gatekeeper and add the programming that checks that all conditions have been met.

FIGURE 15.19 Make Cannon immobile and he won't budge.

You've now seen that creatables can create other creatables. You can use this capability in a lot of different ways. For example, I could easily have created a more powerful but slower Sputnik that is dropped and that fires missiles back at Kodu. And I could have that missile-firing Sputnik creatable drop a super-fast, missile-firing Sputnik when it is destroyed. This becomes a method for upgrading objects in Kodu Game Lab and giving them more powers and abilities.

You can also downgrade an object into another less powerful object when it's bumped by programming the first object to vanish itself and create a creatable that replaces it. They might even look the same, meaning you've downgraded the original creatable and replaced it with an identical object that has weaker powers.

All these creatables are stored in your game as objects that you can use over and over. As *MiniWorld* progresses, I can place more Sputniks, more Cycles, and more coins in the world. Imagine having Kodu buy powers for coins. (Hint: Vanish the old Kodu after delivering a coin and call a new, more powerful Kodu creatable with all new programming.)

Moving On

You learned a lot of new things in this chapter. After seeing how easy it is to create a maze and stadium, you've probably got your own ideas for creating some unique game worlds. It's all about experimenting and pushing the limits of the terrain editing tools.

And don't forget about the capability to print out your game's Kode. This will save you time and stress when you're deep into version 12 of your hot new game. Being able to quickly look on a sheet of paper to remember the basics of all the objects' programming will save you from having to open up earlier versions and later versions to hunt down just when and where you made a certain change or added a bit of additional programming.

And I hope you're starting to pick up on the benefits of not just creatables, but also using the scoreboards for checking whether certain conditions have been met. The When/Do boxes can do a lot of things for you, but sometimes you've got to get a little creative and find a way to do things yourself. Scoreboards, especially the hidden ones that use letters instead of numbers, are a great way to indicate that something has occurred (set a value to 1) or has not occurred (leave its value at 0). You can also use them as counting tools as you know how to check for above, below, equal, and other comparisons (look back to Chapter 12, "Create Quests and Missions: Adding Conversations and In-Game Instructions").

This chapter offered up information in a variety of areas, not just programming, so rather than give you additional programming tasks to complete for homework, I want you to think about these questions:

1. How might you program a two-player game where each player needs to deliver items to a gatekeeper but each player can hinder the other player's progress? (Hint: How would you program hidden scoreboards that could be decremented as well as incremented when certain items are delivered?)

2. Could a water-based object be used to place a land-based creatable on solid ground? (Hint: Where do creatables seem to appear when they are first created/dropped on to the world?)

3. How would you program Cannon to warn a player who had not yet destroyed Cycle about delivering the second coin too early? (Hint: Adding the Say tile to remind the player after giving the first coin away would be a good method.)

Be sure to click the Home Menu button and save any work you've done before selecting Exit to Main Menu. Don't forget to add some additional information to the Description field.

16

The Role of the Storyteller: Scripting Cut-Scenes Between Game Action

In This Chapter

○ Scripting a Cut-Scene

○ Adding a Camera

○ Scripted Conversation

○ Scripted Movement

○ The Second Conversation

Many games created using Kodu Game Lab put the player right into the action. The Play button is pressed, and the player begins dodging and firing or some other action that a mouse and keyboard (or game controller) offers to the player. There's nothing wrong with a game that immediately puts the player on alert, but you have a fun alternative to consider. In Chapter 12, "Create Quests and Missions: Adding Conversations and In-Game Instructions," you learned how to program conversations between objects when the player's object (such as Kodu or Rover) bumps or interacts with another object, triggering the chat. But did you know you can also add preprogrammed movements and conversations that provide your games with what are basically mini-movies? They're called cut-scenes, and they can really make a game stand out from the crowd.

Scripting a Cut-Scene

A *cut-scene* is an action sequence in a game where the player (or players) relinquishes control for a moment. A cut-scene is often used to move a player's object to a certain location in the game world or tell a small story related to the premise of a game. Many video games use multiple cut-scenes to break up a game into parts, inserting a bit of animated storytelling to provide a player with some crucial information, change to a different game locale, or even provide a nice wrap-up movie at the end of a game.

With Kodu Game Lab, you can add your own cut-scene to a game. You can place it at the beginning, middle, or end of your game, and all it requires is good timing and some camera view manipulation.

> **NOTE**
> You learn how to add a cut-scene to the beginning of a game in this chapter, but you can easily change the steps to add a cut-scene to the middle or end of a game.

I show you how to create a simple cut-scene using one of my existing games: *Saucer Hunt Extreme*. I modified the game by adding some additional terrain that you can see in Figure 16.1. The smart saucer starts shooting missiles at the Kodus if they're nearby, so I'm moving them to a safe area so that they can find out what's going on!

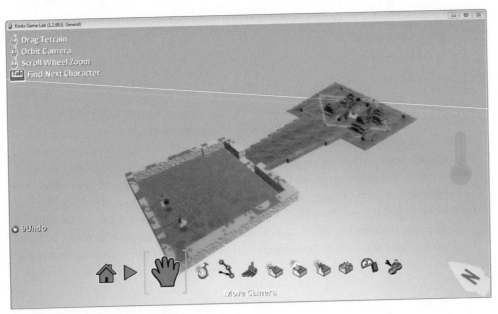

FIGURE 16.1 *Saucer Hunt Extreme* with new terrain.

When the game starts, I want both players to watch as the Blue Kodu (BK) and White Kodu (WK) approach the two gatekeepers and listen as they discuss whether the players are worthy to enter the sacred burial ground that is guarded by the saucers.

Here are the tasks I need to complete:

1. Add Gatekeepers 1 and 2 (G1 and G2).

2. Program BK and WK to discuss approaching G1 and G2.

3. Program BK and WK to move in the direction of G1 and G2.

4. Program Conversation between G1 and G2.

5. Program Conversation between BK/WK and G1.

6. Program G1 to give a warning to players.

7. Program G1 and G2 to disappear.

Adding a Camera

I start by adding G1 and G2 to the game and placing them near the entrance to the game field, as shown in Figure 16.2.

FIGURE 16.2 Adding my two gatekeepers.

Next, I need to program BK and WK to notice the gatekeepers and talk about approaching them. At this point in the game, I do not want the players to be able to move or shoot. I want the players to listen and watch as the opening cut-scene is played. To do this, I use a trick that involves one of the hidden scoreboards you've already learned about.

If I open the programming of the White Kodu right now, you'll see that the movement controls are still active, as shown in Figure 16.3.

FIGURE 16.3 When the game begins, players can immediately move and shoot.

What I need is for a condition to be true that will then allow each player to move and shoot. To do this, I use the **J** scoreboard. Figure 16.4 shows that I've added it to Programming Row 5.

I now drag Programming Row 5 up to the top and indent Programming Rows 1 and 2 so that they work only if the J scoreboard has a value of 1. I add the same programming to the Blue Kodu's program.

> **NOTE**
> If you've never tried this, just click on a programming row's number and hold it while dragging it up or down the list. The programming rows renumber themselves when you drop a row in a new location.

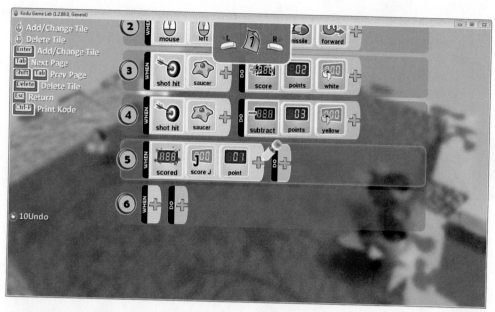

FIGURE 16.4 Creating a new condition that uses the J scoreboard.

All I've done in Figure 16.5 is specify that until the J scoreboard has a value of 1 the moving and firing capabilities of the Kodus won't work. Because I never plan on setting the J scoreboard to a value of 1, the player controls will be disabled until I re-enable them at the end of the cut-scene.

FIGURE 16.5 Moving and firing are limited until the J scoreboard has a value of 1.

Now it's time to have the players watch as BK and WK have a little conversation. Before I program the conversations using the Say tile covered in Chapter 12, here's a little trick for controlling the point of view of the conversation. First, I drop in Stick. Normally he's used as a gun turret, but he also looks like a camera to me. Figure 16.6 shows that I've placed him right in front of the two Kodus and rotated him so that he's looking directly at them. Stick objects are going to serve as my cameras.

> **TIP**
>
> Imagine Stick holding a video camera, and rotate Stick so that he's seeing what you want your players to see.

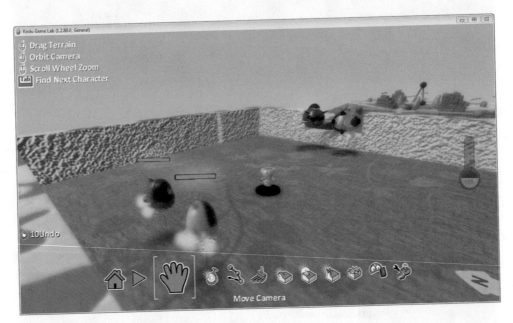

FIGURE 16.6   Stick is looking at White Kodu and Blue Kodu.

When the game begins, I want it to start from Stick's first-person point of view (POV). To do this, I program stick to Always have the 1st Person POV. This simple bit of programming is shown in Figure 16.7.

> **TIP**
>
> To find the 1st Person tile, click the Do box, click the View pie slice, and select the 1st Person pie slice.

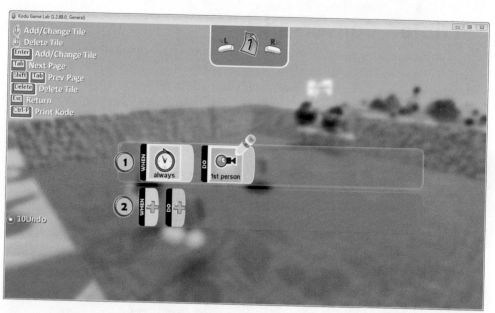

FIGURE 16.7   Program Stick to have 1st Person view when the game begins.

Go ahead and test the game to see what happens. When you click Play, the game should start with Blue Kodu and White Kodu bouncing around (but staying in place), as shown in Figure 16.8.

FIGURE 16.8   Stick's point of view as he stares at Blue Kodu and White Kodu.

Scripted Conversation

This cut-scene requires me to use time to synchronize the various conversations and movements. I use the Timer tile in Programming Row 6 to increment the Green scoreboard, as shown in Figure 16.9. I've also added Programming Row 7, which switches White Kodu to using Page 2 after 5 seconds have elapsed (or when the Green scoreboard equals 5). I also copy Programming Row 7 and copy it into Blue Kodu's Page 1 program.

> **NOTE**
>
> Why didn't I copy Programming Row 6 into the Blue Kodu? As long as one programming row is incrementing the Green scoreboard, that's all that is needed. All other objects can use the Green scoreboard to trigger their own events, so it's not necessary to have every object incrementing the Green scoreboard.

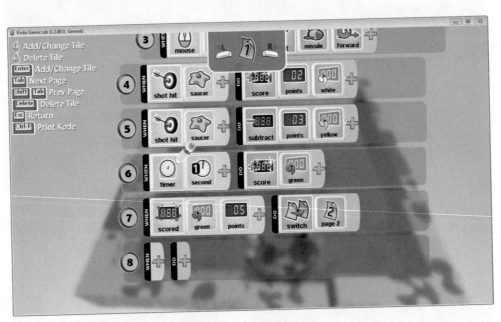

FIGURE 16.9 The Green scoreboard will be the timer used for the cut-scene.

When the game starts, the Green scoreboard increments by a value of 1 every second, so I can use this scoreboard to time the movements and conversations I need for this cut-scene.

Remember that a text bubble appears for about three seconds, so I've programmed the back-and-forth conversation using the Green scoreboard to trigger the proper timing with a one-second pause after each line. Here is the short conversation between the Kodus, with the value of the T scoreboard for each line:

White Kodu: Those two gatekeepers are looking at us! (T = 6)

Blue Kodu: Maybe we should go say hello. (T = 10)

White Kodu: We could just sneak around them. (T = 14)

Blue Kodu: I don't think that's a good idea. (T = 18)

White Kodu: They do look a bit dangerous. (T = 22)

Blue Kodu: Come on… follow me. (T = 26)

Each Kodu has three different lines to say, and Figure 16.10 shows the programming I've added on Page 2 for Blue Kodu. Notice that the conversation is paced using the Green scoreboard.

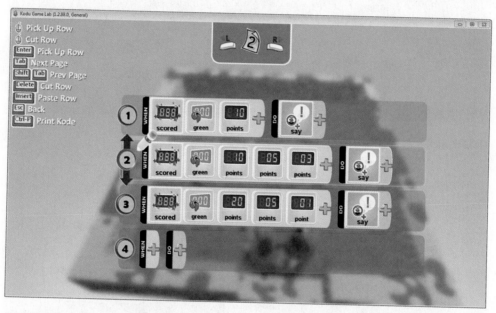

FIGURE 16.10   The Page 2 programming for White Kodu and Blue Kodu.

Now I just test to see whether the pace of the conversation is correct. It is, but now I've noticed a new problem. Take a look at Figure 16.11, and you'll see that part of the conversation between the Kodus is actually not visible.

To fix this, I need to adjust Stick's location and his height. I've pulled him back a little bit (further from the Kodus) and right-clicked him to access the Height option so that I can raise him up a little bit. As you can see in Figure 16.12, now the conversation bubbles are fully visible.

You might find that you need to tweak the timing of the conversation a bit, but that's easy to do after you've got all the Say tiles installed.

FIGURE 16.11 Part of the conversation is off the screen.

FIGURE 16.12 The opening conversation is done and looks good.

After the opening conversation, I want BK and WK to move closer to the gatekeepers. I program this using Page 3 for each of the Kodus, and I've added Programming Row 4 to the Blue Kodu's Page 2 that will switch to Page 3 when the Green scoreboard has a value of 30, as shown in Figure 16.13. Remember to copy this programming row to White Kodu.

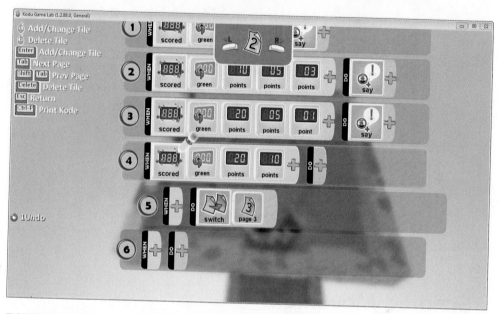

FIGURE 16.13 Move to Page 3 for Blue Kodu and White Kodu.

Before WK and BK begin moving toward the gatekeepers, however, I need to change the POV. I don't want my players to keep looking at the spot where Stick 1 is pointed because after BK and WK move, there's nothing to see there. What's needed is for Stick 1 to relinquish control of the camera and find a new location.

> **NOTE**
>
> I'm numbering Stick now because I'm now going to have to place Stick in Location 2. Every time I place a new Stick object, its number increments by one. This helps me remember the order in which Stick is filming during the cut-scene.

Figure 16.14 shows that I've added Programming Row 2 to Stick's program and configured it to Vanish Stick 1 when the Green scoreboard has a value of 28. This is timed to coincide with BK's final sentence before the Kodus begin moving. After Stick is vanished, the camera changes to a view that enables the players to view BK and WK moving to the gatekeepers.

And now it's time to get WK and BK moving.

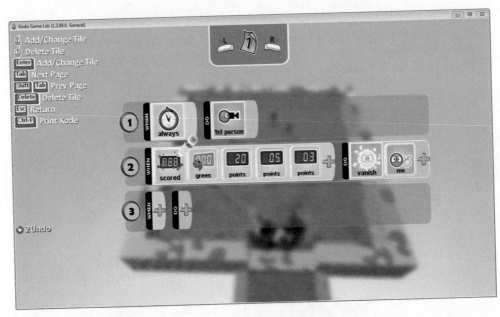

FIGURE 16.14   Stick disappears and the POV changes.

Scripted Movement

Now that BK and WK have had their conversation and Stick has disappeared, it's time to program them to move toward the gatekeepers. I need to move BK and WK from their starting position to a spot a little closer to the gatekeepers. If you guessed that I'll be adding a path, you'd be correct. (Refer back to Chapter 7, "Difficult Targets to Hit: Increasing Game Difficulty and Path Following," for details on adding paths.)

NOTE
I also turned off the Show Hit Points so that White Kodu and Blue Kodu don't have health bars over their heads that could possibly obstruct the view of the text bubbles.

Figure 16.15 shows that I've added two paths: a blue one for BK and a white one for WK.

TIP
Using two colors will allow me to move BK and WK toward the gatekeepers on different paths.

When do I want them to start moving on these paths? The opening conversation ends when the Green scoreboard value is 28. I'll pause an additional 2 seconds, and then when 30 seconds have elapsed, both Kodus' programs jump to Page 3. Page 3 contains the programming that forces the Kodus to follow the paths so that they can approach the gatekeepers.

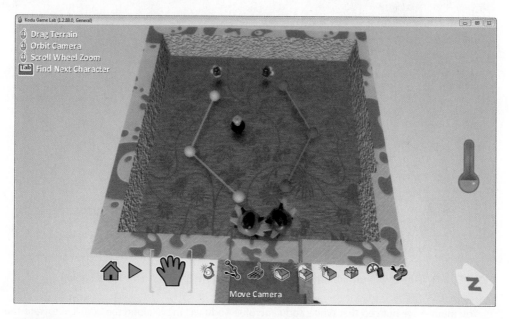

FIGURE 16.15   A blue path for Blue Kodu and a white path for White Kodu.

Figure 16.16 shows the new programming on Programming Rows 2 and 3 (on Page 3) for BK. Programming Row 1 contains the tiles that will keep the Green scoreboard incrementing by one point for every second that passes. (I could have placed Programming Row 1 in WK's Page 3 program, but because BK is leading WK, I put it there.)

> **CAUTION**
> Make certain to copy Programming Rows 2 and 3 to Page 3 of White Kodu's programming and change the path color to White.

Let me explain Programming Rows 2 and 3 quickly. For Programming Row 2, the When box simply checks to see whether BK sees a jet (the Gatekeepers are Jet objects). When BK sees a jet, he moves on the blue path at a fast speed.

For Programming Row 3, the When box checks to see whether BK has reached the end of the blue path (using the End of Path tile) and, if so, switches BK to Page 4.

Identical Programming Rows 2 and 3 appear on Page 3 of White Kodu, but I changed the color tile from Blue to White. Go ahead and test the game and watch what happens.

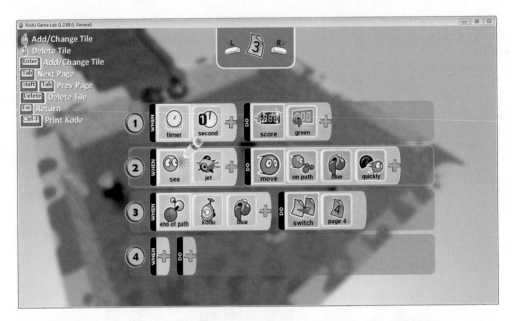

FIGURE 16.16   These two programming rows (2 and 3) move BK toward the gatekeepers.

You might have noticed that White Kodu and Blue Kodu will move along the blue line toward the gatekeepers and then turn right around and move in the opposite direction. They're not stopping!

To make them stop, you need to create an actual end for the path. And to do that, you need to limit the direction that an object can move on a path. When you first place a path on the screen, it can be traveled on in both directions. So, when BK or WK reach the end node (sphere) on a path, they just turn around and go the other direction. And they do this over and over again, never stopping to talk to the gatekeepers. But here's how you fix it:

1. Click the **Path** tool.

2. On a line section of the path (not a sphere), right-click the line.

3. Look carefully and you'll see two small cones, one pointing in one direction and the other pointing in the opposite direction. You can see this in Figure 16.17.

4. Click the Change Direction button (shown in Figure 16.17) and one of the cones will disappear, indicating the only direction that can be traveled on that path.

5. If the cone is not pointing in the direction you want an object to travel, right-click the line again and choose Change Direction again. The wrong-direction cone will disappear, and the cone pointing in the opposite direction will appear.

FIGURE 16.17   Cycle through the three possible direction combinations using Change Direction.

You have three possible options: Cone 1 (pointing one way), Cone 2 (pointing the other way), and dual cones (allowing for bidirectional travel). Select the cone option on both the white lines and the blue lines that forces WK and BK to travel toward the gatekeepers.

> **CAUTION**
>
> You have to specify the direction on every line segment. So, in the case of Figure 16.17, there are four line segments: two for white and two for blue. Each segment ends in a sphere.

If you have the Path tool selected and you hover your mouse pointer over a line segment, you can see in which directions an object can move. Figure 16.18 shows that my direction cone is pointed toward the gatekeepers on one of the line segments, and I've verified that the same direction is configured for the remaining three line segments.

FIGURE 16.18 Travel on this path is allowed only in the direction the cone is pointing. When White Kodu and Blue Kodu reach the gatekeepers, it's time to call up Stick again so that I can continue the cut-scene with the gatekeepers discussing the two new arrivals.

The Second Conversation

I move through the remainder of the cut-scene's programming a bit faster now that you've seen how I'm using the Green scoreboard for scripted conversations and movement and the Stick object for the POV.

Figure 16.19 shows that I've placed Stick 2 so that he's facing the two gatekeepers from the side and BK and WK are just in the scene.

I need to program Stick 2 to grab the 1st Person POV after WK and BK have approached the gatekeepers. Using my Green scoreboard, I have determined that the best time for this to happen is when the Green scoreboard has a value of 40. Figure 16.20 shows Stick 2's new programming.

At this point, I can begin adding this conversation to the gatekeepers:

Gatekeeper 1: Are you looking to enter the sacred burial ground?

Gatekeeper 2: Are you brave and strong?

G1: There are dangers beyond these walls!

G2: Many have entered, but few have returned.

G1: You look ready. We will let you pass.

G2: Good luck, and safe travels.

FIGURE 16.19   Stick has a second camera placement.

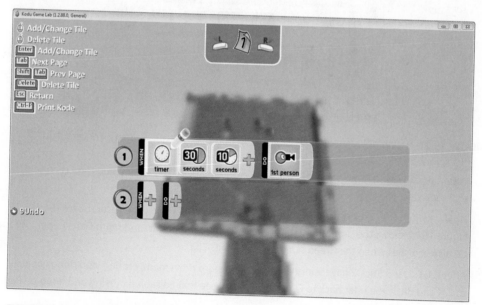

FIGURE 16.20   Stick 2 has new programming.

I don't show you how to program the Say tiles for Gatekeeper 1 and Gatekeeper 2 here; you should be able to figure out how to use the Green scoreboard to time the conversation and end Stick 2's 1st Person POV based on the previous sections.

Just remember, you need to do the following:

1. Program G1 and G2 using Say tiles.

2. Vanish Stick 1 after the gatekeeper's conversation ends.

3. Vanish G1 and G2 to allow BK and WK to pass.

Figure 16.21 shows G2's programming for his part of the conversation. Notice that when the conversation ends the program will switch to Page 2.

FIGURE 16.21 Using a Say tile and the Green scoreboard for the gatekeepers' conversation.

You've already seen how to vanish Stick 1, so program Stick 2 to vanish when the Green scoreboard reaches 70.

Finally, switch to Page 2 of Jet 1's program and vanish it when the Green scoreboard reaches 72. Figure 16.22 shows the programming for this. Add the same programming to Gatekeeper 2 so that G2 also vanishes when the Green scoreboard reaches 72.

After G1, G2, and Stick 2 have vanished, I need to return movement, scoring, and firing capabilities to WK and BK. If you refer back to Figure 16.5, you'll see that I disabled moving and firing on Page 1 using the J scoreboard.

To turn movement, scoring, and firing back on, I go to Page 4 of Blue Kodu's program and add the simple programming row shown in Figure 16.23.

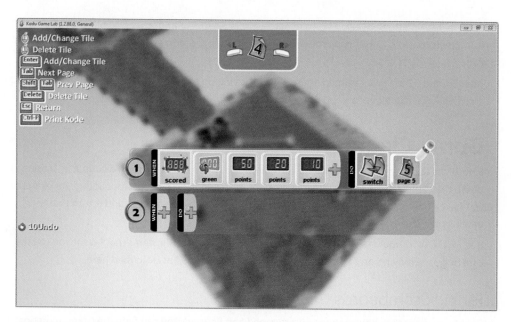

FIGURE 16.22 Vanish G1 and G2 to allow the Kodus to continue the game.

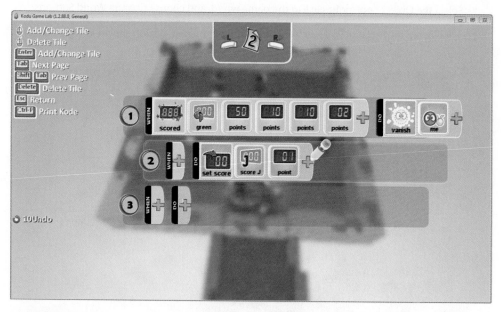

FIGURE 16.23 When the Green scoreboard reaches 80, switch to Page 5.

This creates a pause between when the gatekeepers disappear and when the players can begin using their controls. I'll just copy the movement, firing, and scoring programming from Page 1 to Page 5… and test it out.

After G1 and G2 are programmed, there's some tidying up to do with the game before White Kodu and Blue Kodu can move forward to the sacred burial ground and fight the saucers.

Game Cleanup

Before you're ready to share the game with the world, you need to perform a couple of actions to polish the gameplay. Of course, the game can be expanded and new features added; for example, you haven't programmed an ending after the player's destroy the saucers and return to the gatekeeper. There's plenty of ways to upgrade this game.

But, for the work you've done in this chapter, there are two specific items that I want you to take care of before moving on to Chapter 17, "The Big Bag of Tricks," as described here.

Hiding Scoreboards

Once you've got the conversations programmed and finished, you can hide the Green scoreboard (and you may want to also hide the Yellow scoreboard). To do so, just follow these easy steps:

1. Select the Object Tool, right-click in the game world, and choose Change World Settings.

2. Scroll down the list until you reach the Score Visibility: Green option shown in Figure 16.24.

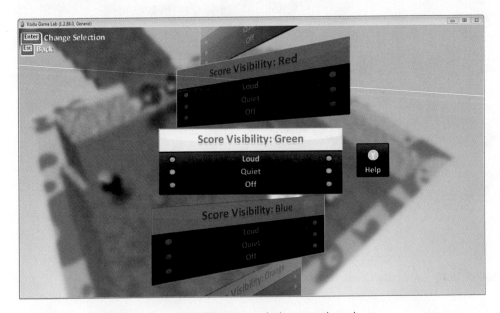

FIGURE 16.24 Modify the Score Visibility option to hide a scoreboard.

3. Select the Off option to completely hide the Green scoreboard from the screen. (Use the **A** button to change selections if using a game controller).

4. Tap the Escape key or the B button to leave the Change World Settings screen.

Now the Green scoreboard will not be visible (and counting up); it will still be needed to time the conversations, so you cannot just delete it. Perform the same steps to hide the Yellow scoreboard that is part of the saucer hunt portion of the game. All that is left at that point are the scores for the Blue and White Kodus.

Making Sticks Invisible

You placed two Stick objects to serve as cameras and to follow the Kodus as they talk and approach the gatekeepers. If you play the game, you'll see them sitting there. But they really shouldn't be visible. Thankfully, it's easy to make them invisible but still fully functional. Follow these steps:

1. Using the Object Tool, right-click a Stick object and select Change Settings.

2. Scroll down the list until you find the Invisible option shown in Figure 16.25.

FIGURE 16.25   Make a Stick object invisible to players.

3. Turn on the Invisible option by clicking its icon; it will turn green to indicate that it is turned on.

4. Return to the game and perform the same steps for the second Stick object.

And that's it. Play the game and you should now see that the two Stick objects are no longer visible as you play the game. As a matter of fact, while you edit the game, the two Stick objects will appear ghost-like, as shown in Figure 16.26, reminding you that they are programmed to be invisible when the game starts.

FIGURE 16.26   The two Stick objects appear as ghosts to remind you they are invisible.

Moving On

Action games are great, but there really is something nice about having a game that allows for some interaction between objects. Using conversations, you can provide your players with instructions, give them hints if they are stuck in a game, and even let enemies taunt players. Conversations can help players forget for a moment that they are playing a game and provide them with a story. Hopefully you'll find some ways to incorporate the Say tile and some hidden cameras (you don't necessarily have to use the Stick object, by the way) into your own games.

Before you move on to Chapter 17, let me offer up three suggestions for you to consider when it comes to modifying the game:

1. After the players destroy all the saucers, consider adding a wrap-up conversation where the gatekeepers congratulate the players on their success. You could add a hidden scoreboard that tracks the number of saucers destroyed and, when the last one goes boom, the players once again lose control and watch as the Kodus return to the gatekeepers.

2. Try to place a third camera (invisible) in the sacred burial grounds so that when the final saucer is destroyed the players can sit back and watch a short discussion between the Kodus where they discuss the adventure they just finished.

3. This game has so much potential for additional tests. You could have another set of gatekeepers that must be approached after completing the sacred burial grounds mission (destroy all saucers). These gatekeepers could block the players from moving into a completely new game area until they destroy the saucers and retrieve a special object that they must deliver to the new gatekeepers.

Be sure to click the Home Menu button and save any work you've done before selecting Exit to Main Menu. Don't forget to add some additional information to the Description field.

17

The Big Bag of Tricks

In This Chapter

Throughout the previous 16 chapters, you learned about a number of Kodu Game Labs features. You use some of these for programming, others for tweaking game settings, and others help you create unique game worlds. You've still got seven more chapters to read, and plenty more to learn. This chapter introduces you to some new and interesting Kodu Game Lab features that you might find useful as you continue to learn and program.

Programming Features You Might Not Have Discovered

Kodu Game Lab is a powerful tool for creating your own video games. As you've explored the user interface, you've no doubt discovered a few programming tiles or object settings that I've yet to use in the previous chapters. Unfortunately, a book puts a page limit on a writer, and this means that it's simply impossible for me to cover every button, tile, setting, and special feature found in Kodu Game Lab. I have to pick and choose those items that I feel will get you enough experience and knowledge so that you'll feel comfortable experimenting with any remaining features that you discover on your own.

Throughout the book, I've squeezed in tips and tricks where I thought they'd be most useful. But I've also had to set aside some tips and tricks because I couldn't fit them into the earlier chapters. I created this chapter specifically to provide you with some advice and programming examples that couldn't be squeezed in elsewhere.

I'm presenting this information to you here in no particular order, so read through it all. You will probably find at least one feature, possibly more, that will help you in your current game.

Modifying Terrain Edit Speed

If you've spent any time editing game terrain, you've probably discovered that Kodu Game Lab will raise and lower terrain (including water) at a high rate of speed. Sometimes you click and release the mouse button quickly to raise the terrain, but instead you find a mountain where you really want a simple hill. This becomes a real problem when you're fine-tuning your game world and need to make small changes in the height of a wall or the level of a lake.

When you need a single click of the mouse to make a very small change in the terrain, you want to modify the terrain edit speed. Here's how you do it:

1. From the Main Menu, select Options, as shown in Figure 17.1.

FIGURE 17.1 On the Main Menu, select Options.

2. Scroll down the list until you find the Terrain Edit Speed drag bar shown in Figure 17.2, and drag it left or right to change the speed at which your edits appear on screen.

FIGURE 17.2 Find Terrain Edit Speed to change how fast terrain edits occur.

The terrain edit speed is a value between 0.25 and 4. The higher the value, the faster terrain edits will occur. If you set the terrain edit speed to 4, for example, a single click-and-release of the left mouse button when using the Up/Down tool will cause a mountain to grow out of the terrain. Try it out to see exactly how fast terrain edits occur with that maximum value.

In my experience, I've found that a value of 1.0 works best for initial placement of terrain, raising of terrain, and addition of water. When you turn the value down to 0.5 or even 0.25, the minimum value, the edits occur at a snail's pace. Again, try it. You'll get to see a single click's effect and better understand how it can help you when it comes time to tweaking your terrain.

My best advice is this: Use a terrain edit speed of between 1.0 and 2.0 when you're raising the initial terrain for a game. Turn the speed down to 0.5 for lowering of terrain (and combine this by shrinking the size of the brush using the left arrow key). This lower value gives you more control over carving away terrain in smaller increments and will produce much smoother and more natural-looking terrain.

Controlling Score Visibility

In Chapter 16, "The Role of the Storyteller Scripting Cut-Scenes Between Game Action," I used the Green scoreboard as a timer that I could view as I developed a cut-scene. When the game is done, however, there really is no need for the players to have to see this scoreboard as it ticks up one point for every one second that elapses.

Still, the Green scoreboard is necessary for the behind-the-scenes conversations and movements of the cut-scene, so I can't delete the Green Score tiles from the various objects' programs.

I can, however, make the Green scoreboard invisible. It's still there, ticking up and helping to trigger the proper conversations and movements of the Kodus and the jets, but the players don't have to see it.

Inside your game, choose the Object tool, right-click any empty piece of terrain, and select Change World Settings. Scroll down the list until you find the Score Visibility: Green option shown in Figure 17.3.

The movement controls are still active, as shown in Figure 17.3.

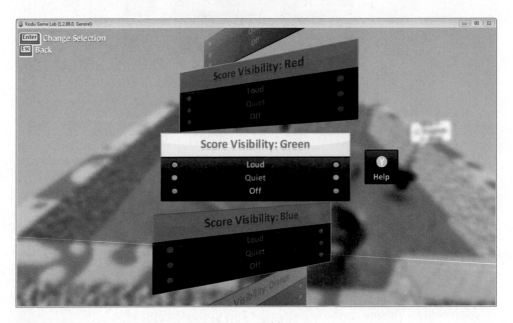

FIGURE 17.3 A scoreboard has three options available.

You can choose from three options when it comes to a color's scoreboard: Loud, Quiet, and Off. Here's how they work:

○ **Loud:** When this option is selected, every increment to the scoreboard will occur with both a sound and an onscreen animation. You'll hear the scoreboard ticking up, plus you'll see a +X appear on the screen and fly toward the scoreboard. The +X is a value that a particular object is adding to the scoreboard. For example, if a missile awards White Kodu with three points when it hits an enemy, the Loud setting shows a +3 flying out of White Kodu and toward the White scoreboard.

○ **Quiet:** With this option, the scoreboard is still visible in the upper-right corner of the screen, but no sound is made as the scoreboard ticks up. Also, the +X animation is turned off, so there is no visible alert as to which object added the points to a particular scoreboard.

○ **Off:** This turns off the scoreboard completely, and it will not be visible in the upper-right corner of the game. There will be no sound and no animation to indicate an increase in the scoreboard.

TIP

I often use the Quiet option during testing of a game. For example, I might assign the S scoreboard to hold a value of 0 when a certain event has not yet happened (Kodu bumps a coin). When the event does happen, I change the S scoreboard to a value of 1 and trigger a conversation. Because I can see the S scoreboard in the upper-right corner of the screen, if I see the S Score change to a value of 1, I'll start watching for the conversation. If I don't see the conversation, I'll know there's something wrong in my programming related to using the S Score tile and can hunt down the problem more easily.

The Great and Powerful Rock

If you refer back to Chapter 8, "Dangerous Targets Programming Enemies That Fire Back," you might notice that in that game I placed a small rock that controlled the game's timer as it counted up to 120. I deleted that rock from the game in Chapter 16 because with White Kodu and Blue Kodu joining forces, I didn't want a time limit on the game.

I did add the Green scoreboard to various objects in Chapter 16's game, and I used it to keep a timer going that I could use to trigger conversations and movements. At the time, it seemed like a great idea, but after the game was done, I smacked my forehead and wondered why I didn't use another rock object to keep the Green scoreboard counting up one point every second.

Even better, I could have made that rock invisible so players wouldn't wonder just what in the world that single rock was doing sitting on the game field.

Controlling a game timer isn't the only use for the great and powerful rock, either. Using colored scoreboards, the rock could also end a game or declare a winner, as shown in Figure 17.4.

Remember to turn the rock invisible, as shown in Figure 17.5 (right-click the rock, choose Change Settings, and turn on the Invisible option) and use it to control things such as timers and special scoreboards that can be used to trigger other in-game events.

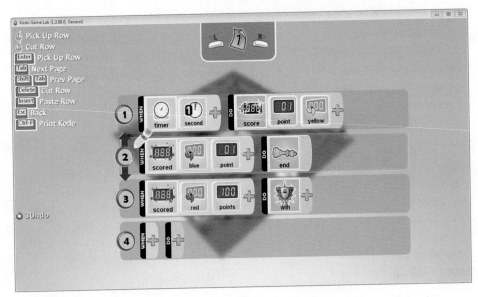

FIGURE 17.4 Multiple conditions can be controlled using the great and powerful rock.

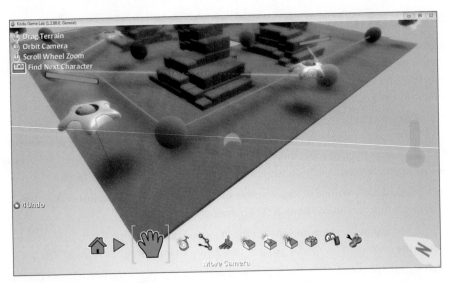

FIGURE 17.5 Turn the rock invisible, so it won't distract the players.

Using Description to Hold Comments

Kodu Game Lab is a visual programming tool with drag-and-drop features. You can use the keyboard to enter text such as conversations and a description of your game, but most everything else is done using a mouse or game controller.

But not all programming tools are visual; as a matter of fact, most programming tools used in the real world are text based. Take a look at Figure 17.6 and you'll see an example of Microsoft X, used by programmers around the world. It has some buttons on the toolbar at the top, but most everything else is typed in with a keyboard.

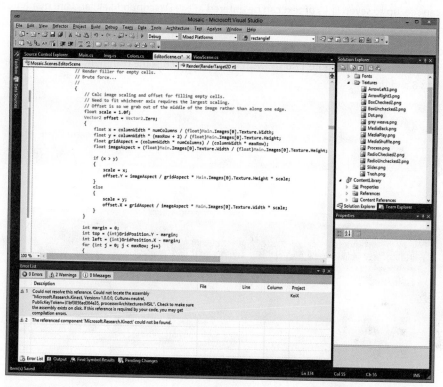

FIGURE 17.6 A text-based programming tool uses a keyboard for most of the work.

When using text-based programming tools, programmers often have a hard time keeping track of all the complex programming that is displayed on the screen. To make it easier for the original programmer and other programmers to figure out exactly what they are looking at and trying to decipher, many programming tools allow programmers to add comments to their programs. Comments are often nothing more than a sentence or two describing what is happening on the screen that is currently visible. Sometimes entire paragraphs are included if a particular part of a program is super complex and difficult to understand.

Unfortunately, because Kodu Game Lab is a graphical programming tool and not a text-based tool, you cannot simply add a note to the White Kodu object to remind yourself next time that you need to tweak the missile-firing speed. You also can't add a note to the Blue Rover object to explain to someone examining your game's programming why you chose to use two Quickly tiles instead of just one.

Although you can't add notes inside objects, there is a way for you to add comments to your games for you and others to see. This is done using the Description field that appears when you choose to save a game. Take a look at Figure 17.7 and you'll see the short Description that appears below my *Saucer Hunt Extreme* v03 game.

As you can see, up to seven lines of text can be entered in the Description field and are guaranteed to appear when browsing through games to open and play.

This means you can hide comments you don't want players to see when they're browsing your game on Line 8 and higher. Figure 17.8 shows that I've provided some commentary on my game using Lines 8 and up.

> **TIP**
> You don't have to include Line 8, Line 9, and so on. I used that only so that you could see which lines were holding comments.

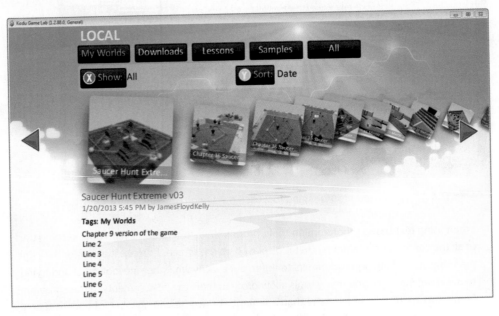

FIGURE 17.7   The Description field holds up to seven lines of text.

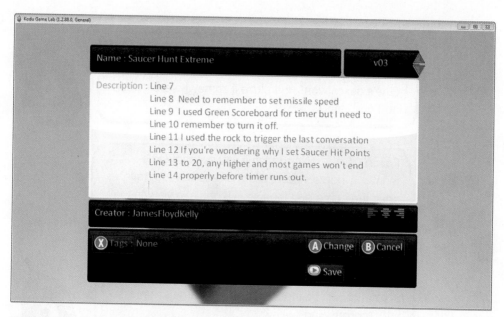

Kodu Game Lab (1.2.88.0, General)

Name : Saucer Hunt Extreme

v03

Description : Line 7
Line 8 Need to remember to set missile speed
Line 9 I used Green Scoreboard for timer but I need to
Line 10 remember to turn it off.
Line 11 I used the rock to trigger the last conversation
Line 12 If you're wondering why I set Saucer Hit Points
Line 13 to 20, any higher and most games won't end
Line 14 properly before timer runs out.

Creator : JamesFloydKelly

(X) Tags : None   (A) Change (B) Cancel
                              (▶) Save

FIGURE 17.8 These lines won't appear when players are reading the game's description.

Comments can be very helpful to you and anyone wanting to examine your game. And although not every professional programmer uses comments, the best ones do, and so should you. Even if it's just a few lines describing why you used the specific programming tiles on Page 2 instead of other tiles, other programmers will appreciate your explanations, especially if they're trying to figure out how you pulled off an amazing display of programming skill.

Rover: It sounds like commenting is a good idea.

Kodu: It definitely helps other Kodu Game Lab programmers to understand an object's tricky programming.

Rover: But how do you know if a game has comments?

Kodu: A good Kodu Game Lab programmer could add "Comments can be found starting on Line 8 in the game's description" and place it somewhere between Line 1 and Line 7.

Rover: Of course. And then if you see that statement in a game's description, all you have to do is open the game and then save it again to view the full Description field and see the comments.

Kodu: You can also print out the Kode; the full Description will be included with the game's name and programming.

Using Say Tiles to Hold Comments

Comments are so useful that I want to give you yet another method for adding comments to your programs. Fortunately, you're already familiar with this method; it uses the Say tile that you've already learned how to use to create conversations between characters.

To use a Say tile for comments, however, you want to make certain that the comments you actually type into a Say tile never appear onscreen. To make this bit of magic happen, all you need to do is have a character programmed with the tiles seen in Programming Row 6 of Figure 17.9.

Figure 17.10 shows the contents of the single Say tile found inside Page 1 of Kodu's program, and explains how this works.

One benefit to using Say tiles to hold your comments is that the comments will be printed out when you choose the Print Kode for Level option.

Using Say tiles to hold comments is a useful method to leave yourself notes when you find yourself having to leave an unfinished game. Just drop in a Say tile using the WHEN SEE ME NOT condition in the last programming row and it'll be there to greet you when you return.

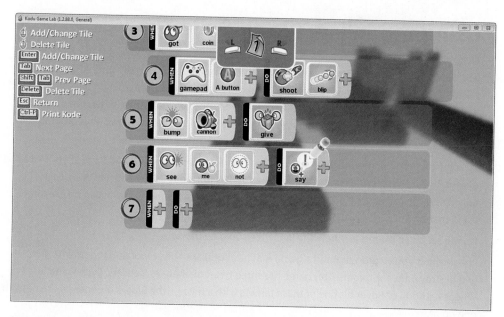

FIGURE 17.9   The content of this Say tile will never be displayed.

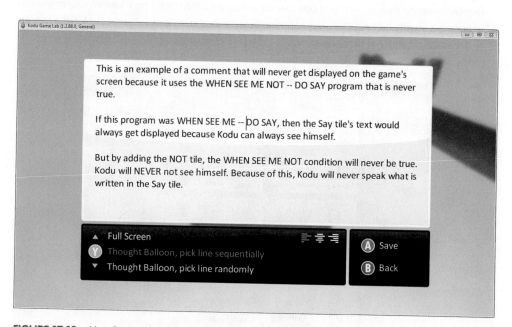

FIGURE 17.10   Use the inside of a Say tile to leave comments for others to read.

Using the Inline Tile to Save Time

There's a very useful tile found in Kodu Game Labs that I've not yet used in this book's example games but that you might have seen used in other Kodu games, especially tutorial games. It's called the Inline tile, and it's used as a way to take another Page's programming and "pull it back" to the page that calls it. Similar to the Switch tile, it has one big difference: When the Inline tile specifies another page, it executes any programming found on that page as if that programming were actually included on the original page.

So, if the programming on Page 1 has WHEN Button A DO Inline Page 2, and Page 2 has WHEN Always DO Fire Missile, it executes as if you had WHEN Button A DO Fire Missile on Page 1. The only difference is that you can include many more rows of programming that can be executed using that single Inline tile that calls another page of programming.

Let me set up an example of how the Inline tile could be used.

Imagine that you've programmed a game that has Kodu and Rover working together to shoot and destroy different targets. This game has three types of enemies: saucers, Cycles, and jets. Whenever Kodu or Rover hit one of these targets with a missile, the Blue scoreboard increments by one point.

Figure 17.11 shows the three programming rows you'd have to add to both Kodu and Rover to increment the Blue scoreboard: one row for detecting a missile hit on a saucer, one row for detecting a missile hit on a Cycle, and another row for detecting a missile hit on a jet. If a missile hit is detected on any of these three objects, the Do box awards the Blue scoreboard a point.

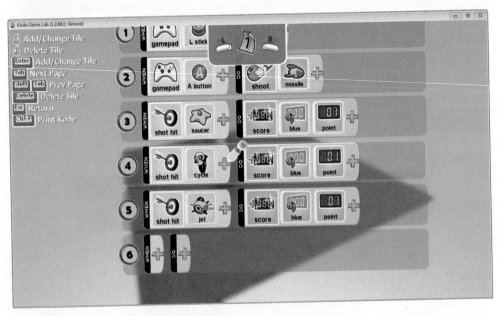

FIGURE 17.11   Three different programming rows dedicated to scoring.

Notice in Figure 17.11 that the Do box for Programming Rows 3, 4, and 5 requires three tiles to award the points. You could copy Row 3 and paste two copies, changing the saucer in Row 4 to a Cycle and the saucer in Row 5 to a jet. That would definitely save a little programming time.

But you could also use the Inline tile, which would execute any programming found on Page 2. The program on Page 2 would simply add one point to the Blue scoreboard, as shown in Figure 17.12, and it wouldn't matter whether Row 3, Row 4, or Row 5 executed the programming on Page 2. Page 2 executes its program immediately as if it were actually executed on Page 1 (adding a point to Blue scoreboard).

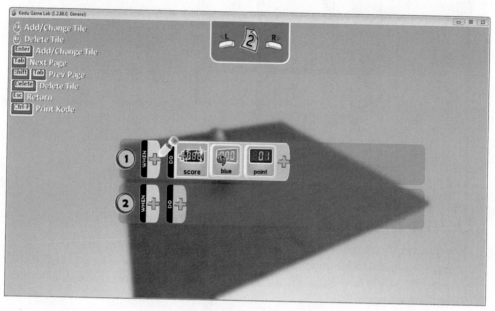

FIGURE 17.12   Page 2 does nothing but increment the Blue scoreboard by one point.

After the program on Page 2 is created, I can delete the three tiles required to add a point to the Blue scoreboard in the Do boxes and replace them with two tiles: the Inline tile and the Page 2 tile shown in Figure 17.13. Yes, I'm not saving much time by adding two tiles instead of three tiles, but hopefully you've got the point that the Inline tile can be used by multiple programming rows and executes immediately without having to change pages.

The purpose of the Inline tile is to give you a method for executing identical programming rows in a game. The Inline tile is tied to a particular object (such as White Kodu), so the Blue Kodu's program can't jump to White Kodu's Page 2—White Kodu's Inline tiles will only jump to White Kodu's other pages.

If you've got a complex game developing, with multiple pages that have repeated programming rows, you could save some time by having Inline tiles jump to a specific Page, execute any programming there, and then jump back to the originating Page.

FIGURE 17.13 Reducing the number of tiles required to increment the Blue scoreboard.

Using Multiple Game Controllers

Throughout this book, I've been demonstrating two-player games with one player using the mouse and keyboard for moving and firing controls, and another player using a game controller. But you don't have to force a player to use a mouse and keyboard if there are two or more game controllers available.

Rover: That's great. So both players can use game controllers in a two-player game.

Kodu: Actually, Kodu Game Lab allows up to four game controllers.

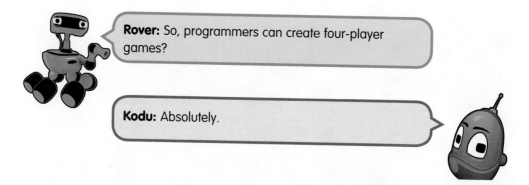

Kodu Game Lab supports up to four game controllers, so you can easily create a four-player game. And it's easy to do.

Take a look at Figure 17.14 and you'll see that I've specified that the Gamepad and L Stick tiles in Programming Row 1 will control White Kodu's movement.

But what if I have two game controllers? Is there a way to control Blue Kodu with a second game controller? Yes, there is. Click the plus sign (+) to the right of the L Stick tile and you'll see a pie menu appear like the one in Figure 17.15.

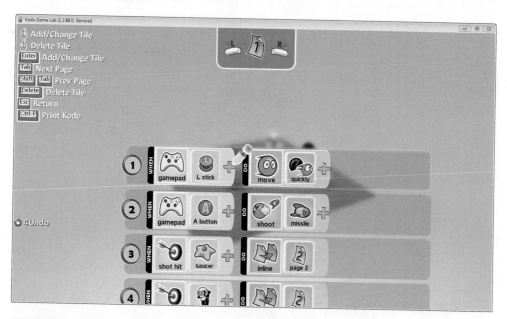

FIGURE 17.14 Standard movement is done with the Gamepad and L Stick tiles.

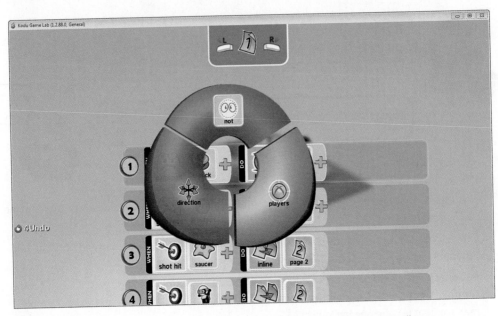

FIGURE 17.15   Adding another tile to the When box will allow more game controllers.

Click the Players pie slice seen in Figure 17.15 and another pie menu appears, like the one in Figure 17.16.

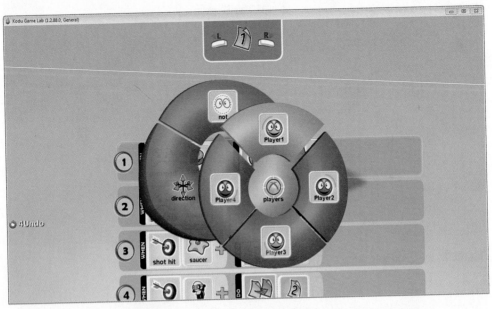

FIGURE 17.16   Up to four players can use game controllers in a Kodu Game Lab game.

Here you can see that four different game controllers can be used; all you have to do is assign a player number (Player 1, Player 2, Player 3, or Player 4).

Figure 17.17 shows that Programming Row 1's When box now has a Player 1 tile added. Remember to do the same for the button controls (as shown in Programming Row 2).

NOTE

You won't have to specify a player number (Player 1, for example) when it comes to scoring. Scoring is usually done using a colored scoreboard tile (such as the Blue scoreboard), so as long as you remember to program each player's object (such as White Kodu) using the proper Player Number tile and use a different colored scoreboard, everything should work fine.

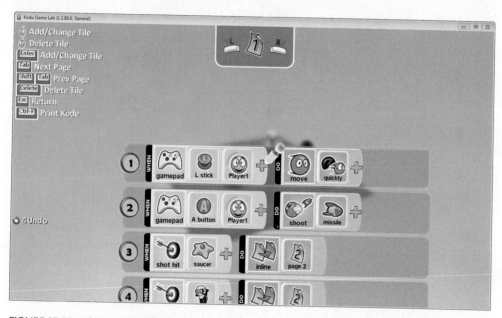

FIGURE 17.17   The Player 1 tile lets you know this program is for Player 1's game controller.

What about extra keyboards? Well, most computers do not recognize multiple keyboards or mouse devices, so Kodu Game Lab does not offer up player number tiles for keyboards and mouse devices.

TIP

One nice thing you can always do for your game players is to let them know in the game description whether a game uses the keyboard/mouse or a game controller. It's also nice to inform players of a two-player game, whether the game is meant to use two game controllers or a single game controller for Player 1 and a mouse/keyboard for Player 2.

Configuring Missile Control

Take a look at Figure 17.18 and you'll notice something interesting. I've got a wall separating Kodu from an enemy target, but when I fire a missile at the target, the missile flies up and over the wall to impact the target.

FIGURE 17.18   That missile flew right over that wall!

You might find Player 2 griping when he is hit by Player 1's missile that flies up and over a large building or mountain that separates the two players. In Figure 17.18, for example, Player 1's missile should fly straight, so when she presses the A button to fire a missile, it should impact the wall, not fly over it. This is an easy fix, and Figure 17.19 shows how it's done.

In Figure 17.19, I've clicked the + to the right of the Missile tile. The two tiles I'm interested in are the Level tile and the Cruise tile. The Cruise tile is the default setting; the missile will fly over mountains and walls. But I can choose the Level tile to specify that any missile fired will fly straight and level with the ground and impact a mountain or wall if it's high enough.

Figure 17.20 shows the missile is now impacting the wall, not flying over it.

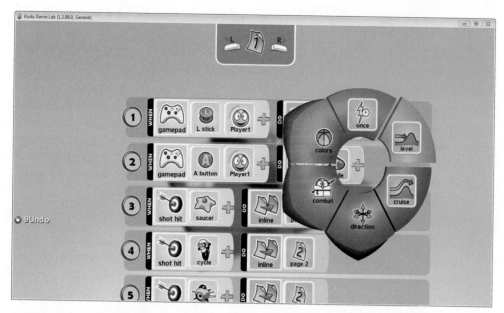

FIGURE 17.19   Two options are available for programming a missile: Cruise and Level.

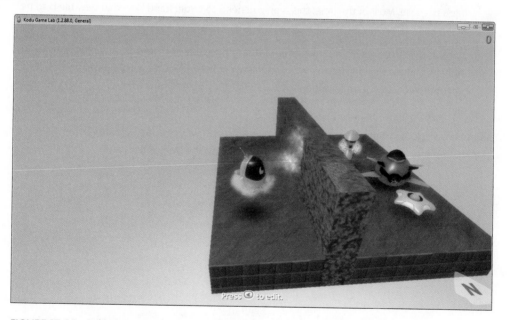

FIGURE 17.20   With the Level tile, the missile hits the wall instead of flying over it.

Moving On

With this chapter, I simply wanted to introduce you to some useful features in Kodu Game Lab that I've not yet had a chance to use in the earlier chapters. One or more of them should prove useful to you as you continue to design your own games.

Kodu Game Lab contains more features to discover, some of which you'll encounter before the end of the book. But this is also where I want to offer you a bit of encouragement to poke around Kodu Game Lab, click some pie slices that you've not yet used, and see what they do. I cannot show you every feature that's built into Kodu Game Lab, but by now you've probably gotten quite comfortable with programming games and should feel confident that you can undo any changes you make to a game that don't work well.

With that said, here's what I want you to do before moving on to Chapter 18, "Join the Community: Online Help and Sharing Games:"

1. Open some of your objects that you've programmed and examine the When boxes. Anytime you see a + to the right of the last tile in a When box, click it and investigate what other options are available. Pick one or two that you've not yet used and try them out.

2. After you add a new tile to a program, right-click it and choose the Help option from the pop-up menu that appears. The Help option is there to give you a very basic description of that tile's purpose. Most of the time, this is all you need to understand how that new tile is to be used.

3. Look at the Do boxes in your own programs and see whether there are any plus signs to the right of the last tile. Click those and examine even more tiles that you've probably not yet encountered. Use the Help option to learn what they do and how they might help your own games.

Be sure to click the Home Menu button and save any work you've done before selecting Exit to Main Menu. Don't forget to add some additional information to the Description field.

18

Join the Community: Online Help and Sharing Games

In This Chapter

○ The Kodu Game Lab Website

○ The Kodu Community Forum

○ Sharing Your Games

You're not alone when it comes to Kodu Game Lab. Microsoft doesn't want you to be creating games and not sharing them with the world, and they've made it very easy to share your games and meet other Kodu programmers out there. This chapter introduces you to some of the services and tools you need to become a useful and respected Kodu Community member.

The Kodu Game Lab Website

If you're viewing the Main Menu in Kodu Game Lab, you can click the link shown in Figure 18.1 (just below Kodu) to open up the official Kodu Game Lab website.

FIGURE 18.1   On the Main Menu, click the www.KoduGameLab.com link.

You can also enter kodugamelab.com into a web browser; either way, you are taken to the page shown in Figure 18.2.

If you've got a friend who would like to download and install Kodu Game Lab, this is the web address to provide. There's a nice big green Get Kodu button in the upper-left corner of the screen that will get your friend started.

The official web page has four different pages for you to view: Home, Worlds, About, and Discussion. Let me briefly introduce you to each of these and I'll go a little deeper with a few of them later in this chapter.

Home

The Home page is where you can find announcements from the Kodu team at Microsoft. Running down the left side of the screen (refer back to Figure 18.2) are the latest news items related to Kodu. The date of the item will be listed along with a brief title; be sure to look for the Read More Here link that can be clicked to open up the full news item.

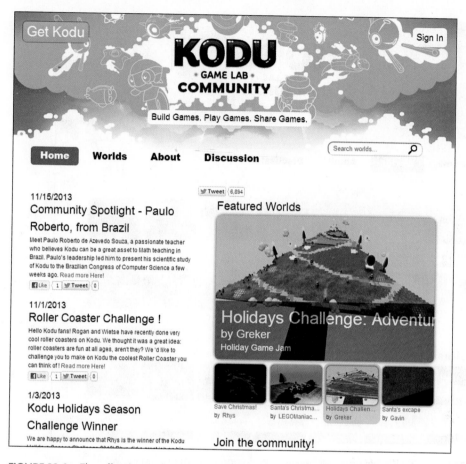

FIGURE 18.2   The official Kodu Game Lab website.

Worlds

If you click the Worlds tab, the Home screen disappears and is replaced with something similar to Figure 18.3.

Here you'll find three categories: Newest, Highest Ratings, and Most Popular. Below each category are small images of games that have been submitted by other Kodu game programmers like you. You can view the game's name, the username of the person who submitted the game, and other information. For the Highest Ratings category, you can view how many stars a game has received from other Kodu Community members, and the Most Popular category displays how many times a game has been downloaded. (I discuss downloading games shortly.)

FIGURE 18.3 The Worlds page lets you view Kodu games from around the world.

> **TIP**
> There's also a Search bar (in Figure 18.3) that you can use to search thousands of existing Kodu games using keywords. Type in a keyword (such as *alien* or *maze*) and you'll get back results that include your keywords in the game title.

To view more details about any game you see on the Worlds page, just click the image above a game's name and you'll be taken to that game's information page. Figure 18.4 shows an information page example.

On the game's information page, you can click the Download button to download and begin playing the game immediately (assuming you have Kodu Game Lab installed on the computer you are currently using), leave a comment (if you are logged in to the Kodu Community; more on this in a moment), and, if you find an uploaded game that is offensive, you can click the Report As Inappropriate link to have it looked over by the Kodu team.

FIGURE 18.4   Read more information about a game.

About

The About page contains basic information about Kodu Game Lab along with some screen captures, as shown in Figure 18.5.

Scroll down a bit and you'll also find links to short tutorials that can get a friend using Kodu Game Lab quickly. You'll find a list of the system requirements needed to run Kodu Game Lab, as well as some links to the Kodu Game Lab Facebook account and Twitter account under the Contact Us section. You'll also find an email address that you can use to contact Kodu Support and a Get Satisfaction link that takes you to a tech support forum, shown in Figure 18.6.

FIGURE 18.5 The About page offers tutorials, system requirements, and more.

Click the **Sign Up** link near the top of the page shown in Figure 18.6 to create an account. After you've got an account, you can post any technical questions you have related to Kodu Game Labs. Keep in mind that this is a place to ask questions related to bugs found in Kodu Game Lab or issues you might encounter with installation.

Rover: Great! I was wondering where I could ask questions about programming in Kodu Game Lab.

Kodu: Actually, this isn't the place to ask those types of questions. This forum is really for posting questions related to issues installing and running Kodu.

Rover: So where do I go for help in programming my Beam tool to examine all these special Martian rocks?

Kodu: For that, you'll want to reach out to the Kodu Community and post a question on the Community Forum.

Rover: Where is the Kodu Community Forum, and how do I post questions?

Kodu: I think those questions are going to be answered next.

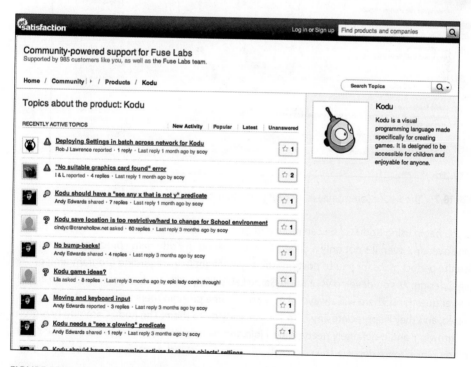

FIGURE 18.6   The tech support page for Kodu Game Lab.

Discussion

The last tab on the KoduGameLab.com website takes you to the Kodu Community forum, shown in Figure 18.7.

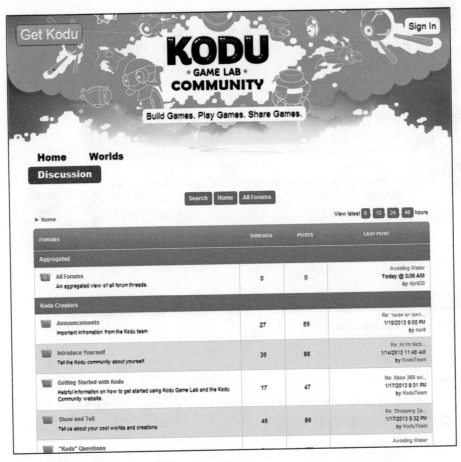

FIGURE 18.7   The Kodu Community is a great place to meet other programmers.

As you begin using Kodu Game Lab more and more, you'll likely find yourself returning to this page over and over. It's not only a great place to meet other Kodu game programmers, but it's also the perfect place for you to post questions you might have regarding programming or game design. As you develop your Kodu Game Lab skills, you'll also find yourself able to actually answer questions! There will always be new Kodu game programmers who are just getting started, and they'll appreciate any help you can provide to them. The Kodu Community is growing and growing, and it definitely needs you to join and participate. I'm going to go over the Kodu Community in more detail in the next section, but for now I just want you to know where to go to find it and gain access.

The Kodu Community Forum

You'll always be able to browse the forum and read questions and responses, but the real benefits will come after you've joined the community and become a Kodu Community member. Please check with a parent to make certain he or she is comfortable with you joining the Kodu Community. Although it's a safe and monitored community, it's always a good idea to make sure Mom or Dad approves!

There are three ways you can do this, but you'll need to click the Discussion tab if you're not already viewing that page. After you're there, click the Sign In button in the top-right corner of the screen (refer back to Figure 18.7) and you will see a screen like the one in Figure 18.8.

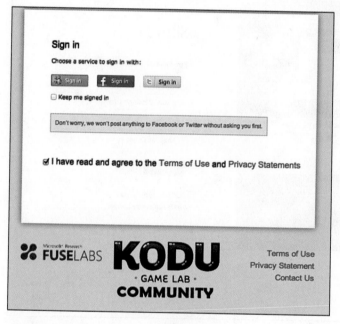

FIGURE 18.8   The Kodu Community login screen.

If you agree to the Terms of Use and Privacy Statements, place a checkmark in the check box.

NOTE
You can click the Terms of Use link or the Privacy Statements link to read those items.

After checking the box, you'll find three methods for logging in to the Kodu Community: using a LiveID account, a Facebook account, or a Twitter account. I'll be using my LiveID account, and I do encourage you to create a LiveID account rather than using Facebook or Twitter. For security reasons, I recommend that you hide your real name when accessing the Kodu Community. Here's how you can create a LiveID account.

Creating a LiveID Account

Click the LiveID button (the orange button in the upper-left corner of Figure 18.8) and you'll see a window open like the one in Figure 18.9 appear.

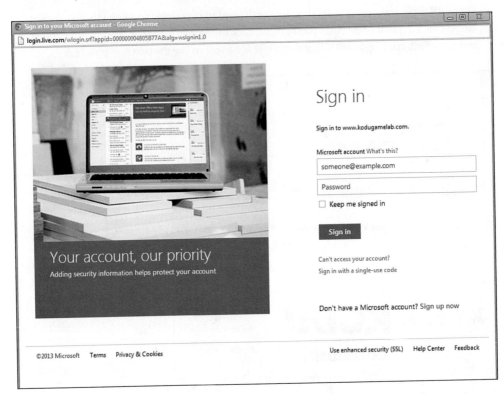

FIGURE 18.9   Create a LiveID account to use the Kodu Community forum.

On this new window, click the Sign Up Now link if you don't already have a LiveID account. If you do have a LiveID account, go ahead and sign in by entering your Microsoft account username and password.

> **CAUTION**
>
> Be sure to ask your parent or teacher for permission to create a LiveID account. There might be rules in place at your school or home regarding accessing the Internet, so don't get in trouble. Ask first!

When you're creating your LiveID, be sure to pick a username that does not give away your real name or location or gender. Don't use RickyHolmes or AtlantaGirl, for example. Feel free to call yourself DeKoder or XpertKoder or anything else you can think of. Just be safe and ask yourself if someone would be able to garner any personal details about you from your username.

After you've got a LiveID created, log in and you'll be asked to create a screen name, as shown in Figure 18.10.

FIGURE 18.10   Create your Kodu Community Forum screen name.

The Kodu Community screen name can differ from your LiveID username if you like. Once again, however, pick something that's not offensive and doesn't give away your real name or gender or location. Click the Submit button and you're ready to start using the Kodu Community Forum.

> **NOTE**
> If you pick a screen name that's already in use, you'll be asked to try another name.

Posting Comments, Questions, and Answers

Now it's time to actually use the Kodu Community Forum. The forum is broken into a number of sections such as Announcements, Show and Tell, and "Kode" Questions. There are currently 12 sections, and I'm certain you'll find a favorite. You can see all the sections in Figure 18.11.

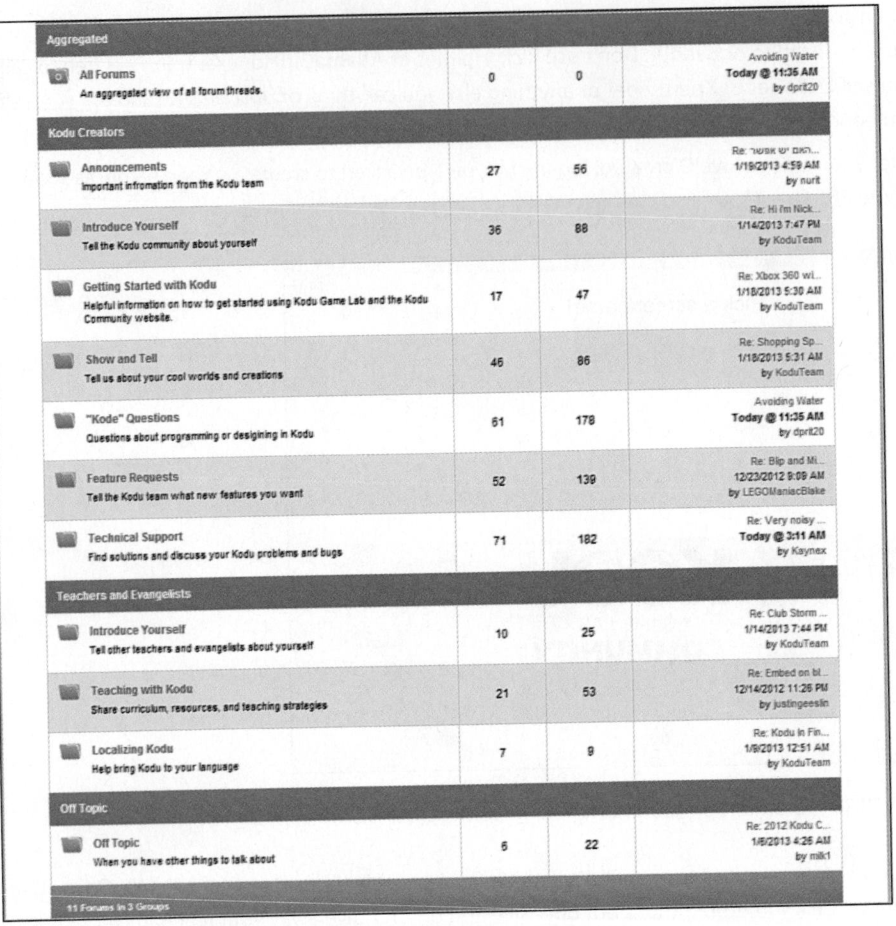

Aggregated			
All Forums An aggregated view of all forum threads.	0	0	Avoiding Water **Today @ 11:35 AM** by dprit20
Kodu Creators			
Announcements Important infromation from the Kodu team	27	56	Re: האם ש אושר... 1/19/2013 4:59 AM by nurit
Introduce Yourself Tell the Kodu community about yourself	36	88	Re: Hi I'm Nick... 1/14/2013 7:47 PM by KoduTeam
Getting Started with Kodu Helpful information on how to get started using Kodu Game Lab and the Kodu Community website.	17	47	Re: Xbox 360 wi... 1/18/2013 5:30 AM by KoduTeam
Show and Tell Tell us about your cool worlds and creations	46	86	Re: Shopping Sp... 1/18/2013 5:31 AM by KoduTeam
"Kode" Questions Questions about programming or designing in Kodu	61	178	Avoiding Water **Today @ 11:35 AM** by dprit20
Feature Requests Tell the Kodu team what new features you want	52	139	Re: Blip and Mi... 12/23/2012 9:09 AM by LEGOManiacBlake
Technical Support Find solutions and discuss your Kodu problems and bugs	71	182	Re: Very noisy ... **Today @ 3:11 AM** by Kaynex
Teachers and Evangelists			
Introduce Yourself Tell other teachers and evangelists about yourself	10	25	Re: Club Storm ... 1/14/2013 7:44 PM by KoduTeam
Teaching with Kodu Share curriculum, resources, and teaching strategies	21	53	Re: Embed on bl... 12/14/2012 11:26 PM by justingeeslin
Localizing Kodu Help bring Kodu to your language	7	9	Re: Kodu In Fin... 1/9/2013 12:51 AM by KoduTeam
Off Topic			
Off Topic When you have other things to talk about	6	22	Re: 2012 Kodu C... 1/6/2013 4:26 AM by milk1

11 Forums in 3 Groups

FIGURE 18.11 The various sections in the Kodu Community Forum.

Each section name is followed by a number indicating how many discussions (threads) currently exist. The next number is the number of posts (these can be comments, questions, or answers) contained in the section, and the last bit of information is the last user to post something in that section and the date and time that post was made.

TIP

The Last Post section is useful when you'd like to see whether there have been any posts made since your last visit. If you've posted a question in a section and are waiting on a response, this is a fast way to see whether someone has possibly provided an answer. But it could also be someone posting a comment or reply to a different thread; the only way to know for sure is to check your question.

To open a section, just click it. I'm going to open the Show and Tell section, which brings up the screen shown in Figure 18.12.

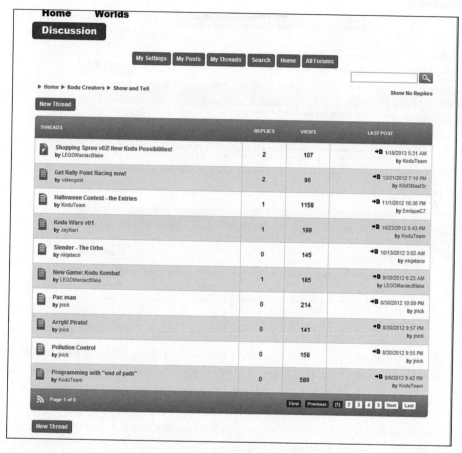

FIGURE 18.12   Click a section to open it and view all threads.

Figure 18.12 shows that on this first page 10 threads (or discussions) are going on. First page? Yep! There are four more pages of discussions, and I can tell this by looking at the lower-left corner of the screen where it says Page 1 of 5. Some sections might have fewer pages, but some will definitely have more.

I can use the Previous and Next buttons to move between the pages in the Show and Tell section. If I see a discussion that interests me, I simply click the title of the discussion. Figure 18.13 shows that I've opened up the discussion thread titled "Hearing program setting doesn't work, this is the solution."

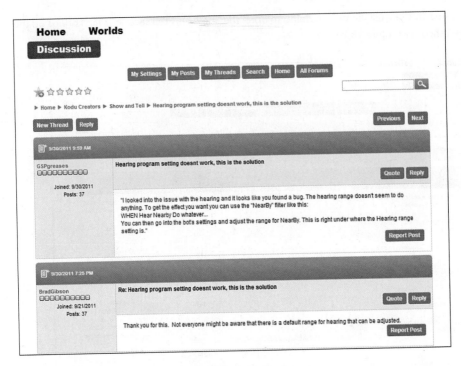

FIGURE 18.13 Opening a thread to read its content.

I can scroll up and down to read other Kodu users' comments, and I can click the Reply button to type up my own response if I want. If the number of comments is getting large, you'll once again find Previous and Next buttons that will allow you to move forward and backward through a discussion.

If you'd like to post your own comment or question as a new thread, you'll first need to pick the proper section. If you've got a programming question, the Show and Tell section probably isn't the best place to create it. Let me try the "Kode" Questions section.

> **TIP**
>
> If you're reading threads inside a section and want to return to the main page, click the Discussion button near the top of the screen and you will be taken to the section listing shown earlier in Figure 18.11.

After opening the "Kode" Questions section, I want to post my question. To do this, I click the New Thread button shown in Figure 18.14.

The New Thread button can be used to post a question, but you can also use it to post other items. Use it to create a post about a new game you've just uploaded to the Community (use the Show and Tell section). Use it to submit an idea for a new Kodu Game Lab feature to the Kodu

Team (use the Feature Requests section). Or use it to introduce yourself to the community (using the Introduce Yourself section). Just remember not to share your real name, location, or gender. Your Kodu Community screen name is all you need to let others know who you are, what kinds of games you enjoy programming, and other Kodu-related information.

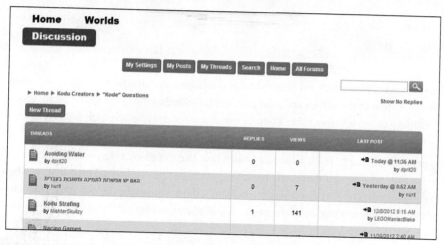

FIGURE 18.14   The New Thread button enables you to create a new thread.

After clicking the New Thread button, you'll see a new screen like the one in Figure 18.15.

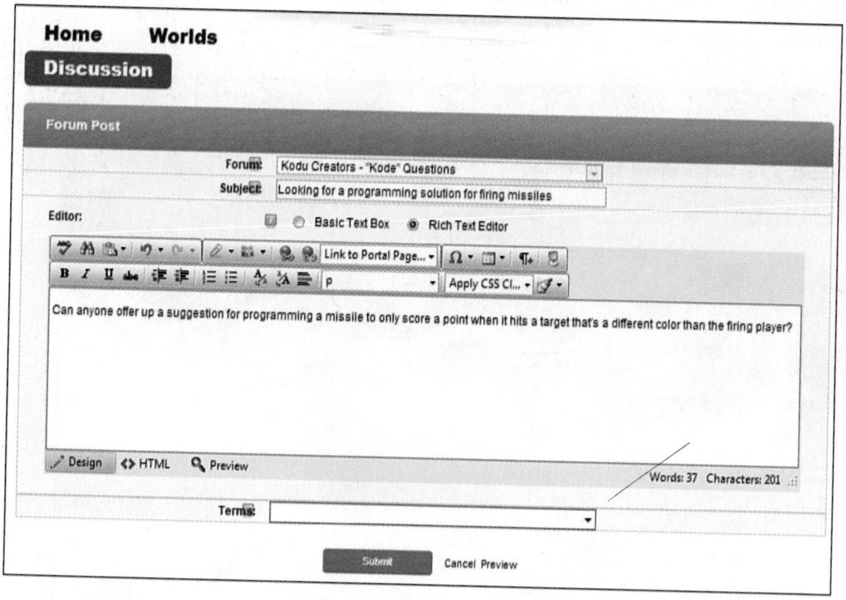

FIGURE 18.15   Create your new forum thread post here.

Type in a subject for your post in the Subject field followed by your question in the text box at the bottom. If you've exported your Kodu game to a file, you can also attach that file if you'd like to share it in the forums before releasing to the community using the Worlds option.

> **NOTE**
>
> I'll show you how to export your game so it can be emailed or included as a thread attachment later in this chapter.

After you've typed in your comment or question and included any attachments, click the Submit button at the bottom of the screen and your post will be added to the community forum! Check back occasionally to see whether other Kodu Community members have responded... and use the Reply button if you want to communicate back to them.

On every page of the forum, you'll also see a Search box. Use this to enter keywords (such as *missile* or *Say tile*); only threads that contain your keywords will be displayed. This is helpful when you're looking for posts related to a question you might have; you might discover that others have had the same question and that answers are already available, saving you from having to create a new post.

The Kodu Community Forum is one of the best places to go when you have questions or want to share what you're working on. But what do you do when you've completed a game and are ready to share it with all the other Kodu game players in the world?

For that, you need to return to Kodu Game Lab's Main Menu, select Load Worlds, and then click the My Worlds button shown in Figure 18.16.

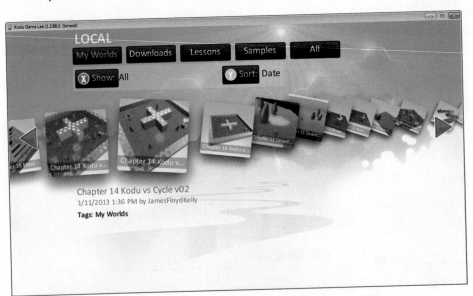

FIGURE 18.16 Open up My Worlds and find a game you want to share with the world.

Sharing Your Games

After you select a game you want to share, click the game and you'll see a small menu of options appear, as shown in Figure 18.17.

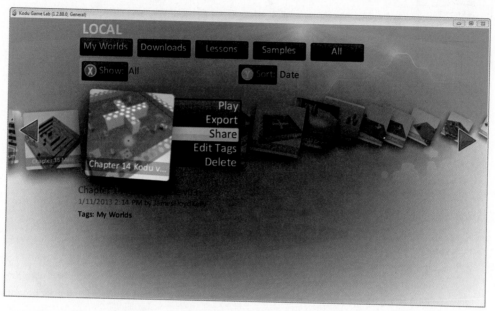

FIGURE 18.17   A small menu offers five options for your games.

As you can see here, you can choose to edit any tags you've assigned to a game (refer back to Chapter 11 "Good Game Design, Part 1: Tips and Tricks for Better Game Programming," for information on using tags), delete a game (this cannot be undone, so be careful!), and play a game. But the other two options, Export and Share, are the ones I need to introduce you to now.

Let's start with the Export option. If you select the Export option, Kodu Game Lab creates a small file on your computer that contains everything needed to play the game on another computer running Kodu Game Lab. If you've got a friend using Kodu Game Lab, you can email this small file to her. She'll receive it as an email attachment, and after saving it to her own computer, she can double-click the file and immediately play it.

TIP

This file can also be modified, so someone could take the file and make changes to it or fix some bugs. It's a great way to get some help with a problem that's got you stuck.

So, try it out. Click the Export option and you'll see a screen open like the one in Figure 18.18.

FIGURE 18.18   Save your Kodu game to your computer's hard drive.

Pick somewhere to save the file that you'll easily remember. I usually use the Desktop so that I can get to it immediately. Name the file or use the one already provided and includes your game name and your name. Notice that the file uses the .kodu extension. Click the Save button and your Kodu game will be bundled up into a nice tidy little file that can be emailed or used as an attachment in the Kodu Community Forum, as shown in Figure 18.19.

FIGURE 18.19   My *Kodu vs. Cycle* game is bundled up and ready to email to a friend.

Now let's go back to that same game in the My Worlds listing, click it, and choose the Share option. When I click the Share option, I get an alert that asks me to sign in to the Kodu Community, as shown in Figure 18.20. You might already be signed in, but if you're not, click the Yes button and provide your LiveID username and password.

After you've provided your login credentials, another message appears like the one in Figure 18.21, telling you your game has now been uploaded to the Worlds section at KoduGameLab.com.

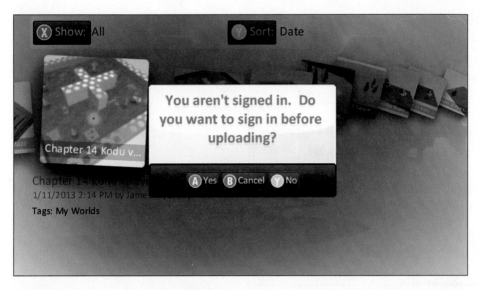

FIGURE 18.20   Log in with your LiveID account so that you can share your game.

> **NOTE**
>
> You can share your levels anonymously if you're not logged in to the Kodu Community, but your name will not be associated with the game.

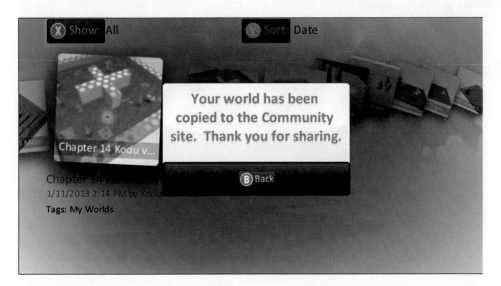

FIGURE 18.21   Your game is now part of the Kodu Game Lab World library.

Congratulations! You've made the Kodu Community a better one by providing a game that others can enjoy, examine, and use to learn some new tricks.

A quick visit to www.kodugamelab.com and a click on the Worlds tab shows me that my game is now resting comfortably in the Newest category, as shown in Figure 18.22.

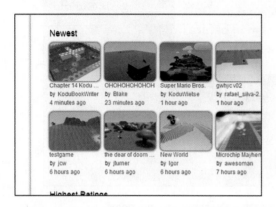

FIGURE 18.22 My *Kodu vs. Cycle* game has been added to the Worlds page.

You can also view newly added games by tapping the Community option on the Main Menu. As you can see in Figure 18.23, my newly added game appears in the scrolling list when I click the All button to see all Kodu Community members' games.

FIGURE 18.23 My *Kodu vs. Cycle* game is also visible within Kodu Game Lab.

Moving On

Designing games with Kodu Game Lab is fun, and it's even more fun when you have a community of friends who are always on the lookout for great games to play and use as inspiration.

With the Kodu Community, you've got access to the Kodu Team, as well as to Kodu Game Lab users from all over the world. Just as you are probably always looking for new programming tips and tricks, so are other Kodu programmers.

Never be afraid to share what you know! If you've figured out some amazing programming trick, don't keep it to yourself. Log in to the forum and create a new post in the Show and Tell section and let all the other programmers know what you've discovered. This kind of sharing inspires others to do the same, and if all Kodu game programmers can start sharing their knowledge and advice, we will all start seeing even more incredible games being added to the Kodu Community worlds.

Before you move on to Chapter 19, "Good Game Design: Part 3: Giving Players a Great Experience," I want to give you three really easy assignments:

1. If you can get permission from a parent or teacher to create a LiveID, go ahead and do so and then create your Kodu screen name for use in the forums.

2. Pick one of your own games that you're proud of and share it with other Kodu programmers. (Even better, log in to the Kodu Community Forum and let everyone know the name of the game you've uploaded and explain how it works and the rules for playing.)

3. Download a game that you've never played before and open it up and examine the programming. You might have to examine a few more games, but I guarantee that if you take a look at half a dozen games or more, you're going to see some programming tricks that you've never encountered. That's how you learn new programming: Look at what others are doing.

Be sure to click the Home Menu button and save any work you've done before selecting Exit to Main Menu. Don't forget to add some additional information to the Description field.

Good Game Design, Part 3: Giving Players a Great Experience

By this point in the book, you've probably either already programmed a game or two of your own design, or you've got some ideas bopping around in your head that you're just itching to create and share with the world. If you've already programmed some of your own games, you probably encountered a few of the typical issues that professional game designers experience every day. And if you're preparing to program one of your own games for the very first time, you might be wondering where to start.

This chapter shares some advice about game design using Kodu Game Lab. As with any advice, you're free to take it or leave it; use what you like, and skip the rest. But one thing is for certain: If you spend a little time up front thinking about your game, listing some of the design requirements and special rules, and possibly sketching out the game world before you start dropping terrain everywhere, you might find that your game comes together a bit easier.

Giving Players a Great Experience

If you want the games you create with Kodu Game Lab to really stand out from the crowd, the key is to give the players a great experience. One of the best compliments you as a game designer will get is to hear a player say "I want to play that again." If players are enjoying your game and keep coming back for more, you've done your job.

But before players can tell you how much they've enjoyed your game and how they can't wait to play it again, you've got to actually create it. But that's what is so amazing about Kodu Game Lab: Designing a game is almost like playing a game! I can't tell you how often I've lost track of the time while putting together a game in Kodu Game Lab. Between the terrain editing, the object programming, and the constant testing, I often feel like I'm having more fun designing the game than I will have playing it.

Because Kodu Game Lab is so fun to use, you may find yourself constantly tweaking and changing things, trying to make the game more fun and more eye-catching.

But sooner or later, you've got to release the game to the players. That's the whole point of creating a game, isn't it? And while you can certainly release games before they're 100% done (often called a *beta release*), your ultimate goal is to release a finished game to the world and then move on to the next game.

> **NOTE**
>
> Of course, you want to listen to players and fix any issues (bugs) they might find with the game. And players might offer up suggestions for how they'd like to see the game improved. So you can certainly stay with a game and keep improving it and adding new features. When this happens, consider releasing the new version with a new name. If players love *Mud Quest* and offer suggestions for new quests in the game, consider releasing *Mud Quest II* with all the suggestions and new game features added to the sequel.

But again, getting to that finished game requires starting from the beginning and creating a great game from the ground up. And there's no better place to start designing a game than by simply sitting down and writing up some details about the game you want to create. It's called a *game design*, and it can be just as fun as programming the objects of your game or laying down tiles of terrain.

Game Design

You should try to brainstorm three things about your game before you begin building it in Kodu Game Lab:

○ **The game world:** The size, terrain used, and the layout such as mountains, roads, buildings, and more.

○ **Number of players**: Your game can host between one and six players (four using game controllers and two using the keyboard—WASD and arrow keys), and knowing how many player-controlled objects you need to program will help you narrow down the type of game you'll create.

○ **The ultimate goal**: Is your game a shoot-em-up where each player is trying to destroy the other? Are players going to cooperate against programmed enemies? Is it a quest where players need to hunt and navigate to solve problems?

If you can write down a few short sentences that describe each of these three game plan items, you've got the skeleton of a game already created. And you don't need to develop these three items in that order. You might know that you want to create a two-player quest and still be uncertain about the layout of the game world, so feel free to develop what you can. Here's an example of how I would start out developing my own game plan.

○ **Number of players**: I want to create a single-player game that will be a mix of quest and shooting at enemies. If the game is popular, I might want to expand the game to allow for two players.

○ **Ultimate goal**: I think it would be fun if the player had to fight through a small group of enemies to get to each of the quest items. Three items should be enough, and I want to hide them so that players won't easily locate the objects.

○ **The game world**: The world will need to be large if the quest items are going to be hidden. I also want to make certain the enemies don't wander away from the objects or fire on the player before a player begins an attempt to retrieve an item. This means a fairly large game world, with lots of hidden areas.

Notice with my three descriptions that I've not come up with a name for the game, and I haven't really decided on terrain colors, which objects will be controlled by players, and which objects will be enemy targets. I also haven't decided on what types of objects that players will hunt for on their quest. All of these are questions that I can decide later… and they're also items that I can change easily enough. If I find I'd rather have the player using Cycle instead of being attacked by a bunch of evil Cycles, I can simply copy programming from the original player object to the new one, and the same goes for the enemy targets.

> **CAUTION**
>
> Remember that not every object in Kodu Game Lab supports every action. Rover, for example, cannot shoot missiles. And the Boat object won't move around on land… only water. Keep limitations of the objects in mind when choosing them for player-controlled objects or enemy objects.

Many Kodu Game Lab programmers will simply sit down and start adding terrain, dropping in enemies, and programming a player object to fire missiles. And there's nothing wrong with this. But if you want to do something different and grab players' attentions with something new and exciting, spend a little time developing your own game plan before opening up Kodu Game Lab.

Game World Planning

You can easily drop in a missile-firing Kodu and a few nonfiring enemy targets on the new world, as shown in Figure 19.1, but that's going to be one boring game and not all that exciting. I call this game *Fast Fight*.

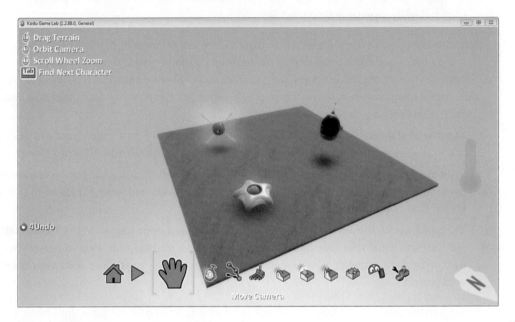

FIGURE 19.1   *Fast Fight* doesn't last long, and Player 1 always wins.

There was no planning here. I took the single square piece of terrain, added Kodu, a saucer, and Sputnik, and programmed Kodu to move and fire. Yawn!

Now, I could try to create many varieties of games, but if all I'm looking for is a simple hunt-and-shoot, with Kodu trying to find enemies to shoot, I can do much better than a simple block of terrain. How much better? Take a look at Figure 19.2 to see a game world that I first sketched out on paper before ever placing a single bit of terrain or touching the terrain editing tools.

With a rough sketch, I'm now able to determine the size of the world I need to create. It's going to include a small maze, a graveyard, a forest, a mountain, and a castle, so I've got to get players a lot of room to wander so they won't see all the surprises.

Just creating this sketch also helped me make another decision about this game. Because I don't want the players to see the entire world, I'm going to program the player's object to view the world using first-person point of view (POV). So I'll make a note to myself to remember to add that bit of programming.

Rover: I'm starting to see that there are a lot of details that a programmer must keep track of when designing a game.

Kodu: One of the best ways is to keep a notebook or a small stack of paper where you can jot down your thoughts and ideas.

Rover: Couldn't I just keep my notes in the computer or type them into the description of my game?

Kodu: Sure you can. But you might not always have access to Kodu Game Lab, so having a place to write down your ideas for your games will be useful, too.

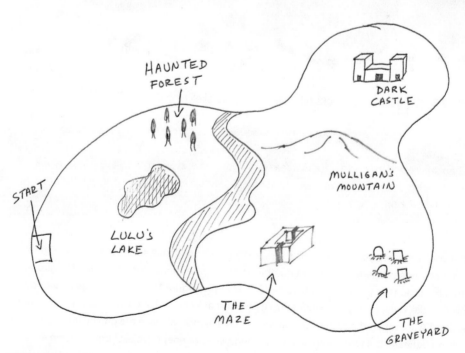

FIGURE 19.2 This world should be suitable for a quest.

I've used some plain printer paper for my sketch, but you could just as easily use graph paper or even sketch out your game world using Paint or another graphics program. Whatever you choose, sketching out your game world can help you make the right decisions when it comes time to selecting the shape of your world, the terrain you'll use, and any obstacles or sites you want to add to your world (such as a castle or a lake).

Figure 19.3 shows how I've taken my sketch and turned it into a game world using Kodu Game Lab. I haven't added items like the castle or graveyard yet, but it's a start.

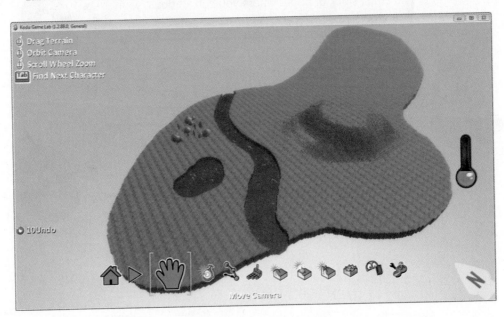

FIGURE 19.3 My game world looks a lot like my original sketch.

> **TIP**
> When drawing a large world, zoom out as far as you can and enlarge the Brush tool so that you can fill in the terrain faster. You can enlarge the Brush tool quite a bit, saving you a lot of time when filling in empty space.

After you've created your game world, be sure to save it and make a note in the Description field that this is the game world with no objects or programming. From this point forward, save different versions as you add new features. For example, Figure 19.3 shows my game world with only the lake, river, forest, and mountain. I'll save this as Version 0 and won't modify it anymore. Version 1 will contain the castle, for example, and Version 2 will have the graveyard added. Version 3 will hold the maze. I won't start actually adding player or enemy objects until Version 4!

One of the benefits to saving the basic game world before adding any additional objects is that should I choose to create another game (maybe a sequel) using the same game world, I won't have to go and remove the castle or graveyard should I decide I don't want to use them in the new game.

You might find yourself constantly refining and updating the game world as you program the game's various objects. For example, the castle's entrance might not be wide enough for a player's object to enter; you might not discover this until you're testing movement. When this happens, adjust your game world accordingly.

It's not uncommon for a game world to be modified numerous times as a game is being created, so don't get too attached to your game world. Be flexible and make changes when they are needed.

Game Rules and Objectives

While I'm thinking about my game world, I'm also looking at the actual terrain and pondering how my player will operate in it. Kodu can float over the ground, but Cycle actually touches it. For small rocks, Kodu simply goes over them. But Cycle has to go around all rocks. This is an example of a game rule that is defined by Kodu Game Lab. No amount of programming is going to enable Kodu to climb out of a deep pit he's falling into; some in-game rules are simply out of your hands.

But there are also those rules that you can create. These are the rules that are applied to your players. Examples include the following:

○ Player 1 cannot pick up a gold coin unless all saucers are destroyed.

○ Player 2 will steal five hit points when Player 1 is hit by a missile.

○ The jets will always fire on the nearest player.

Many gamers tend to look at rules negatively, but without rules a game would be a free-for-all, and a winner would be difficult to determine if players can do whatever they want. You have to create rules to provide a structure for your game.

Going hand in hand with rules are the game's objectives. A game objective is something a player is working toward achieving. Objectives can end a game or even open up new areas of a game to explore. Examples include the following:

○ First player to reach 50 points wins the game.

○ Pay the gatekeeper with a coin to gain access to the castle.

○ Find all stars before the timer runs out.

The rules and objectives are key to creating a fun game for players. If you have too many rules, however, players will get frustrated. And if the objectives aren't clear, players will get confused… and then frustrated.

To avoid these issues with your own games, it can sometimes help to write them down as you develop them. If you're developing a quest-type game, write down the objects a player must retrieve or the special object that must be approached with the secret word. If you're developing a two-player competition game, write down how the winner will be determined. Score? Last man standing? Number of stars retrieved?

Writing down rules and objectives will also help you organize the objects you must place in your game. If an objective is to collect coins, you know you're going to be dropping coins onto the game world. If a gatekeeper is to be approached by a player, you need to pick the best object to fill the gatekeeper's shoes (I favor the jet) and where that object will be placed in your world. If six saucers must be destroyed before a coin is dropped, you know you'll be placing six Saucer objects on the terrain.

Here are some examples of rules and objectives for some of my games and what they tell me I'll need to do or should expect when I begin programming:

- The game ends when the last silver star is delivered to the castle. (I need to create a castle or use the Castle or Hut object. I'll also be using the Silver Star object.)
- When Player 1 or Player 2 reaches 60 points, the game clock starts counting down by two points instead of one. (I need two unique player objects and three scoreboards—two for players and one for the clock.)
- The saucer steals a player's coin if touched. (I need to program a saucer to move toward a player and take a coin if they bump.)
- The game ends when a player's hit points reach zero. (I won't need a scoreboard or timer.)

As you develop the rules and objectives for your game, be sure to write them down either in your notes or in the game's description. You don't want to surprise your players by not explaining how the game works, and documenting your rules and objectives as you create them ensures that you won't forget to include them in the game's description.

Not every rule, however, needs to be provided in the game's description. Sometimes the rules can be provided to players using the Say tile. An in-game object can explain objectives (go find me a coin) or rules (if you get hit three times by the saucer, the game is over).

Take a look at Figure 19.4. It's from the *Mars Rover: Discovery* game.

Here you can see an example of a game's objectives being clearly explained:

- Search out rocks and drill them to score points.
- Avoid hazards.
- The game ends after 90 seconds have elapsed.

Those are clear objectives. But what about the game rules? Take a look at Figure 19.5 and you'll see that after the game begins, the player is told how to play.

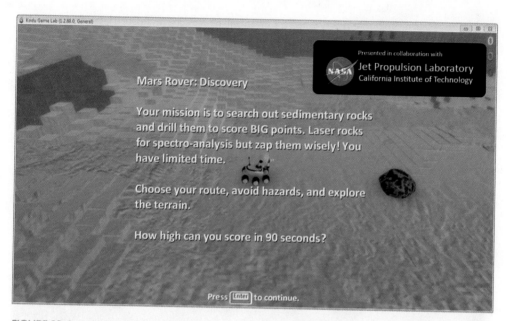

FIGURE 19.4   The *Mars Rover: Discovery* game's opening screen.

FIGURE 19.5   Some rules are provided when the game begins.

Here the player is told that pressing the B button will hit a rock with Rover's laser. So one of the first things a player learns when the game begins is how to hit a rock with the laser beam.

After the player learns to use the B button, the next rock tells the player how to drill a rock: Press the X button. You can see the text bubble that appears in Figure 19.6.

FIGURE 19.6 Another rule that is given as the player is actually playing the game.

By the time the player has moved forward in the game, all the rules have been provided. Ensuring that the player will want to play again, some rules are only mentioned when the player gets into trouble. Figure 19.7, for example, only appears when Rover moves over sand.

If players never roll over the sand, they are unlikely to be shown the rule that explains how Rover moves slower over sand.

TIP

Open up the three *Mars Rover* games by choosing the Load World option and then clicking the **Lessons** button. The three games are *Mars Rover: Discovery*, *Mars Rover: The Expedition*, and *Mars Rover: Set the Course*. The programming for these three games can be examined, showing you how the Kodu Team programmed the in-game rules.

FIGURE 19.7 Some rules are provided only when they are broken.

Kodu: I can fire missiles and blips, but you've got some unique tools of your own.

Rover: I'm on a mission of peace and science to explore and learn about new worlds. My Scanner, Drill, and Laser (Spectroscope, I believe it's called) do come in handy when rolling over the Martian surface.

Kodu: How do you use them?

Rover: Right-click me and select Program. Click a Do box and select the Rover pie slice; you'll see a new pie menu appear that lets me take a picture (Picture tile), use my laser (Beam tile), drill (Inspect tile), and scan (Scan tile). These can be assigned to activate when a game controller button or a keyboard key is pressed.

Kodu: Can your tools also be used in the When box to test for certain conditions?

Rover: Click the When box and you'll see the Scanned (scanner), Inspected (drill), and Beamed (laser) tiles. Each of them can be used on Rock objects. For example, you could program WHEN SCANNED SEDIMENTARY—DO GLOW IT. This would cause a rock that is scanned to glow, indicating it has a unique chemical composition.

Given a choice, most players will choose fewer rules over more rules. Obviously, the fewer rules you place on a game, the easier it is for players to remember the ones that do exist. The same goes for objectives. If your game has 50 objectives that must be accomplished to win, most players are going to lose interest. You've got to find the right balance between rules and objectives so that players will have a memorable game experience.

This balancing takes practice. Many Kodu Game Lab programmers find that their early games are not as engaging or memorable as their more recent game creations. Early games often are more frustrating to players; some are too slow, and other games end too quickly. As with any skill, programming a good game takes practice, and combining the programming tricks you learn with good game design techniques ensures that every game you create will probably be more fun than the previous one.

Balancing Fun and Difficulty

With any game you create, there's a fine balance between how fun the game is to play and how difficult it is to play. If a game is too easy, players won't find it challenging and will rate it low on the Fun Factor. Likewise, make a game too difficult and players will get frustrated, also generating a low Fun Factor score.

The secret to finding this balance is simple: Test your games often.

Here's another secret: You are not the best judge of your own games.

What this means is that as you are creating your game, you're going to need help. This means asking your friends and family to try out your game and give you some feedback.

The easiest way to get this feedback is to let them play and then ask them some questions:

○ What did you like about the game?

○ What did you *not* like about the game?

○ Was it too difficult?

○ Was it too easy?

○ What could I do to improve the game?

Believe it or not, these five simple questions can provide you hours, maybe even days, of work as you fine-tune your game based on the feedback you received.

When getting feedback and suggestions about your game, you're going to be tempted to make many changes all at once. You'll increase the missile speed, reduce the time limit, increase the enemy hit points, decrease the number of coins, and finally add in a power-up that makes the player indestructible for 30 seconds.

But here's the problem: If you make all five of these changes, you'll likely find your players are still frustrated. Why? It's very possible that the only thing that needed changing in the game was the missile speed. With an increase in missile speed, more hits were made, more points were awarded, and your player felt more rewarded.

But what happens if you just increase the missile speed and reduce the time limit? Now your player is getting more points but with less time on the clock, the game ends before the player feels satisfaction.

The more tweaks and changes you make, the more difficult it will be to pin down exactly what you need to do to improve a game. So what's the goal here? Easy. Make as few changes as possible before testing. Change the missile speed and tell the player about the change, and then get the feedback. If the missile speed is acceptable, but the player says the game ended too quickly, now increase the time on the clock. Test again. Now the player says the missiles are firing at the right speed and the game clock is fine, but the enemies are too difficult to destroy. Great! That's an easy one. Reduce the enemy hit points and test again.

That's how you tweak your game. Make a tweak in the programming or settings. Test. Tweak. Test. Tweak. Test. And so on. Yes, it takes time. But the end result is a game that everyone loves because you've listened to the players and made improvements based on their feedback. Everyone wins!

CAUTION

When using other players to test your game, don't overwhelm them with requests to play. Although it's easy for you to go in and make a quick tweak to a game setting (such as missile-firing speed) and then immediately ask your tester to play again, this can get tiring for your players. No one wants to play the same test game (or beta game) over and over and over. You've got to give your testers a break so that it will be easier for them to spot the changes you made. Ask them to play too many times in one day, and they might overlook a good change you've made. Ask them to play too many times in one sitting, and they might get burned out and simply refuse to play anymore.

Be warned: Testing can get frustrating to you, the programmer. If you receive too many negative responses about your game, you might throw up your hands and walk away from a game that's showing real promise. To be a game designer, you're going to have to develop some thick skin if you really want to know what other players think about your game. Remember that if you ask them what they do not like about a game, they're probably going to tell you. Only ask if you can handle the answer.

Moving On

You have learned a lot about Kodu Game Lab programming since Chapter 1, "Get Kodu: Download and Installation." You might have even put the book down for a while and started programming your own games; I'm not offended! The purpose of this book has been to inform but also to encourage you to create your own games. And I really cannot wait to see what types of games you create. You probably have some ideas of your own, but if you're still struggling to come up with a game on your own, I think I might be able to help.

The next four chapters (20 through 23) provide you with four new and unique games as jumping-off points for you to take and make changes and improvements. You'll see how the games started out, see some programming techniques that you can copy, and get some suggestions for updating the games and making them more fun and challenging.

Here's a sneak look at what's coming:

○ Chapter 20, "Sample Game 1: A One-Player Shooter" (first-person POV in a maze)

○ Chapter 21, "Sample Game 2: A Two-Player Competition" (cooperate… or don't)

○ Chapter 22, "Sample Game 3: On a Mission" (a quest game)

○ Chapter 23, "Sample Game 4: The Side-Scroller Experience" (from NASA)

See you in Chapter 20.

20

Sample Game 1:
A One-Player Shooter

In This Chapter

○ Game 1 Overview

○ Creating *The Amazing Maze Chase*

○ Programming the Game

○ Improving the Game

○ Moving On

The first of four sample games begins in this chapter. These games can certainly be played and enjoyed, but the real goal here is to give you the frameworks that you can use to upgrade and improve the games. Throughout this chapter (and the next three chapters), you learn techniques I've used to create and program the game. Ultimately, these four games are provided as both inspiration and as ideas for how to start creating your own games.

Game 1 Overview

When I start thinking about creating a game with Kodu Game Lab, that's what I do: think. I ponder. I consider ideas, throwing some away and keeping others. I look at other games people are playing, and I look at games other Kodu programmers are uploading to the community.

Ultimately, I decide on a theme or style of game, and for this first sample game, I've chosen to create a single-player game. I want the player to be able to use either a mouse/keyboard or a game controller. And I'd like to have some enemy targets to shoot missiles.

But that in itself is not a game. What will the game look like? Which object will the player control? What kind of terrain will the game use? Will it be on dry land or water? Will the enemies shoot back? Will there be a time limit? Do I need a scoreboard for a single player game?

All these questions made me pause and think about my game again. I started to look for inspiration around me. Books, TV shows, and other games—I looked around to see what I could find that would be a fun setting for a single-player game.

My young son was working through a book of various puzzles and asked me to help him. As I helped him trace a line through a maze, I imagined actually being inside that maze and trying to find my way out. And that's how I got the idea for game 1, *The Amazing Maze Chase*.

So, I've decided to create a maze and put the player inside the maze using a first-person point of view (POV). The player will see walls, dead ends, and long hallways, and must try to find a way to the end of the maze. But how and where do I start?

Creating *The Amazing Maze Chase*

I thought about the maze game I wanted to design and considered that actually creating a maze could be somewhat difficult and time-consuming. I'm not a maze designer, so my first job was to find out if I could actually re-create a challenging maze using the Kodu Game Lab terrain tools.

Take a look at Figure 20.1 and you'll see an image of a maze that I created using a free online tool.

FIGURE 20.1 Can I re-create this maze in Kodu Game Lab?

TIP
You can find this maze generator by visiting http://worksheets.theteacherscorner.net/make-your-own/maze/. Select the number of columns and rows, and the generator does all the hard work for you.

I chose to create a 15×15 grid maze. I could have made it smaller or larger, but 15×15 looked good. I would start the player in the upper-left corner of the maze, and the player would need to navigate through the maze to the exit in the lower-right corner.

The maze looks good using thin lines, but the real question is how do you convert a line drawing like the one in Figure 20.1 into a three-dimensional maze using Kodu Game Lab?

There are probably a number of methods, but here's how I did it.

1. Zoom out quite a bit so you can see the single square patch of terrain of a new world.

2. Choose the Ground Brush, select the Square brush shape, and enlarge it to match the same size of the existing square patch of terrain. (Use the right arrow key to enlarge the brush size.)

3. Place individual squares in the world. Place 14 additional squares to the right of the original terrain patch and 14 additional squares above the original terrain patch, as shown in Figure 20.2.

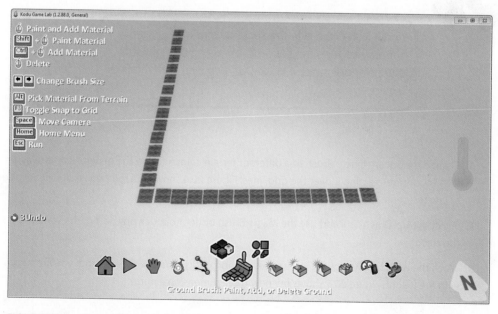

FIGURE 20.2   Create the start of a grid with the Ground Brush.

4. Use the Square Linear Brush to complete a large 15×15 patch of terrain.

5. Shrink the size of the Square Linear Brush, change the terrain color, and draw 14 vertical lines and 14 horizontal lines over the terrain to create a grid system like you see in Figure 20.3.

Rover: Why not just put down one very large square of terrain that will be broken into 15×15 sections?

Kodu: By drawing the initial set of vertical and horizontal square patches with a small space between each, you can use those spaces to trace over with the second terrain color used to create the grid lines.

Rover: Okay, but why use a second color to create the grid lines? Why not just leave the empty space between all the squares?

Kodu: You could skip the second color and just leave spaces between the squares, but using a bright second color will make it easier to trace over with the final wall color.

6. Change the Square Linear Brush to a different terrain color and use the generated maze as a reference for re-creating it over the grid lines. Figure 20.4 shows the red walls that will be raised to create a three-dimensional maze.

7. Select the Up/Down tool and use the Magic Brush option to touch any part of the walls with the cursor.

8. When the walls begin to glow, use a series of short clicks to raise the walls until you are happy with the height. Figure 20.5 shows my new three dimensional maze.

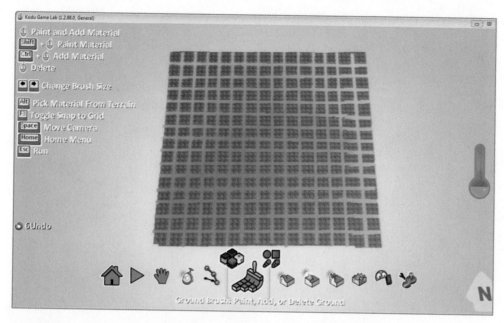

FIGURE 20.3   The grid system will let me easily draw the walls of the maze.

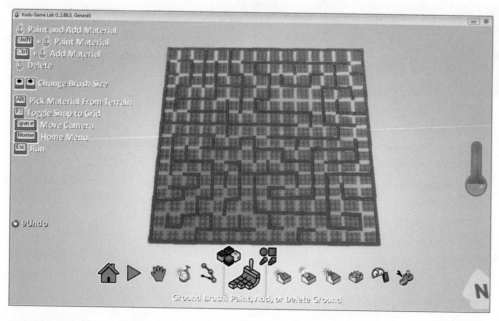

FIGURE 20.4   The two-dimensional maze looks just like the generated maze.

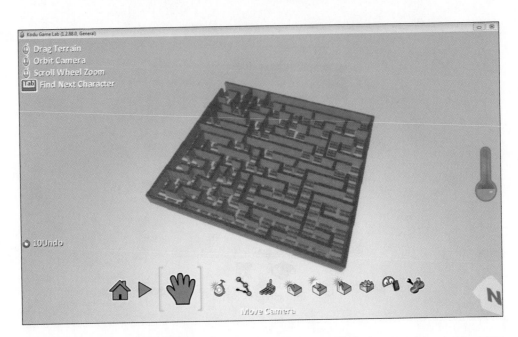

FIGURE 20.5   A real three-dimensional maze.

> **TIP**
> You might have noticed that I enclosed the entire maze with a solid wall. This made it easier to raise the entire maze at once. Instead of an exit, I'll use a different terrain type as the final goal for the player.

All that's left to do now is go back and change the color of the original grid lines to match the green of the terrain squares. I've added a few details such as the word *start* at the entrance, as shown in Figure 20.6.

I'm certainly not done with the maze. I've got to add the player object, the enemies, and maybe a few other surprises. (I'm thinking a couple of water or pit traps that end the game if the player falls in might be fun!)

FIGURE 20.6   When players begin the game, they'll know they're at the entrance.

Programming the Game

Programming the game is fairly straightforward. You already know how to add game controller or keyboard movement controls to the player-controlled object, but to give the player a sense that she is actually in the maze, I'm going to need to force the player to view the game from the first-person POV.

Programming Cycle

To do this, I add a simple programming row that forces the camera view to stay in first person. Figure 20.7 shows the simple programming I've added to the Cycle object so that I can test my maze.

You can find the 1st Person tile by clicking the Do box and selecting the View pie slice. This opens up a new pie menu, and you can click the 1st Person tile to change the game so that the player always sees through Cycle's eyes, as shown in Figure 20.8.

After testing the game and driving Cycle through the maze, I quickly realized that this maze is very large. I got lost often and couldn't even find my way back to the entrance most times.

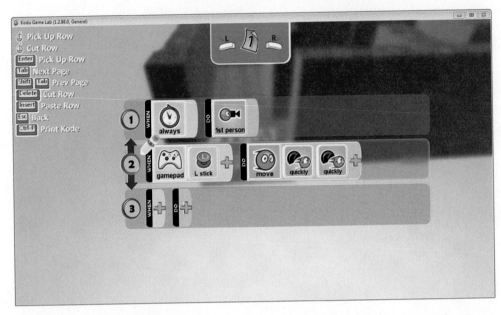

FIGURE 20.7 The player will always view the game from first-person POV.

FIGURE 20.8 The maze as seen from Cycle's point of view.

Kodu: That's a large maze. I don't know if I could find my way to the end.

Rover: I agree. I think the programmer is going to have to add something that will help the player.

Kodu: Maybe something like Hansel and Gretel dropping bread crumbs?

Rover: That's actually not a bad idea. Hey, programmer, the player is going to need some help!

Rover is correct. I need to give the players a tool that will help them navigate the maze. This tool should help them identify dead ends and traps, and alert them if they begin to move down a hallway that they've already explored. Figure 20.9 shows my solution.

This might work! When I tap the B button on the game controller (I'll add in controls for mouse/keyboard players later), Cycle drops an easy-to-spot black rock. As I explore the maze, when I reach a dead end I'll backtrack a little and drop the black rock near the entrance of the hallway that would lead me to the dead end. Figure 20.10 shows the rock warning me away from going down that path again.

After further testing, I also discovered that sometimes I would backtrack too far. After exploring three different paths and finding two were dead ends, I returned to the point where the maze branched off but kept moving. What would be nice is something to alert me to go back no further. I know: a different dropped object.

I'll use a dropped star to prevent me from going too far back in the maze. Through trial and error, I should be able to eliminate certain hallways with the black rock while using the star to remind me where to return for further exploration. But I don't want a lot of stars dropped in the maze, so I'll also program in the capability for Cycle to remove a star and place a new one. You can see the update to Cycle's programming in Figure 20.11.

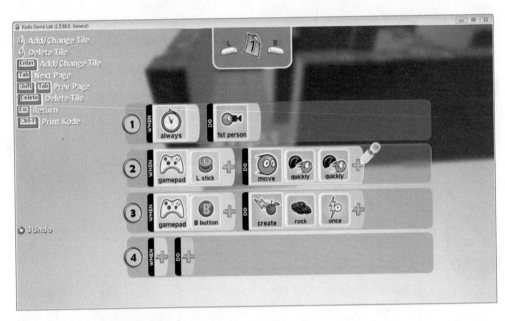

FIGURE 20.9   Additional programming added to Cycle.

FIGURE 20.10   Black rocks will warn players about traps and dead ends.

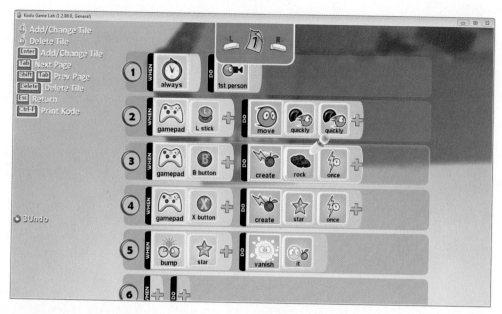

FIGURE 20.11 A star will help me stay on the right path and I can also remove the star.

Now I can mark a point to return with a star, but also remove the star as I move deeper into the maze. All I need to do is bump a star to make it vanish and then I can place another star.

Adding a Trap

Take a look at Figure 20.12 and you'll see that I've added a pit to one of the dead ends. Cycle better not go racing too fast through the maze.

The additional programming for Cycle that will end the game if Cycle touches the pit can be seen in Figure 20.13.

See that Type tile in Figure 20.13? After you add it, click it again and select the Types pie slice shown in Figure 20.14. You need to select the color/pattern terrain that was used to create the pit.

I can add additional pits (I'll use the same color so I don't have to duplicate Programming Row 6 over and over to specify different color terrains) and maybe even a few water hazards. Instead of the On Land tile, I can use the On Water tile to end the game if Cycle falls into the water.

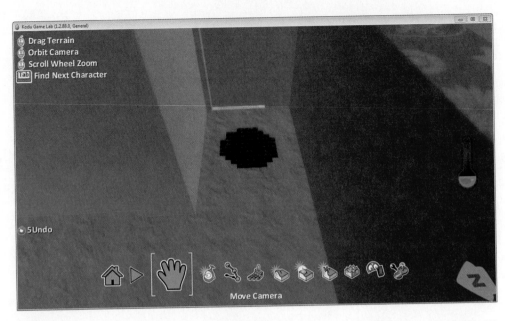

FIGURE 20.12 If Cycle falls into this pit, the game is over.

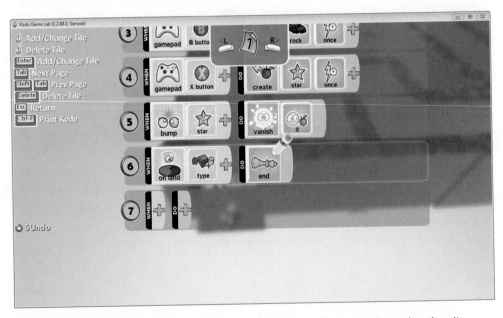

FIGURE 20.13 The On Land and Type tiles are used to detect whether Cycle touches the pit.

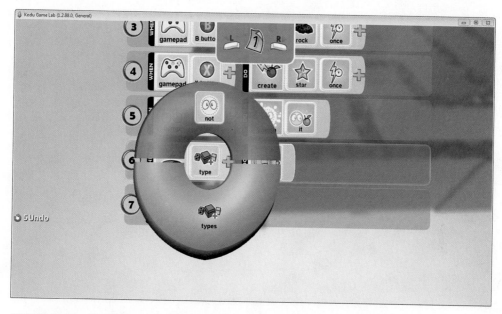

FIGURE 20.14   The Types pie menu lets you select the terrain used for the pit.

Adding an Enemy

This is a shooter, so of course I've programmed Cycle to use button A to fire missiles. But he's going to need an enemy to shoot. With such a large maze, it would be time consuming to create a path that weaves through the entire maze for an enemy to follow. Instead, I can create short paths and use multiple enemies that guard certain hallways. Figure 20.15 shows that I've dropped in a saucer that follows a specific path in one hallway.

To make this work, I program the saucer to follow this bidirectional path and fire missiles when it sees Kodu. Notice that I've lowered the height of the saucer so that Cycle has a chance to hit it with his own missiles. I'll set the hit points for the saucer to 20 (Cycle's missiles do 10 points of damage each) and the saucer's missiles to do 2 points of damage. I'll play around with Cycle's hit points during later testing to find the right balance that gives players a chance to win the game but also keeps them vigilant and watching around corners for enemies.

Ending the Game

Figure 20.16 shows how I end the game. I've placed a circular bit of terrain (with a different color) for Cycle to roll over.

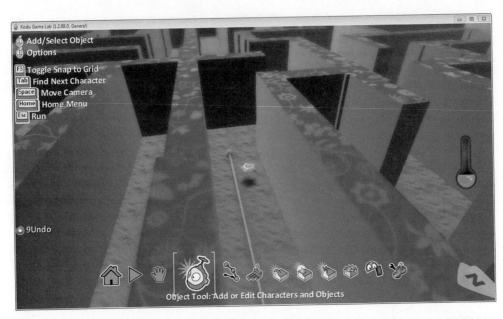

FIGURE 20.15   This saucer will follow the path and fire at Cycle.

FIGURE 20.16   The game ends when Cycle rolls on to this circular patch of terrain.

I'll use that On Land tile and add programming to Cycle that ends the game when he rolls over that pattern of terrain.

Improving the Game

That's the basis of *The Amazing Maze Chase*, but the game is by no means done. I need to add more enemies and more traps. I also need to tweak some of Cycle's settings, such as his speed, hit points, and missile damage.

For you, however, I've got some suggestions for how this game could be upgraded. Previous chapters have given you the knowledge you need to implement these suggested updates, so refer back to earlier chapters if you need help.

Time Limit

A time limit could be almost impossible to add to this game given it's such a large maze. But if you were to use a smaller maze, a sufficiently large time limit (10 minutes? 20 minutes?) could make for a serious challenge for your players.

Enemy Chasers

The enemy I added earlier simply follows a path, but you could easily program an enemy to follow Cycle after he is discovered. Being chased adds an additional challenge to players who run because those players will need to be alert if they run in a direction they've yet to explore. They could easily stumble upon another enemy, fall into a pit, or get cornered in a dead end!

Keys/Quest Items

It's an easy bit of programming to drop an object in a hallway and prevent Cycle from moving forward. Add a special item somewhere else in the maze that Cycle must retrieve (use the Get tile) and give to the blocking object to make it disappear.

Scoring

Drop in special items throughout the maze that have some value to a final score. Instead of players trying to find the end of the maze, the objective can simply be to capture as many special items as possible during a time limit. (Add enemies to make it even more challenging.)

A Cheat Button

This would be a real challenge for you, but consider adding a button press that temporarily removes the first-person POV and allows players to zoom out and above the maze, getting a look at their location in the maze. Add another button that returns the player to first-person POV.

Two Players

You won't be able to give two players the first-person POV, but as long as they stay together, they could navigate the maze and fight off enemies as a team. You'll have to experiment with the size of the maze, too, to allow for both players to fit in hallways and to discover how the camera view works to keep both players on screen at the same time.

Devious Maze

I chose two colors that make it easy to see the twists and turns of the maze. If you're feeling a little devious, you could try to use darker walls and ground color. Players might not like it, so you'll have to experiment to find the right mix of colors that make a game challenging but not too frustrating. You might even try changing the game from day to night; after all, trying to navigate a maze at night could be even more devious. (Be sure to do an evil laugh here.)

The Invisible Hunter

You can make an object invisible by right-clicking the object, choosing **Change Settings**, and turning on the **Invisible** option. Imagine adding in an invisible hunter that stalks the player through the maze? Give this enemy missiles that do a very small amount of damage and give the player a large number of hit points. Tell the player to *run* when the game starts and set a timer to count up. See who can survive the longest!

Moving On

And that's *The Amazing Maze Chase*! There weren't a lot of programming tricks required for this game, but it did require coming up with a method for creating a three-dimensional maze from a two-dimensional drawing. Pretty cool, huh?

If I can re-create a 3D maze from a 2D image, so can you. And it doesn't have to just be a maze. You could re-create the layout of your home or school (*Escape from Junior High* sounds like a great game), or even try to make a game out of famous landmarks such as Mount Rushmore or the Parthenon.

Here's something cool for you to consider: The next time your teacher assigns you a project on a famous location, open up Kodu Game Lab and re-create it as a 3D game that your fellow classmates can walk through and talk to objects who will speak (using the Say tile) and share different facts about the site.

Kodu Game Lab will let you create some amazing game worlds. Your imagination is where you'll start. I saw my son's maze and imagined it as a game. Take a look around and see what you can find to inspire your own game world creation.

21

Sample Game 2: Two-Player Competition

And now we come to the second of the four sample games. This one is for two players, but it can easily be expanded to allow for more players. As you work through this chapter, always be asking yourself how you could modify the game to make it your own. What new features or objects could you add to make it more fun for your friends and family? As with the other sample games, this chapter provides you with another example of how you can develop a game with just a few starting concepts (such as how many players). As you create your own games, you'll continue to gain confidence in your abilities to begin a game from scratch.

Game 2 Overview

As I was thinking about the various two-player games I've played over the years, I realized that most of the time the goal of the game was to beat your opponent's score or reduce his hit points (or health) to 0 first. It occurred to me that a fun two-player game could be created that adds a slight twist to keeping score or having the most hit points to win a game.

So, here's what I came up with as an idea for the second sample game:

○ Each player starts with 100 hit points.

○ Each player has a limited number of blips to fire (100).

○ Each blip you fire reduces your hit points by 3 points.

○ Each blip hit on an opponent subtracts 5 points from your opponent's hit points.

○ Blips can only be fired when you are on certain types of terrain.

○ Remaining blips and hit points will be displayed for both players using scoreboards.

The goal of the game is reduce your opponents hit points to 0. But think about it for a moment. You've got limited ammunition (only 100 blips), and every time you fire a blip you lose 3 hit points. If you fire 34 blips and miss all 34 times, your hit points will reach 0, and the game could end with your opponent winning without ever firing a shot! But if your opponent fires 20 blips, each hitting you and doing 5 points of damage, the game will also end with your hit points reaching 0. Because both players are losing hit points every time they fire blips, the best strategy would be to conserve blips until you've got an easy, no-miss shot.

You might be thinking that you could win games by simply never firing a single blip and letting your opponents fire on you, reducing their hit points to 0 while you hide and avoid getting hit. That would work if there weren't two additional game changers added to the game:

○ Every 20 seconds a recharger will appear, awarding 10 extra blips and 15 hit points to the player who successfully retrieves it.

○ A couple of path-following enemies will also be able to fire on players, reducing their hit points.

How does that sound for a fun two-person competition? I'm going to call it *Blip Bam Boom*. Both players have an equal number of obstacles (terrain and enemies) and a symmetrical game world to navigate. It won't be a maze, but it will have a suitable number of places for players to hide, as well as a couple of locations to retrieve rechargers.

Creating *Blip Bam Boom*

I'm not going to go into extreme detail on how I made the game world for *Blip Bam Boom*. You can see the game world I've created in Figure 21.1. Notice that there are two colors of terrain. When a player is on one type of terrain, firing is possible (the green terrain). When a player is on another type of terrain, firing is impossible (the dotted terrain in the center of the game world).

Notice that both players (White Kodu and Red Kodu) cannot see each other when the game starts. Walls between them prevent the players from firing a lucky blip when the game first begins.

To encourage the players to try and hunt their opponent, I place some path-following enemies that will also fire on players. These will be used to "encourage" players to stay more in the center of the game world and to try to eliminate the other player rather than simply hiding.

FIGURE 21.1   A small arena with two types of terrain and walls. No enemies... yet.

Figure 21.2 shows where I've placed two enemy saucers, each following their own line.

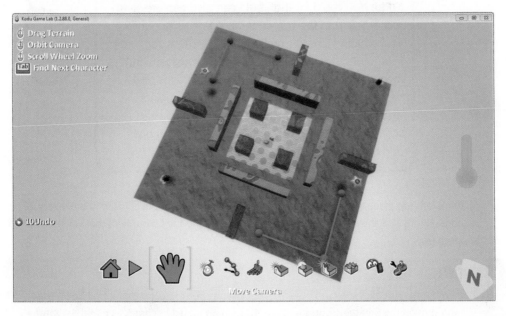

FIGURE 21.2   Two path-following enemies will fire on any player that gets close.

I program these two saucers to fire on any player that comes too close. The saucers' missiles will be programmed to do 5 points of damage.

Rover: So the saucers can help me win?

Kodu: That's right! If I'm hit by a saucer's missile, I lose hit points even if I haven't fired a single blip.

Rover: So I could just hide and save my blips and only shoot at you when I've got a guaranteed shot?

Kodu: You could do that, but I can also capture recharges from the center of the game world while you're hiding. There's no limit on how many recharges I can collect, so I can just hoard the recharges, and then when I have a sufficient number of blips and hit points, I'll just rush you. Remember, hit points and blips will be displayed for both players using scoreboards, so I'll know where you stand on blips and hit points.

All that's left is to place two Rovers, who will each drop a recharger (a coin creatable) every 20 seconds. Figure 21.3 shows the placement of the Rovers and the Coin object that will represent a blip recharge.

NOTE

Remember to right-click the Coin object, select Change Settings, and then scroll down the list and turn on the Creatable option, so that the Ammo object becomes a creatable that the Rovers will create every 20 seconds. If you want, you can choose to turn the Rovers invisible by going into their settings (right-click Change Settings) and turning on the Invisible option.

FIGURE 21.3   The Rovers will create blip recharge creatables every 20 seconds.

That's it for the game elements. I might find during testing that I need to add or subtract walls, increase or decrease the time between recharger drops, or vary the damage done by the Kodus' blips and saucers' missiles.

But before I can begin testing, I need to go and add in all the object programming.

Programming the Game

A total of seven objects must be programmed for *Blip Bam Boom*: two Kodus, two saucers, two Rovers, and a coin creatable. I'm going to start with some of the easiest programming first—the Rovers and the coin creatable.

Programming the Rovers and Coin Creatable

The Rovers will simply drop a Coin object every 20 seconds, but that Coin object must be a creatable. So, after placing a single coin on the game world, I right-click it, select Change Settings, and turn on the Creatable option in the scrolling list. Once that's done, I add the program shown in Figure 21.4.

As you can see in Figure 21.4, I've programmed the coin creatable to vanish after it's bumped by a Kodu. Before vanishing, however, that bump triggers the addition of 10 points to the blip scoreboard and 15 points to the hit points scoreboard for the Kodu that bumped it.

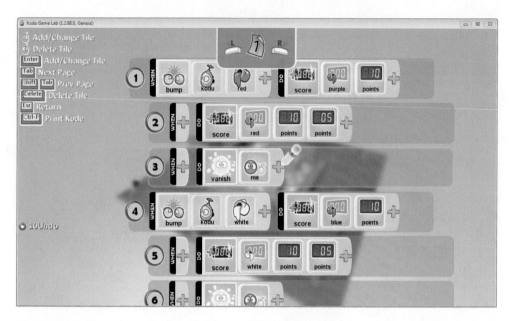

FIGURE 21.4 The coin creatable adds blips and hit points to a Kodu.

With this game, I'll be programming the White Kodu to have a White scoreboard that shows the number of hit points remaining, and a Blue scoreboard that shows how many blips the White Kodu player currently has available. The Red Kodu will have a Red scoreboard that shows the Red player's hit points, and a Purple scoreboard showing how many blips the Red Kodu has remaining.

Both Kodus have matching programming, so Figure 21.5 shows the single programming row that will release a single coin creatable every 20 seconds.

> **TIP**
>
> The 20 Seconds tile is all that needs to be modified during testing to increase or decrease the drop rate of the blip recharges. Simply left-click the 20 Seconds tile and select a different value or click the plus sign (+) to the right of the 20 Seconds tile to add more time.

Programming the Saucers

Now it's time to program the two saucers. Once again, the programming will be identical except for the color of the line that each saucer will follow.

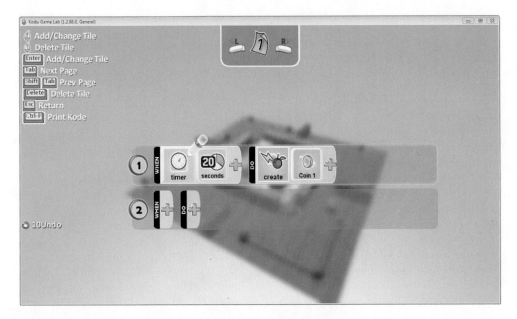

FIGURE 21.5   The Rover objects will drop a coin creatable every 20 seconds.

> **NOTE**
>
> I could easily have used the same color line for both paths; any object that is programmed to follow a path will always pick the closest path to follow if a color isn't specified. But later on, I might choose to give these two saucers different powers or modify them so that they are no longer identical. Because of this, I've decided to create two unique colored paths and to program each saucer to follow a specific color path.

Figure 21.6 shows the programming for one of the saucers.

From Figure 21.6, you can see that the saucer will always follow a specific colored path, and the saucer will also be keeping an eye open for Kodus. It doesn't matter which color Kodu comes near, either. When it sees a Kodu, it fires a missile at that player, reducing that player's hit points by 5 points if the missile hits.

> **TIP**
>
> During testing, try adjusting the damage and speed of that missile to find a speed and damage amount that makes the game more fun. You'll want to get some feedback from players to find the right balance.

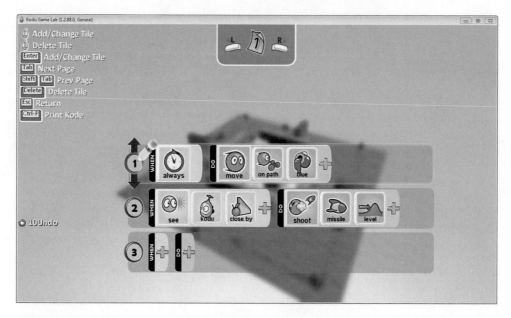

FIGURE 21.6   The blue saucer will follow a blue path and fire missiles at any Kodu it sees.

Be sure to copy this program to the other saucer, changing the color of the path to match the color of the path you added in your own game world.

Programming the Kodus

The last two objects to be programmed will be the players' Kodus. As with the Rovers and saucers, the programming I've created is identical for both, but you might need to modify the movement and firing controls depending on whether you are giving players a keyboard/mouse option or a game controller option. (I'm using the game controller option for both players, so I also need to specify the Player #. You'll see this in Figure 21.8, where I use the Player1 tile.)

I start with the White Kodu. Figure 21.7 shows Page 1 of the White Kodu's programming.

Notice that there is no movement or firing programming on Page 1. This page is all about setting up the scoreboards.

Programming Row 1 shows that I've set the White scoreboard to a value of 100. This matches how many hit points I've configured for the White Kodu.

Programming Row 2 sets the Blue scoreboard to a value of 500; this is the number of blips that White Kodu will possess when the game begins.

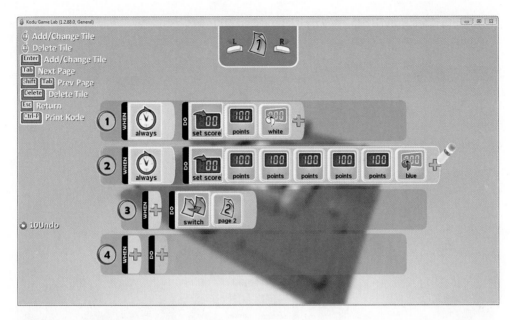

FIGURE 21.7 White Kodu's programming for Page 1.

CAUTION

500 points per row is the maximum you can program for any colored scoreboard because the highest value tile available is the 100 Points tile. You could add another 100 Points tile in Figure 21.7, but then you would not be able to add the White Tile because Programming Row 1's Do box can hold a maximum of seven tiles; one is the Set Score tile, then five 100 Points tiles, and then the final White Scoreboard tile. To set a score or value (such as number of blips) above 500 points, simply use another programming row to add more points by indenting and adding DO Score 100 100 100 100 100 Blue, for example.

After both of White Kodu's scoreboards have been set (100 hit points and 500 blips), Programming Row 3 jumps to Page 2.

Page 2 of White Kodu's programming is a bit long, so Figure 21.8 shows only Programming Rows 1 through 5.

Programming Row 1 simply specifies that Player 1 will use the left thumbstick to control movement.

Programming Row 2 uses the On Land tile along with the Type and Not tiles to create a unique condition. The Type tile specifies the Blue Dotted terrain that makes up the center of the game world. Programming Row 2 basically says: When Kodu is not on blue dotted terrain, do something. That *something* is specified in the indented Programming Row 3 where the game controller's A button will fire a single blip every time it is pushed. (This prevents a player from holding down the A button for a continuous stream of blips.)

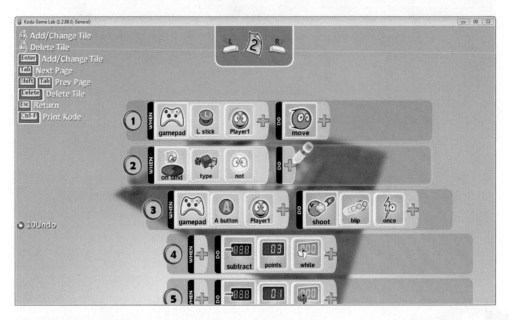

FIGURE 21.8   Part of White Kodu's Page 2 programming.

If either Kodu is on the blue dotted terrain, that player's ability to fire is disabled. Although players crossing the blue dotted terrain cannot fire, they can be fired upon by the other player if that player is not currently over the blue dotted terrain.

Now take a look at Figure 21.9, which shows the remaining programming rows for Page 2.

Notice that Programming Rows 4, 5, and 6 are indented below Programming Row 3. These three rows affect scoring and hit points.

Programming Row 4 subtracts 3 points from White Kodu's White scoreboard every time that player fires a blip. Note that this doesn't subtract 3 points from White Kodu's actual hit points; that is done with the programming in Row 5. Every time a blip is fired, 3 points are deducted from White Kodu's actual hit points.

Programming Row 6 subtracts one point from the Blue scoreboard that tracks the number of blips White Kodu has remaining.

Programming Row 7 simply deducts 5 points if White Kodu is hit by a blip fired from Red Kodu or a missile fired by a saucer.

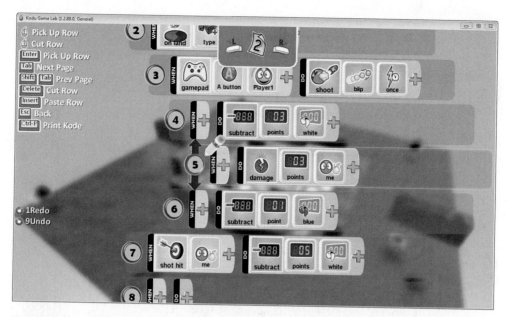

FIGURE 21.9   The remaining programming rows for White Kodu's Page 2.

So, to recap:

○ White Kodu can only fire (use the A button) when he is over green terrain.

○ When White Kodu fires a blip, 3 points are deducted from White Kodu's White scoreboard that tracks his total hit points, and one blip is deducted from White Kodu's Blue scoreboard that tracks the number of remaining blips.

○ If Kodu is hit by a blip or a missile, 5 points are deducted from the White scoreboard.

CAUTION

Programming Row 5 is required. Without that row, firing a blip will deduct 3 points from the White scoreboard, but Kodu's actual hit points will not decrease by 3 points. The White scoreboards are there simply to remind both players about the number of hit points and blips remaining.

That's it!

Now all you need to do is copy White Kodu's programming (Page 1 and Page 2) to Red Kodu and change all White Score tiles to Red Score tiles, and all Blue Score tiles to Purple Score tiles. Run the game and you'll see a game like the one in Figure 21.10.

Kodu: Those saucers are fast.

Rover: Yes, they are… and my movement speed feels a bit sluggish.

Kodu: So, I guess one of the first things to try out is to decrease the movement speeds of the saucers.

Rover: And increase the Kodus' speeds.

FIGURE 21.10   A sample test game shows that the scoreboards are set.

All that's left now is to add the programming that will help determine the winner. I add Programming Row 8 to each of the Kodus' Page 2 programming. Figure 21.11 shows the simple programming I've added to (Player 1) White Kodu's Page 2 that checks to see whether his hit points drop to 0 (or less). If so, Player 2 wins. Copy Programming Row 8 to Red Kodu's Page 2, but change the Player 2 tile to the Player 1 tile.

> **TIP**
>
> You can also specify a color (such as red) rather than a player number. Using colors may make it easier for players to determine the winner if you color-code each player object. Rather than say DO Win Player2, just program DO Win Red (assuming Player 2's object is colored red).

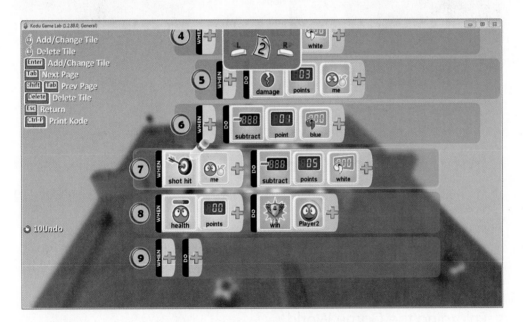

FIGURE 21.11   If White Kodu's hit points reach 0, Red Kodu (Player 2) wins.

Figure 21.12 shows the screen that appears after Player 1 (White Kodu) has defeated Player 2 (Red Kodu).

> **NOTE**
>
> The negative score shown in Figure 21.12 is due to 5 points of damage being done to Player 2 when Player 2's hit points were at 1 point. One last blip hit Player 2, subtracting 5 hit points from 1 hit point, which leaves −4 hit points.

FIGURE 21.12 Player 1 wins.

Improving the Game

Blip Bam Boom is fun. I've been playing it with my family, and there is definitely a benefit to being sneaky and trying to grab those rechargers as often as possible.

Still, even after plenty of testing and tweaking the various settings, such as the saucer's missile speed or Kodu's movement speed, I can think of numerous ways this game can be improved or expanded. Here are some of my ideas, but I'm sure you can come up with many more on your own.

Enlarging the Game World

You'll quickly figure out that when you make your game world too large, two-player games become more difficult to play because the camera view will have to pull back enough for both players to be visible on the screen. Still, this world could be enlarged a bit more to allow for more enemies or even four players.

Imposing a Time Limit

If you're finding that players just aren't attacking one another at a fast enough pace, consider throwing in a timer. Give players 3 or 4 minutes, and the winner will be the person with the most hit points left over. Expand the paths for the saucers, too, so that they fly by the players and take a few shots at them; this will encourage players to move toward the center of the game world to try and grab rechargers as well as avoid the saucers' missiles.

Adding a Super Recharger

Consider adding in a super recharger that appears in the very center of the game world at a random time in the game. This super recharger could affect hit points, blips, or both. If the benefits are high enough, players will rush to the center to try and grab it. Of course, you might want to remove the limitation that prevents players from shooting blips over the blue dotted terrain.

Using Power-Ups

Here's a sneak-peek of what's to come: You're going to learn how to give players power-ups in Chapter 22, "Sample Game 3: On a Mission." After you know how this is done, consider returning to *Blip Bam Boom* and throwing in some random power-ups that can give a player temporary immunity to blips. Another power-up could provide a player with 10 seconds of missile-firing capability, with each missile delivering 20 points of damage. Another power-up could provide a player with a major boost of speed, allowing that player to sneak around and attack the opponent from behind. Use your imagination. (And don't skip Chapter 22, which explains how to use power-ups.)

Encouraging Duels

Place both players in the center of the game world and have them race to the edges to retrieve rechargers that you've placed to charge up their blip inventory. (Start them out with 0 blips.) Some rechargers might add to their hit points, others to the blips. Make rechargers different colors so that players can decide whether they want to race for blips or hit points.

Providing Missiles

Consider adding the capability to fire missiles as well as blips. Give each player two or three missiles that do high damage, but when they're gone, they're gone—players better make that shot count. Or go crazy and let rechargers provide additional missiles as well as blips and hit points. Consider shortening the missile range so that players must get close to their opponents for a missile to have a chance to hit.

Deploying Decoys

This can be a bit tricky, but I think you can figure it out. Suppose that a special creatable allows a player to press a button and create two or three additional Kodus of the same color that wander randomly. The opponent will have to figure out which Kodu is the player and which are decoys. Remember to add some randomness to your own movements to trick your opponent into thinking you're one of the decoys.

A Game of Chase

Modify the game so that players take turns being the pursuer and the target. Create a start and an end location on the game world. When the game begins, the target must move from the start to the end, avoiding the hunter. Throw in some power-ups or rechargers for the target and consider using a timer to see who can complete the game the fastest.

Moving On

Two-player competitions are often some of the most fun games you can create, giving you something that can be enjoyed by you *and* your friends. *Blip Bam Boom* offers up a lot of ways to modify the game; I've given you eight suggestions, but I'll bet you can come up with some great variations, too.

I cannot stress enough how useful scoreboard tiles can be when it comes to providing information to players. The health bar that appears over a player's head (if you've enabled that feature) is useful, but it doesn't tell you exactly how many hit points you have left. By now, you should understand how easy it is to configure a scoreboard to show the actual hit point value, and how you add programming to deduct from that value when damage is sustained.

Scoreboards can be used for timers, for inventory (I used them to tell players how many blips they had left, but you could use it to track coins, stars, and even missiles), and of course, for keeping an actual score. Just remember to always duplicate scoreboard programming for all players; if you're showing Player 1's hit points, it's only fair to display Player 2's hit points, too.

> **TIP**
>
> A new feature with Kodu Game Lab that was added as this book was being finished allows you to assign labels to the scoreboards. So, instead of just seeing 0 or 50 or some other score in red, you can actually put "Player 1" or "Hit Points Left" next to the value so that players can quickly determine what the value means. Look for this new feature in the Score pie menu.

Two-player games are everywhere and can often provide great inspiration for designing your own two-player games. Always be on the lookout for games that can be given a completely new twist by changing a rule or two.

Sample Game 3: On a Mission

In This Chapter

○ Game 3 Overview

○ Creating *The Dune Treasure*

○ Programming the Game

○ Improving the Game

○ Moving On

I had an idea for a single-player quest game that involves a treasure map that is broken into six pieces. This chapter shows how I brainstormed the entire game (six challenges in all) and then shows you how I developed the opening challenge.

Game 3 Overview

I've always enjoyed quest games, and maybe you do, too. The best quest games usually contain a mix of action and puzzle-solving, and for my quest game, that's exactly what I want to provide to the player.

I started by writing down all the features I wanted to include in my quest game, and here's the basic list I came up with:

○ Seven locales

○ Six bosses (A *boss* is an enemy that is often very hard to destroy.)

○ A treasure map broken into six parts

○ A treasure that can only be discovered using the assembled map

○ Power-ups (bonus powers for the player to grab)

I created a hand-sketch that you can see in Figure 22.1 that gives you an idea of how I want to create my game world.

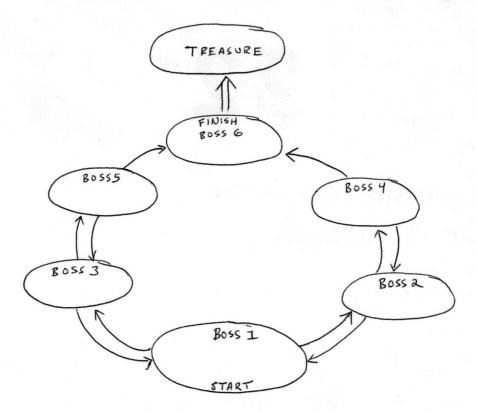

FIGURE 22.1   My quest game will involve seven locales and six bosses.

The player will be able to hunt down five pieces of the treasure map by moving back and forth between five different locales (each with a unique boss to fight). When ready, the player moves to the sixth locale, fights the boss there, obtains the final piece of the treasure map, and then moves to the seventh locale, where the player locates the treasure by assembling the map pieces.

I'm going to call this game *The Dune Treasure*. Now it's time for me to show you how I've begun to create it.

Creating *The Dune Treasure*

I'm going with a desert dune theme, so first I create a section of game world using a sand-colored terrain. I also start this opening challenge by dropping in the outline of an abandoned castle, as shown in Figure 22.2.

> **TIP**
>
> Refer back to Chapter 20, "Sample Game 1: A One-Player Shooter," for instructions on using a 2D tracing of a building to create a 3D version using the Up/Down tool.

FIGURE 22.2 My desert dunes and the outline of a castle I need to build.

To get this opening challenge started, I need to complete the following tasks:

1. Drop in Kodu and configure for movement (game controller, hit points set to 50) and missile firing (damage set to 5 points each).

2. Drop in a Push Pad object as Boss 1 and configure to fire missiles (50 damage) when Kodu gets too close (set boss hit points to 1,000).

3. Drop in a saucer to protect the first section of the treasure map (set saucer to Invulnerable).

Rover: One missile hit will destroy you, Kodu! That doesn't sound like fun.

Kodu: I'm going to have to be sneaky and find a way to increase my missile damage and raise my hit points.

Rover: It would be great if there were some power-ups hidden in other areas of the castle.

Kodu: I'll definitely go look around before I try to fight the first boss.

Figure 22.3 shows that I've raised the walls of my castle outline using the Up/Down tool, and I've dropped in the Saucer and Push Pad objects. The push pad will serve as Boss 1, and it's guarding the saucer that is inside the castle walls.

If Kodu gets too close to the boss, he's in big trouble. Figure 22.4 shows the simple bit of programming I've added that lets Boss 1 fire a missile if Kodu gets near.

The saucer sits over a piece of the treasure map, so in Figure 22.5 I've dragged the saucer to the right so that you can see how I've created the treasure map.

The map was made using the Ground Brush and the smallest square brush shape possible (use the left arrow to shrink it down) to apply a few black squares and a single blue square over a larger sand-colored square.

The player needs to sketch this piece of the treasure map on a small scrap of paper. After Boss 1 is destroyed, when the saucer sees Kodu approaching, he will explain that the blue dot is used to orient the drawing properly. (In this case, the square sketch should be rotated so the blue dot is on top.) Figure 22.6 shows the programming I've applied to the saucer that will allow him to explain the map, and then tell Kodu to bump him to make him vanish.

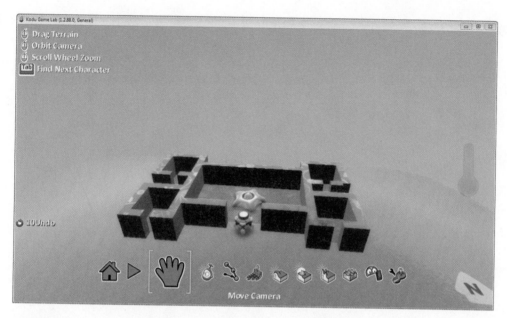

FIGURE 22.3   The boss guards the entrance to the castle, blocking access to saucer.

FIGURE 22.4   Boss 1 fires a missile that can destroy Kodu.

FIGURE 22.5   The first piece of the treasure map will be hidden underneath the saucer.

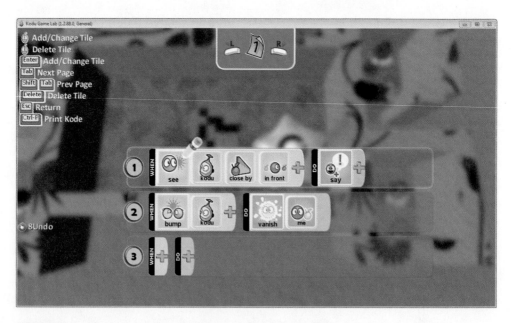

FIGURE 22.6   The Saucer will explain the map and then vanish.

> **NOTE**
>
> Here's the text I've added to the Say tile in Figure 22.6:
>
> *Thank you for rescuing me.*
>
> *Copy this drawing.*
>
> *Rotate the drawing so the blue dot is on top.*
>
> *Retrieve the remaining five drawings.*
>
> *These six drawings will form an emblem.*
>
> *This emblem will help you locate the treasure.*
>
> *Bump me and I'll vanish.*
>
> As long as Kodu stands in front of the saucer and doesn't bump him, the instructions repeat.

Now, after putting the saucer over the treasure map fragment and placing Boss 1 at the castle's entrance, there are a few remaining tasks to perform:

1. Add power-ups (because Kodu will not be strong enough to fight Boss 1 when the game starts).

2. Add a wise sage who can warn Kodu about approaching the boss without power-ups.

Adding the wise sage is an easy bit. You already know how to use the Say block to create a conversation, so I won't go over that bit of programming. Instead, I'll simply drop in a Blue Kodu (bigger in size than the player Kodu, too) and place him far away from Kodu's starting position, as shown in Figure 22.7.

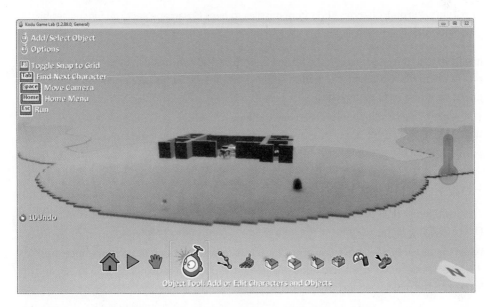

FIGURE 22.7 The wise sage can provide warnings and hints to Kodu.

When the game begins, the player can rush in and try to fight the boss, but one missile hit will end the game immediately. If the player is cautious and approaches the wise sage (Blue Kodu), the player will learn that the boss can only be defeated using a power-up. These power-ups are the key to winning the first challenge, so I focus on programming them properly in the next section.

Programming the Game

With this first challenge, there is simply no way for Kodu to defeat Boss 1. Kodu's missiles only do 5 points of damage, and the range of the missiles has been decreased to a value of 10. Kodu will need to be very close for his missiles to hit! As for Boss 1, however, his missiles do 50 points of damage. Kodu's hit points are set to 50, so one missile hit will end the game.

A smart player might try to get close enough to hit with a missile while staying out of Boss 1's vision range. I've tweaked the settings and tested the game so that it might be possible for the player to get close enough for Kodu's missiles to hit Boss 1, but just far enough away that Boss 1's own missiles aren't triggered. But given that Boss 1's hit points are set to 1,000, it would take 200 missile hits to destroy him. That's going to take a while, so the player is probably going to find it more fun to go hunt down the power-ups.

Let's return to the idea of these power-ups. I've added four power-ups, one in each corner of the castle. These power-ups are simply Kodu objects with a different color, and here is what they do:

○ **Kodu 2 (Red):** Increase Kodu's hit points (500) and missile damage (50)

○ **Kodu 3 (Yellow):** Increase Kodu's missile speed (10) and missile range (30)

○ **Kodu 4 (Green):** Increase Kodu's speed (2.0) and missile damage (30)

○ **Kodu 5 (Purple):** Changes Kodu from missiles to blips (5 damage each) and increases hit points (500)

It will be up to the player to find the best power-up to use; only one can be selected. Each power-up makes two changes to Kodu's settings, and these changes are explained by the Kodu power-up when Kodu approaches.

You might be wondering how you can make changes to Kodu's settings while a game is in play. Well, normally you can't. But with a simple programming trick, you'll see how easy it is to apply power-ups to a player's object.

How Power-Ups Work

The first thing I'll do is add four new Kodus, one in each of the rooms surrounding the castle. Figure 22.8 shows the locations of the Red, Yellow, Green, and Purple Kodus.

When the player bumps into a power-up, I want the player to obtain those power increases described earlier (such as the Red Kodu increasing the player's hit points from 50 to 500 and increasing the missile damage from 5 to 50).

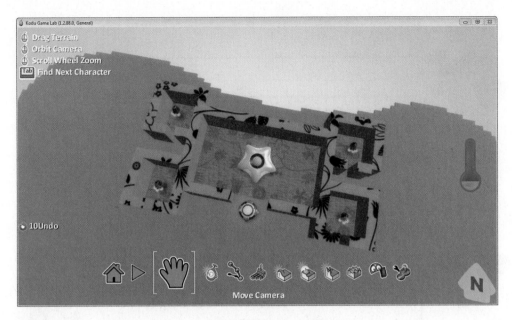

FIGURE 22.8 A Kodu power-up waits in each of the four rooms.

I first program the power-up Red Kodu to explain what increase in power this power-up will provide. Figure 22.9 shows Programming Row 1 for the power-up Red Kodu.

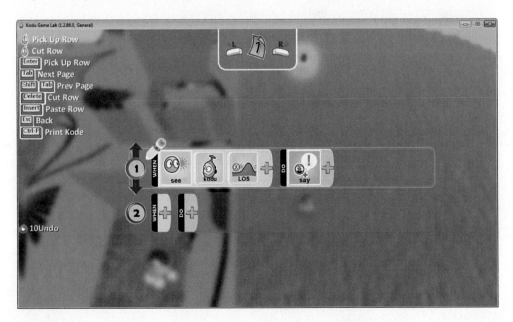

FIGURE 22.9 This power-up explains what increases in power it offers.

Rover: What is that LOS tile?

Kodu: The Line-of-Sight tile simply means that an object must see an object before beginning what is programmed in the Do box.

Rover: So the power-up Red Kodu won't start talking until Kodu is visible in the doorway?

Kodu: Correct. Kodu can be right outside the door, but if the wall is blocking the power-up Kodu from seeing him, the Say tile won't be executed.

I've programmed the power-up Red Kodu to say the following:

I will increase your hit points to 500.

I will increase missile damage to 50.

Earlier I told you how the saucer will explain the treasure map and disappear once bumped, and I'm going to use that bit of programming again now, but in addition to vanishing the power-up Red Kodu, I'm going to vanish the player object, too!

But don't worry. To replace the player's Kodu object, I'm going to have a Red Kodu creatable appear that will be programmed to move and fire missiles. The color will indicate which power-up the player is using, and that creatable will have its settings changed so that missile damage and hit points are increased. When the player's original Kodu is vanished, the player will simply take over the controls of the Red Kodu creatable.

Program a Power-Up

To start this, I drop a copy of the player's Kodu object, and then paste a copy of it on the game world (it doesn't matter where you place it), as shown in Figure 22.10. I also change its color to red.

FIGURE 22.10 The Red Kodu creatable appears when the power-up Red Kodu vanishes.

> **NOTE**
>
> You will create four new creatables, one for each power-up color. You cannot use the same creatable for each power-up because each creatable Kodu will have different powers such as more powerful missiles, longer missile range, more hit points, and other improvements.

Remember to right-click the new object, select Change Settings, and then scroll down the list and turn this object into a creatable, as shown in Figure 22.11.

Next, I program the power-up Red Kodu so that when it's bumped by another Kodu (in this case, the player), the power-up Kodu will vanish, the new creatable will be created, and the original player's Kodu will vanish. Figure 22.12 shows the programming required to do this trick.

The order in which these events occur is important! First, you vanish the original player Kodu. This triggers the creatable to be added and the power-up to be vanished. Programming Rows 3 and 4 are indented below Programming Row 2, meaning they will happen when the actions in Programming Row 2 are triggered and finished.

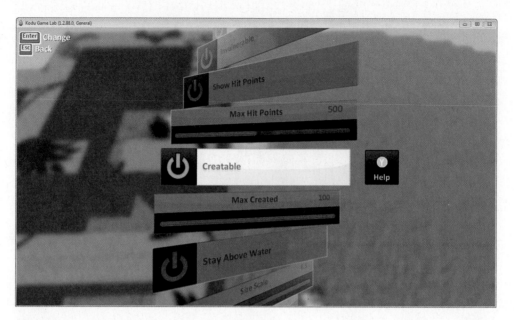

FIGURE 22.11 Change the new object to a creatable.

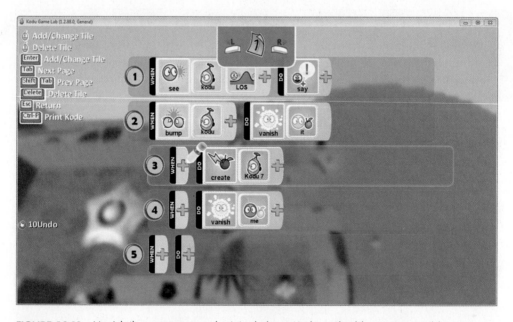

FIGURE 22.12 Vanish the power-up and original player Kodu and add a new creatable.

CAUTION

If you vanish the power-up first, it won't exist to vanish the original player object or the new creatable. Try changing Programming Row 2 to vanish the power-up (use the Me tile) and then test the game. Does the creatable ever show up?

Now all that's needed is to program the Red Kodu creatable to move and fire missiles and change its settings so that hit points are 500 and missile damage is set to 50. When the player bumps into the Red power-up, the power-up vanishes, the original Kodu vanishes, and the player is left controlling the Red Kodu creatable. Cool!

Just repeat these steps for the remaining three power-ups. Remember to copy the original Kodu and then paste three copies. Change their color to match the power-up color, and then program them with the Say tile to inform the player about their respective power increases. Also, remember to add the programming to the power-ups so that they create their specific creatable object before vanishing both the player's object and themselves.

After creating and programming all the power-ups and creatables, I test the game and see how it holds up before moving on to the remaining five challenges and bosses.

Improving the Game

And there's the starting challenge for *The Dune Treasure*. I've got a difficult enemy that must be vanquished, a wise sage who can provide hints to the player, four power-ups to test out, and a mysterious saucer that is covering up one of the six pieces of a treasure map. It's a good start, but there's plenty left to do, so here are some suggestions for how the game could be improved or modified.

Including a Wandering Boss

After the player has a power-up, the boss becomes less of a challenge just sitting there. Consider adding a path for the boss to begin following after it's been hit by a single missile. Keep the boss close to the castle, but give it enough room to wander away and take an occasional shot at the player.

Adding Healing Water

With the desert theme of the game, you could easily add an oasis that can heal the player. For an added challenge, consider placing a less-powerful boss that wanders around the oasis (via a path) and must be destroyed before the player can take a healing drink.

Defeating an Unfriendly Saucer

In the original game, the saucer is being held prisoner by the boss. But you can add an additional challenge that requires the player to defeat the saucer. When the saucer's hit points drop to 0, program it to explain the treasure map before disappearing.

Using Mystery Power-Ups

You don't have to tell the player what bonuses the power-ups provide. You can easily make it more of a challenge by letting players grab a power-up and then they just see what happens.

Creating Boss Minions

If you think it might be a bit too easy on the player to have bosses that have limited movement, consider enabling your bosses to send out their own little minions. You could easily program a boss to start sending out a creatable object, one every 10 to 20 seconds of game time (using the Timer), that is programmed to chase and fire at the player. I'm thinking that Boss 1 could send out some sand bugs (tiny Sputniks) to keep the player engaged.

Introducing a Super Boss

When the six pieces of the map are found and arranged to form a special emblem, that emblem could be placed at the entrance to one of four castles. If the player has copied the treasure maps properly and oriented them in the right direction, they should be able to find this emblem painted on the ground in front of one of the castles. But...deep inside that castle guarding the final treasure could be one very large super boss that might require additional power-ups that you'll add somewhere in the other three castles to defeat.

Changing Terrain

Although I've called the game *The Dune Treasure*, I don't have to limit myself to the sandy terrain. You might consider creating five additional challenges, with each having a unique terrain. Try a water challenge or a maze challenge, for example. And you don't have to have a boss in every challenge. You could simply find one of the treasure map pieces at the end of the maze, for example.

Adding Scoring

Consider adding a scoring element to the game. Players will not be able to enter certain areas if the score isn't high enough, or maybe a gatekeeper protects a super power-up until the player returns from defeating a few more bosses, or destroying a certain number of minions. Scoring can be used to limit access to other challenges by placing gatekeepers in front of the paths between each challenge. Figure 22.13 shows that I've already created the next two challenge areas and the small roads that allow movement. A gatekeeper placed in front of a small doorway can keep players from leaving a challenge area until a specific score is reached.

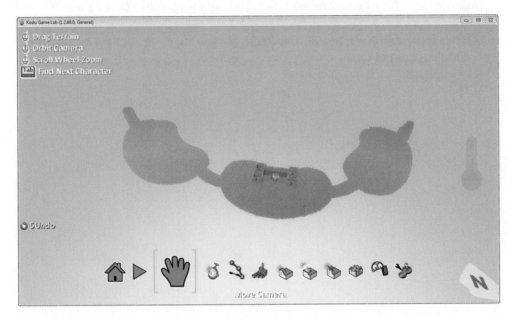

FIGURE 22.13 Additional challenges are ready to be added to *The Dune Treasure*.

Moving On

I hope you've enjoyed learning about the development of *The Dune Treasure*. As you can see, it's not even close to being completed. I might decide to finish it up and post the entire game for the community to play, but I'm actually more interested in seeing how you might finish up the remaining challenges.

Keep in mind that a quest game doesn't have to involve gold coins or enemies to fight. A quest game can easily be created for a school project. Consider a historical event, for example, where you add a bit of terrain that Lewis and Clark crossed during their famous expedition. Instead of humans, however, you substitute Kodu Game Lab objects and program a mini-game for your fellow students to play that lets them learn some interesting facts that you've researched.

> **NOTE**
>
> For more information about one of the most amazing explorations of a new country, visit http://wikipedia.org/wiki/Lewis_and_Clark_Expedition and read about the adventures that took place between 1804 and 1806.

A quest game allows you to slow down a game and use Say blocks to provide information to your players. Quest games also allow you to release a series of games to the community. Instead of six challenges in *The Dune Treasure*, for example, I could easily have created *Dune Treasure Part I* and released it as a stand-alone quest game. Then, over time, I'd upload *Dune Treasure Part II*, then *Part III*, and so on. It's a great way to build a reputation as a good game designer, but be warned: If it's a good game, don't be surprised when other players begin asking over and over when the next game in the series will be released.

23

Sample Game 4: The Side-Scroller Experience

Most games that you've seen created in this book enable the player (or players) to wander around a game world, with no limitations as to where they can go (except for maybe areas blocked by a gatekeeper, for example). In this chapter, however, you will see a game that does put a limitation on the player. This kind of game is called a *side-scroller*, and as the name implies, the action moves from one side of the screen to the other.

Sample Game 4 Overview

The game you're going to learn about in this chapter is called *Octo's Aquarium*, and it was created by Scott Fintel, a member of the Kodu Development Team. Scott provided me with his notes about the game's development, and I'm inserting some of those (in *italics*) into this chapter so that you'll get some first-hand details about how he developed the idea for the game and some of the key programming aspects that make it work. Here's a little explanation about Scott's initial thoughts on a side-scroller game:

I've always loved side-scrolling games. There is something about having a definitive path that you must go toward, a goal that you know you must hit, and a very tough final battle at the end of the level, which you will fight hard. Side-scrollers are also fun because there are many tricks that you can do as a game programmer to make these experiences more exciting. From how your character moves, to the types of levels you create, as well as the type of environment the level has. All the skills come into play when you make a level. They are very important because you also have to understand how your friends will play it and how you want them to play it.

For *Octo's Aquarium*, Scott chose to create a game that takes place completely underwater! How's that for unique and different? Scott created a fish tank, which you'll learn more about shortly, and then added programming that follows Octo as he crosses from one side of the fish tank to the other side. The game is a simple one, and there are plenty of places where you can expand and improve on the game, but as Scott says, "Let's start simple." The idea is to collect as many points as possible as Octo crosses the fish tank.

For this simple version, the player is going to help Octo try to steer around obstacles and collect items as he moves to the other side of the fish tank. On the opposite side of the tank, a strong current pushes him backward. There are fish and turtles to avoid; bumping into them ends the game.

Take a look at Figure 23.1 and you'll see the end result of the fish tank that you need to create. Your fish tank probably won't look exactly like this one, but that's okay.

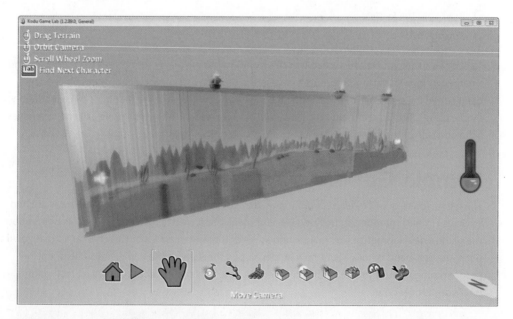

FIGURE 23.1   *Octo's Aquarium* is a side-scrolling game.

In this chapter, you learn how to design the fish tank and then how to program some of the game elements, including a strong current that pushes Octo around and some of the other objects that inhabit Octo's tank.

Creating *Octo's Aquarium*

To create the fish tank, you first want to create a length of terrain that resembles what you'd see on the bottom of an actual fish tank. Think about starfish, sea grass, and rocks. Scott says:

> *The first thing that I did was use the smallest possible brush size to paint a long stripe of green. This is my first "foreground" layer of ground, which helps set perspective. Next, I switched terrain to brown and painted another line. Then I changed to yellow and painted another line. Finally, I switched back to brown and completed that line. You can use any color you want, but the trick is to make the environment look good without looking confusing. Choose materials that you think actually exist in the water.*

Figure 23.2 shows a length of terrain that Scott created. Notice that it has some greenery near the back and a strip of yellow and green terrain running down the center that will be the track that Octo will move along. Also notice that the tank moves east to west. You can tell because of the north-pointing graphic in the lower-right corner of the screen. As you create your own terrain, make certain that it runs east to west or north to south. (The reason for this is explained later, but it basically comes down to the fact that when programming you can limit an object's movement to north, south, east, or west… or a combination of those.)

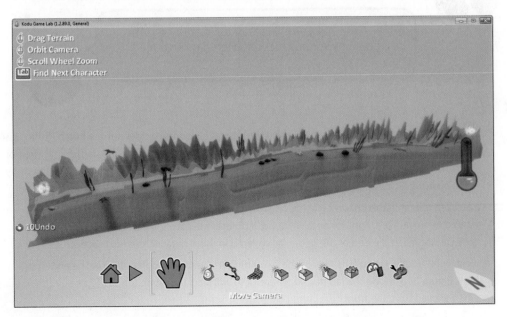

FIGURE 23.2   The fish tank starts with terrain and some greenery added.

Again, before you begin creating your terrain, use the **Move Camera** tool to orient your terrain placement so that it runs east-west.

Scott's game relies heavily on creatables, so here's an interesting trick he used for keeping all his creatables in one place. Hidden behind the fish tank is a small square of terrain where he's placed all his creatables. Remember that when a game starts, creatables disappear and only appear when another object creates them; so the player won't see any of these objects. (Not only will the player not see the creatables, but the camera view is going to be locked, so the player will never see the patch of terrain holding the creatables shown in Figure 23.3.)

Rover: So what objects are going to actually create the creatables?

Kodu: The game will have Ship objects creating turtles that the player must avoid.

Rover: What about the fish? And is Octo a creatable, too?

Kodu: When the game starts, the fish and Octo are all created by various rocks scattered around the fish tank.

Figure 23.4 shows the final fish tank with all the creatables on the hidden terrain patch. Notice also the path running right down the center of the fish tank, which has only a few starfish scattered on the surface. All the sea grass and rocks are pushed to the front or rear of the fish tank so that they don't obstruct Octo's movement.

You'll learn later in this chapter why this is so important in a side-scrolling game. Octo will be limited in moving left/right (or east/west); so, if objects are placed incorrectly, players might find they cannot reach the end of the game (as covered in more detail in the next section).

Next, Scott added in two fans: one at the beginning of the tank and the other at the end of the tank. Figure 23.5 shows the fan placed where Octo will start the game (on the left side of the tank when viewed from the front).

FIGURE 23.3 All the creatables are hidden from view behind the fish tank.

FIGURE 23.4 The fish tank has a clear path running down the middle.

FIGURE 23.5 Place one fan at each end of the aquarium.

When the game starts, the fans really shouldn't be visible, so right-click them, select Change Settings, and scroll down and turn on the Invisible feature for both. Figure 23.6 shows the fan is now clear (see-through), indicating it won't be seen when the game starts.

FIGURE 23.6 Make the fans invisible so that they're not seen as the game is played.

> **NOTE**
> You complete the fan programming in the next section. The fans are used to push objects away from them, simulating a strong underwater current.

All that's left now is to add a few additional items: three ships that will drop turtles that will act as obstacles (and that Octo must navigate around and avoid touching) and the water.

Adding water is easy! Figure 23.7 shows that I've selected the Water tool (and the Clear water, Option 1) and added a sufficient depth in which the fish, turtles, and Octo can swim. (You can experiment with different depths of water during testing to find the best depth to offer a good challenge without being too difficult.)

Look closely at Figure 23.7 and you'll see three Ship objects floating on the surface, as well as the other (invisible) fan located on the far right of the fish tank.

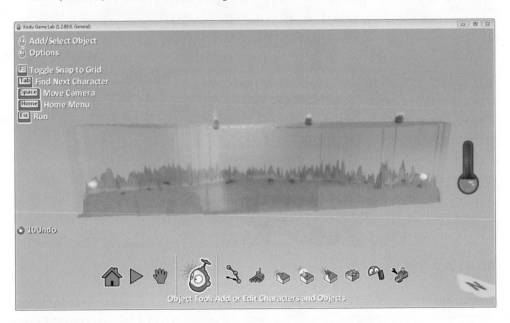

FIGURE 23.7   Water and ships added and ready for programming.

Now that all the objects and creatables have been added, it's time for the programming.

Programming the Game

This is a side-scrolling game, so the action is going to follow Octo as he starts on the left side of the tank and moves toward the right side. This means limiting not only the player (Octo) to left and right movement, but also making certain the camera follows at a proper distance so that Octo is always on the screen and the player is viewing the action from the side, as if looking through the front of the fishbowl at all the characters inside.

Earlier you were told the importance of having the terrain running east to west (or north to south). That's because later you'll be programming limits on Octo that allow him to only move east or west. But there's another reason we chose to have the game running east to west, and it involves the camera mode.

Refer back to Chapter 10, "The Cameras Are Rolling: Camera Controls for Solo and Multiplayer Games," for details about the various camera modes. For the side-scroller, you're going to want to use the Fixed Offset option. Right-click your game world's terrain, select Change World Settings, scroll down to Camera Mode, and select Fixed Offset, as shown in Figure 23.8. Don't exit the Camera Mode option yet, however.

FIGURE 23.8   Choose the Fixed Offset camera mode for side-scrolling games.

This option keeps the camera a fixed distance and angle from the player-controlled object (Octo) as it moves through the game. This setting forces the camera to follow the player object, but you'll still need to set the distance and angle where the camera starts when the game begins. Exit the World Settings and return to your game world terrain.

Follow these steps to set the Starting Camera location:

1. While still using the Camera Mode option (shown in Figure 23.8) click the X (Set Camera) option with your mouse cursor or press the X button on a game controller.

2. Move the camera to the starting position you want to use for the game, as shown in Figure 23.9.

3. Press the Enter key to lock in the Starting Camera location.

FIGURE 23.9   Move the camera around until you're happy with the distance and angle.

That's it for defining the camera view for the game. Now it's time to do some programming.

Programming Octo

This section does not explain where to find every tile used to program Octo's movement. Instead, you can view the basics of Octo's movement controls in their entirety in Figure 23.10.

As shown in Figure 23.10, keys on the keyboard are being used for movement. The D key moves Octo to the east (toward the right side of the fish tank), the A key moves Octo to the west (back toward his starting position), and the W and S keys move Octo up and down, respectively.

Look at Programming Row 5; the C key has been assigned to a camouflage ability! This will let Octo hide if a fish or turtle spots him and begins to swim toward him. Remember that if a fish or turtle bumps Octo, the game is over, so this is a great way to give players a special ability. Take a look at Figure 23.11 and you'll see Programming Rows 6 and 7 indented under Row 5.

When the player presses the C button, Octo disappears for 4 seconds. This is done using the White scoreboard. Programming Row 6 sets its value to 4, and then Octo's programming jumps to Page 3. Figure 23.12 shows Page 3's programming.

FIGURE 23.10 Select where the camera starts and the distance from the player object.

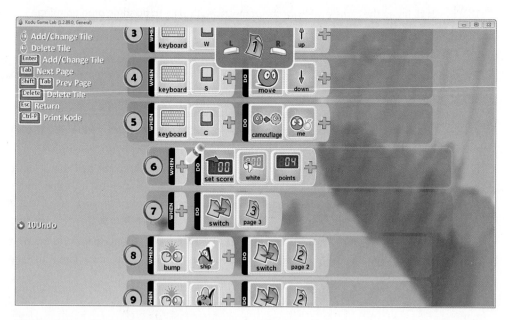

FIGURE 23.11 The camouflage special ability has a limit.

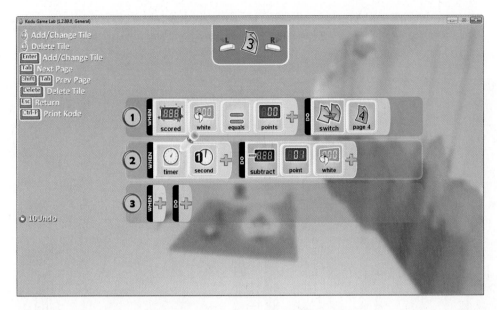

FIGURE 23.12 The four-second countdown for the camouflage ability.

Programming Row 1 (on Page 3) first checks to see whether the White score is equal to a value of 1. If it is, Octo's programming jumps to Page 4. If it isn't, the White score is reduced by 1 point every second, as shown in Programming Row 2. This gives Octo four seconds of camouflage. When the four seconds are up, Page 4, shown in Figure 23.13, is executed.

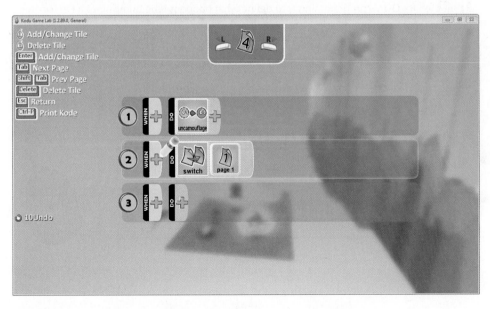

FIGURE 23.13 After four seconds, the camouflage ability is turned off.

When the camouflage ability wears off, Octo's programming jumps back to Page 1. Scrolling down Page 1 a bit more, you can now see that the remaining programming rows all point to Page 2 if Octo bumps a turtle, ship, or fish.

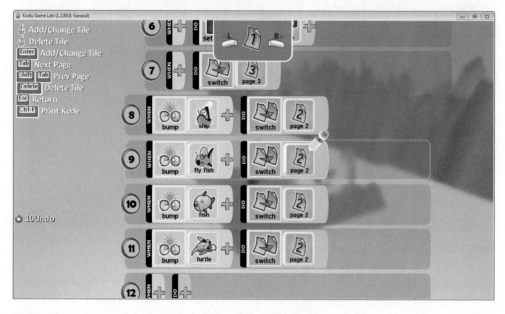

FIGURE 23.14   If Octo bumps a fish, ship, or turtle, the programming jumps to Page 2.

All that's left for Octo's programming is to define what happens if he bumps into a Fish or Ship object, and that's shown on Page 2, shown in Figure 23.15.

Rover: Whoa! I've never seen that Sky tile before in Programming Row 1.

Kodu: It's brand new, and only just became available when the author began writing Chapter 23. It's a shortcut to changing the color of the sky. Simply click the tile and choose a color.

Rover: And I see a new Lighting tile, too, on Row 2.

Kodu: Yep, that tile is new, too. Click that tile and you can define the lighting of the game. It's used here to dim all the lights when the game ends.

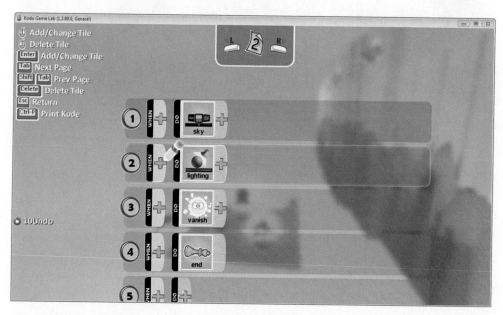

FIGURE 23.15 Night comes, the light dims, and the game ends.

Guess what? Kodu Game Lab is always adding new features. Take a look at Figure 23.15 and you'll see the new Sky and Lighting tiles. These arrived in an update as this book was finishing up. Now you can change the color of the sky and the lighting while the game is running. Cool, huh?

Well, that does it for Octo's programming. Now it's time to check out a few of the creatables' programming.

Programming the Creatables

This game contains a lot of different creatables, and you can certainly make more. There isn't room in this chapter to cover them all, so just examine the ones provided here and you should be able to figure out how to make the others work. (For example, there are two types of fish, but they both end the game if they touch Octo.)

Let's start with the ship. There are three of them, and you can see their simple programming in Figure 23.16. Their job is to create a turtle creatable.

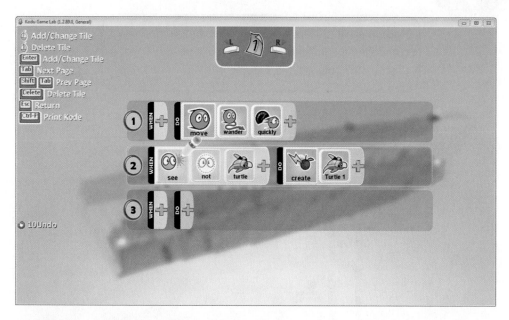

FIGURE 23.16   There are three ships and they each create a turtle.

Notice in Programming Row 2 that when the ships no longer see a turtle they'll create a new one. Notice also that these ships can wander randomly on the surface of the water.

Figure 23.17 shows the programming that's found in the turtle creatable and the two fish creatables (Fish and Flyfish are the two objects used).

Now you can see why it was so important to orient your terrain to run from east to west. Programming Row 1 constrains the creatable so that it can only move (wander) slowly along an east/west path. The E/W tile forces these creatables to only move left or right in the fish tank (corresponding to an east or west movement). When they see Octo, they are programmed to move toward him. (Now you see the value of the camouflage special ability.)

Programming the Fans

The last thing to be added is the programming for the two Fan objects. Figure 23.18 shows the simple programming. The fans simply push anything in front of them.

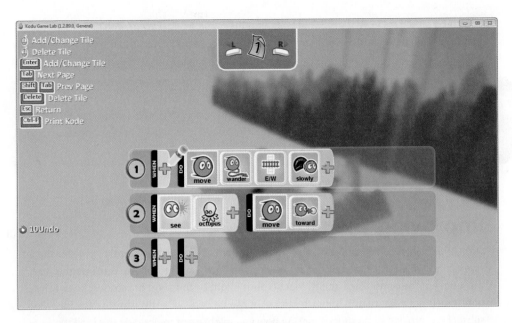

FIGURE 23.17 These creatables move toward Octo when they spot him.

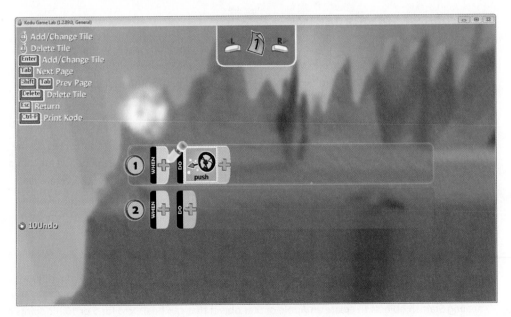

FIGURE 23.18 The fans push Octo or any other object in front of them.

You could place fans in various locations around the game world. Players won't see them, so they won't know which tricky locations could possibly push poor Octo into the path of an enemy object.

> **NOTE**
> You can further define the strength of the fan's push by clicking the plus sign (+) to the right of the Push tile and choosing Weak or Strong. There's even a Pull tile that does the reverse and pulls objects in front toward the object.

Improving the Game

Octo's Aquarium is a very simple game: Avoid the enemies (fish, turtles, ships) and get to the far side of the fish tank. Use the camouflage ability if an enemy gets too close. You'll want to test the length of the camouflage ability; four seconds might be too short or too long, so tweak it until it feels right. But there's so much more that can be done with this game, so the following subsections provide some suggestions on how you might want to upgrade this fun little side-scroller.

Including Underwater Weapons

Why not give poor Octo a fighting chance? A fish tank is a dangerous place, so maybe you can figure out how to use a Score tile to give Octo three or four missiles to fire. If players use them all up, they'll just have to be fast and avoid the enemies and get to the other side of the tank.

Enabling Ink Clouds

A new ability added to Kodu Game Lab lets Octo fire up an ink cloud. Assign it to the I key on the keyboard and press it to put up an inky black cloud for Octo to hide in. You can find the Ink Cloud tile by adding the Create tile to Octo's Do box and then clicking + to the right of the Create tile; you should then see Ink Cloud in the pie menu that appears.

Introducing Healing Starfish

Instead of ending the game when Octo bumps an enemy, consider giving Octo some hit points and having each enemy bump subtract some points. Throw up Octo's hit points using a scoreboard so that players know exactly how many points they have left, and perhaps add a few healing Starfish objects to create an Apple or Star object that can heal Octo for 5 or 10 hit points if he collects them.

Don't Forget Music

You learned all about how to add music and sound effects in Chapter 14, "Games Should Be Heard: Programming Music and Sound Effects." Most of the games in this book have focused on programming and ignored adding music to save both on page space and because we all have different tastes in music. But don't forget the music! Pick a rock or piece of sea grass and program it with an Always tile and select a fun bit of music that will always be playing as Octo races to the end of the tank.

Getting There and Back

There's nothing to stop you from requiring your players to race to the end of the tank and then back to the start. To ensure fairness, consider placing a coin or star that Octo must pick up on the far side of the tank. Add a unique bit of terrain or another object that will constantly be checking to see when the coin or star is brought back. Or turn it into a quest! Have a friendly tank character assign Octo a mission in the tank. Feel free to enlarge that tank, but if you want it to remain a side-scroller, remember to limit the tank's growth to running east or west.

You Sank My Ship!

Those three ships sure do like dropping turtles in the water, but feel free to give Octo the ability to sink a ship by bumping it. Change Octo's programming so that if Octo bumps a ship the ship vanishes. No more turtles!

Creating an Invisible Maze

Remove the enemies (fish, turtles, ships) and instead add in a bunch of invisible fans. Some push, and some pull, but the player won't know their locations or which ones are pushing and which ones are pulling. Using these fans, you can create an invisible maze of sorts, where there are only a limited number of ways to cross from one side of the tank to the other. Change the strength of the fans to **Strong** and really give your players a challenge.

Using Depth Charges

Using paths (which are invisible after the game begins), you could remove the turtle creatable and instead have the ships drop soccer balls. Soccer balls will sink in water (straight down, away from the ship that created them) toward the bottom of the tank. You could add programming that will vanish the ball if it bumps Kodu, doing a certain amount of hit-point damage or ending the game altogether. Time the release of the balls so that they don't litter the bottom of the fish tank. If players decide to get too close to the fish tank bottom, however, it's not your fault if they bump a soccer ball, right?

Moving On

The addition of water makes for some interesting game ideas. Not only do you have objects that can float on or hover over the surface (like a ship or Kodu), you also have objects that are meant for underwater activities.

Octo's Aquarium showed you that you could design an entire underwater game, but there's nothing to stop you from creating a game that mixes both underwater and above-water action. Because you can change Kodu's settings to allow him to go underwater, you can easily create a game that lets players experience the best of both environments. Think about a quest game that has a hidden treasure underneath the water that must be retrieved… that would really add a new and fun element to a standard quest game.

> **NOTE**
>
> If you can't remember how to disable Kodu's hover ability so that he can go underwater, just right-click him, select Change Settings, scroll down the list to the Stay Above Water option, and turn it off. Likewise, you can give Octo or a fish the ability to float over dry land by turning on the Stay Above Water option.

Over the past four chapters, you've read how four different games were developed: a single-player maze, a two-player competition, a quest/mission, and now a side-scroller. You can easily mix and match these games, creating an underwater maze, a side-scrolling two-player quest, and much more.

Now it's your turn. You're ready! You've probably got a list of game ideas in your head or written down, and your only choice now is which one to create first. You've got all the time you need, and you have a good grasp on game design and using Kodu Game Lab. Let's wrap things up in Chapter 24, "Closing Thoughts and Challenges," so that you can get moving on creating the next great Kodu game.

24

Closing Thoughts and Challenges

In This Chapter

- ○ Consider All You've Learned
- ○ Where to Go from Here
- ○ A Challenge For You
- ○ Moving On

Congratulations! You've worked your way through 23 chapters, but there's one more to go. This chapter offers some suggestions and challenges for you to consider as you move forward with your own game development. And because Kodu Game Lab is continually being updated with new features, new tiles, and new objects, by the time you're reading this and have installed the latest version you might find a number of new things you'll need to learn.

Consider All You've Learned

I'm not going to list every tile and every setting that you've seen used in this book, but let me list just a few that stand out in my mind:

- ○ **Scoreboard tiles**: Useful for scorekeeping, inventory, and object features such as hit points.
- ○ **Path following**: Program smarter enemies and helpful characters and enable them to navigate around your game world rather than sitting still.
- ○ **Terrain editing**: With all the various editing tools, you can create unique worlds as well as duplicate existing landmarks. Water adds in even more capabilities for water-based object programming.

- ○ **Movement controls**: You've seen how to program games that can use both the game controller and mouse and keyboard for controlling player objects.

- ○ **Pages**: Using pages, you can change behaviors, create new scenes (such as cut-scenes), and give your player controlled objects and non-player-controlled objects much more interesting movements and powers.

- ○ **Creatables**: Program an object once and then unleash as many of them as you need. Creatables can be spawned by players or programmed to be released by non-player-controlled objects.

- ○ **Bump/grab/vanish**: Enabling players to pick up items in a game opens up a variety of options. Vanishing objects (both player and non-player) allow you to apply power-ups by dropping in a new player-controlled object that can immediately be controlled by the player.

The list goes on, too. I'm sure that you've discovered some of your favorite programming tricks, and there's nothing wrong with sticking with what works best. If you're good at creating two-player games, keep creating them, but always be on the lookout for new programming tricks to improve your games and make the next one even better than the last one.

What this means is taking an honest look at the skills you are comfortable with, and the skills you are still working on improving. If you're still struggling to use scoreboards for uses other than keeping score, you might try and create games that don't use scoreboard tiles. I challenge you to do the opposite: Identify the areas in Kodu Game Lab where you are weak and push yourself to incorporate those areas into your new games.

Mistakes are part of learning. You might spend 30 minutes programming an object to do something unusual, and during testing discover that it just doesn't work.

You didn't fail.

You discovered something that doesn't work!

Sometimes you have to start over from the beginning, but more often than not, you can simply start peeling away the programming, tile by tile, until you discover the error or the right combination of tiles that's required to make your great idea work.

Where to Go from Here

You learned in Chapter 18, "Join the Community: Online Help and Sharing Games," about the Kodu Community. I highly encourage you to join the community and discover other Kodu Game Lab fans who are creating their own games, sharing their programming tricks, asking questions, and providing answers.

I also want to point out that the Kodu Game Lab development team isn't sitting still. As I was writing this book, some new features were added just as I putting the finishing touches on Chapter 22, "Sample Game 3: On a Mission." You might have noticed the new Octo in Chapter 23, "Sample Game 4: The Side-Scroller Experience," which hasn't been seen in many of the earlier screenshots. That's right. Some new characters and some new tiles have been added. As Kodu Game Lab continues to be updated, you'll find new features not covered in this book. Don't let that bother you. If you've completed all the activities in this book, you've got a solid understanding of Kodu Game Lab, and any new features you discover will simply require you to try them out to find out what they can offer you as a game designer. (Of course, you can always turn to the Kodu Community members for help if you really need assistance with new features.)

You can use this book as a reference book should you need a reminder about a certain programming trick, but it's only one source of information. The Kodu Community is a much larger source of information and inspiration, where you can upload your games and ask for feedback, provide your own solutions to questions from Kodu novices, and find out information about upgrades to Kodu Game Lab, contests, and what others are doing with the game development software.

Are you looking for some additional online resources? I can help you there:

○ **10 Tips for Building a Better Game**: Not all of this advice is relevant to Kodu Game Lab, but you'll find some great tips in this short article; it's well worth a read.

  http://www.netmagazine.com/features/10-tips-building-better-game

○ **A Game Design Method Empowering Children and Adults**: This article is a bit more complex, but you'll find a great three-phase method for brainstorming and developing games. It can be used by individuals or teams and offers the right mix of brainstorming, planning, and hands-on programming.

  http://www.academia.edu/548125/A_Game_Design_Method_Empowering_Children_and_Adults

○ **Three Steps to Designing Your Game**: BAFTA (British Academy of Film and Television Arts) has a great website for young game designers (YGD), with dozens of articles. Much of the content isn't specific to Kodu Game Lab, but you'll find plenty of inspiration by exploring the website.

  http://ygd.bafta.org/top-tips-for-entry/3-steps-to-designing-your-game

  http://ygd.bafta.org

○ **Planet Kodu**: Planet Kodu is not an official Microsoft Kodu website, but it is another online resource that you should definitely check out. It offers tutorials, a Kwestion section, and even regular challenges for you to accept and try your hand at solving using Kodu Game Lab.

  http://planetkodu.com

If you really enjoy creating games with Kodu Game lab… I mean *really, really, really* enjoy creating games with Kodu Game Lab—I have two additional recommendations for you.

The first is a book titled *The Art of Game Design: A Book of Lenses*, written by Jesse Schell. I purchased a copy of this book a few years back, and it's one of the most interesting books on game design that you'll ever read. It's a thick book, a little pricey, and it's got some extremely complex topics tucked in those pages. But if you're imagining that game design is something you might like to dive deeper into and maybe even consider as a career, well, this is the book for you.

Just be warned, it's 500 pages, so it's going to add some weight to a book bag! (Summer vacation might be the best time to tackle it.)

Another book recommendation that comes straight from the Kodu Game Lab team is *Building XNA 2.0 Games: A Practical Guide for Independent Game Developers*, by John Sedlak and James Silva. It's a more advanced book that uses a text-based programming language called C#, but you might find it useful as you develop your game designing and programming skills.

A Challenge for You

Programming is an art and a skill. Just like painting or writing, programming is something that you never really stop learning about if you enjoy doing it. But unlike painting or writing, programming isn't a talent that you have to develop solo.

So, here's a final challenge for you:

If you enjoy programming games with Kodu Game Lab, be sure to share your enjoyment with your friends, family members, and even your teachers.

Imagine creating a new game with your best buddies. Now you can design a two-player game that both players will enjoy, and one in which both players will have contributed some special features.

Imagine creating a new game with your parents or a sibling… or even creating a game for a younger sibling to show her how much fun playing video games can be. Family game night can take on a whole new meaning when the game is one that the family created itself.

Imagine being able to share your Kodu Game Lab experiences with your class. Liven up your next report by having a conversation with Kodu. (You'll need to practice the timing to get it right.) And maybe your school might be interested in starting up a Kodu Game Lab club, with members getting together occasionally to create a game just for the school. (You could re-create the school's layout and create a digital treasure hunt that takes new students on a tour of the school.)

That's more than a single challenge, isn't it? That's okay. It all comes down to sharing. Share your games. Share what you've learned. Share your answers. Share your questions. And share your excitement.

Moving On

You're done! With the book, that is. But you're definitely not done when it comes to creating games with Kodu Game Lab. Now it's time to take everything you've learned from the book, combine it with your own exploration of Kodu Game Lab and any other resources (such as the Kodu Community) that you've used to learn more and more, and go create some amazing games.

You are going to have so much fun! Game design tests your creativity skills and your programming skills at the same time. You will be smiling from ear to ear when you start hearing from players who are enjoying your games. Remember, though, that getting from the idea of a game to a fully functional (and fun) game takes time, and there will be much testing in between, and possibly frustration. But remember to treat the frustration that comes from game design as a puzzle that you can solve.

And you can solve it.

Change the programming a bit.

Add or remove an object that is causing the trouble.

Post a question or two on a forum and ask for help.

Try a different tile or two to see whether there's a better method.

Share your games.

Ask for feedback.

Fix what you can.

Post a game as final version.

Move on to the next game.

Smile and have fun!

James Floyd Kelly

Atlanta, Georgia

February 1, 2013

A

The Kodu Developers

Stephen Coy

When we first began the Kodu project, we were looking for a fun project that would do some good for people. We had just finished working on Windows Vista and were brainstorming ideas for a research project. One of the issues we discussed was the declining rate of enrollment in computer science degree programs. At the time, enrollment had been in decline for almost a decade. Working for Microsoft, this is a concern. Our business depends on being able to hire talented programmers. So we thought back to the experiences that had led each of us to a career in programming.

I did my first programming in the late 1970s and early 1980s. At the time, when you turned on a computer, it generally went "beep" and displayed a command prompt where you could start typing in a program using the BASIC language. I was immediately hooked. For me, programming was like an endless puzzle. I was also drawn to the sense of control I had. The machine did as I told it, even if it was nothing more than bouncing a box around on the screen. Modern computers no longer start up at a BASIC prompt. In fact, they don't come with any programming languages at all. Sure, lots of free languages are available, but the learning curve has just gotten steeper over time. We also realized that a generation of kids raised on smart phones and game consoles wasn't going to get too excited about drawing a box on the screen. We wanted to design a new computer language that was easy to grasp while still being powerful enough to be useful. We also wanted to take advantage of the graphics power of modern PCs.

The missing piece of the puzzle fell into place when Microsoft announced the first version of XNA Game Studio. XNA would allow us to build Kodu and make it run on the Xbox and PC. The choice to make Kodu run on the Xbox was quite significant. We would have great hardware for 3D graphics, making Kodu look like an application built in the twenty-first century rather than in the 1980s. More importantly, the choice of Xbox meant that our programming language had to be accessible with a game pad controller sans keyboard. What at first seemed like a limitation helped us focus on keeping everything as approachable as possible. Even with the addition of keyboard and mouse support for the PC version, we've tried to keep this sense of simplicity at the core of everything Kodu.

It's been more than six years now since we started Kodu, and this has been by far the most rewarding project I've worked on in my career. With the startup beep of my Apple][+, I had found what I wanted to do with my life. For me, programming has been an endlessly rewarding career and hobby. My personal goal with Kodu is not to try to turn every kid into a programmer but to make sure that every potential great programmer has the opportunity to find the same joy and success in his or her life.

Matt MacLaurin

Some years ago, I stood in the kitchen with some friends on a workday evening. As we chatted, I idly watched my daughter—then 3 years old—as she watched my wife using the computer for a typical browsing session: social networks, email, a few links. Not sure if Facebook was even out yet.

It struck me that my daughter was watching her mother use the computer so that she could understand *what the computer was for*. I decided to imagine what concepts my daughter was forming about the use and value of computers.

What *are* computers for?

Here's what my daughter saw that evening: pictures scrolling by, a movie snippet playing, a bunch of text, some pictures, a movie preview, an ad, and so on.

I compared this to my own experience learning to use a computer at age 14—a Commodore PET with 8K of RAM and a cassette drive. This computer was black and white, and its entire memory could hold only a few dozen pages of text—but could still do crude animation and graphics. To me, the main use of this computer was for was playing really simple games…and, very quickly, for *programming* really simple games.

Programming was a revelation: a creative canvas with extreme magical powers. Through the right incantations, I could create interactive story worlds with strange physics, unpredictable enemies, spaceships, tanks, robots, interactive dungeons, and 3D visualizations.

To me at that age, computers were like some ultimate descendant of pen and ink, writing and drawing, filmmaking, and music composition. The personal computer was a creative breakthrough for the arts. I was hooked. I'm still hooked.

To a child today, a computer is different. It's a communication device, a broadcast medium, a tool for writing and audiovisual design, and a crystal ball for searching knowledge. This is great. This is amazing.

But the creative power unique to computers—software—remains hidden to most people. As the popularity of computers has spread, this core creative capacity has become coated in a thick candy shell of mass consumption. Is software passé? Are we done, as a culture, with programming? Not hardly.

We are surrounded by software. We are embedded in banking, media, government, and social algorithms. Fortunes are created and destroyed over lines of code—text in a document, with the power to connect the planet and keep it entranced.

Software design is the only modern form of design. It intersects with all others—almost assimilates them—but software goes beyond previous media. Only software can react to the world around it in complex and specific ways. Software is a fundamentally new medium whose impact on our life and culture grows daily.

But we don't treat software as a design medium. We actually don't teach software design at all to our children. Not even 1 in every 100 public school teachers spends *any time at all* teaching programming. If you experienced even a single programming class before college, you are an extremely rare person.

It's worse for girls. Girls who are not interested in technology by the time they reach seventh grade are very unlikely to ever pursue a technical career. Yet we don't offer even basic programming until college.

Software is amazing; it's transforming the world. It's one of the most satisfying jobs in the world, primarily for creative and intellectual reasons. We really need to give more kids an opportunity to try it, because many will enjoy it and add it to their life's options.

This is why we made Kodu. We wanted to create the most creative possible way for kids to enjoy learning what programming is about. In some ways, Kodu is like a programming simulator because it is so forgiving. You toss a few symbols together, and things start reacting to other things and to the environment.

As you dig deeper, though, the creative powers expand to provide deep and real algorithm design abilities. Characters can change moods, swapping in new combinations of actions and reactions. Sculpted worlds can provide unexpected challenges and adventures. Kids people their worlds with actors in their own original stories—but actors who can think for themselves, and in which the story continuously evolves. In Kodu worlds, kids are often surprised by their own creations, actors combine in different ways, and complex phenomena arise that can be harnessed and directed with further refinement.

This form of learning is powerful and extremely far-reaching. Kids are learning three things:

○ How to predict how a system behaves by examining its design

○ How to design a system to achieve a particular effect

○ That software design offers endlessly unique creative possibilities

Because we involved K-12 teachers in the design of Kodu from the very beginning, we are mindful of the environment they're in. Most teachers using Kodu in the classroom don't have computer science degrees. They are English teachers, art teachers, and math teachers. And this is fine.

In schools around the world, for hundreds of thousands of students in more than 200 countries and more than a dozen languages, kids have agreed with us—it's magic, and they love it. And teachers have agreed as well: These kids are really thinking, they're really engaging with this medium and creatively with each other, and they're growing in some ways that are different from what they get out of other fundamental literacies.

Some kids engage with software in ways in which they haven't engaged with anything else; they finally see a way to make their thoughts visible, and to demonstrate their own unique ways of solving problems and telling stories. These have been some of my favorite stories of Kodu in schools.

Kodu is by far the best thing that has ever happened to me—aside from my family—and by far the best thing I have ever helped to create with my own hands. My partners in crime Stephen, Eric, Mark, Brad, Brian, Michael, and most of all Lili—champions forever.

Mark Finch

When I was a young sprout, way before I started programming computers, I built models. My favorites were the old three-masted sailing vessels, especially the clipper ships. I enjoyed the whole bit, from carving the pieces out of wood to running thread for the riggings to starching the sails. My other hobby, which was really the same hobby, was growing terrariums. I was always on the lookout for tiny plants that looked like their larger cousins, for mosses and ferns to fill out my landscapes. And I would lay out rolling lawns and stepped terraces as a backdrop for beautiful lush gardens or sometimes even create harsh desert badlands. I would create an entire world in a large glass bottle, then cork it up and see how it grew on its own.

I really enjoyed creating these worlds, but always wound up at the same frustration. I could build a ship, but I couldn't sail it. I could plant a garden, but I couldn't stroll through it.

At the time, I had a dream of getting a small video camera and that someday I would be able to virtually visit my gardens by remote control. If I could send my little camera into the garden and see what it saw, it would be like being there myself. I never got that little camera. But what I got was better.

When I started programming, it didn't take me long to realize that I was getting back to creating worlds. Only the worlds I was creating through code were bigger, richer, and more detailed than anything I had made out of wood and paint or plants and soil. In the virtual world of a computer, I can build as detailed a ship as I want. But why stop there? I can make a whole crew to sail the ship and an ocean for her to sail in. And not only can I go sailing on the ship myself, I can take other people there, too.

And there's another, hidden, even more beautiful world that I can create. The program itself is a world, a complex clockwork realm hidden from everyone except coders. The complex and precise dance of events, data, and logic exists only in the computer, but is only realized in the programmer's mind.

Some people might think Kodu lets you make games without learning to program. But we built Kodu to let you start programming without having to learn a bunch of other stuff. In Kodu, you can create a world of your own design. And then you can build up the logic of that world, the cause and effects, the rewards and losses, the goals and traps. You decide what you want your world to be, and then you make it that way.

And that's what programming is. It's breaking big and hard problems into smaller and easier chunks. It's keeping track of the big picture even when you're trying to work out the tiniest detail. It's creating worlds out of imagination.

Michael Miller

For many years before starting on Kodu, one of my hobbies was robotics. Not the type of robotics that would put a car together using an arc welder, but hobby robotics that you build and program yourself and that you might use to scurry around and scare your cat. I even built a BattleBot and participated one year in that event. I learned a lot about the mechanical makeup of bots and how messy the real world is for robots. I had been a member of the Seattle Robotics Society, one of the longest-running robotics groups, for some years, so I had others to whom I could ask questions to see how they solved problems.

I built many robots but only finished a few. It's strange to look back to see how many I never really finished and how this resembles lots of my programming projects. I guess that shows how similar engineering is in these fields. I mostly built mobile robots, which means their primary action was just moving around on wheels, tracks, or legs. I was working on AI systems to allow them to move around the real world without stopping at every out-of-place carpet thread or table leg. I needed a system that was robust in how it sensed and reacted to objects and then moved my bots. There are a lot of great books on the subject with varying systems that solve different problems. I focused on a behavioral AI model that fit this problem well. One nice effect of this system is that it would make my robots "feel" like living things. I was still playing around with solutions to my hobby robotics when we started Kodu.

One day I came into work and Matt MacLaurin was talking about this idea of creating a tool that would inspire the next generation to learn programming. His pitch included a few examples of applications that most of us had used on our own journey of learning programming. We reflected on how they just didn't feel "modern" as they once did. He provided his first pass at goals and had shown concepts from another prototype that used "cards." With his infectious passion and this great kernel of an idea, he had me hooked.

I remember reviewing all the research pointers he had collected and shared a few of my own, and we spotted a key problem that kept coming up. There seemed to be a barrier in the age of person who could comprehend all the current systems, with references to requiring algebra-level understanding before they were useful. We took this as one goal: to create a modern tool that could break this barrier.

So, like all technical workers (researchers/engineers/and so on) who need to convince someone to pay for their work, I put together a PowerPoint slide deck on my concept about how the programming could be done. I included some of the high-level "code" I exposed in my robot projects, mixed with some visual concepts from the initial ideas, drew up some initial artwork icons for the programming concepts, and made a pitch on how we could make it work. The idea went over really well. I was given the green light and started working on architecture for programming the next day.

Within a few weeks, I was demonstrating that the basics worked, and we all could see the vision actually coming to life. We all continued to brainstorm and iterate on the programming tile concepts. Stephen Coy continued to expand on other aspects of Kodu, including the world-editing features. Within a few months, we had a fully functioning and usable game, and we started demonstrating Kodu to the rest of Microsoft. Everyone who played with it loved it. Shortly after that, we were doing UR studies and expanding the features.

It was always great to sit in on the UR studies and the early "play fests." I was surprised by how well it was received. The parents and educators liked it. The kids loved the many aspects of it, from having a virtual playground they built, having objects to place in it, and being able to make those objects come to life. I think they often didn't even realize they were programming; it was just play to them. I believe we reached our goal.

My career moved on, and I separated from the Kodu project before it went widely public. I continue to stay in touch with Stephen Coy, and I hear about all the great work being done with it. Today, I can't think of a project I am more proud of having participated on.

INDEX

Where Are the Companion Content Files?

Register this version of

Kodu for Kids: The Official Guide to Creating Your Own Video Games

to access important downloads.

Register this book to unlock the companion files that are included on with this book. Follow the steps below.

1. Go to www.quepublishing.com/register and log in or create a new account.

2. Enter this ISBN: 9780789750761

3. Answer the challenge question as proof of purchase.

4. Click on the "Access Bonus Content" link in the "Registered Products" section of your account page, which will take you to the page where your download-able content is available.

The Professional and Personal Technology Brands of Pearson

 Addison Wesley   Cisco Press   IBM Press.   informIT   PEARSON IT Certification   PRENTICE HALL   QUE   SAMS   vmware PRESS

FREE
Online Edition

Your purchase of **Kodu for Kids** includes access to a free online edition for 45 days through the **Safari Books Online** subscription service. Nearly every Que book is available online through **Safari Books Online**, along with thousands of books and videos from publishers such as Addison-Wesley Professional, Cisco Press, Exam Cram, IBM Press, O'Reilly Media, Prentice Hall, Sams, and VMware Press.

Safari Books Online is a digital library providing searchable, on-demand access to thousands of technology, digital media, and professional development books and videos from leading publishers. With one monthly or yearly subscription price, you get unlimited access to learning tools and information on topics including mobile app and software development, tips and tricks on using your favorite gadgets, networking, project management, graphic design, and much more.

Activate your FREE Online Edition at
informit.com/safarifree

STEP 1: Enter the coupon code: MMJBOVH.

STEP 2: New Safari users, complete the brief registration form. Safari subscribers, just log in.

If you have difficulty registering on Safari or accessing the online edition, please e-mail customer-service@safaribooksonline.com